HOUSE OF COLLECTIBLES PRICE GUIDE TO

STAR WARS® COLLECTIBLES

HOUSE OF COLLECTIBLES PRICE GUIDE TO

STAR WARS® COLLECTIBLES

SUE CORNWELL AND MIKE KOTT

FOURTH EDITION

HOUSE OF COLLECTIBLES

THE BALLANTINE PUBLISHING GROUP • NEW YORK

Important Notice. All of the information, including valuations, in this book has been compiled from the most reliable sources, and every effort has been made to eliminate errors and questionable data. Nevertheless, the possibility of error, in a work of such immense scope, always exists. The publisher will not be held responsible for losses that may occur in the purchase, sale, or other transaction of items because of information contained herein. Readers who feel they have discovered errors are invited to *write* and inform us, so they may be corrected in subsequent editions. Those seeking further information on the topics covered in this book are advised to refer to the complete line of *Official Price Guides* published by the House of Collectibles.

 This is a registered trademark of Random House, Inc.

Published by: House of Collectibles
The Ballantine Publishing Group
201 East 50th Street
New York, NY 10022

Distributed by The Ballantine Publishing Group, a division of Random House, Inc., New York, and simultaneously in Canada by Random House of Canada Limited, Toronto.

http://www.randomhouse.com

Manufactured in the United States of America

ISSN: 1096-729X

ISBN: 0-876-37995-1

Text design by Holly Johnson

Cover design by Michelle T. Gengaro
Background cover art © Telegraph Colour Library/FPG International Corp.
Foreground cover art © George Kerrigan

Fourth Edition: November 1997
10 9 8 7 6 5 4 3 2 1

CONTENTS

PREFACE

The primary aim of this book is to help the ordinary collector, and especially the novice, to buy and sell *Star Wars* collectibles. To this end we have focused on the areas of collecting that we think would be most useful to this audience.

We know that some people in the more established collecting community may take exception to some aspects of this book. Some longtime collectors will probably say our prices on key collectibles are too high. Our prices are based not only on consulting other dealers and trade publications but also on twenty years of selling all kinds of *Star Wars* merchandise to a worldwide market on a daily basis. We know that these items sell regularly at these prices through experience, and wishing that the prices of the things you want will stay low forever won't make it so.

Dealers are probably going to be unhappy with us for criticizing some of their favorite cash cows, most particularly charging extravagant premiums on variations and overgraded items. The simple fact is that aside from picking the pockets of collectors, these practices aren't good for the industry. It's hurt other collectible fields and it can hurt ours. Ask anyone who collected silver dollars in the '80s.

Some licensees aren't going to be particularly happy with us for pointing out that "contrived collectibles" are just that. The great advantage of writing an "unauthorized" book is that we can tell the absolute truth without interference from the powers that be, and we have done just that.

And last, but not least, supercollectors are probably going to say our listings aren't complete enough, but as we pointed out at the beginning, this book is primarily for the ordinary collector who is buying and selling in the regular market. We do not believe that it's possible to put an honest price on an extremely rare item.

All we can say to those of you holding this volume, whether you are happy with what we have written or not, is that we can assure you this book reflects an honest evaluation of the market today and in that respect, at least, we hope you find it useful.

Thank you to all of the people who have contributed information to this book. It would not have been possible without you. If you have comments or information you think should be included in future editions, please direct them to:

Sue Cornwell
P.O. Box 521516
Longwood, FL 23752

Please provide as much information as you can about items for future listings including, when known, description of both the item and the packaging, manufacturer, date of manufacture, price, and any other details you may find pertinent.

HOUSE OF COLLECTIBLES PRICE GUIDE TO

STAR WARS® COLLECTIBLES

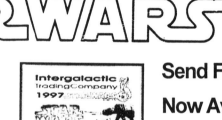

INTRODUCTION

Star Wars is, quite simply, the most significant film in movie history. You can find better acting in the great films of moviemaking's golden era, and there have been more spectacular special effects movies since *Star Wars*' premiere in 1977, but no film has had as much impact on moviemaking itself as *Star Wars*. From the first moment when that Imperial Cruiser slid overhead in pursuit of Leia's Rebel transport, viewers realized what movies really could do, and the movie industry has never been the same. Since *Star Wars*, virtually every blockbuster film to hit theaters has relied heavily on special effects. As we write this, *Lost World* is busy shattering records set just last year by *Independence Day*. We now accept as a given that space battles, T-Rexs or anything else the mind of man can imagine can be translated onto a movie screen.

But *Star Wars* started more than one revolution; *Star Wars* also started a revolution in merchandising. There was, of course, licensed media merchandise before *Star Wars,* but it was never taken seriously by the studios. Licenses were cheap, and in most circles merchandise was considered as a sort of backhanded publicity campaign for the movie or TV show. With *Star Wars*, merchandising became a carefully orchestrated moneymaking endeavor in its own right. Licenses were no longer cheap, royalties (often a ho-hum afterthought in pre-*Star Wars* days) were carefully monitored, and the merchandise itself was at least marginally regulated to make sure it stayed true to the films. None of this discouraged potential licensees. Everyone wanted a piece of the *Star Wars* gold mine. The result was one of the most eclectic assortments of merchandise in history. Everything from soap dishes to candy dispensers were now being made with a *Star Wars* theme, and though they could not have known it at the time, these manufacturers were laying the foundation for one of the largest, and frankly most fun, collecting booms of all time.

Star Wars collecting first started gaining momentum in the lean years after the movies (and assorted TV offerings) were through. In the mid '80s most *Star Wars* merchandise was being "dumped" by retail stores. Walls of heavily discounted action figures, toys, and other merchandise could be found in virtually any chain store. If we only knew then what we know now! Nevertheless, this seems to be the point when many people began to seriously collect *Star Wars* items. When the movies were being released every couple of years, it seemed that *Star Wars* merchandise would be around forever. Now it was slowly becoming apparent that it would eventually all disappear. Collectors picked up everything they could at discount prices and then began to fill in gaps. *Star Wars* items truly started to become "collectibles." Since then, *Star Wars* collectibles, especially action figures and toys, have had (and continue to have) one of the most astounding ascendances in the history of collectibles. In what other field could you have bought a $2 item that was worth $500 in only ten years? And now, with the re-release of the Special Edition movies and looking forward to the "prequel" trilogy, it's starting all over again. The current list of domestic *Star Wars* licensees is fourteen pages long and encompasses products ranging from Christmas ornaments to boxer shorts.

The bottom line is that whether you want to bet the farm that this new wave of merchandise is going to bring the hot collectibles of tomorrow, stick with the oldies but goodies, or simply pick up a few trinkets just for the fun of it; this is a party that's simply too good to miss! Happy collecting and May the Force Be with You.

BUYING AND SELLING

BUYING

What Should I Collect?

The only real answer to this question is to collect what you like. This is the only guarantee that you will get full enjoyment from your hobby. No matter how obscure or insignificant it is to the collecting world in general, how important it is to you is all that really counts. However, if you are also looking at collecting *Star Wars* from an investment standpoint, there are a few things you may wish to keep in mind.

First, if it's easy and inexpensive to make in small quantities, it's never going to be very valuable. Why? Because just as soon as a potential bootlegger sees that there is a substantial profit to be made by making copies of an item, he is going to do just that. Licensed or not, the temptation to make some easy money is simply too great. What kinds of items fit into this category? Most costume jewelry, patches, buttons, most sticker items, and almost any item made by a simple printing process, whether it's paper (simple stationery items, for example) or some other material (T-shirts, many mugs). And with ever-increasing values on *Star Wars* collectibles, the list is expanding into areas that used to be thought safe. Color movie posters and even plastic action figure accessories are all being counterfeited these days.

Second, certain categories of merchandise simply aren't widely collected. This does tend to change somewhat, especially in a field like *Star Wars* collectibles, where prices rise so dramatically that people are forced by economic restraints to change the focus of their collecting. For example, puzzles and crafts have gotten more popular as toys have gotten more expensive. Still, some areas seem to remain perpetually weak; greeting cards, sheet music, and most clothing items, especially children's clothes, are good examples. Some lackluster collectibles cover a range of merchandise categories. *Star Tours* items have never really caught on and many die-hard live-action fans don't even consider the Droids and Ewoks animated series as part of *Star Wars*. Ewoks in general don't seem to be one of George Lucas's more popular inventions. In any line of merchandise offering a choice of characters, Ewoks are invariably the poorest sellers.

Good potential investment categories are often "crossover" collectibles; that is, items that are in demand by more than one group of collectors. For example, lunch-box collecting is a relatively strong collectible field. A lunch-box collector who has no other *Star Wars* collectibles at all may need a *Star Wars* lunch box to complete his collection. This same lunch box may be needed by a *Star Wars* collector to complete his collection of *Star Wars* housewares. The more an item is in demand, the more likely it is to escalate in value. More good crossover collectibles are toys, action figures, trading cards, comic books, plates, records, movie memorabilia, models, and watches, all of which have strong collectible markets in their own right.

Finally, it is almost impossible, these days, to place too much emphasis on condition. In some of the most active categories of *Star Wars* collectibles, toys and action figures, the package is just as important, in some cases more so than the actual item. To be in even marginal collectible condition, any item should at least be complete and free of major damage. Past this, the more the item looks like you would expect it to originally, new on the store shelf, the better.

Where Do I Find It?

There are quite a few options, all with advantages and disadvantages.

CHAIN STORES

This is probably the first place most people would consider. The advantage of chain stores for new items is that because of their profit structure they are going to be the cheapest, and because of their buying clout with manufacturers they often have products first. The disadvantage is that they are never going to have out-of-production items, and unless you are both very diligent and lucky (or know a stock clerk), you are never going to get any harder-to-find merchandise at a chain store (for example, the action figure that comes only one to the case).

LOCAL SPECIALTY STORES

These are usually found in the phone book under categories such as Toys and Comics. More and more of these kinds of stores are selling *Star Wars* collectibles these days and they are becoming fairly common, especially in more urban areas. The advantage of these stores is that they will often have a much broader range of merchandise, especially of production merchandise, than chain stores. Also, since they have a vested interest in cultivating you as a customer, they will often be more flexible in price than other sources, as well as offering services (subscription service or search service, for example) not available elsewhere. The disadvantage, especially for more advanced collectors, is that these stores are often small, in terms of both space and financial resources, and the time may come when they are no longer able to adequately meet your collecting needs.

MEDIA SCIENCE FICTION CONVENTIONS AND SPECIALTY SHOWS (TOY, CARD, ETC.)

The advantage to these is that a large one will offer the greatest possible selection of merchandise available for actual on-site inspection, prices are usually negotiable, especially toward the end of the show, and they are just plain fun to attend. The disadvantage is that to attend one large enough to be worthwhile, you may have to travel if you don't live in a large metropolitan area, and they charge admission fees which can (particularly in the case of the science fiction conventions) be fairly steep.

MAIL ORDER

Catalogs and direct ads for *Star Wars* merchandise can be found in specialty and science fiction magazines and (for the computer literate) on the Internet. Advantages are that this option offers the widest possible range of merchandise and is available to everyone no matter how remote your residence or limited your means of transportation. The disadvantage is that you are buying sight unseen. For this reason it is only prudent to investigate the source before you buy. In general, larger, better-established companies and dealers are your safest bet. By law, merchandise bought through the mail must have a money-back guarantee (as long as it is returned promptly in the condition in which it was sent). Any company that doesn't offer you this option is suspect. You may want to believe that a small fan-run company or an individual wouldn't want to rip off another fan, but the truth is, it happens all too often.

FLEA MARKETS AND GARAGE SALES

Everyone has heard stories of a rare toy or action figure bought for pennies in this manner. In truth, this almost never happens, especially these days. Most regular flea market dealers are all too aware of collectibility of *Star Wars* items, and as for garage and yard sales, it's much more common to drive for hours to find only a sad array of worn and incomplete items that no one could legitimately call collectible. So unless you really enjoy the thrill of the hunt, this is not a particularly good option.

SELLING

Just as with buying, you have several options when you go to sell your collectibles, each with its own advantages and disadvantages. Since the option that is best for you is somewhat dependent on what you have to sell and what you expect to get for your collectibles, you should first organize your items and consider your goals as well. Pertinent factors include whether you have only a few pieces to sell (or even just one) or a large collection. If you are selling a large collection, are you willing to break it up or do you want to sell it all at once and be done with it? Are you willing to pack up your pieces and ship them? Are you determined to get full retail value for your items or will you sell them at a discount to make a quick sale? Are you interested in trade credit for other items you may be interested in? Think about which options are best for your situation and proceed from there.

Where Do I Sell It?

LOCAL SPECIALTY STORES

If there is a store (or stores) near you that sells *Star Wars* collectibles, this is probably going to be your most convenient option. But before you go to the trouble of loading your stuff up in the car and driving around town, call to make sure that the store (or stores) is interested in what you have. If the answer is yes, arrange a convenient time to show your items to the store owner or manager. Take a little time preparing your collectibles before you go. Make sure they are clean looking and free of dust, and package them carefully for the trip. Not just so they arrive in good condition but also to impress upon the buyer that you are aware of their value as collectibles. If the buyer likes what he sees, expect to be offered anywhere from 30 percent to 60 percent of retail value for your items (depending on how badly the buyer needs these particular things for stock). If you are interested in trade credit, be sure to say so. Most dealers make better offers in credit than cash. If you have a large collection, decide in advance whether you will sell individual pieces. Given the choice, most buyers would rather pick out only the pieces they really need. You will probably get more money per piece this way, but what remains will almost certainly be harder to sell elsewhere. A disadvantage with local stores is that they usually do not have a lot of capital to invest in stock. So if you have a very large collection or very expensive items, this may not be your best option. You could also ask if you could leave your items on consignment, though many store owners won't want to bother, especially with very inexpensive or very bulky items. If the owner does agree, however, make sure you have a clear understanding of how long you expect to leave the piece (pieces) and how much money you expect to get for it.

LARGE DEALERS

If you have a very large collection you wish to sell as a whole, or very expensive items, this is probably going to be your best option, since large dealers are the only ones with enough capital to lay out for stock that may take several months to sell. In most cases, selling to large dealers means dealing by phone or mail. Start by making a list of the items you wish to sell, noting any details that affect value (packaged/ unpackaged, condition, *Star Wars* or *Empire* package, etc.). Be honest in your evaluation. The buyer is making an offer based on your description of the items. They will not feel obligated to honor that offer if what they receive is not as presented. As with the store buyer, expect to be offered 30 percent to 60 percent of retail value. Since you will probably need to ship your items, decide at this time who is going to cover that cost. Once an agreement has been reached, arrangements will need to be made to send your collectibles to the buyer. Keep in mind that no dealer is going to pay you before they have had a chance to inspect the merchandise (no C.O.D.s), so it is important to deal only with reputable companies. Pack your items carefully for shipping. The dealer made an offer based on the condition you described, and if it doesn't arrive in that condition he'll feel no obligation to pay you the agreed amount no matter whose fault it is. UPS is probably your best shipping option. They are convenient to most locations, have an excellent tracking system, and insure the first $100 of value free (additional insurance is available for a nominal fee). Insurance is available from the Post Office, but collecting on losses is a long, drawn-out, and frankly unpleasant experience. Once the dealer has received your items and decided they are acceptable, you should receive payment promptly. If there is some problem, you should similarly be promptly informed.

PRINT ADS

If you have only a few pieces to sell or are willing to break up a large collection and you are determined to get full retail value for your items, this may be an option. There are, of course, all kinds of publications that sell advertising space. Some are more suitable to your purpose than others. You can start by eliminating the ones that don't target your focus audience, namely people who want to buy *Star Wars* collectibles. The classified section of your local newspaper is convenient and probably cheap, but the chances that someone interested in what you are selling just might run across your ad the day(s) it is running are probably not good. Trade publications (toy, card, antique) are a better bet but more expensive, and while media science fiction publications offer the best possible venue for your ad, they are probably too expensive to be practical in most circumstances. Remember that you buy ad space by the line or column inch, so consider carefully the items you wish to run. If the items you advertise are of interest to too few people or your prices are too steep, you will have wasted your money on the ad. It also isn't usually worthwhile running very inexpensive items; the money from their sale won't cover the cost of advertising them. Unlike the first two selling options, where you were dealing with professionals, you are now trying to sell to individuals. Almost everyone is going to want to ask questions about the items you have for sale, so in addition to your name and address, be sure to list your phone number in the ad. Even if you have an answering machine, it's a good idea to list times when you will be available. Not only will it make potential customers happy to have a live person to speak to, but it can also save you money on your long-distance bill. If it irks you to have people make counteroffers on your prices, be sure that your ad reads "prices firm." If someone says he or she wants a particular piece, make it clear you will only hold it for as long a time as it would reasonably take a check to reach you. Many sales are lost endlessly holding articles for people who never follow through. Once you do receive the check, cash it immediately but don't send the item until it clears the bank. Once you're sure the check is good, package the item carefully and send it promptly to its new owner. Be sure to insure the package. And remember, just like the big mail-order houses, you are required by law to refund the customer's money if he is dissatisfied with his purchase, so it might be a good idea to hold on to his money for a while.

NOTE: Most tips for selling through print ads apply to the Internet too!

CARE

Star Wars collectibles encompass an enormous range of different types of items that run the gamut from fragile to practically indestructible. Most of them require some degree of care for storage or display in order to remain in the best possible collectible condition. Preservation of collectibles is, for the most part, merely an exercise in common sense. Certain categories of items need to be protected from creases and tears. Others can be damaged by water or heat. Many will fade with long exposure to sunlight. Glassware and ceramics should be stored and displayed where they are safe from breakage. To help you maintain your collectible investments, a whole plethora of boxes, bags, cases, and inserts are readily available from most comic, toy, or hobby stores or through mail-order companies. Their use is highly recommended. Below are a few additional tips on care.

• *Toys and Other Boxed Items (Games, Housewares, etc.).* First of all, *never* throw away the box. Even if you wish to use the item or display it without the box, don't discard the box, any interior packaging (cardboard or styrofoam), or instruction sheets. Make sure the box is stored where it won't get crushed or damaged, and if it will fit, it's not a bad idea to store the box in a plastic collectibles bag. If you want to retain absolute maximum collectibility, leave decal sheets that come with toys and punchable counters and playing pieces in games intact. Once out of the box, make sure all small parts stay with the item.

• *Action Figures and Other Blister-Carded Items. Don't* open them. To do so, no matter how carefully, and regardless of how good of condition you keep the card, reduces the value of your collectible nearly to the level of a loose item. If you absolutely can't resist the urge to touch it, buy two, one to open and one to keep. There are now some excellent inexpensive, soft plastic protective cases available to collectors that fit both old and new *Star Wars* figures. They are suitable for both storage and display and more expensive, hard plastic ones are also available for your really expensive figures. For larger blister-carded items, plastic collectible bags are still the best bet, preferably with a cardboard backing board to further help prevent tears and creases in cards and dents in plastic bubbles. Store loose figures and small toys in plastic bags or boxes. This not only keeps them clean but prevents any small pieces from being lost.

• *Paper Items (Books, Comic Books, Magazines, Posters).* When reading books, be careful not to break the spine or dog-ear pages or roll over the pages of magazines and comics, and never write on any paper collectible. Plastic collectible bags are made in a variety of shapes and sizes to fit almost any book, comic, or magazine, and there are even sizes that fit record albums and most calendars. With flimsy publications, magazines, comics, and thin paperback books, cardboard backing boards should be used. Sturdy boxes in magazine and comic sizes are made for storage of large collections. For display, posters can be shrink-wrapped onto backing boards if framing is too expensive an option. Never punch pinholes in the corners and don't fold a poster if it isn't folded already. For storage, sturdy cardboard tubes are your best option. They protect the poster, and several posters can be rolled into one tube to save space.

• *Trading Cards.* Keep sets in hard plastic storage boxes designed for that purpose. They come in several different sizes that will fit most sets. Never use rubber bands to keep stacks of cards together. They ruin the edges of the cards. For display, plastic notebook pages with pockets (pages with several different pocket sizes are available) designed for three-ring binders are an excellent choice not only for cards but for many other small items as well (postcards, action figure coins, buttons, bookmarks, etc.). Licensed *Star Wars* logo binders are available to hold the pages, or, better yet, get a plain binder and decorate it yourself.

A FEW ADDITIONAL THOUGHTS ON COLLECTING IN TODAY'S MARKET

In recent years, there has been a trend on the part of both manufacturers of licensed *Star Wars* merchandise and secondary market dealers to take advantage of an aspect in human nature that makes us yearn to find that one special item, a unique or at least rare piece that simply isn't available to the common hordes. Unfortunately, nearly all of us, and especially *Star Wars* fans, seem all too ready to leap on these perceived treasures, perhaps without properly analyzing exactly how "special" these things really are. While to a large extent collectibles, like beauty, are in the eye of the beholder and therefore nothing of value to the owner, no matter how humble, is a waste, there are a few things you might want to consider before you plop down your hard-earned cash.

1. Just because it's old, is it automatically valuable? Absolutely not. For example, a very pretty "May the Force Be with You" button was given out at the original premiere of *Star Wars*. The words were in white on a dark blue star background. It was probably the first *Star Wars* item, along with the theater program book, readily available to the general public. Despite the fact that it is one of the earliest *Star Wars* collectibles (and has a nice nostalgia aspect as well), it is not very valuable and never will be. Why? Well, besides the fact that the original L.A. manufacturer would sell anyone who asked as many as they wanted (things were a little more informal in those days), all you would have to do is give one to any button manufacturer today and you could have a truckload of indistinguishable copies by next week. Other items, no matter how old or rare, simply aren't in much demand. Factors Etc. sold some very nice T-shirt transfers both on and off shirts as early as 1977. But people who collect old T-shirts are few and far between. Of course, unlike the buttons, the shirts aren't likely to be bootlegged and T-shirts could one day become collectible—but I wouldn't hold my breath.

2. But an authorized source said it's limited—sure it is. And there are only so many cups of water in the Atlantic Ocean. Examples of this one are so numerous these days, I don't know where to begin, but there are several basic tricks. One is to put numbers on things. Your $250 Genuine Authorized Limited Edition Darth Vader Petrified Gummi Bear Sculpture (on genuine imitation wood base) is one of only 100,000 EVER TO BE PRODUCED!!! Oh, and by the way, we cut off sales at precisely 12 noon, May 13, 2146. But are there really 100,000 people out there willing to fork out $250 for a Darth Vader Gummi Bear sculpture? For that matter, are there 10,000 or 10?

Another trick is to take, say, an autographed color 8″ × 10″ photo of one of the secondary actors. Price, $25—fair enough. The XYZ home shopping network puts it in a frame ($12.95 at Wal-Mart) with a GENUINE AUTHORIZED CERTIFICATE OF AUTHENTICITY (same approximate value as two paper towels) and sells it on their OFFICIAL AUTHORIZED *Star Wars* Home Shopping Show for *only* $199.99. And don't forget, you better have your credit card ready because we only have a few of these left. Of course, the actor, who is sitting right there on the set, could always duck into the back room between telling amusing anecdotes and sign a few more pictures while helper A runs to Wal-Mart for more frames and helper B runs off more certificates of authenticity on the copy machine.

Of course there are some real limited collectibles being made these days that are worth every penny of their price, but it's still a good idea to let certain "hype" words like Limited, Official, and Authorized ring the alarm bell that kicks your common sense into action.

3. See, it says right here it's worth $150. Yes, and it's correct. The one being described, the complete one, in the new condition box with all accessories, interior packing, instructions, and unapplied decal sheets is worth at least $150. The one this guy is trying to sell you, the one that someone's grandmother gave to Goodwill after Grandpa accidently ran over it with the lawn tractor, is worth about $1.50. Condition is the most important word in collectibles today, but it also

seems to be a very easy word to forget (by both sellers and buyers) when it's convenient.

4. Of course it's worth three times as much. It's a C-10, absolute mint! This is the flip side of number three. The word "mint" is bandied about extensively in the collectibles field, undoubtedly because it conjures up visions of shiny golden treasure. Strictly speaking, it is a complete misnomer when used in conjunction with anything but coins, since they are the only products that are actually "minted" (unless you're talking about a flavor of toothpaste). But it is nevertheless widely used in the *Star Wars* collectibles market, mostly when referring to toys and action figures. In toy and collectible publications you will often see the initials MOC (Mint on Card) or MIB (Mint in Box). This can be especially misleading because technically speaking it's only referring to the toy itself (yes, the toy is mint, but the box had an unfortunate run-in with the neighbor's Rottweiler). So all MIB is really saying is that the box is present. And since the box is 50 percent or more of the value in some *Star Wars* collectibles, it can be a pretty important detail. If the toy really does have a nice box, the fact will usually be emphasized, sometimes with the abbreviations MMB (Mint in Mint Box) or MMC (Mint on Mint Card) for action figures.

You may also see, especially with packaged action figures, the use of a numbering system (C-1 through C-10), and here's where the problem starts. The system, loosely speaking, is a lot like the old "on a scale of one to ten" question except that it gets a little crazy at the high end. No one would argue that a C-1 figure is in pretty bad shape, but by the time you get to the other end, you're worrying about nearly microscopic white specks on the mostly dark cards and whether or not that little piece of cardboard has been punched out of the hole made for hanging the figure on a display. This nitpicking would all be academic except that so many people try to charge astronomic premiums for what are, in actuality, extremely minor differences in condition. There is no question that condition is an extremely important factor in collectibility. An item in truly collectible condition looks like you would have expected it to when it was first put out on the store shelf. Should you, if at all feasible, buy collectibles in near-new condition? Absolutely. But should you pay two or three times the going rate to get *the* absolutely most perfect specimen? You decide.

5. Honest, it's right off the set. George Lucas gave it to my cousin for delivering a pizza. If you get caught by this one I only hope you can find your way back to the turnip truck. Contrary to the popular notion that once a film is through shooting they just take all that neat stuff out to the Dumpster, studios take an extremely dim view of props and costumes disappearing from their custody. And of all the studios, Lucasfilm is by far the most tightfisted. If you are seriously thinking of buying an item purported to be an original off a *Star Wars* movie set, no amount of research into its authenticity is too much. And then you can start to worry about how you can pay for it.

6. Who is leading who? Variations. This one is a little less clear-cut because to a large extent it's being foisted on fans by the fans themselves. But if you were, say, Kenner, and you found out that you could create a feeding frenzy for your product merely by changing the color of your product's package (or the picture on the package or the length of Obi-Wan's lightsaber or the paint job on Boba Fett's hand, etc., etc., etc.), what would you do? Especially when all these products are still being made. Consider that they have never said how many long lightsabers they have made. And they are under no obligation, either legal or moral, not to make more. If you could boost your company's profits by adding another inch of plastic to an action figure accessory, what would you do? Yes, it's fun to hunt down variations; almost everyone does it. But should you pay a big premium for one? I believe the moral of this one is to try and take the long view of collecting. In ten years is the Luke Jedi with brown outfit really going to be that much more valuable than the other twenty-seven Luke Jedi variations that will have appeared by then?

USING THIS BOOK

Because there is such a wide range of different types of *Star Wars* items, we have organized the various sections in different ways (chronologically, alphabetically, by title, by type of item, etc.) in order to access the information more easily. Short notes at the head of each section or subsection tell which way was used for that particular part of the book. We have tried to concentrate the focus of this book on the areas of greater general interest. We felt this was important, since the purpose of the book is more as a price guide than a checklist. If we have, to this end, skimmed over something of particular importance to you, we apologize.

In that same vein, you will find that a great many unique or very rare items are not presented here. Included in this list are such things as prototypes, artwork, original props, and some very rare or obscure items, primarily from outside the United States. After much consideration, we decided not to include many of these kinds of things even though we know they exist, because this book is first and foremost a price guide, and the type of items just mentioned are for the most part unquantifiable. In other words, we simply don't know what a *Star Wars* painting by Boris, an original model from a *Star Wars* movie set, or a toy of which only two are known to exist would bring in today's market. Pricing is based on our experience buying and selling similar items over a period of time, and any figure we chose to put on such unique collectibles would only be a number pulled from thin air. About the only thing we are reasonably certain of is that any amount we selected would be low.

Please note that the prices for all the items listed in this book assume that they are absolutely complete and in basically new condition for both the item and the original packaging (if applicable) unless specifically stated otherwise. Do not expect anyone in the collectibles field to evaluate a piece in any lesser condition at anywhere near the prices in this book.

Finally, please remember that this is a price GUIDE, not the final word in *Star Wars* collectibles. To see the figures here as fixed amounts will hamper your abilities as either a buyer or a seller.

ACTION FIGURE TOYS

ORIGINAL SERIES ACTION FIGURE TOYS

These toys were designed by Kenner to be used with their original small action figure line. Values for unpackaged toys assume toys are complete with all small parts, clean and in excellent condition. Values for packaged toys assume toy and box are complete and in excellent condition with all interior packaging, instructions and decal sheets. Boxes in lesser condition are still in demand, though the value is proportionately reduced. Incomplete or damaged toys are of little interest to serious

collectors. Boxes show color photos of toy depicted in action scenes with figures. Like the small action figures, packaging for many toys was updated as each film in the series was released. "Power of the Force" packaging was done after the completion of the movie trilogy and was apparently designed as a general title. In actuality, very few toys were done in "Power of the Force" boxes, and these tend to be more valuable. There was also a late series in which a few original toys were reissued in packaging identical to the original except for a "Collector's Series" seal printed on the box. These are worth only slightly less than original counterparts. Droids packaging was limited to a few very late toys, and while Ewok packaging is shown in Kenner advertising of the time, it was apparently never used except for a few items in Kenner's preschool line (see TOYS). Some variations in box art and logos do occur, including some triple language boxes for foreign markets, but package variations for the toys is not nearly so common as it is with the original Kenner action figure line. Foreign packaging by companies other than Kenner was done, but other than Palitoy (Britain) came late in the trilogy and is relatively rare. In most cases, Palitoy toys have only minor changes, and prices are comparable to the U.S. versions. Exceptions are noted where this is not the case. Packaging is similar but not identical to their U.S. counterparts. Unique to the European market were some combined toy and action figure sets done primarily with the smaller toys. These are relatively rare, especially in the United States, and for this reason tend to bring premium prices ($500 and up) when complete and in good condition.

This section is organized alphabetically by item.

Action Figure Accessories, 1981–1983

These came boxed in $4\frac{1}{2}'' \times 6''$ boxes with color photo of toy similar to the Mini-Rigs packaging but without the side headers.

Kenner, Ewok Assault Catapult

Ewok Assault Catapult Dark brown. Base, arm, release hook and string, two boulders.

- **No package** .... $20–$30
- **Jedi box** .... $40–$55

Ewok Combat Glider Tan "wings," two boulders.

- **No package** .... $20–$30
- **Jedi box** .... $40–$55

Radar Laser Cannon Dark gray. Base and dish.

- **No package** .... $10–$20
- **Empire box** .... $25–$35
- **Jedi box** .... $20–$30

Kenner, Tri-Pod Laser Cannon, Radar Laser Cannon, and Vehicle Maintenance Energizer action figure accessories

Tri-Pod Laser Cannon Dark gray cannon on tri-pod with power hose and power unit.

- **No package** .... $15–$25
- **Empire box** .... $25–$35
- **Jedi box** .... $20–$30

Vehicle Maintenance Energizer White plastic container opens for storage of eight plastic "tools." Two power hoses.

- **No package** .... $20–$30
- **Empire box** .... $35–$40
- **Jedi box** .... $30–$35

Action Figure Holders

NOTE: Action figure cases (except for Chewbacca Bandolier) came with paper inserts showing color photos of small action figures.

Collector's Cases, 1979–1983. Black vinyl with illustrated color covers. Holds 24 figures.

- **Star Wars** .... $25–$35
- **Empire** .... $25–$35
- **Jedi** .... $50–$75

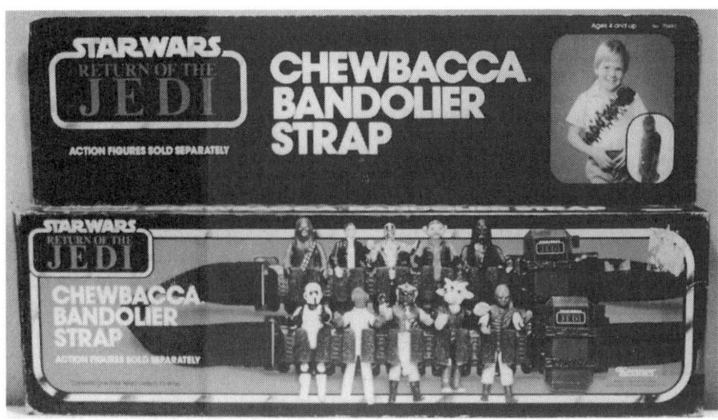

Kenner, Chewbacca Bandolier Strap action figure holder

Chewbacca Bandolier Strap, 1983. Holds ten figures plus two containers for accessories. Came boxed.

No package .... $15–$25
Jedi box .... $30–$40

C-3PO Collector's Case, 1983. Gold plastic bust of C-3PO. Holds 40 figures. Packaging was wrapper with color photos around base.

Each .... $25–$40

Darth Vader Collector's Case, 1980. Black plastic bust of Darth Vader. Holds 31 figures. Wrapper with color photos around base.

Each .... $15–$25

Laser Rifle Case, 1984. Shaped like a rifle. Holds 19 figures. Came packaged in color cardboard base.

Each .... $35–$55

Mini-Rigs, 1981–1983

These are small, one-figure vehicles that came uniformly packaged in 6″ × 4½″ boxes with side headers showing color photos of the toy.

Armored Sentinel Transport (AST-5) Orange. Two side guns and hatch.

No package .... $15–$20
Jedi box .... $25–$35

Captivator (CAP-2) Dark gray. Four arms, front gun and hatch.

No package .... $10–$15
Empire box .... $20–$25

Desert Sail Skiff Green with overhead orange "sail," two rear side fins and two side guns.

No package .... $15–$20
Jedi box .... $25–$35

Endor Forest Ranger Green, drum-shaped. One front and two side guns and front hatch.

No package .... $15–$20
Jedi box .... $25–$35

Interceptor (INT-4) Dark gray. Two fold-down wings, hatch and front gun.

No package .... $10–$15
Empire box .... $25–$30
Jedi box .... $20–$25

Imperial Shuttle Pod (ISP-6) White with fold-up wings, dorsal fin, hatch and two wing guns.

No package .... $15–$20
Jedi box .... $25–$35

Mobile Laser Cannon (MLC-3) White mini-tank. Hatch and two front guns.

No package .... $15–$20
Empire box .... $25–$35
Jedi box .... $25–$35

Multi Terrain Vehicle (MTV-7) White on two high wheels. Front gun.

No package .... $15–$20
Empire box .... $25–$35
Jedi box .... $25–$35

Personnel Deployment Transport (PDT-8) White with front and back openings and side guns.

No package .... $15–$20
Empire box .... $25–$35
Jedi box .... $25–$35

Miscellaneous

AT-AT (All-Terrain Armored Transport), 1981. Posable legs, movable control center. 17½″ high, battery functions. Small parts include two clear plastic "jaw" guns, battery cover, top hatch and side hatch.

No package .... $125–$150
Empire box .... $250–$300
Jedi box .... $225–$275

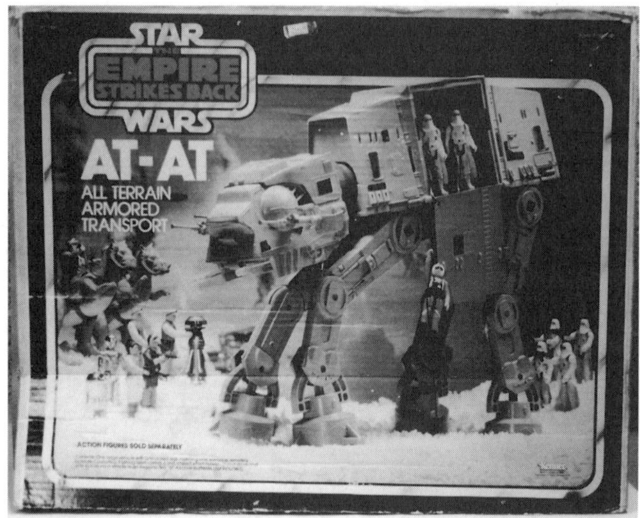

Kenner, AT-AT (Empire box)

Action Figure Collector's Stand, 1977. Gray plastic stand for action figures with cardboard backdrops. Produced for early bird package. Available through mail-in offer.

NOTE: A very few display box versions of this item appear that were probably intended for store sales. Display box stands are extremely rare.

Each .... $20–$30

ATL (Air-To-Land) Interceptor Vehicle, 1985. Approximately 7″ long with fold-down front extensions. Small parts include hatch cover. Originally came with "Planetary Map."

No package .... $35–$45
Droids box .... $50–$60

A-Wing Fighter, 1985. Battery-operated sound. Approximately 12″ long with swivelling side guns and two rear "fins." No easily removable small parts. Originally came with "Planetary Map."

No package .... $350–$500
Droids box .... $650–$950

B-Wing Fighter, 1983. Battery-operated sound. Approximately 22″ long. Rotating cockpit and two fold-out side "wings" which are easily removable. Small parts include cockpit canopy and two wing guns.

No package .... $85–$115
Jedi box .... $125–$165

Cantina Adventure Set, 1978. Sears promotional set. Base and backdrop plus four figures: Greedo, Hammerhead, Tall (blue) Snaggletooth and Walrusman.

No package .... $300–$375
Star Wars box .... $550–$700

Cloud City Playset, 1981. Sears promotional item. Included base, backdrop and four figures: Han Solo, Ugnaught, Lando Calrissian and Boba Fett.

No package .... $150–$200
Empire box .... $350–$500

Creature Cantina, 1977. Consisted of plastic base and scenic cardboard backdrop with lever-activated functions. Small parts include door frame and two-piece door.

NOTE: Palitoy version of this toy called simply "Cantina" differs slightly from U.S. version. Plastic table and movable action figure turntables are separate pieces and bar is in two parts with a plastic counter and cardboard base.

No package .... $35–$45
Star Wars box .... $65–$95
Palitoy version .... $150–$250

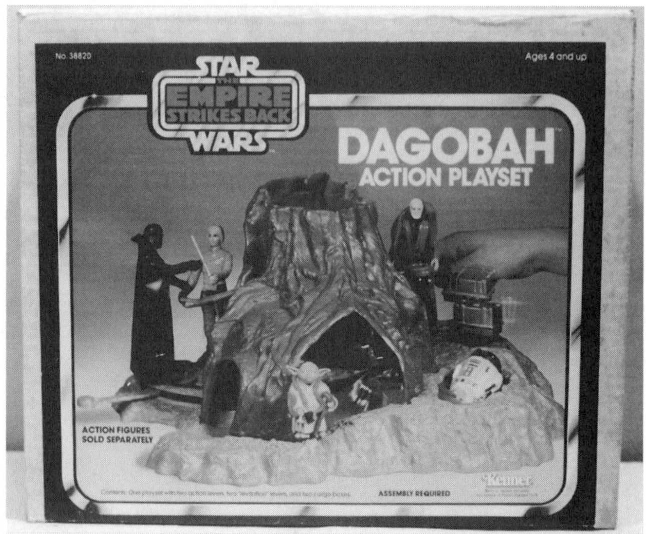

Kenner, Dagobah Action Playset (Empire box)

Dagobah Action Playset, 1981. Plastic base with detachable hut, a levitation lever and two two-piece action figure lever assemblies. Small parts include two-piece "levitator" rod, two plastic cargo boxes and adapter for an R2-D2 figure. Sponge "swamp" tends to deteriorate with age.

No package .... $25–$35
Empire box .... $55–$75

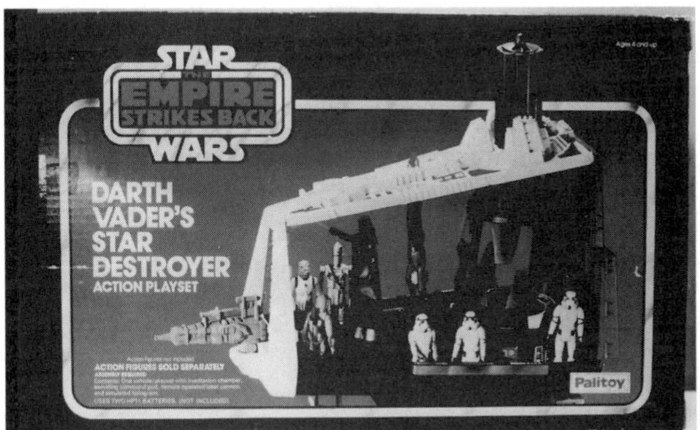

Palitoy, Darth Vader's Star Destroyer Action Playset (Empire box)

Darth Vader's Star Destroyer, 1980. Approximately 20″ long. Cross section of ship consisting of base with three supports and front, rear and top housings. Interior includes two-piece Darth Vader's Meditation Chamber. Small parts include trapdoor and two-piece laser cannon and for meditation chamber, hologram, console, window, three-piece bulb and three-piece battery assemblies for light effect.

No package .... $65–$85
Empire box .... $175–$225

Darth Vader's TIE Fighter, 1977. Approximately 11″ across. Battery light and sound. Two pop-off solar panels with separate connectors. Other small parts include two doors to interior and battery cover.

No package .... $65–$95
Star Wars box .... $125–$150

Death Star (Space Station), 1978. Approximately 23″ high when assembled. Toy consists of two "floors" and roof connected by elevator shaft, two plastic wall panels and nine plastic struts. Other parts include two thin cardboard backdrops, ledge, rope, laser cannon and trash compactor with sponge "trash" and trash monster.

No package .... $65–$85
Star Wars box .... $225–$325

Kenner, Death Star Space Station (Star Wars box)

Palitoy version of Death Star (Space Station)

Death Star Space Station Palitoy (British version), 1978. Toy is significantly different; dome shape and made primarily of cardboard instead of plastic.

No package .... $200–$350
Star Wars box .... $650–$950

Kenner, Droid Factory (Star Wars box)

Display Arena, 1981. Four L-shaped plastic stands for action figures and eight two-sided backdrop cards with scenes from Star Wars and Empire. Mail-order item (plain shipping box).

Each .... $45–$65

Droid Factory, 1977. Plastic base with two-piece movable crane. Small parts include pivot pin, hook, hydraulic tubing, two axles, base stand, radar unit, antenna, computer housing, four wheels, two tank treads, two wheel supports, sixteen connector pins, six assorted droid bases (including R2-D2), one droid body, one R2-D2 top, seven assorted droid legs and four assorted tool arms.

No package .... $50–$75
Star Wars box .... $115–$135
Empire box .... $175–$200
Palitoy (British) version, has manually operated conveyor belt instead of crane .... $200–$225

Ewok Battle Wagon, 1984. Approximately 12″ long. Free rolling. Originally came with "Planetary Map."

No package .... $75–$95
Power of the Force package .... $125–$175

Ewok Village Action Playset, 1983. Approximately 12″ high. Two-story plastic playset consisting of three "trees" and main platform. Small parts include three two-piece side platforms, net with rope and T-cap, three-piece carrying chair, elevator with winch rope, boulder, drum, three railings, spit with two side supports and firepit.

No package .... $45–$75
Jedi box .... $85–$125

Hoth Ice Planet Adventure Set, 1980. Plastic base with cardboard AT-AT backdrop. Small parts include five-piece elevator assembly, four-piece lever assemblies, five-piece Radar Laser Cannon and four pegs for figures.

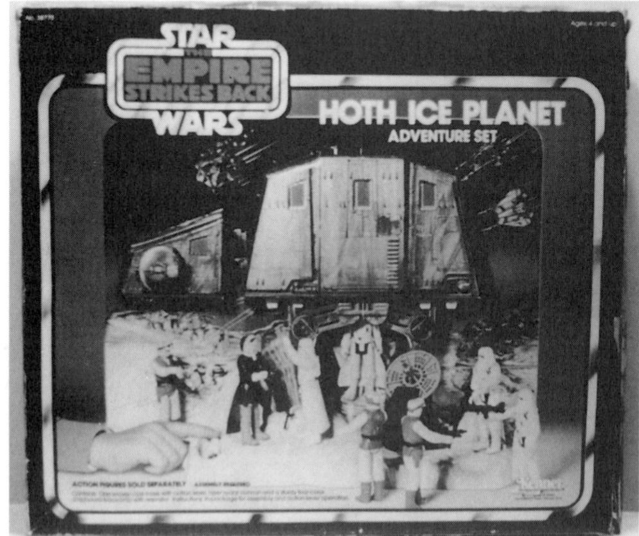

Kenner, Hoth Ice Planet Adventure Set (Empire box)

No package .... $55–$65
Empire box .... $165–$215

Hoth Wampa, 1981. 6″ tall. Movable arms and legs. No accessories.

No package .... $15–$25
Empire box .... $35–$45

Imperial Attack Base (Hoth scene), 1980. White plastic base with lever-activated functions. Small parts include two-piece "ice" arch, dark gray plastic hut with separate two-piece roof and removable white back wall, two dark gray plastic lever covers and laser cannon.

Kenner, Imperial Attack Base (Empire box)

No package .... $40–$60
Empire box .... $85–$115

Imperial Cruiser SEE Imperial Troop Transporter.

Imperial Shuttle, 1984. Approximately 18″ tall with wings folded. Battery sound. Dorsal fin is removable. Small parts include two-piece ramp, cockpit canopy, side hatch, battery cover, landing gear, two wing guns, two front and one rear cannon.

No package .... $150–$195
Jedi box .... $350–$450

Imperial Sniper Vehicle, 1984. Gray one-man vehicle with overhead wings. Figure sat in seat under wings. Came blister-packed on color cardboard header.

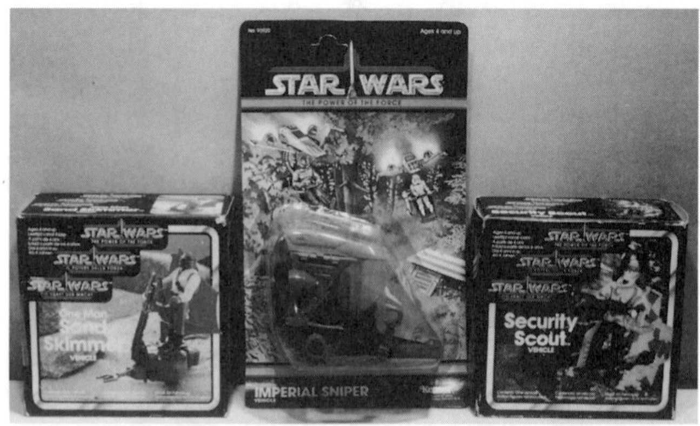

Kenner version of Imperial Sniper vehicle *(center)*, with European packaging of two other toys in the series, Sand Skimmer and Security Scout

No package .... $35–$50
Power of the Force package .... $85–$125

Imperial TIE Fighter, 1977. Approximately 12″ wide. White plastic. Pop-off solar panels with connectors. Battery light and sound. Small parts include access doors and battery cover.

No package .... $70–$95
Star Wars box .... $150–$200
Empire box .... $195–$250

Four TIE toys from the original series. ***Clockwise from upper left,*** **Imperial TIE Fighter, Imperial TIE Fighter (Battle Damaged), Darth Vader TIE Fighter, and TIE Interceptor**

Imperial TIE Fighter (Battle Damaged), 1983. Battery functions. Same mold as official TIE but in blue plastic with "battle damage" decals.

No package .... $65–$75
Jedi box .... $125–$150

Imperial Troop Transporter, 1979. Wheeled vehicle with compartments for figures on sides and six different battery-operated sounds. Also called "Imperial Cruiser" on some packaging. Small parts include two "Prisoner Immobilization Units" and battery cover.

NOTE: Versions of this toy with and without sound exist. Value is approximately the same.

Kenner, Imperial Troop Transporter (Star Wars box)

No package .... $45–$65
Star Wars box .... $115–$145
Empire box .... $125–$155

Jabba the Hutt Action Playset, 1983. Includes Jabba action figure and platform with trapdoors. Small parts include Salacious Crumb figure, two-piece water pipe and collar and string.

No package .... $25–$40
Jedi box .... $75–$95

Jabba the Hutt Dungeon Action Playset Two different variations; both utilize reworked base and crane from earlier Droid Factory toy. Difference in value is due primarily to scarcity of different action figures included with the sets. For this reason, unboxed sets have very little value over that of the figures.

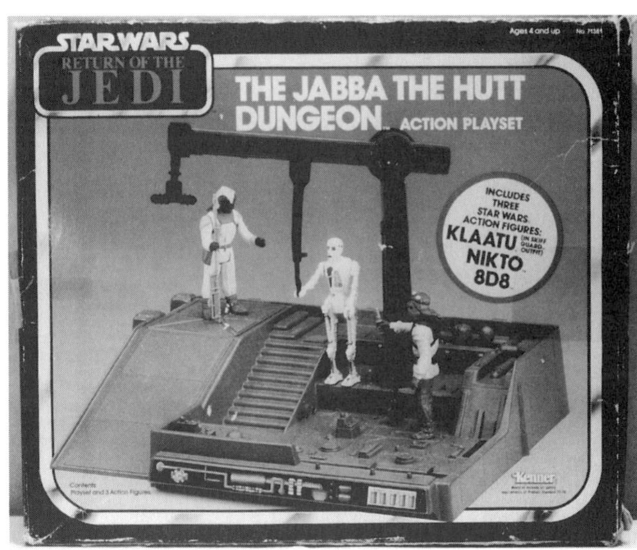

Kenner, Jabba the Hutt Dungeon Action Playset. This version includes the more common action figures

1983, includes Klaatu (Skiff Guard), Nikto and 8D8 action figures. Jedi box has red background .... $150–$195

1984, includes EV-9D9, Amanaman and Barada figures. Jedi box has green background .... $325–$450

Land of the Jawas Action Playset, 1977. Plastic base with cardboard Sandcrawler backdrop and two-piece plastic escape pod. Small parts include five-piece elevator assembly and four-piece lever assemblies.

NOTE: Palitoy version of this toy did not include escape pod but did include separate action figure disks and Jawa action figure.

No package .... $65–$85
Star Wars box .... $150–$225
Empire box .... $250–$400

Landspeeder, 1977. Rolls on spring wheels. Seats and windshield are occasionally missing on this toy.

No package .... $25–$35
Star Wars box .... $65–$80

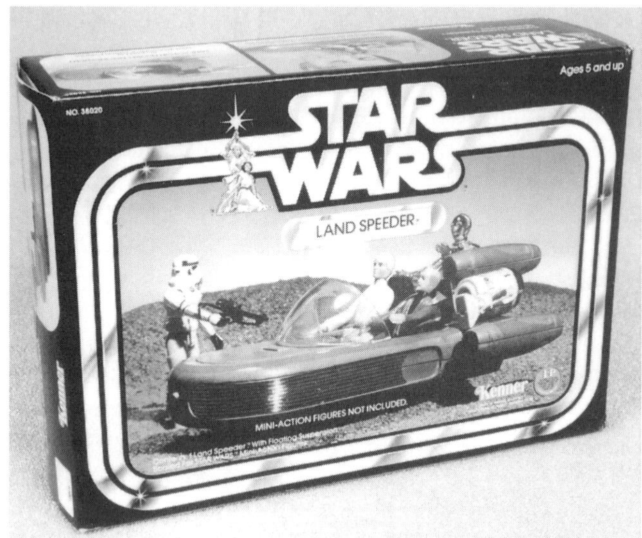

Kenner, Land Speeder (Star Wars box)

Millennium Falcon, 1977. 23″ with removable top cover. Battery sound. Small parts include two landing legs, ramp with two struts, false floor, lightsaber practice ball with support rod and string, game table, four-piece cannon assembly and three-piece radar dish.

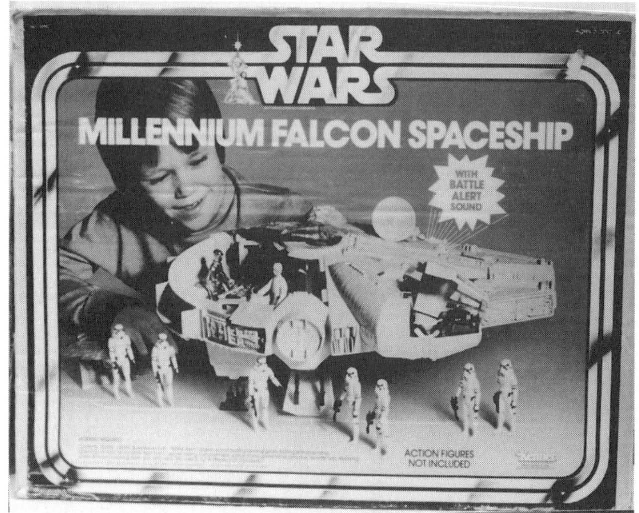

Kenner, Millennium Falcon Spaceship (Star Wars box)

No package .... $115–$135
Star Wars box .... $250–$325
Empire box .... $200–$250
Jedi box .... $175–$200

One Man Sand Skimmer, 1984. Small dark green and orange vehicle. Figure stands on platform with controls in front and sail behind. Came blister-packed on color artwork header.

No package .... $35–$50
Power of the Force .... $85–$125

Patrol Dewback, 1977. Approximately 10″ long. Movable head, legs and tail. Small parts include saddle and reins.

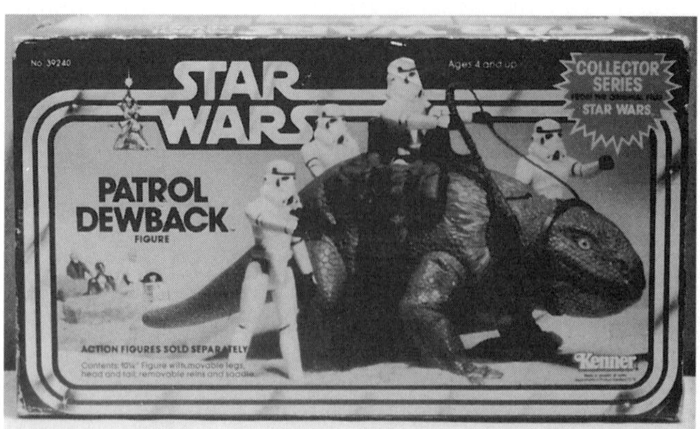

Kenner, Patrol Dewback (Star Wars box)

No package .... $35–$45
Star Wars box .... $50–$85
Empire box .... $95–$125

Radio Controlled Jawa Sandcrawler, 1977. Brown wheeled vehicle with top and side doors opening into interior. Comes with antennaed radio control unit.

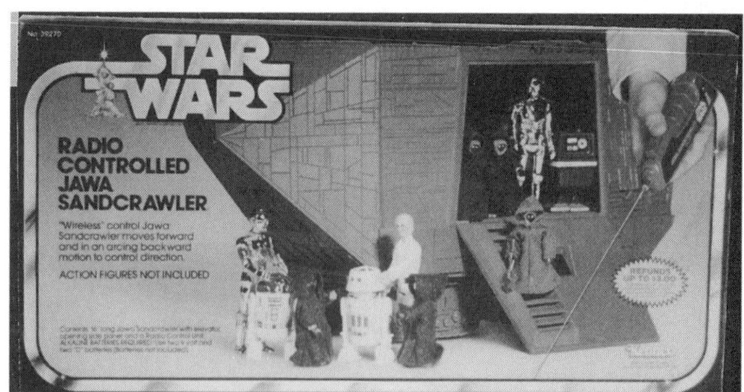

Kenner, Radio-Controlled Jawa Sandcrawler (Star Wars box)

No package .... $175–$250
Star Wars box .... $550–$650
Empire box .... $700–$850

Rancor Monster, 1983. Approximately 10″ high. Movable joints. Spring-loaded arm action. No accessories.

No package .... $30–$50
Jedi box .... $70–$95

Rebel Command Center Adventure Set, 1981. Sears promotional set. Includes cardboard playset and three action figures, R2-D2 (sensorscape), Luke (Hoth outfit) and AT-AT Commander.

No package .... $125–$195
Empire box .... $275–$400

Rebel Transport, 1982. Approximately 20″ long. Removable front and back hatches and cannons. Top is removable. Includes five backpacks and four gas masks.

No package..$50–$75
Empire box..$150–$225

Scout Walker, 1982. Approximately 10″ tall. Hand-operated walking mechanism. Small parts include entrance door with small detachable hatch cover, breast plate and top gun.

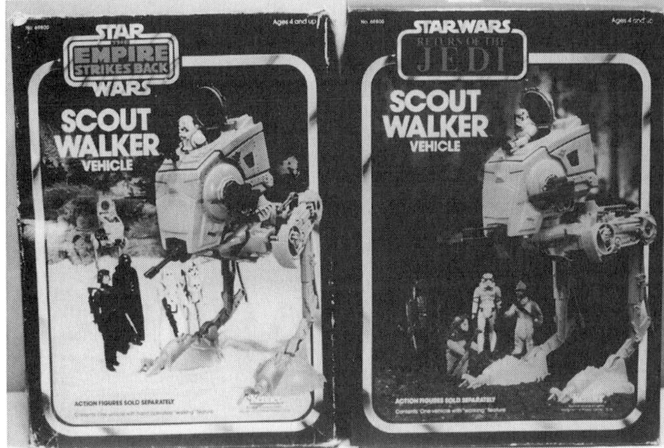

Scout Walkers in Empire and Jedi boxes

No package..$45–$65
Empire box..$95–$125
Jedi box...$85–$115

Security Scout, 1984. Small one-man vehicle. Camouflage-colored. Figure was placed in front with guns on either side. Came blister-packed on color artwork header.

No package..$35–$50
Power of the Force package............................$85–$125

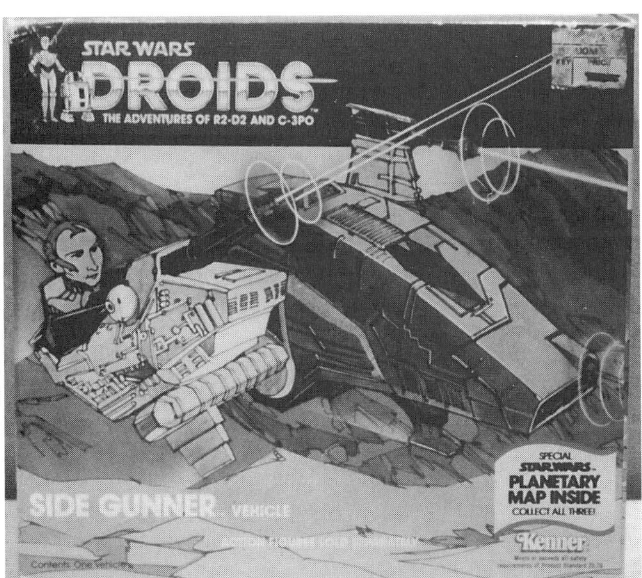

Kenner, Side Gunner vehicle (Droids box)

Side Gunner, 1985. From Droids animated series. Side car portion is removable from main toy. Small parts include hatch cover, pop-up side car seat and two side guns. Also originally included "Planetary Map."

No package..$40–$50
Droids box..$65–$85

Slave I, 1982. Approximately 12″ long. Removable wings and ramp. Adjustable seat. Includes one-piece Han Solo in carbonite figure exclusive to this set. (Not the same as two-piece action figure.)

Kenner, Slave I (Empire box)

No package..$85–$115
Empire box..$145–$175

Snow Speeder, 1982. Approximately 12″ long. Battery light and sound. Small parts include two front cannons, two rear cannons, cockpit cover, harpoon mount, harpoon and harpoon spool and string.

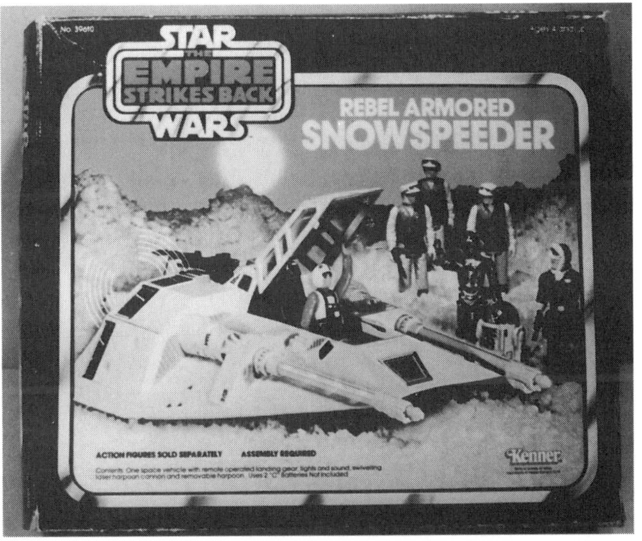

Kenner, Rebel Armored Snow Speeder (Empire box)

No package..$55–$75
Empire box..$135–$165

Sonic Controlled Land Speeder, 1977. Slightly larger than regular Land Speeder. Battery operated with rotated front wheel. Direction is controlled with a mechanical clicker shaped like R2-D2.

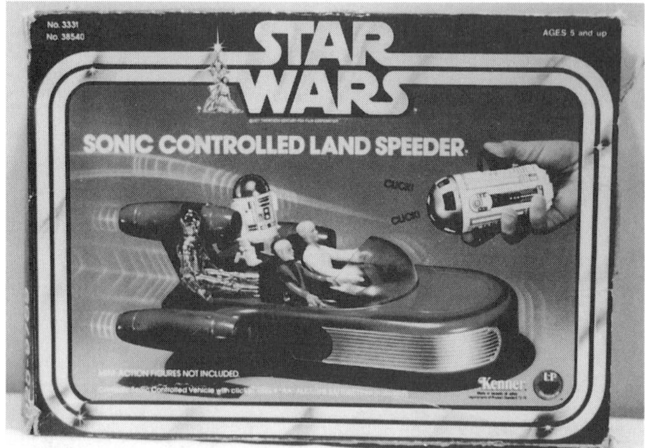

Kenner, Sonic-Controlled Land Speeder (Star Wars box)

No package .... $200–$250
Star Wars box .... $500–$700

Speeder Bike, 1983. Approximately 8″ long. Movable flaps, brakes and handlebars. Toy is designed to "explode." Main body of toy is three-piece (top, bottom and front extension). Small parts include one-piece front fin assembly and two tiny rear speed flaps.

No package .... $15–$25
Jedi box .... $35–$45

Survival Kit, 1980. Mail order only. Packet of accessories for action figures. Grappling hook, belt, Jedi training harness, two backpacks, three gas masks and five different weapons. Came in clear plastic bag.

Each .... $10–$15

Sy Snootles and the Rebo Band, 1983. Set includes three action figures available only in this set. Figures and accessories came blister-packed in shallow tray box. Droopy McCool, Max Rebo and Sy Snootles. Set also includes Max's pianolike instrument, Droopy's flute and two microphones.

No package .... $40–$60
Jedi box .... $75–$115

Tatooine Skiff, 1985. Approximately 12″ long with fold-down legs. Small parts include two side railings, two rear fins and hinged end of gangplank. Also originally included "Planetary Map." Not to be confused with the Desert Sail Skiff Mini-Rig.

No package .... $175–$225
Power of the Force box .... $750–$950

Tauntaun, 1980. Approximately 8″ tall. Movable front and rear legs. Removable saddle and reins. Trapdoor in back for placement of action figure.

No package .... $25–$35
Empire box .... $65–$85

Regular *(left)* and Open-Belly Tauntauns (Empire boxes)

Tauntaun (Open Belly), 1980. Same as the regular model except for slot in belly for placement of action figure.

No package .... $20–$30
Empire box .... $60–$75

TIE Interceptor, 1983. Approximately 12″ wide. Pop-off solar panels with connectors. Battery light and sound. Small parts include access doors and battery cover.

No package .... $50–$70
Jedi box .... $125–$150

Turret and Probot, 1980. White plastic lever action base, five-piece turret and four-piece probot.

No package .... $45–$60
Empire box .... $135–$175

Twin Pod Cloud Car, 1980. Approximately 10″ wide, molded in orange plastic. Canopies are removable.

Kenner, Twin Pod Cloud Car (Empire box)

No package .... $35–$45
Empire box .... $85–$125

X-Wing Fighter, 1977. Approximately 14″ long. White plastic. Movable wings, landing gear and canopy. Battery-operated light and sound. Small parts include four wing guns and canopy cover.

No package .... $65–$85

X-Wing Fighter (*top,* Star Wars box) and X-Wing Battle Damaged (Jedi box)

Star Wars box .... $145–$165
Empire box .... $175–$250

X-Wing (Battle Damaged), 1980. Battery functions. Same basic toy as original X-Wing but in light gray plastic with "battle damage" decals.

No package .... $55–$75
Empire box .... $150–$200
Jedi box .... $115–$145

Kenner, Y-Wing Fighter (Jedi box)

Y-Wing Fighter, 1983. Approximately 20″ long. Battery sound. Small parts consist of two removable engine pods each containing four long rods and an endcap, two small front and one larger top gun, battery cover and two-piece bomb.

No package .... $75–$95
Jedi box .... $150–$225

CURRENT SERIES ACTION FIGURE TOYS

The current series of toys produced by Kenner (now part of the Hasbro Group) began manufacture in 1995. Most, to date, are re-issues of ships done for Kenner's Original Action Figure Toy line and, unlike the action figures themselves, utilize the same molds as the originals. Though the detailing of the pieces has changed, the basic toys themselves are identical to the originals despite the fact that they are now slightly out of scale with the new, larger figures. Box art, which depicts a photo of the product, is new and carries either "Star Wars" or "Star Wars, Shadows of the Empire" logos. Since this is a current toy line, with most toys still readily available in near-new, in-the-package condition, unpackaged toys have yet to attain any appreciable collectible value. For this reason, all toys in this section will be assumed to be in basically new-in-the-box condition.

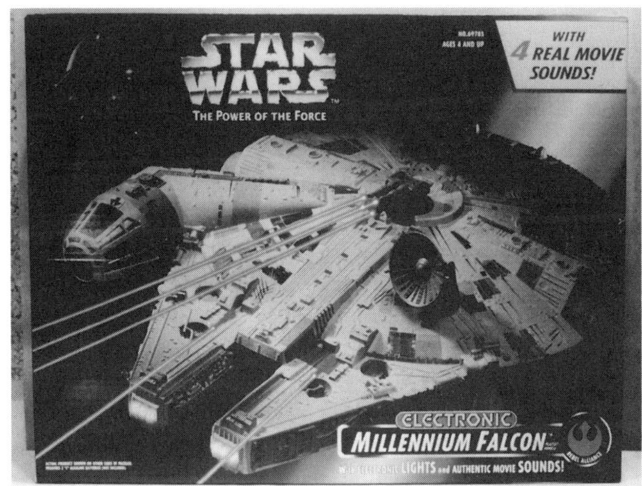

Kenner's "new" Millennium Falcon

Darth Vader Figure Case, (Just Toys) slightly different from original .... $10–$20
Dash Rendar's Outrider, new vehicle .... $20–$30
Imperial AT-ST .... $15–$25
Imperial Speeder Bike, with Biker Scout figure .... $25–$35
Landspeeder .... $10–$20
Millennium Falcon .... $45–$55
Power of the Force Figure Case .... $10–$20
Slave I .... $50–$60
Snowspeeder .... $50–$60
Swoop, new vehicle, with Swoop Trooper figure .... $15–$25
TIE Fighter .... $20–$30
X-Wing Fighter .... $20–$30

ACTION FIGURES, DOLLS AND PVC FIGURES

There are, in this section, two major categories of figures. The first group are unjointed (or nearly so) and on the whole are not taken particularly seriously by collectors. The second, dolls or action figures, are probably the hottest field of collectibles in the United States today. Because they are so heavily scrutinized by collectors, condition is even more important than in most collectible categories, especially with the older carded figures. Extra-nice figures can be sold for considerable premiums to particularly picky collectors who have devised complex grading systems and worry about even the tiniest flaws.

Practically speaking, the collector should buy older figures in as good condition as he or she can afford, passing entirely on packages with major flaws such as large creases and tears and making sure loose figures have all weapons and equipment appropriate for the particular figure.

For other three-dimensional figural representations, see GAMES, PEWTER and TOYS AND CRAFTS. This section is organized alphabetically by manufacturer.

NOTE: The plastic used in Kenner's original line of Jedi, Power of the Force and Droids small action figures turns yellow with age (this generally does not occur in older figures or in Triple Language or Ewoks figures). Though clear plastic bubbles are, of course, more desirable, they may soon be impossible to find for these particular figures.

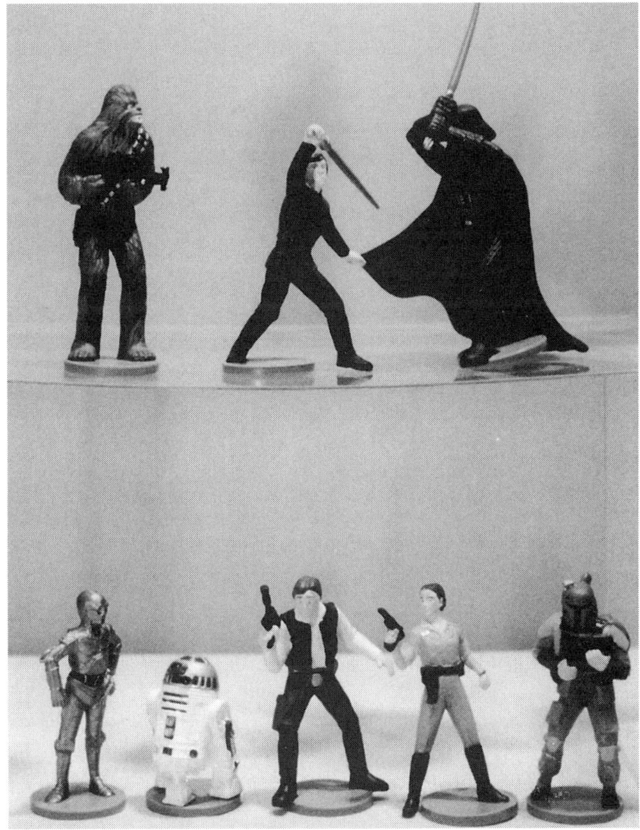

Applause, Star Wars Collectors Series PVC figurines

APPLAUSE

Star Wars Collectors Series PVC Figurines, 1995

Figurines have no moving parts and range in size from 2″ to 4 1/2″. Those not packaged in sets were expected to be sold as single pieces from counter displays and have no individual packaging.

Individual Figures

- **Boba Fett** .... $4–$5
- **Chewbacca** .... $4–$5
- **C-3PO** .... $4–$5
- **Darth Vader** .... $4–$5
- **Emperor** .... $4–$5
- **Han Solo** .... $4–$5
- **Luke Skywalker** .... $4–$5

Princess Leia .... $4–$5
R2-D2 .... $4–$5
Stormtrooper .... $4–$5

Seven-Piece Set Window boxes have artwork to left and are individually numbered. Includes C-3PO, R2-D2, Han Solo, Chewbacca, Boba Fett, Darth Vader, Luke and stand for figures.
Each .... $15–$20

Collector Series Large Vinyl Dolls, 1995 to present. Figures are between 9″ and 11″ tall and either are permanently posed or have only one or two movable features. No packaging other than a protective plastic cover. An information card on the character is attached to each doll. "Shadows of the Empire" as well as regular Star Wars saga figures are included in the series.

Applause, Collector Series large vinyl dolls

Boba Fett .... $15–$20
Chewbacca and C-3PO .... $15–$20
Darth Vader .... $15–$20
Dash Rendar .... $15–$20
Emperor Palpatine .... $15–$20
Greedo .... $15–$20
Han Solo, Stormtrooper .... $15–$20
Lando, Skiff Guard .... $15–$20
Luke Skywalker and Yoda .... $15–$20
Obi-Wan Kenobi .... $15–$20
Princess Leia Organa .... $15–$20
Prince Xizor .... $15–$20
Tusken Raider .... $15–$20

COMICS SPAIN

1986. 2″ to 3″ non-posable. Based on animated shows.

C-3PO .... $10–$15
Ewok, hat with green feather .... $10–$15
Ewok, hat with pink feather .... $10–$15
Ewok, with flaver .... $10–$15
Ewok, with horn .... $10–$15
Ewok, with spear .... $10–$15
Kez-Iban .... $10–$15
R2-D2 .... $10–$15

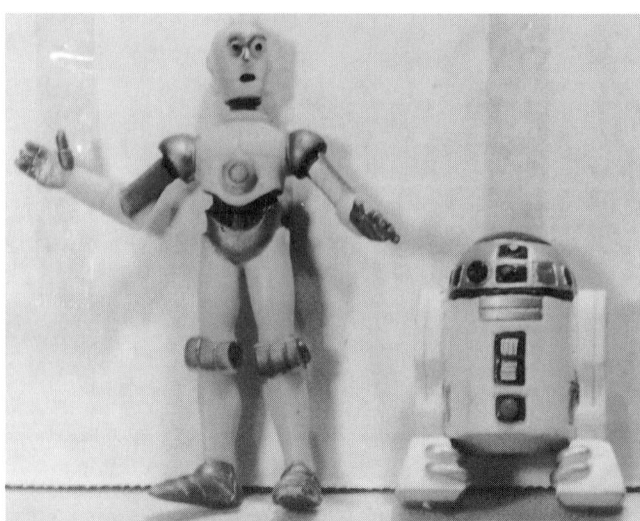

Comics Spain, C-3PO and R2-D2

JUST TOYS

Star Wars BendEms, 1993

Flexible plastic figures range in height from approximately $2^{1}/_{2}$″ to 5″. Single figures came blister-packed on color header cards. Sets had figures blister-carded onto backings set in shallow tray boxes. Both single figures and sets often included bonus Topps Star Wars Galaxy trading cards, which add very little to the value. Prices are for packaged figures. Unpackaged figures have yet to accrue any collectible value. Slight variations do occur.

Single Figures
C-3PO .... $5–$10
Chewbacca .... $5–$10
Darth Vader .... $5–$10
Emperor .... $5–$10
Han Solo .... $5–$10
Luke Skywalker .... $5–$10
Obi-Wan Kenobi .... $5–$10
Princess Leia .... $5–$10
R2-D2 .... $5–$10
Wicket .... $5–$10
Yoda .... $5–$10

Four-Piece Sets
Emperor, R2-D2, Luke, Darth Vader .... $20–$30
Obi-Wan, Leia, Han, C-3PO .... $20–$30
Stormtrooper, R2-D2, C-3PO, Darth Vader ..... $20–$30
Stormtrooper, Wicket, Yoda, Chewbacca .... $20–$30

Six-Piece Set Promotional.
Admiral Ackbar, Chewbacca, Darth Vader, Emperor, Emperor's Royal Guard, Lando .... $35–$50

Eight-Piece Set Three variations.

Just Toys, eight-piece BendEms boxed set

Darth Vader, Stormtrooper, Luke, R2-D2, C-3PO, Leia, Wicket and either Emperor, Obi-Wan or Yoda .... $30–$40

Gift Set Nine figures plus coin and cards.

Admiral Ackbar, Bib Fortuna, Chewbacca, Darth Vader, Emperor's Royal Guard, Han, Luke, R2-D2, Stormtrooper .... $40–$50

KENNER

NOTE: For figures intended for sale only in playsets, see ACTION FIGURE TOYS. For loose Kenner aluminum character coins, see COINS.

Large Star Wars Action Figures, 1977–1980

When originally marketed, this series of figures did not compete well against Kenner's own line of small action figures, which were selling concurrently with these. Consequently, Kenner soon lost interest in the large action figure line and discontinued their production. Because of this relative scarcity, these dolls have become extremely collectible. Dolls come packaged in window boxes with side panels depicting a photograph of the character. Boxes originally came with colored cardboard liners which were slotted to hold weapons (if any). All easily removable clothing and accessories are listed with figure.

NOTE: Kenner large action figures were marketed in some foreign countries by Palitoy and Denys Fisher in Europe and Lili-Lily in Mexico. Prices for foreign packaging are approximately the same.

Ben (Obi-Wan) Kenobi, 12″ tall. White robe with black collar, brown robe with hood, brown boots, yellow lightsaber.

Boxed .... $200–$350
Unboxed .... $150–$200

Boba Fett, 13½″ tall. Swing-up "range-finder," green cape, rifle, backpack with string and "rocket," two "Wookiee-scalps," belt.

Boxed .... $250–$450
Unboxed .... $150–$200

Chewbacca, 15″ tall. Crossbow rifle, bandolier with 16 removable gray plastic inserts.

Boxed .... $150–$225
Unboxed .... $65–$100

C-3PO, 12½″ tall. No clothing or accessories.

Boxed .... $135–$195
Unboxed .... $50–$75

Darth Vader, 15″ tall. Black cape, red lightsaber.

Boxed .... $165–$250
Unboxed .... $75–$100

Han Solo, 12½″ tall. Black pants, white shirt, black vinyl vest, boots, pistol, holster, gold plastic medallion on red ribbon.

Boxed .... $450–$675
Unboxed .... $250–$350

IG-88, 15″ tall. Brown bandolier with four red "grenades," pistol (approximately 3½″ in length) and rifle (approximately 7½″ in length).

Boxed .... $500–$800
Unboxed .... $275–$350

Jawa, 8″ tall. Brown hooded robe, X-shaped bandolier, rifle (approximately 4″ long).

Boxed .... $200–$325
Unboxed .... $100–$150

Luke Skywalker, 12″ tall. Tan pants, white shirt, white boots, belt, grappling hook on string, blue lightsaber.

Boxed .... $300–$400
Unboxed .... $200–$250

Princess Leia, 12″ tall. Fiber hair is held in original bun style by two plastic rings. White dress with hood, silver plastic belt, white stockings, white plastic shoes, blue plastic comb and brush. (A hairstyle booklet also originally came with this figure.)

Boxed .... $300–$400
Unboxed .... $175–$250

R2-D2, 7½″ tall. Back panel opens to hold two removable "circuit boards."

Boxed .... $150–$250
Unboxed .... $60–$95

Stormtrooper, 12″ tall. Rifle (approximately 5″ long) can be secured to waist of figure with black thread loop.

Boxed .... $250–$350
Unboxed .... $125–$195

Collector Series Large Star Wars Action Figures, 1996

Though approximately the same size, figures are made from different molds than Kenner's original series of large figures. Box has fold-over flap with color character photo opening to window box with figure and accessories wired and blister-packed onto an interior cardboard liner. Prices are for packaged figures only, as unpackaged figures have little collectible value at this time. Minor package variations have occurred in this series, but to date none are appreciably more valuable.

Boba Fett .... $50–$75
Darth Vader .... $60–$95
Han Solo .... $40–$60
Lando Calrissian .... $50–$75
Luke Skywalker .... $50–$75

Kenner, original *(left)* and Collector Series large Luke Skywalker figures

Luke Skywalker, Bespin .... $60–$95
Luke X-Wing Pilot .... $40–$60
Obi-Wan Kenobi .... $60–$95
Princess Leia .... $40–$60
Stormtrooper .... $40–$60
Tusken Raider, with Gaffi Stick .... $50–$75
Tusken Raider, with blaster .... $40–$60

Star Wars Trilogy Small Action Figures (Original Issue), 1978–1983

Figures range in size from approximately 2¼″ to 4¼″ in height and come blister-packed on color header cards. They were released in series with new figures being added as time progressed. Older figures were not dropped from the line but instead were packaged to display the logo of the most current film. Consequently, figures that had been in production longer accumulated the most package logo variations. These were Star Wars, The Empire Strikes Back, Return of the Jedi, Power of the Force (done at the end of the trilogy and designed as an all-encompassing logo), which included an aluminum character coin and Triple Language, designed as common packaging for foreign markets. Other packaging exists for figures sold in various countries, but the packages mentioned above are by far the most commonly collected. As a general rule, earlier package logos and Power of the Force logos are more rare and therefore more valuable (earlier ones because more of those figures tended to be removed from cards and Power of the Force because demand for the figures was waning by the time these were being sold and fewer were produced). Values given here for loose figures assume that figures are complete with all original weapons and equipment. Incomplete figures retain only a fraction of the value of their complete counterparts. Values for packaged figures assume packaging is in excellent, near new condition. Wear and damage to packaging reduces the value of figures proportionally. Open packages reduce their value drastically. Though collecting variations is very popular with this particular figure line, separate values will be listed only for figures with major structural differences. Package variations within the five major categories and paint variations on the figures will not be listed, the first because so many exist that only the most dedicated collector could ever hope to come near completing a collection, and the second because paint variations are extremely easy to counterfeit and therefore never likely to become significantly more valuable. Since only one value is listed for each variation, a 10 percent plus or minus range in the price may be assumed. Also keep in mind that this is a very volatile collector's market, even for the active action figure field, and collectors are advised to keep as up-to-date on changing prices as possible. A blank entry for a particular variation denotes that the figure was not commonly produced in that packaging.

NOTE: Recently, counterfeiting of harder-to-find weapons and equipment for loose figures has become common, and most probably will lead to the eventual devaluation of many of these figures.

Admiral Ackbar

Type of Package	*None*	*SW*	*Empire*	*Jedi*	*POF*	*3-Lang*
Admiral Ackbar	10.00	—	—	25.00	—	25.00
Amanaman	100.00	—	—	—	225.00	200.00

Anakin Skywalker

Type of Package	None	SW	Empire	Jedi	POF	3-Lang
Anakin Skywalker	35.00	—	—	—	600.00	75.00
AT-AT Commander	10.00	—	35.00	15.00	—	15.00
AT-AT Driver	10.00	—	45.00	35.00	250.00	35.00
AT-ST Driver	10.00	—	—	15.00	75.00	15.00
A-Wing Pilot	65.00	—	—	—	85.00	65.00

Barada

Type of Package	None	SW	Empire	Jedi	POF	3-Lang
Barada	65.00	—	—	—	135.00	85.00
Bespin Security Guard (Black)	15.00	—	50.00	45.00	—	45.00
Bespin Security Guard (White)	15.00	—	50.00	45.00	—	45.00

Bib Fortuna

Type of Package	None	SW	Empire	Jedi	POF	3-Lang
Bib Fortuna	20.00	—	—	30.00	—	30.00
Biker Scout	20.00	—	—	25.00	75.00	25.00
Boba Fett	35.00	600.00	275.00	175.00	—	175.00

Bossk

Type of Package	None	SW	Empire	Jedi	POF	3-Lang
Bossk	10.00	—	75.00	35.00	—	35.00
B-Wing Pilot	20.00	—	—	30.00	35.00	30.00
C-3PO	15.00	150.00	85.00	50.00	—	50.00
C-3PO (Removable Limbs)	10.00	—	50.00	40.00	95.00	40.00
Chewbacca	10.00	200.00	95.00	45.00	—	45.00
Chief Chirpa	15.00	—	—	20.00	—	20.00
Cloud Car Pilot	20.00	—	60.00	50.00	—	50.00
Darth Vader	20.00	200.00	115.00	50.00	125.00	50.00

Type of Package	*None*	*SW*	*Empire*	*Jedi*	*POF*	*3-Lang*
Death Star Droid	15.00	150.00	150.00	75.00	—	75.00
Dengar	15.00	—	35.00	35.00	—	35.00
8D8	10.00	—	—	20.00	—	20.00

Emperor

Type of Package	*None*	*SW*	*Empire*	*Jedi*	*POF*	*3-Lang*
Emperor	25.00	—	—	35.00	60.00	35.00
Emperor's Royal Guard	10.00	—	—	35.00	—	35.00
EV-9D9	125.00	—	—	—	165.00	145.00
4-LOM	20.00	—	75.00	45.00	—	45.00
FX-7	10.00	—	65.00	45.00	—	45.00
Gamorrean Guard	15.00	—	—	20.00	175.00	20.00
General Madine	15.00	—	—	20.00	—	20.00

Greedo

Type of Package	*None*	*SW*	*Empire*	*Jedi*	*POF*	*3-Lang*
Greedo	20.00	175.00	150.00	65.00	—	65.00

Hammerhead

Type of Package	*None*	*SW*	*Empire*	*Jedi*	*POF*	*3-Lang*
Hammerhead	10.00	165.00	135.00	65.00	—	65.00
Han Solo (Large Head)	30.00	500.00	275.00	135.00	—	135.00
Han Solo (Small Head)	30.00	500.00	275.00	—	—	—
Han Solo (Bespin)	30.00	—	95.00	65.00	—	65.00
Han Solo (Carbonite)	125.00	—	—	—	250.00	200.00
Han Solo (Hoth)	15.00	—	75.00	65.00	—	65.00
Han Solo (Trench Coat)	15.00	—	—	35.00	250.00	35.00

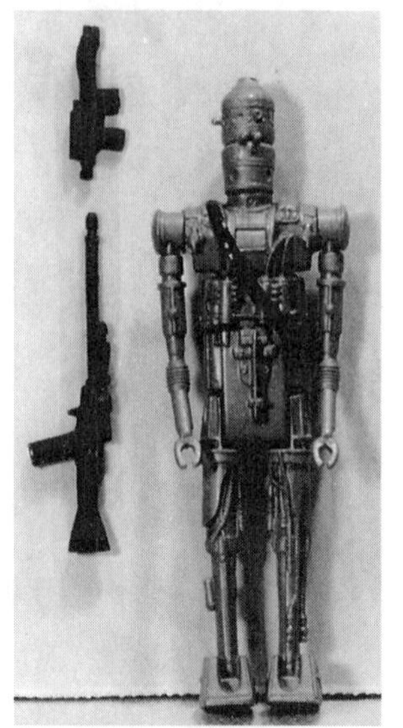

IG88

Type of Package	*None*	*SW*	*Empire*	*Jedi*	*POF*	*3-Lang*
IG88	15.00	—	75.00	45.00	—	45.00

Type of Package	*None*	*SW*	*Empire*	*Jedi*	*POF*	*3-Lang*
Imperial Commander	15.00	—	35.00	25.00	—	25.00
Imperial Dignitary	55.00	—	—	—	135.00	115.00
Imperial Gunner	85.00	—	—	—	150.00	125.00
Imperial Stormtrooper	15.00	225.00	175.00	75.00	175.00	75.00
Imperial Stormtrooper (Hoth)	20.00	—	75.00	55.00	—	55.00
Imperial TIE Pilot	35.00	—	95.00	70.00	—	70.00
Jawa	15.00	225.00	150.00	75.00	125.00	75.00
Jawa (Plastic Cape)	350.00	1500.00	—	—	—	—

NOTE: This figure is widely counterfeited.

Type of Package	*None*	*SW*	*Empire*	*Jedi*	*POF*	*3-Lang*
Klaatu	10.00	—	—	20.00	—	20.00

Klaatu (Skiff Guard)

Type of Package	*None*	*SW*	*Empire*	*Jedi*	*POF*	*3-Lang*
Klaatu (Skiff Guard)	15.00	—	—	20.00	—	20.00

Lando Calrissian

Type of Package	*None*	*SW*	*Empire*	*Jedi*	*POF*	*3-Lang*
Lando Calrissian	15.00	—	60.00	35.00	—	35.00
Lando (General Pilot)	85.00	—	—	—	145.00	125.00
Lando (Skiff Guard)	15.00	—	—	20.00	—	20.00
Lobot	15.00	—	35.00	25.00	—	25.00
Logray	10.00	—	—	20.00	—	20.00
Luke Skywalker	45.00	400.00	300.00	150.00	—	150.00
Luke Skywalker (extendable saber)	175.00	—	—	—	—	—
Luke (Battle Poncho)	95.00	—	—	—	125.00	115.00
Luke (Bespin)	35.00	—	125.00	95.00	—	95.00

Luke (Hoth)

Type of Package	*None*	*SW*	*Empire*	*Jedi*	*POF*	*3-Lang*
Luke (Hoth)	45.00	—	95.00	75.00	—	75.00
Luke (Jedi Knight)	75.00	—	—	135.00	250.00	135.00
Luke (Stormtrooper)	150.00	—	—	—	400.00	325.00
Luke (X-Wing Pilot)	15.00	200.00	150.00	65.00	175.00	65.00
Lumat	30.00	—	—	35.00	—	35.00

Nien Nunb

Type of Package	*None*	*SW*	*Empire*	*Jedi*	*POF*	*3-Lang*
Nien Nunb	15.00	—	—	25.00	—	25.00

Obi-Wan Kenobi

Obi Wan Kenobi	15.00	250.00	175.00	65.00	150.00	65.00

Nikto

Nikto	20.00	—	—	25.00	225.00	25.00
Paploo	20.00	—	—	25.00	95.00	25.00
Power Droid	10.00	150.00	125.00	85.00	—	85.00
Princess Leia	45.00	350.00	300.00	325.00	—	275.00
Princess Leia (Bespin)	35.00	—	150.00	65.00	—	65.00
Princess Leia (Boushh)	35.00	—	—	65.00	—	65.00
Princess Leia (Hoth)	45.00	—	95.00	75.00	—	75.00

Princess Leia

Type of Package	*None*	*SW*	*Empire*	*Jedi*	*POF*	*3-Lang*
Princess Leia (Poncho)	25.00	—	—	35.00	95.00	35.00

Prune Face

Prune Face	10.00	—	—	20.00	—	20.00
Rancor Keeper	15.00	—	—	20.00	—	20.00
Rebel Commander	10.00	—	40.00	30.00	—	30.00
Rebel Commando	10.00	—	—	30.00	—	30.00
Rebel Soldier	10.00	—	40.00	30.00	—	30.00
Ree-Yees	15.00	—	—	25.00	—	25.00
R2-D2	20.00	175.00	125.00	50.00	—	50.00
R2-D2 (Lightsaber)	95.00	—	—	—	150.00	125.00
R2-D2 (Sensorscope)	10.00	—	50.00	30.00	—	30.00
R5-D4	20.00	175.00	125.00	75.00	—	75.00
Romba	35.00	—	—	—	60.00	50.00

Type of Package	*None*	*SW*	*Empire*	*Jedi*	*POF*	*3-Lang*
Snaggletooth (Tall)	175.00	—	—	—	—	—
Snaggletooth (Short)	15.00	145.00	135.00	50.00	—	50.00
Star Destroyer Comm (Death Squad Comm.)	20.00	195.00	95.00	45.00	—	45.00
Squid Head	20.00	—	—	30.00	—	30.00
Teebo	15.00	—	—	25.00	125.00	25.00
2-1B	20.00	—	65.00	40.00	—	40.00
Tusken Raider (Sand People)	15.00	195.00	85.00	45.00	—	45.00

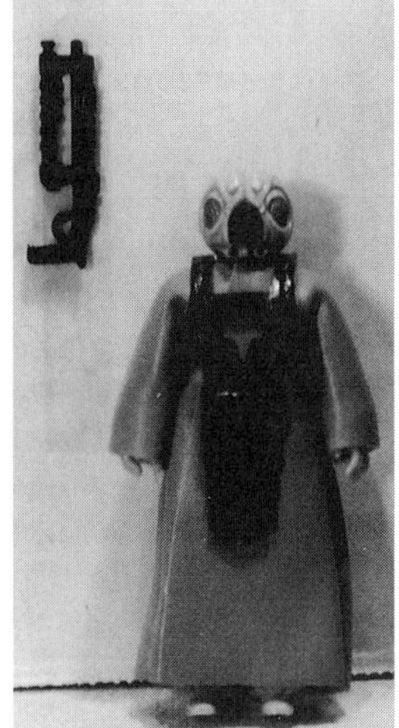

Tusken (Sand People)

Ugnaught	15.00	—	75.00	50.00	—	50.00
Walrusman	20.00	175.00	125.00	65.00	—	65.00
Warok	35.00	—	—	—	50.00	40.00

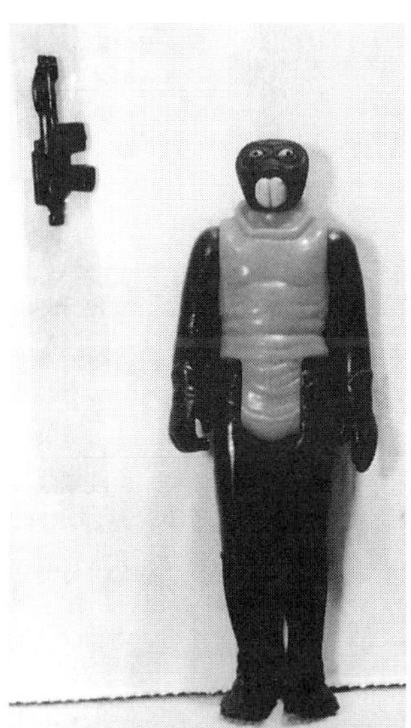

Walrusman

Weequay

Type of Package	*None*	*SW*	*Empire*	*Jedi*	*POF*	*3-Lang*
Weequay	15.00	—	—	25.00	—	25.00
Wicket	20.00	—	—	25.00	125.00	25.00

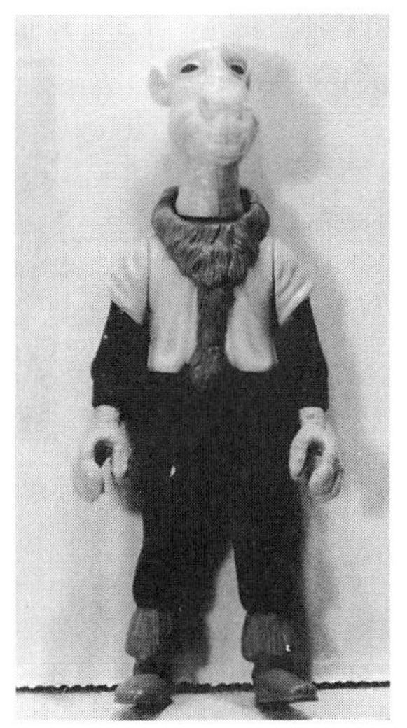

Yak Face

Yak Face	175.00	—	—	—	750.00	350.00
Yoda	30.00	—	95.00	75.00	—	75.00
Zuckuss	15.00	—	45.00	25.00	—	25.00

EARLY BIRD CERTIFICATE PACKAGE, 1977

Light cardboard envelope with Star Wars logo at top and color photos of characters across middle. Sold by stores before the small figures were actually manufactured in order to offer something for sale from Star Wars during the Christmas sales season. The certificate could be sent to Kenner and redeemed for the figures after they were actually made.

Complete kit..$300–$500

Foreign small figure packaging

MULTIPLE PACKAGING

Kenner offered several send-in promotions for small action figures during the course of their manufacture. These were sent in plain white mailing boxes, sometimes with a color photo sticker of the figures it included on the front. Their value is essentially the sum of the figures it contained, which must be considered as loose figures, since they are not blister-carded. There were some extremely rare three-figure blister-carded sets (Star Wars, Empire and Jedi cards were made), none of which sell for less than $500. There are also at least two extremely rare six-figure Empire boxed sets. Much less rare are blister-packed two-figure sets. These were packaged on Jedi cards, which unlike both single-carded figures and the above-mentioned sets, did not have the figure's or figures' names printed on the card. These were most likely an attempt by Kenner to move excess stock through repackaging. Bubbles were made of a size and shape to accommodate almost any of the figures, and weapons were usually not included. Many different figure combinations exist. Two-packs are valued at $50–$75.

FOREIGN PACKAGING

Kenner small action figures were marketed in foreign countries by several different companies including Palitoy (Britain), Meccano (France), Harbert (Italy), Glassite (Brazil), Lili-Lily (Mexico) and Popy (Japan). Though artwork on foreign packaging differs, all except the Japanese figures (a boxed Empire series) used blister cards similar to the U.S. version. Only Palitoy's line was nearly as extensive as the U.S. Kenner releases. While all foreign figures sell for higher prices than their Kenner counterparts, the margin is usually not more than 25 percent and the market for these figures is relatively small.

Droids (Cartoon) Action Figures, 1985

Based on the animated series, figures were similar in size and construction to Kenner's movie line. Figures are blister-packed on color header cards and each includes a gold-colored aluminum character coin.

NOTE: Unlike the other two characters (C-3PO and R2-D2) carried over from the movies, the A-Wing Pilot and Boba Fett figures were the same as those produced for Kenner's movie action figure line and are therefore indistinguishable unpackaged.

A-Wing Pilot
Unpackaged
Packaged .... $200–$250
Boba Fett
Unpackaged
Packaged .... $250–$350
C-3PO
Unpackaged .... $15–$20
Packaged .... $50–$75
Jann Tosh
Unpackaged .... $10–$15
Packaged .... $35–$50
Jord Dusat
Unpackaged .... $10–$15
Packaged .... $30–$45
Kea Moll
Unpackaged .... $10–$15
Packaged .... $30–$45
Kez-Iban
Unpackaged .... $10–$15

Packaged..$25–$40

R2-D2

Unpackaged..$15–$20

Packaged..$45–$65

Sise Fromm

Unpackaged..$20–$25

Packaged..$50–$75

Thall Joben

Unpackaged..$10–$15

Packaged..$25–$40

Tig Fromm

Unpackaged..$20–$25

Packaged..$50–$75

Uncle Gundy

Unpackaged..$10–$15

Packaged..$20–$30

Ewoks (Cartoon) Action Figures, 1985

Based on the animated series figures were similar in size and construction to Kenner's movie line. Figures are blister packed on color header cards and each includes a copper-colored header coin.

Dulok Scout

Unpackaged..$10–$15

Packaged..$20–$25

Dulok Shaman

Unpackaged..$10–$15

Packaged..$20–$25

King Gorneesh

Unpackaged..$10–$15

Packaged..$20–$25

Logray

Unpackaged..$10–$15

Packaged..$20–$25

Urgah Lady Gorneesh

Unpackaged..$10–$15

Packaged..$20–$25

Wicket

Unpackaged..$10–$15

Packaged..$20–$25

Star Wars Original Action Figure Re-Issue Set (Classic Edition Four-Pack), 1995

This was a boxed set of four figures (Luke, Han Solo, Darth Vader and Chewbacca) made from the original series molds. The limited edition set was made to promote Kenner's new Star Wars action figure series. Figures are blister-carded inside shallow open tray boxes.

Price for unopened set..$75–$100

Star Wars Small Action Figures (Current Series), 1995-Present

This line of Kenner figures is made from new molds and is considerably different from the older series. Figures are slightly taller than their original counterparts, averaging approximately $3^{3}/_{4}''$, and have been designed to more closely resemble other current action figure lines. They have a distinctly more muscular look and have been given more dynamic poses. Figures are blister-carded on die-cut color header cards featuring a Darth Vader head and "Star Wars" logo, and the series incorporates characters and outfits from written Star Wars adventures (Shadows of the Empire) in addition to the familiar screen characters. Cards for regular movie characters originally had a red/orange background (Shadows of the Empire characters were on purplish cards), but the background changed to green shortly after the fourth "wave" of figures was released by the manufacturer. This resulted in some figures being available on either red OR green cards, though to date green cards seem far more prevalent. Additionally, some cards have a foil "hologram" sticker placed over the character picture. At this time, neither of these package styles appears more common than the other. Kenner seems to be determined to capitalize on the current collecting craze of acquiring variations. Not only have they varied figure packaging but they have also produced several minor differences in paint and equipment. Since this is a current line of figures, and it cannot be determined at this point in time how many of these variations will ultimately be produced, it is therefore impossible to predict how this might eventually affect the value of figures in this line.

NOTE: As with the older figure line, only major structural variations in figures will be individually listed, despite the current mania for package variations. Though not noted separately, the price range for a figure does take into consideration any paint or package variations that may occur. Because this is a current, ongoing line of figures, prices are for packaged figures only. Unpackaged figures have very little collectible value at this time. Figures available only as accessories to toys are considered as part of the applicable set (see ACTION FIGURE TOYS).

Boba Fett..$15–$35

Chewbacca..$10–$15

Chewbacca, Bounty Hunter......................................$10–$15

C-3PO...$10–$15

Darth Vader, long lightsaber....................................$20–$25

Darth Vader, short lightsaber...................................$10–$20

Dash Rendar...$10–$15

Death Star Gunner...$10–$15

Greedo..$10–$30

Hammerhead, Momaw Nadon..................................$10–$25

Han Solo...$10–$15

Han Solo, Carbonite...$10–$15

Han Solo, Hoth...$10–$20

Han Solo, Stormtrooper (mail premium, no package) $30–$45

Jawa, two-pack..$25–$50

Lando Calrissian..$10–$20

Luke Skywalker, long lightsaber..............................$20–$30

Luke Skywalker, short lightsaber.............................$15–$20

Kenner, original Luke figure *(left)* and Luke figure from the current action figure line

Luke Skywalker, Imperial Guard ....$10–$15
Luke Skywalker, Dagobah - long lightsaber ....$20–$25
Luke Skywalker, Dagobah - short lightsaber ....$10–$20
Luke Skywalker, Jedi Knight ....$10–$50
Luke Skywalker, Stormtrooper ....$10–$25
Luke Skywalker, X-Wing - long lightsaber ....$10–$20
Luke Skywalker, X-Wing - short lightsaber ....$10–$20
Obi-Wan Kenobi, long lightsaber ....$50–$60
Obi-Wan Kenobi, short lightsaber ....$10–$15
Princess Leia ....$15–$25
Princess Leia, Boushh....................$10–$15
Prince Xizor ....$10–$15
R2-D2 ....$10–$15
R5-D4 ....$10–$20
Stormtrooper ....$20–$35
Tatooine Sandtrooper ....$20–$45
TIE Fighter Pilot ....$10–$25
Tusken Raider ....$15–$25
Yoda ....$10–$20

Two-Packs Pairs come blister-packed on color header.

Boba Fett vs. IG-88 ....$15–$20
Darth Vader vs. Prince Xizor ....$15–$20

Three-Packs

Lando, Chewbacca, Han Solo ....$35–$50
Luke, Obi-Wan, Darth Vader ....$35–$50
R2-D2, Stormtrooper, C-3PO ....$30–$40

Deluxe Packs These figures each include a backpack-like accessory

Crowd Control Stormtrooper ....$10–$20
Han Solo with Smuggler Flight ....$10–$20
Luke with Desert Sport Skiff ....$10–$20

Kenner, deluxe Luke with Desert Sport Skiff

Theater Premiere Packaging Available only at Special Edition premiere of Return of the Jedi. Special Edition logo and "Not for Retail Sale" are printed on the header card.

Luke, Jedi Knight ....$75–$100

1997 Hong Kong Commemorative Editions Set of three figures posed on a silver plastic commemorative base. Packaged in window box with Hong Kong skyline at bottom.

Set I, Princess Leia, Luke Skywalker, C-3PO.....$125–$200
Set II, Boba Fett, Darth Vader, Stormtrooper.....$125–$200

Kenner, Small Action Figure Three-Pack

OUT-OF-CHARACTER

Large Vinyl Dolls, 1993

Permanently posed figures approximately 12″ high. Made exclusively for Suncoast stores.

C-3PO .... $13–$18
Chewbacca .... $13–$18
Darth Vader, two minor size variations .... $13–$18
Han Solo .... $13–$18
Leia .... $13–$18
Luke .... $13–$18
Luke, X-Wing .... $13–$18
Obi-Wan .... $13–$18
R2-D2 .... $13–$18

TAKARA

Star Wars Action Figures, 1978, Japan

Figures are approximately 7″ high and came blister-packed on color header cards. Figures are articulated only at arm and leg joints. Only four different figures were produced.

Chewbacca .... $350–$500
C-3PO .... $350–$500
Darth Vader .... $350–$500
Stormtrooper .... $350–$500

BADGES, BUTTONS, DECALS AND STICKERS

This section is divided into badges, buttons, and decals and stickers, then organized alphabetically by manufacturer.

BADGES

A.H. Prismatic, 1994

2″ square plastic pinback badges with foil hologram stickers affixed to front.

FIRST SERIES

AT-AT .... $4–$6
B-Wing .... $4–$6
Darth Vader .... $4–$6
Darth TIE .... $4–$6
Imperial Cruiser .... $4–$6
Millennium Falcon .... $4–$6
Millennium Falcon, with logo .... $4–$6
TIE Interceptor .... $4–$6
X-Wing .... $4–$6

SECOND SERIES

Darth Vader .... $4–$6
C-3PO and R2-D2 .... $4–$6
Millennium Falcon .... $4–$6
X-Wing .... $4–$6

BUTTONS

In this section the word "button" refers to either a printed metal surface or printed paper and plastic affixed to a metal surface attached to a pinback. For pewter, enamel, cloisonne or epoxy surfaced pins sometimes referred to as buttons, see the JEWELRY section of this book. Buttons are probably the best example of a category of merchandise that, because they are so easy to reproduce, have very little chance of ever attaining any significant collectible value. Simple button-making machines are available to the hobbyist for as little as $25, and professional manufacturers will make buttons to order in relatively small quantities for only pennies a piece.

NOTE: In addition to bootleg copies of licensed buttons or illegal use of other images, logos, etc., countless, perfectly legal buttons made from magazines and books have been manufactured over the years. Since these types of buttons have even less collectible merit than their licensed counterparts, neither category is listed in this section.

Adam Joseph, 1983

2¼″ Buttons were originally sold either blister-carded or loose in boxed selections depending on the requirements of the retailer.

Adam Joseph, Return of the Jedi buttons

RETURN OF THE JEDI

Baby Ewok .... $1–$2
Chewbacca .... $1–$2
Darth Vader, artwork from prerelease, one-sheet .... $1–$2

Darth Vader ..... $1–$2
Droopy, from Rebo Band ..... $1–$2
Gamorrean Guard ..... $1–$2
Group Shot, heroes in woods ..... $1–$2
Imperial Guard ..... $1–$2
Jabba the Hutt ..... $1–$2
Logo from Return of the Jedi ..... $1–$2
R2-D2 and C-3PO ..... $1–$2
Yoda ..... $1–$2

EWOK ANIMATED

Babies ..... $1–$2
Carrying Basket ..... $1–$2
Flying Gliders ..... $1–$2
Group ..... $1–$2
In Village ..... $1–$2
In Woods ..... $1–$2
Logo ..... $1–$2
Riding Animal ..... $1–$2
Sitting ..... $1–$2
Swinging on Vine ..... $1–$2
With Animal ..... $1–$2
With R2-D2 ..... $1–$2

Factors Etc, 1977–1980

WORD BUTTONS, 3″

Factors Etc. Star Wars word buttons

Darth Vader Lives ..... $2–$3
May the Force Be With You ..... $2–$3

PICTURE BUTTONS—STAR WARS, 3″

Chewbacca ..... $2–$3
C-3PO ..... $2–$3
C-3PO/R2-D2, with Star Wars logo ..... $2–$3
Darth Vader ..... $2–$3
Luke Skywalker ..... $2–$3
Obi-Wan ..... $2–$3
Princess Leia ..... $2–$3
R2-D2 ..... $2–$3
Han and Chewie ..... $2–$3

PICTURE BUTTONS—EMPIRE STRIKES BACK, 3″

Boba Fett ..... $2–$3
Chewbacca ..... $2–$3
Darth Vader ..... $2–$3
Luke Skywalker ..... $2–$3
R2-D2/C-3PO ..... $2–$3
Yoda ..... $2–$3

Promotional

"May the Force Be With You," 1977. 2¾″. Given away at original L.A. movie premiere. Blue and white ..... $1–$2
Revenge of the Jedi, 1982. Red on black. 2¼″ ..... $1–$2
Tenth Anniversary Logo, 1987. Color logo button on silver rectangular pinback ..... $3–$5

Star Tours

Star Tours Logo, 3″ glow in the dark ..... $3–$4
Star Tours and Disney-MGM Logos, on blue ..... $1–$2
Star Tours Logo and C-3PO/R2-D2 ..... $1–$2
Star Tours, Disney-MGM Logos and C-3PO/R2-D2 ... $1–$2

Star Wars Fan Club, 1978

PICTURE WITH LOGO AND CHARACTER NAME 1″
FIRST SERIES

Chewbacca ..... $2–$3
George Lucas ..... $2–$3
Han Solo ..... $2–$3
Logo ..... $2–$3
Luke ..... $2–$3
Princess Leia ..... $2–$3
Tusken Raider ..... $2–$3

SECOND SERIES

Ben Kenobi ..... $2–$3
Moff Tarkin ..... $2–$3
Darth Vader ..... $2–$3
R2-D2 ..... $2–$3
C-3PO ..... $2–$3
Jawa ..... $2–$3
Stormtrooper ..... $2–$3

DECALS AND STICKERS

NOTE: For sticker book sets and stickers designed to accompany trading card sets, see TRADING CARDS section of this book.

A.H. Prismatic (British)

HOLOGRAPHIC STICKERS, 1994

Foil hologram stickers approximately 2″ square. Packaged shrink-wrapped on header cards.

> *NOTE: These stickers have been incorporated in many other products, including bookmarks, plastic boxes, pin-back badges, key chains, stand-ups, magnets and pencil boxes (see appropriate sections).*

AT-AT .... $1–$3
B-Wing .... $1–$3
Darth Vader .... $1–$3
Darth TIE .... $1–$3
Imperial Cruiser .... $1–$3
Millennium Falcon .... $1–$3
Millennium Falcon, with logo .... $1–$3
TIE Interceptor .... $1–$3
X-Wing .... $1–$3
Uncut sheet of all 9 .... $8–$10

Creation Entertainment, 1987

10th Anniversary convention bumper sticker .... $2–$5

Drawing Board

PERK UP STICKERS, 1980

Three sheets per package. Three designs.
Bad Guys .... $5–$10
Good Guys .... $5–$10
Ewoks .... $5–$10

PERK UP STICKERS, 1983

Three sheets per package. Three different sets, two characters and one of vehicles.
Per set .... $5–$10

PUFFY STICKERS, 1983

3-D Perk Ups. Three different assortments.
Ewoks and other characters .... $5–$10
Heroes .... $5–$10
Villains .... $5–$10

Fantasma, 1992

Bumper Sticker, Star Wars logo on holographic foil ... $4–$6

Fun Products (British), 1983

CHARACTER STICKERS

4 1/2″ high, color plastic stickers. Packaged mixed packs on blue, 4 1/2″ × 7″ header cards with artwork of characters and Jedi logo.

Three-pack .... $15–$20
Six-pack .... $25–$35

Fun Products (British), character sticker pack

CHARACTER PUFFY STICKERS, 1983

3-D version of this company's regular stickers (above). Come one to a package on same cards.
Admiral Ackbar .... $5–$10
C-3PO .... $5–$10
Chewbacca .... $5–$10
Darth Vader .... $5–$10
Gamorrean Guard .... $5–$10
Jabba the Hutt .... $5–$10
Klaatu .... $5–$10
Ewoks .... $5–$10
Paploo .... $5–$10
P3-D2 .... $5–$10
Shuttle Tydirium .... $5–$10
Yoda .... $5–$10

Fun Products (British), character puffy sticker

Topps, character puffy stickers

Happymates, 1983

PUFFY STICKERS

Two different sets of Return of the Jedi stickers.
Per set .... $5–$10

Star Tours

MGM Logos and Droids, on silver .... $1–$2
Commander Rebel Alliance, Luke. Red on white. ...... $1–$2
Moon of Endor, Ewok Village. White on red .... $1–$2
Millennium Falcon, Battle Station. White on red......... $1–$2
Headquarters—X-Wing Fighting Squadron, white on black .... $1–$2
Imperial Lord—Darth Vader, white on black .... $1–$2
Star Tours Triangular Logo, glow in the dark............ $1–$2

Star Wars Fan Club (Original)

New Hope Triangular design .... $1–$2
"Vader-in-Flames" .... $1–$2
Yoda .... $1–$2
Bounty Hunters, McQuarrie art........................ $1–$2

Star Wars Fan Club (Current), 1987

10th Anniversary logo sticker, 3″ × 5″ .... $1–$2

Topps, 1980

PUFFY STICKERS

Eight different color plastic 3-D character stickers packaged with color header with Darth Vader head and Empire logo.
Each .... $5–$10

BOOKS, CALENDARS AND OTHER PUBLICATIONS

To be in collectible condition, a book, like almost all other categories of Star Wars items, should be in basically new condition. Tears, writing or other marks, broken spines and missing dust jackets are all major faults, especially in older children's books, which have often seen more wear and tear. As it is used in the book industry, the term "trade paperback" refers to any oversize paperback book (cover dimensions, not thickness). Many books have also been translated into foreign languages, including German, Dutch, French, Spanish and Japanese. Though in theory their prices are generally comparable to U.S. books, relatively few collectors are interested in books outside of English-language editions.

This section is organized into calendars, children's books, novels and reference books, and then is alphabetical by title within these sections. For hardcover British annuals, graphic novels and other comic adaptations, see COMICS. For gaming and computer games books, see GAMES.

NOTE: Ballantine, Del Rey and Random House are all divisions of the same publishing company.

CALENDARS

1978

BALLANTINE

Star Wars, black cover with "Star Wars" in blue and photos of Han, Luke, Leia and X-Wing chasing TIE Fighter. Interior has photos from movie. Came boxed ....$25–$30

1979

BALLANTINE

Star Wars, black cover with "Star Wars" in red. Interior has photos from movie. Last boxed calendar ....$25–$30

1980

BALLANTINE

Star Wars, blue cover with triangular "A New Hope" art. Interior has different movie posters from around the world........ ....$20–$25

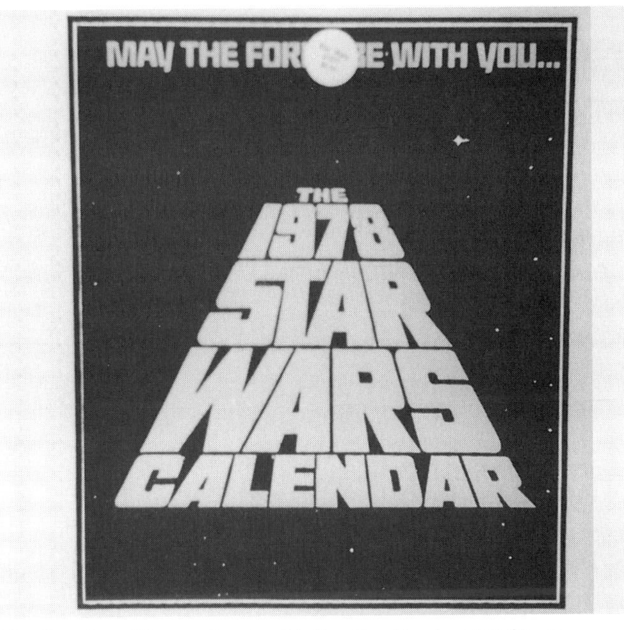

The first Star Wars calendar (Ballantine Books, 1978) in the original box

1981

BALLANTINE

Empire Strikes Back, cover shows color "Kissing Scene" art from Empire. Interior has photos from movie............$15–$20

The first Empire Strikes Back calendar (Ballantine Books, 1981)

1982

THOMAS FORMAN AND SONS (BRITISH)

Star Wars/Empire, 12 color scenes from the movies .... $20–$25

1984

BALLANTINE

Return of the Jedi, black cover with "Lightsaber" movie art. Interior has photos from movie .... $15–$20

RANDOM HOUSE

Ewok calendar, yellow cover with cartoon artwork of Ewoks hang-gliding. Interior has Ewok animated artwork and 48 peel-off stickers .... $5–$10

1990

CEDCO

Return of the Jedi/Star Wars and Empire, cover shows color artwork of characters originally done as promotional art for Return of the Jedi. Interior has photos from all three of the original Star Wars saga films .... $12–$15

1991

CEDCO

Star Wars, cover art shows montage of characters originally used as promotional art for first movie....................... $12–$15

1994

ANTIOCH

Star Wars Book of Days, illustrated day planner with four-year calendar in back.. $12–$15

1995

ANDREWS & MCMEEL

3-D Artwork calendar.. $12–$15

ANTIOCH

Calendar, cover and interior show artwork from novels and comics... $12–$15

LANDMARK

Calendar, cover is Empire artwork by Boris. Interior has promotional and poster artwork from all three films .... $12–$15

1996

CEDCO

Star Wars, photos from Star Wars (cover and interior).......... .... $12–$15

Datebook, 5″ × 7″ format. Photos from Star Wars. Darth and Obi-Wan dueling on cover.. $10–$12

HALLMARK

Store exclusive .... $15–$20

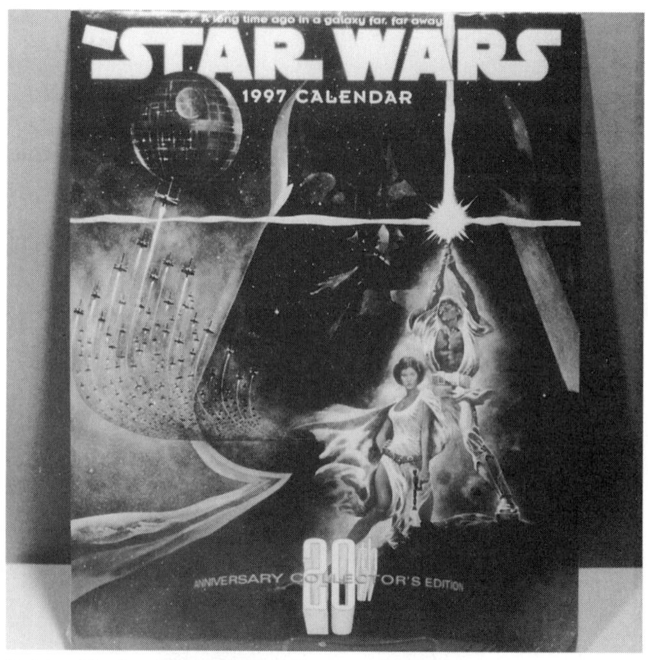

Golden Turtle, 1997 20th anniversary calendar

1997

CEDCO

Art of Star Wars calendar ....$13–$15
Art of Star Wars datebook ....$10–$12

CHRONICLE

Vehicle calendar, artwork with fold-out blueprints ....$12–$15

GOLDEN TURTLE

20th Anniversary edition, movie poster artwork (cover and interior) ....$12–$15

CHILDREN'S BOOKS

Activity Books

All softcover.

FUN WORKS (DISNEY), 1997

Star Wars Flip Books. Forty-page booklets where action seems to move as pages are flipped.

Star Wars ....$3–$4
Empire Strikes Back ....$3–$4
Return of the Jedi ....$3–$4

GOLDEN BOOKS, 1997

Star Wars Mark & See Magic ....$3–$5
Star Wars Puzzles & Mazes, The Rebel Alliance vs. the Imperial Forces ....$3–$5
Star Wars Puzzles & Mazes, The Training of a Jedi Knight. ....$3–$5
Star Wars Tell-a-Story Sticker Book ....$3–$5

PUBLICATIONS INTERNATIONAL, LTD.

Play-a-Sound-Star Wars: A New Hope, hardback storybook with electronic side panel with picture icons for sixteen phrases and sound effects ....$10–$15

RANDOM HOUSE

Artoo Detoo's Activity Book, Star Wars, 1979........$10–$15
Chewbacca's Activity Book, Star Wars, 1979.........$10–$15
Darth Vader's Activity Book, Star Wars, 1979.......$10–$15
Luke Skywalker's Activity Book, Star Wars, 1979....$10–$15
Yoda's Activity Book, James Razzi. Empire Strikes Back, 1981 ....$10–$15
Dot-to-Dot Fun, Return of the Jedi, 1983 ....$10–$15
Mazes, Return of the Jedi, 1983 ....$10–$15
Monster Activity Book, Return of the Jedi, 1983 ....$10–$15
Picture Puzzle Book, Return of the Jedi, 1983.........$10–$15
Word Puzzle Book, Return of the Jedi, 1983 ....$10–$15

SCHOLASTIC, 1997.

Star Wars Trilogy Pull-Out Poster Books. Booklets of fifteen (each) perforated color "mini-poster" pages.

Star Wars ....$4–$6
Empire Strikes Back ....$4–$6
Return of the Jedi ....$4–$6

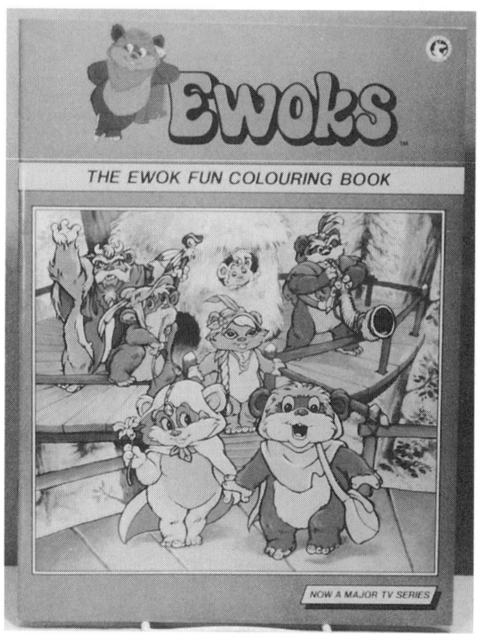

Kenner, coloring books

Coloring Books

GOLDEN BOOKS, 1997

Star Wars—An Ewok Adventure .... $3–$5
Star Wars—Galactic Adventures .... $3–$5
Star Wars—Heroes & Villains .... $3–$5
Star Wars Posters to Color, large format .... $3–$5

KENNER

Chewbacca and Han, cover; Star Wars, 1977 .... $10–$15
R2-D2, cover; Star Wars, 1977 .... $10–$15
Chewbacca, cover; Star Wars, 1977 .... $10–$15
C-3PO and Luke, cover; Star Wars, 1977 .... $10–$15
Cast, cover; Empire Strikes Back, 1980 .... $10–$15
Chewbacca and C-3PO, cover; Empire Strikes Back, 1980 .... $10–$15
Chewbacca and Leia, cover; Empire Strikes Back, 1980 .... $10–$15
Darth Vader and Stormtroopers, cover; Empire Strikes Back, 1980 .... $10–$15
Han, Chewbacca, Lando and Leia, cover; Empire Strikes Back, 1980 .... $10–$15
Luke Skywalker, cover; Empire Strikes Back, 1980 .... $10–$15
R2-D2, cover; Empire Strikes Back, 1980 .... $10–$15
Yoda, cover; Empire Strikes Back, 1980 .... $10–$15
Lando, cover; Return of the Jedi, 1983 .... $10–$15
Lando and Skiff Guard, cover; Return of the Jedi, 1983 .... $10–$15
Luke, cover; Return of the Jedi, 1983 .... $10–$15
Max Rebo Band, cover; Return of the Jedi, 1983 .... $10–$15
Wicket, cover; Return of the Jedi, 1983 .... $10–$15
Wicket and Kneesa, cover; Return of the Jedi, 1983 .... $10–$15
Wicket, Kneesa and Logray, cover; Return of the Jedi, 1983 .... $10–$15

Educational Books

RANDOM HOUSE

Star Wars Attack on Reading, Comprehension #1, 1977 .... $10–$15
Star Wars Attack on Reading, Comprehension #2, 1977 .... $10–$15
Star Wars Attack on Reading, Word Study, 1977..$10–$15
Star Wars Attack on Reading, Study Skills, 1977..$10–$15
Star Wars Book About Flight, 1983, softcover....... $15–$20

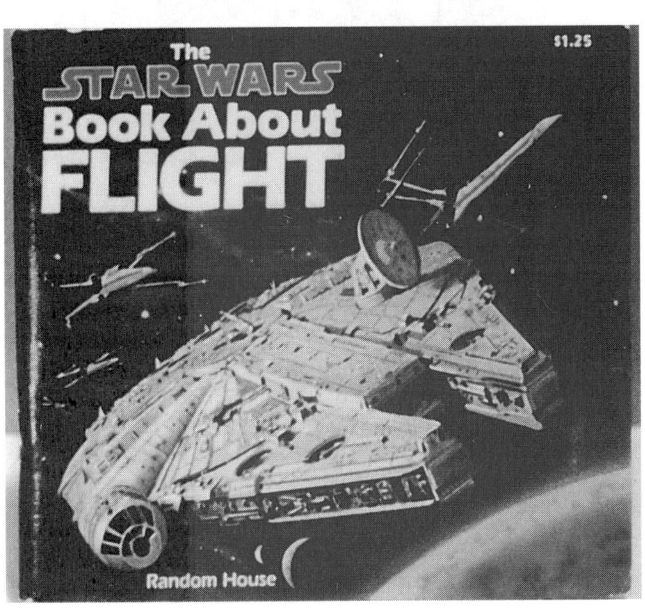

Educational books (Random House)

Star Wars: C-3PO's Book About Robots, 1983, softcover.. ....$15–$20

Star Wars Question and Answer Book About Computers, 1983, softcover ....$15–$20

Star Wars Question and Answer Book About Space, 1983, hardcover..$20–$25

Star Wars Question and Answer Book About Space, 1983, softcover (published by Scholastic) ....$15–$20

Return of the Jedi Educational Workbooks, Happy House (Random House), ABC Readiness, 1983 ....$10–$15

Return of the Jedi Educational Workbooks, Happy House (Random House), Addition and Subtraction, 1983 ..$10–$15

Return of the Jedi Educational Workbooks, Happy House (Random House), Early Numbers, 1983 ....$10–$15

Return of the Jedi Educational Workbooks, Happy House (Random House), Spelling, 1983 ....$10–$15

Return of the Jedi Educational Workbooks, Happy House (Random House), Multiplication, 1983...................$10–$15

Return of the Jedi Educational Workbooks, Happy House (Random House), Reading and Writing, 1983 ....$10–$15

Ewok Books, ABC Fun, 1985 ....$5–$10

Ewok Books, Learn-to-Read, 1985 ....$5–$10

Junior Novels

BANTAM, 1992-PRESENT

Paul Davids and Hollace Davids. Trade paperbacks.

Galaxy of Fear, #1 Eaten Alive ....$5–$6

Galaxy of Fear, #2 City of the Dead............................$5–$6

Galaxy of Fear, #3 Planet Plague ....$5–$6

Star Wars, #1 The Glove of Darth Vader.....................$5–$6

Star Wars, #2 The Lost City of the Jedi ....$5–$6

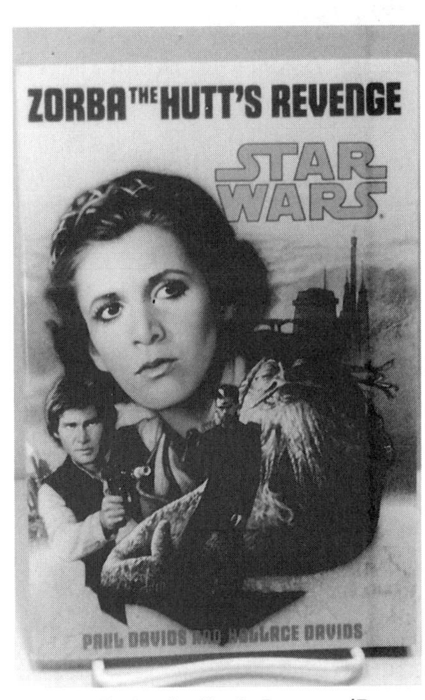

Junior Novel #3, *Zorba the Hutt's Revenge* (Bantam Books)

Star Wars, #3 Zorba the Hutt's Revenge.....................$5–$6

Star Wars, #4 Mission from Mount Yoda ....$5–$6

Star Wars, #5 Queen of the Empire............................$5–$6

Star Wars, #6 Prophets of the Dark Side......................$5–$6

Shadows of the Empire ....$5–$6

Pop-up Books

DARK HORSE

Battle of the Bounty Hunters, 1996. Comic artwork, hardcover ....$18–$20

FUN WORKS (DISNEY)

Star Wars: Heroes in Hiding, 1997. Five spreads ....$9–$12

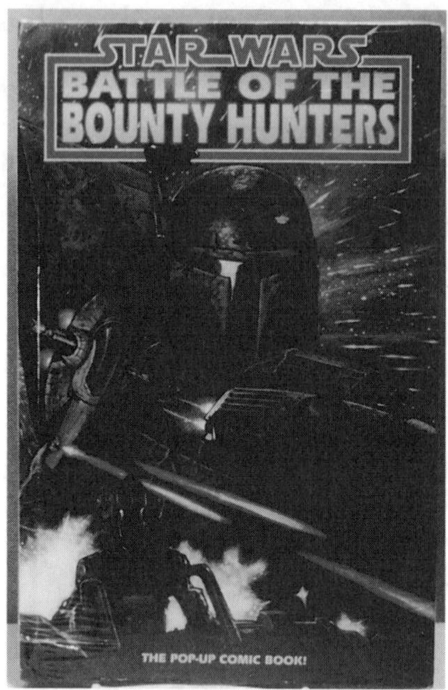

***Battle of the Bounty Hunters,* a pop-up comic book (Dark Horse)**

LITTLE, BROWN

Galactic Empire, The, 1996. Bill Smith. Ships. Horizontal format, hardcover ....$16–$18

Mos Eisley Cantina, Kevin J. Anderson and Rebecca Moesta. Hardcover with light and sound effects........$20–$22

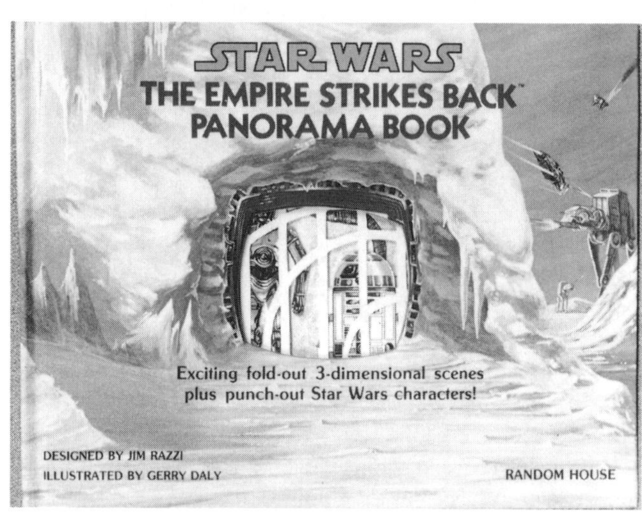

***The Empire Strikes Back Panorama Book* (Random House)**

Rebel Alliance, The, 1996. Bill Smith. Ships. Horizontal format, hardcover..$16–$18

RANDOM HOUSE

Star Wars Pop-up Book, (Collins in Britain), 1978. Hardcover, twelve scenes ....$35–$45

Empire Strikes Back, The, 1980. Hardcover, fourteen scenes ....$30–$40

Empire Strikes Back Panorama Book, The, 1981. Two pop-up scenes plus punch-out figures ....$30–$40

Return of the Jedi Pop-up Book, 1983. Hardcover, ten scenes ....$25–$35

Ewoks Save the Day, The, 1983. Little Pops, 5¼″ × 6″ hardcover. Six scenes ....$10–$15

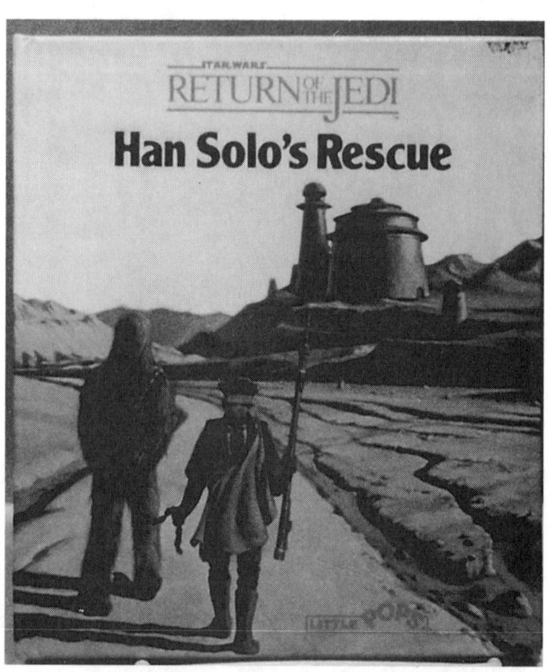

***Han Solo's Rescue* (Little Pops, Random House)**

Han Solo's Rescue, 1983. Little Pops, 5¼″ × 6″ hardcover. Six scenes ....$10–$15

Empire Strikes Back Mix or Match Storybook, 1980. Flip book with different scenes. Spiral bound..................$30–$45

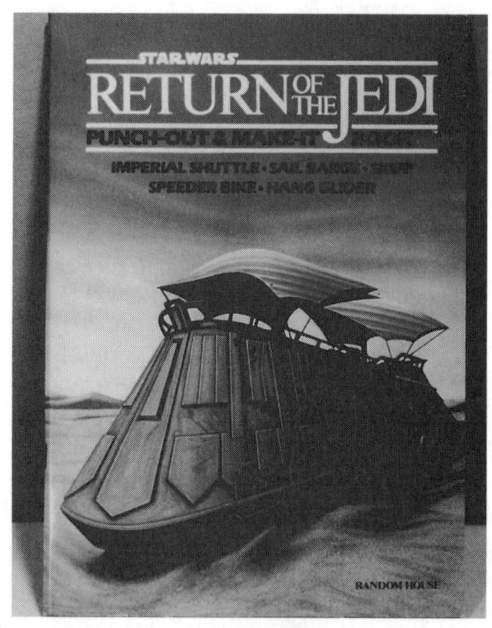

Return of the Jedi punch-out book (Random House)

Punch-out Books

FUN WORKS (DISNEY)

Star Wars: Millennium Falcon, 1997 ....$10–$15

RANDOM HOUSE

Star Wars Punch Out and Make It Book, 1978.....$15–$20
Empire Strikes Back Punch Out and Make It Book, The, 1980 ....$15–$20
Return of the Jedi Punch Out and Make It Book, 1983 ....$10–$15
Star Wars Book of Masks, The, 1983. Nine punch-out masks ....$20–$30

Step-Up Books

These are illustrated easy-to-read books for children who are slightly above the beginning reader stage.

RANDOM HOUSE

Star Wars Step-Up, 1985 ....$10–$15
Empire Strikes Back, The, 1985 ....$10–$15
Return of the Jedi, 1985 ....$10–$15
Star Wars, The Making of the Movie, 1980 ....$10–$15

***The Star Wars Storybook* (Ballantine Books)**

Storybooks

NOTE: Paperback versions of the original U.S. movie adaptation storybooks were done by Scholastic. They were also compiled into a set with a slipcover, the "Star Wars Treasury." Values are approximately equal to the hardcover versions.

BALLANTINE

Star Wars Storybook, 1978. Oversized hardcover......$10–$15

CHRONICLE

Little Chronicles, 1997. Thick, illustrated hardcovers with small (3½″ × 4″) cover dimensions.
- **Star Wars** ....$8–$10
- **The Empire Strikes Back** ....$8–$10
- **Return of the Jedi** ....$8–$10

COLLINS (BRITISH), 1978

Star Wars Storybook, plain blue hardcover with dust jacket picturing R2-D2 and C-3PO ....$25–$35

FUN WORKS (DISNEY), 1997

Darth Vader's Mission: The Search for the Secret Plans, Action Toy Books; die-cut storybook with action figure affixed to spine ....$7–$10
R2-D2's Mission: A Little Hero's Journey, Action Toy Books; die-cut storybook with action figure affixed to spine... ....$7–$10
Star Wars Shimmer Book, hardcover Star Wars storybook decorated with foil throughout ....$9–$12

FUTURA (BRITISH), 1983

Return of the Jedi "Special Junior Edition" ....$15–$20

GOLDEN BOOKS, 1997

8″ × 8″ paperbacks. Movie adaptations each include sheet of twenty temporary tattoos.
Star Wars—A New Hope ....$3–$5
Star Wars—The Empire Strikes Back ....$3–$5
Star Wars—Return of the Jedi ....$3–$5
Star Wars—Pilots and Spacecraft, glow-in-the-dark ....$3–$5

RANDOM HOUSE—BULLSEYE, 1997

Star Wars Trilogy Re-release Storybook Editions. New covers and eight-page color photo insert.
Star Wars ....$5–$6
Empire Strikes Back ....$5–$6
Return of the Jedi ....$5–$6

RANDOM HOUSE—DROIDS STORYBOOKS, 1985

Droids ....$10–$15
Escape from the Monster Ship ....$10–$15
Lost Prince, The ....$10–$15
Pirates of Tarnoonga ....$10–$15
Shiny as a Droid ....$10–$15

RANDOM HOUSE—EWOKS STORYBOOKS, 1985

Fuzzy as an Ewok ....$10–$15
Red Ghost, The ....$10–$15
School Days ....$10–$15
Wicket and the Danelion Warrior ....$10–$15
Wicket Goes Fishing ....$10–$15

RANDOM HOUSE—SOFTCOVER ILLUSTRATED STORIES

(Armada in Britain). Color artwork.

Droid Dilemma, The, 1979; Star Wars ....$10–$15

Maverick Moon, The, 1979; Star Wars....................$10–$15

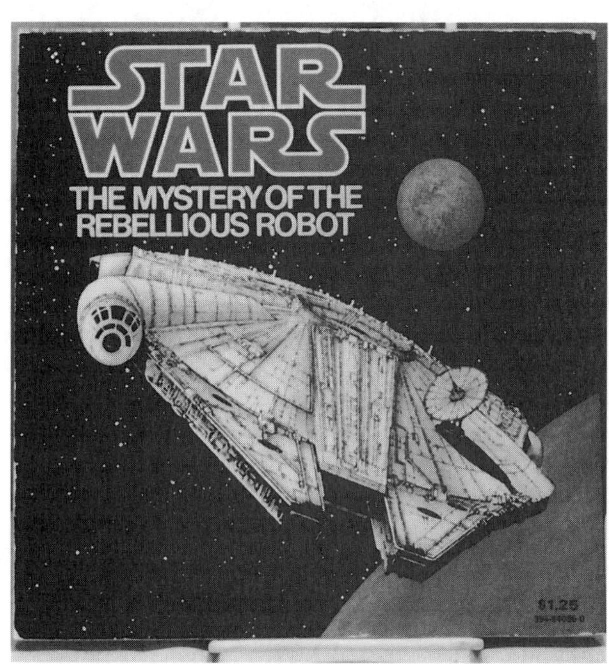

***The Mystery of the Rebellious Robot* (Random House)**

Mystery of the Rebellious Robot, The, 1979; Star Wars ....$10–$15

Ewoks Join the Fight, The, 1983; Return of the Jedi ....$10–$15

RANDOM HOUSE—SOFTCOVER MINI-STORYBOOKS, 1984

5″ × 5½″ format. Return of the Jedi logo.

Baby Ewoks' Picnic Surprise ....$5–$10

Ewoks' Hang-Gliding Adventure ....$5–$10

Three Cheers for Kneesa ....$5–$10

Wicket Finds a Way ....$5–$10

SCHOLASTIC, 1997

Star Wars Trilogy Re-release Storybook Editions. Stories adapted by J. J. Gardner.

Star Wars ....$5–$6

Empire Strikes Back ....$5–$6

Return of the Jedi ....$5–$6

Young Adult Novels

BOULEVARD (BERKLEY), 1995/1996

Young Jedi Knights series. Kevin J. Anderson and Rebecca Moesta.

Heirs of the Force ....$5–$7

Shadow Academy ....$5–$7

The Lost Ones ....$5–$7

***Heirs of the Force,* a Young Jedi Knights young adult novel (Boulevard)**

Lightsabers ....$5–$7

Darkest Knight ....$5–$7

Jedi Under Siege ....$5–$7

Young Reader Editions

SPHERE (BRITISH)

Star Wars, 1978 ....$20–$25

Empire Strikes Back, The, 1980....................$15–$20

NOVELS (MOVIE ADAPTATIONS AND ORIGINAL)

NOTE: Novels are listed alphabetically by title. Though "Star Wars" is part of the official title of most novels, it has been omitted from most of the titles in this list to simplify reference.

Assault at Selonia

Paperback, Bantam, 1995. Roger McBride Allen ...$6–$8

Before the Storm

Paperback, Bantam, 1996. Michael P. Kube...........$6–$8

Champions of the Force Bantam, 1995. Kevin J. Anderson.

Hardcover ....$20–$23

Paperback ....$6–$8

Children of the Jedi, Bantam, 1996. Barbara Hambly.

Hardcover ....$20–$23

Paperback ....$6–$8

Crystal Star, The, Bantam, 1994. Vonda McIntyre.

Hardcover ....$20–$23
Paperback ....$6–$8
Courtship of Princess Leia, The, Bantam, 1995. Dave Wolverton.
Hardcover ....$20–$23
Paperback ....$6–$8
Dark Apprentice, Bantam, 1994. Kevin J. Anderson.
Hardcover ....$20–$23
Paperback ....$6–$8
Dark Force Rising, Bantam, 1992. Timothy Zahn.
Hardcover ....$20–$23
Paperback ....$6–$8
Darksaber, Bantam, 1995. Kevin J. Anderson.
Hardcover ....$20–$23
Paperback ....$6–$8
Empire Strikes Back, The, Del Rey (Sphere in Britain), 1980. Donald F. Glut. Paperback original.
Paperback, original and reprints ....$6–$8
Hardcover book club edition ....$15–$20

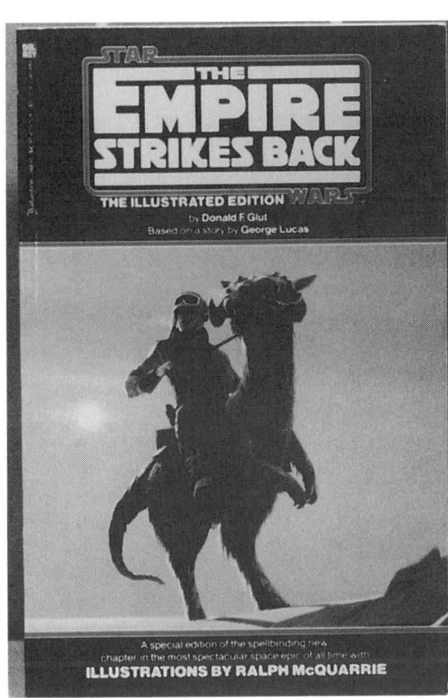

The Empire Strikes Back Illustrated Edition (Del Rey, 1980)

Empire Strikes Back, The (Illustrated Edition), Del Rey, 1980. Donald F. Glut. Illustrations by Ralph McQuarrie.
Trade paperback ....$15–$20
Han Solo Adventures, The, Del Rey, 1992. All three Han Solo novels in one book.
Paperback ....$6–$8
Han Solo and the Lost Legacy, Del Rey (Sphere in Britain), 1980. Brian Daley. Original novel.
Hardcover ....$12–$18
Paperback, original and reprints ....$6–$8
Han Solo at Stars' End, Del Rey (Sphere in Britain), 1979. Brian Daley. Original novel.

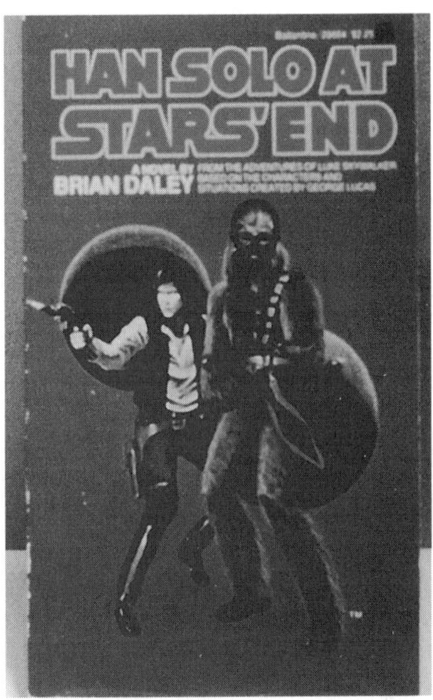

Han Solo at Stars' End (Del Rey and Sphere, 1979)

Hardcover ....$12–$18
Paperback, original and reprints ....$6–$8
Han Solo's Revenge, Del Rey (Sphere in Britain), 1979. Brian Daley. Original novel.
Hardcover ....$12–$18
Paperback, original and reprints ....$6–$8
Heir to the Empire, Bantam, 1991. Timothy Zahn.
Hardcover ....$20–$23
Paperback ....$6–$8
Jedi Search, Bantam, 1994. Kevin J. Anderson.
Hardcover ....$20–$23
Paperback ....$6–$8
Lando Calrissian Adventures, The, Del Rey, 1994. All three Lando Calrissian novels in one book.
Trade Paperback ....$10–$15
Lando Calrissian and the Flamewind of Osceon, Del Rey, 1983. L. Neil Smith.
Hardcover ....$12–$18
Paperback, original and reprints ....$6–$8
Lando Calrissian and the Mindharp of Sharu, Del Rey, 1983. L. Neil Smith.
Hardcover ....$12–$18
Paperback, original and reprints ....$6–$8
Lando Calrissian and the Starcave of Thonboka, Del Rey, 1983. L. Neil Smith.
Hardcover ....$12–$18
Paperback, original and reprints ....$6–$8
Last Command, The, Bantam, 1993. Timothy Zahn.
Hardcover ....$20–$23
Paperback ....$6–$8
New Rebellion, The, Bantam, 1996. Kristine Kathryn Rusch.
Hardcover ....$20–$23
Paperback ....$6–$8

Planet of Twilight, Bantam, 1997. Barbara Hambly.
Hardcover .... $20–$23
Paperback .... $6–$8

Return of the Jedi, Del Rey (Futura in Britain), 1983. Novel. James Kahn.
Paperback, original and reprints .... $6–$8
Hardcover book club edition .... $15–$20

Return of the Jedi (Illustrated Edition) Del Rey, 1983.
Trade paperback .... $15–$20

Shadows of the Empire, Bantam, 1992. Steve Perry.
Hardcover .... $20–$23
Paperback .... $6–$8

Shield of Lies, Bantam, 1996. Michael P. Kube.
Paperback .... $6–$8

Showdown at Centerpoint, Bantam, 1995. Roger McBride Allen.
Paperback .... $6–$8

Splinter of the Mind's Eye, Del Rey, 1978. Alan Dean Foster. Several editions.

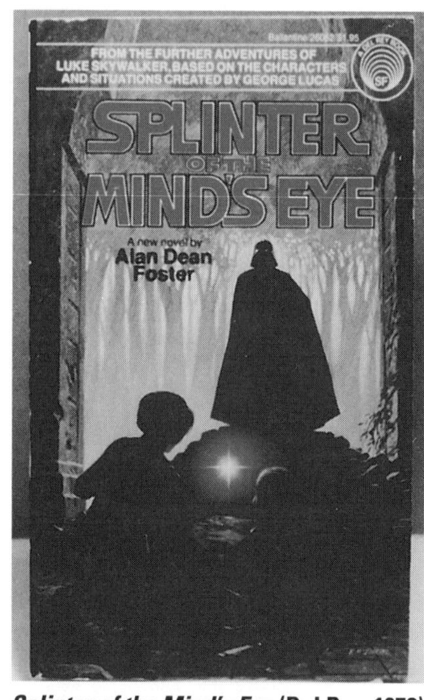

Splinter of the Mind's Eye **(Del Rey, 1978)**

Hardcover .... $10–$15
Paperback, original and reprints .... $6–$8

Star Wars, From the Adventures of Luke Skywalker, Ballantine (Sphere in Britain). George Lucas.
Original novel, 1976, paperback .... $15–$20
Later paperback version, 1977; sixteen-page color photo section .... $10–$15
Original hardcover edition, 1977 .... $30–$35
Hardcover book club edition, 1977 .... $15–$20
All later reprints .... $6–$8

Star Wars Trilogy, Random House, 1987. All three stories in one book.
Several editions .... $10–$20

Tales from the Mos Eisley Cantina, Bantam, 1995. Kevin J. Anderson.
Paperback .... $6–$8

Tales of Jabba's Palace, Bantam, 1996. Kevin J. Anderson.
Paperback .... $6–$8

Tales of the Bounty Hunters, Bantam, 1996. Kevin J. Anderson.
Paperback .... $6–$8

Truce at Bakura, The, Bantam, 1994. Kathy Tyres.
Hardcover .... $20–$23
Paperback .... $6–$8

Tyrant's Test, Bantam, 1996. Michael P. Kube.
Paperback .... $6–$8

X-Wing: Bacta Trap, Bantam, 1997. Michael A. Stockpole.
Paperback .... $6–$8

X-Wing: Krypto's Trap, Bantam, 1996. Michael A. Stockpole.
Paperback .... $6–$8

X-Wing: Rogue Squadron, Bantam, 1996. Michael A. Stockpole.
Paperback .... $6–$8

REFERENCE AND NONFICTION BOOKS (ADULT)

All About the Star Wars, Japanese. Shueisha, 1983.
Oversized paperback .... $30–$40

Art of Dave Dorman, FPG, 1996. Stephen D. Smith/Laureen Haines.
Trade paperback .... $20–$30

Art of The Empire Strikes Back, The, Ballantine, 1981. Artistic and technical accomplishments of the movie. Does not include script.
Oversized hardcover .... $30–$40
Trade paperback .... $20–$30
Del Rey (Ballantine) reprint, 1994 .... $18–$22

Art of Return of the Jedi, Ballantine, 1983. Art and photos plus complete script.
Oversized hardcover .... $30–$40
Trade paperback .... $20–$30
Del Rey (Ballantine) reprint, 1994 .... $18–$22

Art of Star Wars, The, Ballantine, 1979. Illustrations, stills and artists' concepts from the movie. Includes script.
Oversized hardcover .... $35–$45
Trade paperback .... $20–$30
Del Rey (Ballantine) reprint, 1994 .... $18–$22

Art of Star Wars Galaxy, The, Topps, 1993. Fantasy and comic art from trading cards. Trade paperbacks.
Volume I .... $20–$25
Volume II .... $20–$25
Limited Edition, (1000), signed by fourteen artists. Leatherbound with slipcase (Underwood-Miller for Topps) .... $150–$200

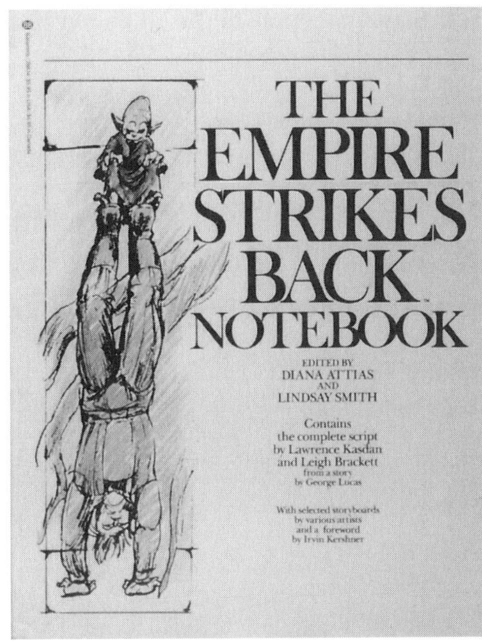

The Empire Strikes Back notebook (Ballantine Books, 1980)

Empire Strikes Back Notebook Ballantine, 1980. Illustrated script.
Trade paperback .... $25–$35

Empire Strikes Back Original Movie Script Premiere, 1995.
Trade paperback .... $20–$25

Empire Strikes Back Sketchbook, The Ballantine, 1980. Joe Johnston and Nilo Rodis-Jamero.
Trade paperback .... $30–$40

Force of Star Wars, The Bible Voice, 1977. Frank Allnutt.
Trade paperback .... $10–$15

425 Questions and Answers About Star Wars and The Empire Strikes Back. Del Rey, 1977.
Trade paperback .... $15–$20

Guide to the Star Wars Universe, A Del Rey, 1994. Bill Slavicsek. Revised, expanded edition.
Trade paperback .... $8–$10

Guide to the Star Wars Universe, A Del Rey (Sphere in Britain), 1984. Raymond L. Velasco.
Paperback .... $5–$8

How to Draw Star Wars Heroes, Creatures, Spaceships and Other Fantastic Things. Random House, 1984. Lee J. Ames.
Paperback .... $20–$30

I'd Just As Soon Kiss a Wookiee Del Rey, 1997. Stephen J. Sansweet. Quote book.
Paperback .... $5–$6

Illustrated Star Wars Universe, The Bantam, 1995. McQuarrie/Anderson.
Oversized hardcover .... $35–$40

Jedi Master Quizbook, The Del Rey, 1982. Rusty Melter.
Paperback .... $10–$15

Making of Return of the Jedi, The Ballantine (Sphere in Britain), 1983.
Paperback .... $15–$20

My Jedi Journal Ballantine, 1983. Blank book.
Hardcover .... $10–$15

National Public Empire Strikes Back Radio Dramatization Del Rey, 1996. Brian Daley. Script.
Trade paperback .... $10–$11

National Public Return of the Jedi Radio Dramatization Del Rey, 1996. Script.
Trade paperback .... $10–$11

National Public Star Wars Radio Dramatization Del Rey, 1996. Brian Daley. Script.
Trade paperback .... $10–$11

Once Upon a Galaxy A Journal of the Making of The Empire Strikes Back. Del Rey, 1980. Alan Arnold.
Paperback .... $20–$25

Return of the Jedi (Japanese picture book), Keibunsha, 1983.
Small trade paperback with dust jacket .... $15–$25

Return of the Jedi Original Movie Script Premiere, 1995.
Trade paperback .... $20–$25

Return of the Jedi Sketchbook Ballantine, 1983. Joe Johnston and Nilo Rodis-Jamero.
Trade paperback .... $25–$35

Star Wars Album Ballantine (Sphere in Britain), 1977.
Trade paperback .... $30–$40

Star Wars Blueprints Ballantine, 1977. Fifteen plans from original set designs in plastic pouch with cover sheet.
Each .... $15–$25

Star Wars Chronicles Chronicle Books, 1997.
NOTE: This book was originally published in Japan.
Hardcover, coffee table book comes with die-cut slipcase $150–$175

Star Wars: The Essential Guide to Characters Del Rey, 1995. Andy Mangels.
Trade paperback .... $18–$20

Star Wars: The Essential Guide to Vehicles and Vessels Del Rey, 1996. Bill Smith.
Trade paperback .... $18–$20

Star Wars: From Concept to Screen to Collectible Chronicle, 1992. Stephen J. Sansweet.
Hardcover .... $25–$30
Trade paperback .... $20–$25

Star Wars Intergalactic Passport Ballantine, 1983. Passport-style booklet with stamps from Star Wars Saga locations.
Each .... $3–$5

Star Wars Iron-on Transfer Book Ballantine, 1977. Sixteen color T-shirt transfers in book form.
Paperback .... $15–$20

Star Wars Original Movie Script Premiere, 1995.
Trade paperback .... $20–$25

Star Wars Sketchbook Ballantine, 1977. Joe Johnston.
Trade paperback .... $35–$50

Star Wars: From Concept to Screen to Collectible **(Chronicle Books, 1992)**

Star Wars, Star Trek and the 21st Century Christians Bible Voice, 1978. Winkie Pratney.

Paperback..$15–$20

Star Wars Technical Journal Del Rey, 1994. Shane Johnson. Compilation of three-volume Starlog magazine specials.

Oversized hardcover...$30–$35

Tomart's Price Guide to Worldwide Star Wars Tomart, 1994. Sansweet/Tombusch.

Trade paperback...$20–$25

Ultimate Unauthorized Star Wars Trilogy Challenge Kensington, 1997. James Hatfield/George Burt.

Trade paperback...$15–$20

CELS, HOLOGRAMS AND PRINTS

This section is divided into cels, holograms and prints categories and is then arranged alphabetically by manufacturer within these categories.

CELS

Cels are the transparencies on which the action parts of an animated film are printed. There are thousands of cels for each half hour of Star Wars animation. Until fairly recently, the value of cels as original art had gone largely unrecognized by the general public. This has changed dramatically in recent years, and the price of cels has skyrocketed. Even so, Star Wars animation has yet to reach the level of notoriety that some other animation enjoys, probably because many collectors who may be avid fans of live-action Star Wars are not nearly so enthusiastic about the Droids and Ewoks series, which have supplied the bulk of Star Wars original animation art. Desirable features in cels are complete well-centered figures and, of course, main characters and groups. Authentic cels seldom have backgrounds, since one backdrop could serve for many "action" sequences. If a background is present, it increases the value of a cel dramatically, but it should be noted that counterfeit backgrounds are common in the cel market. A good-quality cel should sell for about $75–$150 without a background, at least double that amount if a genuine background is present. There has also been a recent trend in selling reproductions of various animation cels, including Star Wars cels (see below), called sericels. It must be emphasized that these are NOT original cels, and no reputable dealer would represent them as anything but copies.

Royal Animation Art, 1996/1997

SERICELS

Reproductions of animation cels with backgrounds from Droids and Ewoks animated series. Come matted.

Price per cel, 15″ × 17″ .... $75–$90

HOLOGRAMS

These are true holograms, as opposed to foil or lenticular holograms employed in various other Star Wars products, most notably as special additions to various recent trading card sets.

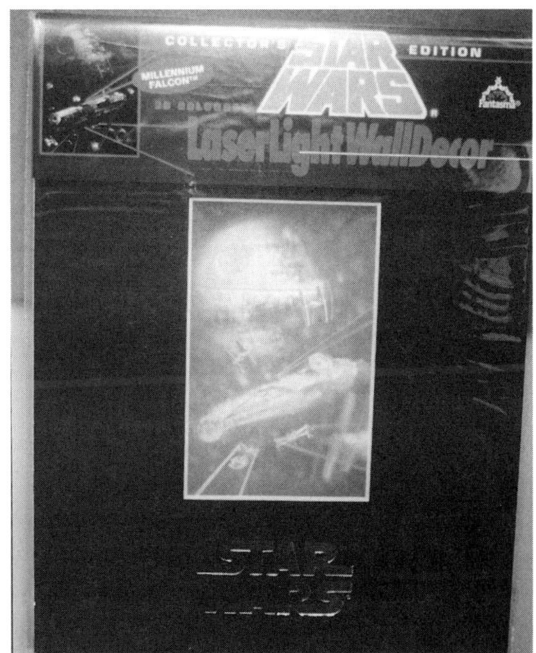

Fantasma, LaserLight hologram

A.H. Prismatic (British), 1994

Millennium Falcon, 5″ × 7″, matted ....$15–$20

Fantasma, 1993

Darth Vader, 8″ × 10″, matted ....$25–$30
Space Battle, 8″ × 10″, matted................................$25–$30

PRINTS

Ballantine

Portfolios of color prints of concept paintings by Ralph McQuarrie. Each comes in a light cardstock folder.

Star Wars Portfolio, 1977.
Each portfolio, 20 prints ....$35–$50
Empire Strikes Back, 1980.
Each portfolio, 24 prints ....$35–$50
Return of the Jedi, 1983.
Each portfolio, 20 prints ....$30–$45

Gifted Images, 1994

LITHOGRAPH

Limited edition (500 copies) by Ken Steacy.

Darth Vader, 23$^{1}/_{2}$″ × 30″ ....$600–$650

Icarus (British), 1982

ARTWORK PRINTS

Silver plastic frames, six different.

Luke...$5–$10
R2-D2 and C3PO...$5–$10
Boba Fett...$5–$10
Yoda...$5–$10
Darth Vader...$5–$10
Chewbacca ....$5–$10

Rolling Thunder, 1996/1997

ART PRINTS

Signed and numbered color prints by Dave Dorman. Limited to 1500 each; six planned in series.

Price each, 16″ × 20″ ....$45–$60

Star Struck

LITHOGRAPH

Limited edition (3000 copies) of three X-Wings and the Death Star II by Michael David Ward.

Price each..$250–$300

Willetts Design, 1996

ART PRINTS

Framed art prints of concept paintings by Ralph McQuarrie. Limited to 2500 pieces. Signed and numbered. Each incorporates a 70mm film clip into the lower corner of the print.

Battle of Hoth, 18″ × 12″ ....$200–$225
Cloud City, 18″ × 12″..$200–$225
Mos Eisley Cantina, 18″ × 12″ ....$200–$225
Millennium Falcon, 18″ × 12″ ....$200–$225
Rebel Ceremony, 18″ × 12″ ....$200–$225

Zanart, 1994–1996

CHROME ART

Matted 11″ × 14″ color photo or art print with metallic highlights.

Zanart, ChromArt Collectibles print

AT-ATs...$10–$15
Bounty Hunters ....$10–$15
B-Wing ....$10–$15
B-Wing, blueprint style ....$10–$15
Darth Vader, photo...$10–$15
Darth Vader, artwork ....$10–$15
Darth Vader, half-face artwork ....$10–$15
Empire Strikes Back, theater poster ....$10–$15
Empire Strikes Back, video box art.........................$10–$15
Escape from Hoth...$10–$15
Prince Xizor ....$10–$15

Return of the Jedi, theater poster ....$10–$15
Return of the Jedi, video box art.............................$10–$15
R2-D2 and C-3PO ....$10–$15
Shadows of the Empire ....$10–$15
Space Battle ....$10–$15
Star Destroyer ....$10–$15
Star Destroyer, blueprint style ....$10–$15
Star Wars, theater poster ....$10–$15
Star Wars, video box art..$10–$15
Stormtrooper, half-face artwork..............................$10–$15
TIE Fighter, blueprint style ....$10–$15
X-Wing, blueprint style ....$10–$15
Yoda, half-face artwork ....$10–$15

STAR WARS TRILOGY PORTFOLIO, 1994

Set of eight 11″ × 14″ color card stock "Moviecards" in light cardstock envelope with color Space Battle cover.
Per portfolio ....$15–$20

VEHICLE BLUEPRINT PORTFOLIO, 1994

Set of eight 11″ × 14″ prints in light cardstock envelope.
Per portfolio ....$15–$20

CLOTHING AND ACCESSORIES

This section is organized alphabetically by item type.

BELTS AND BELT BUCKLES

NOTE: Belts and buckles were also produced for several foreign markets, including Japan, Mexico and several European countries.

American Greeting, 1980/83

STRETCH BELTS

Child's size in assorted background colors with logos stitched into fabric and small metal logo or character buckles (Lee), some with color poly appliques. Came stretched on display hanger. Slight design variations exist.

American Greetings, Star Wars stretch belt

Star Wars .... $35–$40
May the Force Be With You .... $35–$40
Star Wars/Empire Strikes Back .... $35–$40
Star Wars/Return of the Jedi .... $35–$40
Droids .... $35–$40
Ewoks .... $35–$40

Basic Tool & Supply, 1977

Series of buckles in heavy brass. Copies of these by assorted manufacturers also exist.

C-3PO and R2-D2 .... $25–$35
Darth Vader .... $25–$35
R2-D2 .... $25–$35
Star Wars, logo .... $25–$35
X-Wing, with Star Wars logo .... $25–$35

Lee, 1980/83

Belt buckles. Sold primarily on plain brown or black leather belts with enameled copies of Basic Tool & Supply buckles or small brass character buckles (Darth, Jabba or Yoda). Adult and child's sizes. An enameled Empire logo buckle was also produced. Buckles with belts had two packaging variations. Clear plastic boxes with Star Wars logo, characters and scenes or plain rack hangers.

BRASS BUCKLES

Darth (oval), Jabba (rectangular), Yoda (round).

Boxes .... $50–$65
Hangers .... $50–$65
Buckles, no belt .... $20–$30

ENAMEL BUCKLES

Boxes .... $40–$55
Hangers .... $40–$55
Buckles, no belt .... $15–$25

CHARACTER BELTS, 1980/83

Leather belts with characters and scenes embossed the entire length of the belt in either black or color designs. Usually equipped with plain buckle. Several logo and character variations.

Each .... $50–$75

BILLFOLDS AND WALLETS

Billfolds

ADAM JOSEPH, 1983

Color vinyl. Horizontal folding style. Came blister-packed on cardboard header with Jedi logo.

Darth Vader and Imperial Guards, black .... $15–$25
R2-D2 and C-3PO, blue .... $15–$25
Yoda, red .... $15–$25

Coin Holders

ADAM JOSEPH, 1983

Small pouches with color artwork of characters. Vertical fold-over with Velcro closure. Packaged in clear plastic bag atttached to header with Jedi logo.

Darth Vader and Imperial Guards, black .... $10–$15
R2-D2 and C-3PO, blue .... $10–$15
Yoda, red .... $10–$15

TOUCHLINE (BRITISH), 1983

Plastic 3″ oval in assorted colors. Eight different characters. Originally came blister-packed on cardboard header with Jedi logo.

Price each .... $15–$25

Touchline (British), Jabba the Hutt coin holder

Pocket Pals

ADAM JOSEPH, 1983

Similar to coin holders but with extra compartment for photos and ring for keys. More square in shape.

Darth Vader and Imperial Guards, black .... $15–$20
R2-D2 and C-3PO, blue .... $15–$20
Yoda, red .... $15–$20

Wallets

ADAM JOSEPH, 1983

Color vinyl. Similar to billfolds but with side snap closure.

Darth Vader and Imperial Guards, black .... $20–$25
R2-D2 and C-3PO, blue .... $20–$25
Yoda, red .... $20–$25

ADAM JOSEPH, 1983

Vinyl with cartoon Ewok artwork. Came blister-packed on header card with Ewoks cartoon logo.

Kneesa .... $15–$20
Wicket .... $15–$20

ADAM JOSEPH, 1983

Velcro closure type. Vertical fold-over. Package is similar to coin holders.

Darth Vader and Imperial Guards, black .... $15–$20
R2-D2 and C-3PO, blue .... $15–$20
Yoda, red .... $15–$20

STAR TOURS

Black nylon with Velcro closure and "Star Tours" screen printed in corner.

Each .... $10–$15

CAPS AND HATS

Fresh Caps, 1996

Baseball caps.

Character Caps Embroidered half face of character and logo on front of black caps and short saying embroidered on back. Adjustable adult size.

- **Darth Vader** .... $15–$20
- **Stormtrooper** .... $15–$20
- **Yoda** .... $15–$20

Character/Name Caps Embroidered on front of cap.

- **Darth Vader,** on blue cap .... $15–$20
- **Jedi Master Yoda,** on green cap .... $15–$20

Logo Scene Cap, 1996. Black cap with space battle scene embroidered in color surrounded by "Star Wars" logo in heavier gold embroidery.

- **Each** .... $15–$20

20th Anniversary Logo Cap Gold embroidered on black.

- **Each** .... $15–$20

X-Wing Holo-foil Cap Ship in holographic material with Star Wars logo embroidered in red. Adjustable adult size.

- **Each** .... $15–$20

Marlin Tease (Ralph Marlin), 1996

Baseball Cap Black adjustable adult-size cap with either solid or outline-style Star Wars logo embroidered on front.

- **Each** .... $15–$20

Sales Corporation of America, 1983

Baseball Caps Adjustable children's size baseball-style caps with solid fronts and mesh backs in assorted colors. Color artwork design was silk-screened on hat.

Admiral Ackbar, name and picture of character .... $15–$25
Darth Vader and Emperor's Guards .... $15–$25
Gamorrean Guard, name and four guards .... $15–$25
Jabba the Hutt, name and picture of Jabba .... $15–$25
Luke and Darth, logo and characters dueling ..... $15–$25
Return of the Jedi, logo .... $15–$25

Ski Caps Knit, two-tone caps in assorted colors topped with pompoms. Embroidered character applique is applied to cuff of cap. Adult and children's sizes.

C-3PO .... $25–$40
Chewbacca... $25–$40
Ewok .... $25–$40
Gamorrean Guard... $25–$40
Jedi logo... $25–$40
R2-D2... $25–$40

Star Tours

Star Tours at all Disney parks have since the attractions opened done several variations of the Star Tours logo on a variety of baseball and painter-style caps and also visors.

Price for any .... $10–$15

Star Wars Fan Club

Hat Special promotional item.

Each .... $10–$15

Thinking Cap Co., Imperial Guard hat

Thinking Cap Co., 1980/81

Empire Strikes Back Logo Cap Embroidered white, red and black emblem on front of adjustable baseball-style cap.

Each, assorted colors .... $10–$15

Imperial Guard Hat Solid black hat with short bill styled after those worn by Imperial officers in the movies. Metal silver medallion on front of hat reads "Star Wars" and "Imperial Guard."

Each, adult sizes.. $35–$50

Rebel Forces Cap Tan billed cap with flap in back. Round red, blue and yellow embroidered patch on front reads "Star Wars" and "Rebel Forces."

Each, adult sizes.. $25–$40

Yoda Ears Cap Red adjustable baseball-style cap. Green stuffed cloth "ears" and artificial hair on sides. Yellow and black embroidered "Yoda" patch on front.

Each .... $25–$40

CARRYING BAGS

See HOUSEWARES (Luggage and Tote Bags).

GLOVES AND MITTENS

Sales Corporation of America, 1983

Knit Gloves Assorted colors with leatherette facings with characters embroidered on back.

C-3PO .... $30–$50
Chewbacca .... $30–$50
Darth Vader .... $30–$50
R2-D2.. $30–$50

Mittens Nylon children's size with character on back.

C-3PO .... $25–$45
Chewbacca.. $25–$45
Darth Vader .... $25–$45
Ewok .... $25–$45
R2-D2 .... $25–$45

JACKETS

The Fan Club Inc., 1995

Denim, with Boba Fett embroidered on back .... $125–$150

Denim, with Darth Vader head, Star Wars logo embroidered on back .... $100–$125

Miscellaneous

Fatigue type, features Luke Skywalker and Bespin Guard..... .... $50–$75

Short tan fitted style, copy of jacket worn by Luke in The Empire Strikes Back. Originally produced by original Star Wars fan club in adult and children's sizes. Recently reissued in adult sizes by current fan club ....$60–$75

Star Tours, Since the opening of ride in the various Disney parks, jackets in various styles incorporating the Star Tours logo have been in continuous production. Value depends on style and quality of jacket ....$50–$90

LEG WARMERS

Sales Corporation of America, 1983

22″ long. Knit stripes in assorted colors with embroidered applique applied at top.

C-3PO ....$35–$45
Chewbacca ....$35–$45
Darth Vader ....$35–$45
Ewok ....$35–$45
Jedi logo, applique ....$35–$45
Jedi logo, knit ....$35–$45
R2-D2 ....$35–$45

PAJAMAS

Miscellaneous

Three different styles.

Star Wars, C-3PO and X-Wing, gold ....$15–$20
Star Wars, Darth Vader, C-3PO and R2-D2, blue ...$15–$20

Wilker Bros., child's pajama top

May the Force Be With You, Darth and R2-D2, blue ....$15–$20

Wilker Bros.

Pajamas, Sleepers and Nightshirts Several different one- and two-piece outfits in children's sizes with Empire, Jedi and Ewok (cartoon) artwork. Many minor variations.
Price each ....$15–$25

POLO SHIRTS

Star Tours

Shirt, color embroidered pocket logo on white or black shirt. ....$20–$25

RAINWEAR

Ponchos

ADAM JOSEPH, 1983

Plastic children's size with characters and Jedi logo.

C-3PO and R2-D2 ....$35–$45
Darth Vader and Imperial Guard ....$35–$45

Raincoat

ADAM JOSEPH, 1983

Plastic children's size with characters and Jedi logo.

C-3PO and R2-D2 ....$40–$55
Darth Vader and Imperial Guard ....$40–$55

SCARVES

Sales Corporation of America, 1983

Fringed, striped knit scarves in assorted colors with embroidered character applique at end.

C-3PO ....$35–$45
Chewbacca ....$35–$45
Darth Vader ....$35–$45
Ewok ....$35–$45
Jedi logo ....$35–$45
R2-D2 ....$35–$45

Darth Vader flip-flop sandals

SHOES

Sandals

FLIP-FLOPS

Darth Vader, 1977. Plastic Darth Vader head and Star Wars logo .... $35–$40
Darth Vader, plastic head, no logo .... $30–$35
C-3PO, plastic head, no logo .... $30–$35
R2-D2, plastic head, no logo .... $30–$35
Yoda, "May the Force Be With You" on sides .... $30–$35

Shoes—Clarks, 1997

Children's Sneakers Decorated with characters on sides and soles. Assorted colors and characters.
Price per pair, (any) .... $60–$95
Leather Children's Shoes Several different styles and colors named after Star Wars characters, with Star Wars logo inside shoe. Packaged in boxes with color Star Wars artwork.
Price per pair, (any) .... $75–$115

Shoes—KidNATION, Inc., 1997

Children's shoes. Box art for all is all over Darth Vader design.
Darth Vader, low sneakers .... $16–$20
Darth Vader, high sneakers .... $16–$20
Darth Vader, sandals with hologram .... $16–$20
Stormtrooper, low sneakers .... $16–$20
Stormtrooper, high sneakers .... $16–$20
Stormtrooper, sandals .... $16–$20

Shoes—Stride Rite, 1983

Children's Athletic Shoes Decorated with cut-outs of characters on sides and bottoms of shoes. Came in boxes decorated with Star Wars artwork.
Assorted colors .... $70–$115

Shoelaces

STRIDE RITE, 1983

Came blister-packed on header card with spaceships and Jedi logo.
Ewoks .... $10–$15
Return of the Jedi, logo .... $10–$15
Star Wars logo, with Darth Vader .... $10–$15
Star Wars logo, with R2-D2 and C-3PO .... $10–$15

Slippers

BRITISH SHOE, 1983

Boys' and girls' slippers decorated with artwork of characters on front of shoe.
Price per pair, (any) .... $45–$65

STRIDE RITE, 1983

Decorated with cut-out character artwork on front of shoe. Packaged in carrying bags with Jedi logo on front.
C-3PO and R2-D2 .... $35–$50
Ewok .... $35–$50
Darth Vader .... $35–$50

Slipper Socks

STRIDE RITE, 1983

Character on front. Packaged in bags with Darth and Jedi logo headers.
C-3PO .... $30–$45
Darth Vader .... $30–$45

SOCKS

Charleston Hosiery

1977

Tube-style socks in assorted colors with small square color photo transfers on cuff.
C-3PO .... $15–$25
Chewbacca .... $15–$25
"Darth Vader Lives" .... $15–$25
R2-D2 .... $15–$25
Space Battle .... $15–$25

1980

Square color photo transfer on cuff with Empire logo.
Boba Fett .... $15–$25

Charleston Hosiery, Star Wars socks

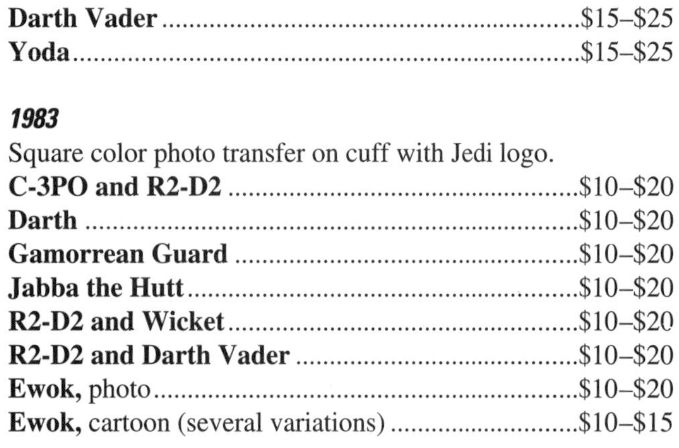

Darth Vader .... $15–$25
Yoda .... $15–$25

1983

Square color photo transfer on cuff with Jedi logo.

C-3PO and R2-D2 .... $10–$20
Darth .... $10–$20
Gamorrean Guard .... $10–$20
Jabba the Hutt .... $10–$20
R2-D2 and Wicket .... $10–$20
R2-D2 and Darth Vader .... $10–$20
Ewok, photo .... $10–$20
Ewok, cartoon (several variations) .... $10–$15

SUSPENDERS

Lee Co., 1980

Children's Suspenders With flat or three-dimensional plastic character badge attached where suspenders cross. Came on Empire logo header with artwork of Darth Vader.

- **Darth Vader,** flat and three-dimensional variations .... $35–$50
- **R2-D2 and C-3PO** .... $35–$50
- **Yoda** .... $35–$50

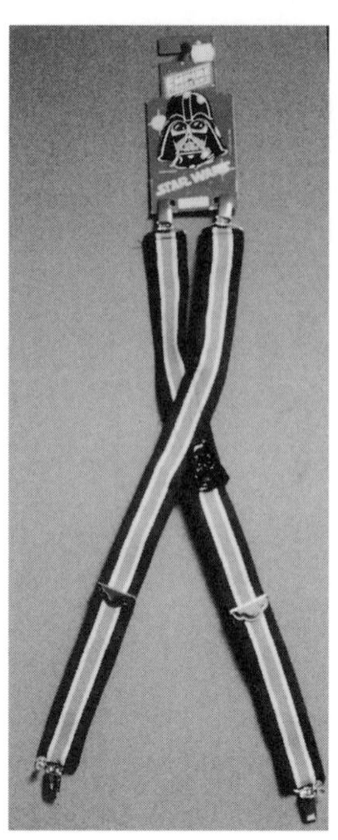

Lee, child's suspenders

SWEATSHIRTS

Star Tours

Sweatshirt, word logo in glitter on black shirt .... $30–$35
Sweatshirt, embroidered pocket logo on gray shirt .... $30–$35

TIES

Ralph Marlin, 1995 to present

Adult Neckties Polyester unless otherwise noted.

- **AT-AT,** all over .... $13–$18
- **C-3PO and R2-D2,** line art with inset photo .... $13–$18
- **Character collage,** two variations .... $13–$18
- **Chewbacca,** line art with inset photo .... $13–$18

Assorted Ralph Marlin Star Wars ties

Darth Vader, lightsaber, silk ....$20–$25
Darth Vader, lightsaber and characters ....$13–$18
Darth Vader, line art with inset photo ....$13–$18
Darth Vader, all over, silk ....$20–$25
Darth Vader, half-face ....$13–$18
Death Star and X-Wings ....$13–$18
Death Star trench scene ....$13–$18
Obi-Wan and characters ....$13–$18
Ships, all over, silk ....$20–$25
Stormtrooper, half-face ....$13–$18
X-Wing and TIE Fighter ....$13–$18
Yoda, half face ....$13–$18
Yoda, line art and inset photo ....$13–$18

T-SHIRTS AND T-SHIRT TRANSFERS

At the time the Star Wars movies were first being shown the popular method of applying a design to a T-shirt was by means of iron-on decals made primarily from plastisal, a thin rubber-like material. Unfortunately for collectors, these transfers do not age well, either on or off shirts. They are sensitive to both temperature and humidity and often crack, peel or bubble. Another type of transfer, done by a method called sublimation, was used for the Star Wars Transfer Book (see BOOKS), but these could only be used on polyester shirts and never gained much popularity. By the end of the Star Wars Saga, the much more durable silk-screen shirt process was coming into general usage and has been used on virtually all subsequent shirts.

NOTE: All of the following shirts and transfers are licensed. Though a few unlicensed Star Wars shirts and transfers have been made, none were ever extensively produced.

Transfers

FACTORS, ETC, 1977

Color photo or artwork designs. Usually sold to the retail customer on shirts, sweatshirts, totebags or other cloth accessories. Price here is for transfer only.

Chewy ....$1–$3
Darth Vader helmet, with ships ....$1–$3
"Darth Vader Lives," with Vader helmet ....$1–$3
Darth Vader, full figure ....$1–$3
Droids, blue background ....$1–$3
Han Solo and Chewbacca ....$1–$3
"May the Force Be With You" ....$1–$3
Jawas ....$1–$3
Luke and C-3PO ....$1–$3
Poster art, Hildebrandt ....$1–$3
Princess Leia ....$1–$3
R2-D2 and C-3PO, in ship corridor ....$1–$3
Star Wars logo, glitter ....$1–$3

FACTORS, ETC, 1980

Color photo or artwork designs. Empire designs were glossier transfer material than earlier ones and made greater use of glitter detail.

Boba Fett ....$1–$3
Empire Strikes Back, logo ....$1–$3
Han Solo ....$1–$3
Lando Calrissian ....$1–$3
Luke on Tauntaun ....$1–$3
Luke with X-Wing ....$1–$3
Millennium Falcon ....$1–$3
Poster art, kissing scene ....$1–$3
Star Destroyer ....$1–$3
The Way of the Force, Luke and Yoda ....$1–$3
TIE Fighter ....$1–$3
X-Wing ....$1–$3
Yoda ....$1–$3

T-Shirts

AMERICAN MARKETING, 1996

Color artwork based on Star Wars Art Trading Card series.

Boba Fett ....$15–$20
Bounty Hunters ....$15–$20
Chewbacca ....$15–$20
Darth Vader ....$15–$20
Darth Vader, with two lightsabers ....$15–$20
Emperor ....$15–$20
Han Solo ....$15–$20
Jawa, with wrench ....$15–$20
Luke and Leia ....$15–$20
Rancor Monster ....$15–$20
Theater poster art, Star Wars domestic ....$15–$20
Theater poster art, Jedi two droids design ....$15–$20
Villains ....$15–$20
Yoda ....$15–$20

ANVIL, 1995

Cream-color shirts with movie logo front design and color montage artwork for movie on back.

Star Wars ....$15–$20
Empire Strikes Back ....$15–$20
Return of the Jedi ....$15–$20

CHANGES, 1996

Break-through T-shirts. Silk-screened background character with foreground character seeming to "break through" design.

Obi-Wan and Darth Vader ....$15–$20
R2-D2 and C-3PO ....$15–$20
Stormtrooper ....$15–$20
TIE and X-Wing ....$15–$20

CHANGES, 1996

Characters silk-screened on shirt.

Boba Fett ....$15–$20
C-3PO ....$15–$20
Darth Vader ....$15–$20
Emperor ....$15–$20
Imperial Guard ....$15–$20
Jabba, two-sided ....$18–$22
Sand Person ....$15–$20
Xizor ....$15–$20
Yoda ....$15–$20

CHANGES, 1996

Black and white collage design on colored shirts.

Creatures ....$15–$20
Imperial characters ....$15–$20
Rebel characters ....$15–$20

CHANGES, 1996

Black or white T-shirts with head of character done in black and white, dot pattern silk-screen artwork.

Boba Fett ....$15–$20
Chewbacca ....$15–$20
C-3PO ....$15–$20
Darth Vader ....$15–$20
Princess Leia ....$15–$20
Stormtrooper ....$15–$20
Yoda ....$15–$20

CHANGES, 1996

Han in carbonite, raised design ....$18–$20

CHANGES, 1996

White shirts with blue or red ringers. Slightly reworked artwork from original Factors Etc. transfer designs (no glitter).

Any ....$12–$15

CHANGES, 1996

Scene T-shirts.

Speeder Bike, two-sided ....$18–$22
Ice Planet, two-sided ....$18–$22
Space Battle, glow-in-the-dark ....$18–$22
Darth/Space Battle, glow-in-the-dark ....$18–$22
Kissing scene ....$18–$22

CHANGES, 1996

Slogan shirts.

Darth Vader "I Want You" recruiting poster parody, black ....$15–$20
Boba Fett for Hire, with artwork ....$15–$20
Darth Vader Imperial Wear, two-sided ....$16–$20
Mos Eisley Cantina, with artwork ....$15–$20
Star Wars Rebel Wear, two-sided ....$16–$20

COLOR-ME-TEE, PATTI M. PRODUCTIONS, 1987

Four different line drawings of Ewoks. Came packaged in clear plastic box with four markers.

Price each ....$12–$15

FREEZE, 1997

Exaggerated cartoon artwork of characters.

Boba Fett and Darth Vader ....$12–$18
Droids ....$12–$18
May the Force Be With You logo, transfer ....$12–$18
Vader and Friends ....$12–$18
Vader and TIE blueprints ....$12–$18
Vader on Red Square, transfer ....$12–$18

HANES, 1996

Several designs in children's and adult sizes.

Darth Vader "The Empire Wants You" ....$15–$20
Darth Vader, glow-in-the-dark X-ray effect ....$15–$20
Darth Vader "Join the Dark Side" ....$15–$20
Darth Vader with Lightsaber ....$15–$20
Jedi, scenes in logo design ....$15–$20
Rancor ....$15–$20
Space Battle ....$15–$20
Star Wars logo ....$15–$20

HI-C, 1983

T-shirt and cap, promotional set. Shirt had montage of Jedi characters. White and navy hat shows Luke and Darth Vader.

Per set ....$15–$20

JUNIOR STARS, 1983

T-shirts with photo transfers applied. Transfers were not sold separately even to wholesalers. Shirts came in assorted colors.

Chewbacca, R2-D2 and C-3PO ....$10–$15
Han Solo, insets of Sarlacc and Ewok ....$10–$15
Luke Skywalker and Darth Vader ....$10–$15
Luke, Darth and Emperor ....$10–$15
Princess Leia, inset of Leia and Han ....$10–$15
R2-D2 and Wicket ....$10–$15
Wicket ....$10–$15

LIQUID BLUE, 1996

Large images silk-screened onto tie-dyed effect background.

Boba Fett ....$25–$30
Chewbacca ....$25–$30
Death Star, two-sided ....$27–$30
Planet Hoth, two-sided ....$27–$30
Sand People, two-sided ....$27–$30
TIE Fighter ....$25–$30
Yoda ....$25–$30

MARLIN TEASE, 1993

Color Death Star battle scene on black shirt.

Each ....$15–$20

NATIONAL SCREENPRINT, 1990

Line artwork on white shirts.

AT-AT .... $10–$15
C-3PO .... $10–$15
R2-D2 .... $10–$15

STAR TOURS

Star Tours at all Disney parks has, since the introduction of the attraction, produced an extensive line of Star Tours T-shirts in both adult and children's sizes. Disney marketing policy dictates that designs go into and out of production rapidly, which has resulted in the production of dozens of different T-shirts and tank tops with Star Tours or generalized Star Wars designs unique to Disney. Though many of the designs are very appealing, these, like all T-shirts, have limited collector appeal and are generally purchased simply to be worn. Price range based primarily on style and quality of shirt and complexity of design.

Any shirt .... $10–$35

STAR WARS FAN CLUB (ORIGINAL)

Promotional. Shows club's Bantha logo.

Each .... $15–$20

STUDIO PROMOTIONAL

Star Wars logo on front and "May the Force Be With You" on back.

Each .... $20–$25

UBI, 1997

Bright artwork designs often with metallic highlights.

Bad guy aliens, monotone blue and silver .... $16–$20
Boba Fett face .... $16–$20
Darth Vader and Stormtroopers .... $16–$20
Yoda— "A Jedi's Strength Flows From the Force" .... $16–$20
Yoda and Lightsaber— "You Must Unlearn What You Have Learned" .... $16–$20

UNDERWEAR

Briefly Stated, 1997

Knit Boxers All-over designs with logo waistbands. Boys' sizes.

- **Droids** .... $8–$10
- **Hoth scene** .... $8–$10
- **Space Battle** .... $8–$10
- **Stormtroopers** .... $8–$10

Marlin Tease (Ralph Marlin), 1995 to present

Cotton Boxers Blue shorts in adult sizes with all-over pattern of ships in space.

- **Each** .... $15–$20

Marlin Tease, Star Wars boxer shorts

Silk Boxers All-over Darth Vader design on black.

- **Each** .... $20–$25

Union Underwear, Underoos, 1983

Children's shirt and pants sets. Color decals on shirts. Packaged in flat square cardboard envelope with color photo of product and Underoos and Jedi logos. Includes "Jedi Knight Certificate."

Boba Fett .... $25–$35
C-3PO .... $25–$35
Darth Vader .... $25–$35
Han Solo .... $25–$35
Luke Skywalker .... $25–$35
Princess Leia .... $25–$35
R2-D2 .... $25–$35
Wicket .... $25–$35
Yoda .... $25–$35

UMBRELLAS

Adam Joseph, 1983

Clear plastic with color design and Jedi logo.

Darth Vader .... $35–$50
R2-D2 and C-3PO .... $35–$50

VESTS

Black vest with pockets, replica of one worn by Han Solo in movies. First made as promotion by original Star Wars Fan Club. Recently reissued by current club .... $75–$85

COINS

Kenner action figure coins are organized alphabetically by character. Rarities Mint and Fan Club coins follow this list.

Kenner, 1984–1985

Aluminum coins with characters portrayed on front and short description under logo on back. The silver-colored coins were included with "Power of the Force" carded action figures and the copper- and gold-colored coins came with "Ewoks" and "Droids" figures, respectively. A few other coins were intended for toys but never packaged with them. Since many of the "Power of the Force" figures are relatively rare, most of the coins did not get widely distributed. It was possible to receive the coins by mail from Kenner and many of the more rare coins in collections today were obtained this way. "Ewoks" and most "Droids" coins are much more common. A few variations exist as well as some prototype coins for figures planned but never mass produced. Both of these categories bring considerable premiums ($200 and up).

SILVER COLOR

"Star Wars" or "Power of the Force" logos on reverse.

Silver Star Wars coins were included with Kenner Power of the Force action figures

Amanaman .... $10–$15
Anakin Skywalker .... $20–$25
AT-AT .... $30–$40
AT-ST Driver .... $15–$20
A-Wing Pilot .... $10–$15
Barada .... $10–$15
Bib Fortuna .... $40–$50
Biker Scout .... $15–$20
Boba Fett .... $35–$45
B-Wing Pilot .... $15–$20
Chewbacca .... $25–$35
Chief Chirpa .... $20–$25
Creatures .... $30–$40
C-3PO .... $25–$35
Darth Vader .... $25–$35
Droids .... $40–$50
Emperor .... $15–$20
Emperor's Royal Guard .... $30–$40
EV-9D9 .... $10–$15
FX-7 .... $50–$65
Gamorrean Guard .... $20–$30
Greedo .... $50–$65
Han Solo, carbon freeze .... $10–$15
Han Solo, Rebel .... $25–$35
Han Solo, Rebel fighter .... $15–$25
Han Solo, Rebel hero .... $30–$40
Hoth Stormtrooper .... $50–$65
Imperial Commander .... $25–$35
Imperial Dignitary .... $10–$15
Imperial Gunner .... $10–$15
Jawas .... $25–$35
Lando Calrissian, Bespin .... $30–$40
Lando Calrissian, Millennium Falcon .... $20–$25
Logray .... $20–$25
Luke Skywalker .... $25–$35
Luke Skywalker, Tatooine outfit .... $25–$35
Luke Skywalker, X-Wing outfit close-up .... $25–$35

Luke Skywalker, X-Wing in background .... $25–$35
Luke Skywalker, Jedi Knight close-up .... $10–$15
Luke Skywalker, Jedi Knight, Dagobah .... $50–$65
Luke Skywalker, on Taun Taun .... $35–$50
Luke Skywalker, on Speeder Bike .... $10–$15
Lumat .... $10–$15
Millennium Falcon .... $40–$50
Obi-Wan Kenobi .... $25–$35
Paploo .... $20–$25
Princess Leia, Boushh .... $50–$65
Princess Leia, wearing helmet .... $10–$15
Princess Leia, original hairstyle .... $50–$65
Romba .... $10–$15
R2-D2 .... $10–$15
Sail Skiff .... $50–$65
Star Destroyer Commander .... $40–$50
Stormtrooper .... $25–$35
Teebo .... $20–$25
TIE Fighter Pilot .... $25–$35
Too-OneBee .... $50–$65
Tusken Raider .... $50–$65
Warok .... $10–$15
Wicket .... $25–$35
Yak Face .... $25–$35
Yoda .... $50–$65
Zuckuss .... $50–$65

Copper Ewoks coins were included with Kenner Ewoks action figures

COPPER COLOR

Ewok coins.

Dulok Scout .... $2–$3
Dulok Shaman .... $2–$3
King Gorneesh .... $2–$3
Logray .... $2–$3
Wicket W. Warrick .... $2–$3
Urgah Lady Gorneesh .... $2–$3

GOLD COLOR

Droid coins.

A-Wing Pilot .... $35–$45
Boba Fett .... $35–$45

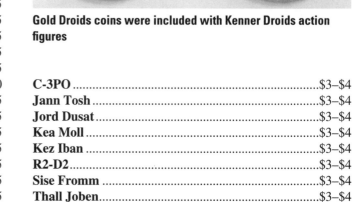

Gold Droids coins were included with Kenner Droids action figures

C-3PO .... $3–$4
Jann Tosh .... $3–$4
Jord Dusat .... $3–$4
Kea Moll .... $3–$4
Kez Iban .... $3–$4
R2-D2 .... $3–$4
Sise Fromm .... $3–$4
Thall Joben .... $3–$4
Tig Fromm .... $3–$4
Uncle Gundy .... $3–$4

Rarities Mint, outside folder

Rarities Mint, 1987–1988

This series of limited edition, numbered collectors' coins in fine metals was released over a period of about a year by the manufacturer. Coins are .999 pure gold or silver with proof finishes. All coins come in plastic coin holders inside of their respective packaging. The five-ounce silver coins come in hinged velveteen jewelry boxes. For all others, the plastic coin cases are embedded in a cardboard card which is slipped into a pocket of a paper folder. Both the card and the folder show color artwork of the characters depicted on the coin. The front of the folders of all coins show the Star Wars Tenth Anniversary logo. In the case of all but the one-ounce silver coins, mintages were very low.

NOTE: Collectible coins are produced by a special minting process intended to give the surface of the coin a lustrous shine. To preserve its value, the coin should be handled only by the edge in order not to mar this surface finish. Silver coins are subject to a process called "toning," where the surface of the coin tarnishes with age. As long as this coloring was caused naturally, it is not considered a defect and should not be removed.

Rarities Mint, one-ounce silver coin

ONE-OUNCE SILVER COINS

NOTE: A 1/10th-ounce silver coin with "The Epic Begins" art was manufactured to be incorporated into souvenirs for foreign markets but is relatively rare.

#I The Epic Begins .... $100–$150
#II R2-D2 and C-3PO .... $100–$150
#III Han Solo and Chewbacca .... $100–$150
#IV Imperial Stormtroopers .... $100–$150
#V Mos Eisley Cantina Band .... $100–$150
#VI Darth Vader and Ben (Obi-Wan) Kenobi .... $100–$150

FIVE-OUNCE SILVER COINS

#I The Epic Begins .... $200–$300
#II R2-D2 and C-3PO .... $200–$300
#III Han Solo and Chewbacca .... $200–$300
#IV Imperial Stormtroopers .... $200–$300
#V Mos Eisley Cantina Band .... $200–$300
#VI Darth Vader and Ben (Obi-Wan) Kenobi .... $200–$300

ONE-QUARTER-OUNCE GOLD COINS

#I The Epic Begins .... $400–$600
#II R2-D2 and C-3PO .... $400–$600
#III Han Solo and Chewbacca .... $400–$600
#IV Imperial Stormtroopers .... $400–$600
#V Mos Eisley Cantina Band .... $400–$600
#VI Darth Vader and Ben (Obi-Wan) Kenobi .... $400–$600

ONE-OUNCE GOLD COINS

#I The Epic Begins .... $2000–$5000
#II R2-D2 and C-3PO .... $2000–$5000
#III Han Solo and Chewbacca .... $2000–$5000
#IV Imperial Stormtroopers .... $2000–$5000
#V Mos Eisley Cantina Band .... $2000–$5000
#VI Darth Vader and Ben (Obi-Wan) Kenobi .... $2000–$5000

Star Wars Fan Club (Rawcliffe), 1995

PEWTER MEDALLIONS

4″ in diameter. Each comes with plastic stand. Same artwork as three of Rawcliffe's keychains in a slightly larger size.

Darth Vader .... $35–$40
Obi-Wan Kenobi .... $35–$40
Yoda .... $35–$40

COLLECTOR PLATES

All authorized Star Wars plates to date have been licensed through Hamilton. They are divided chronologically by series.

NOTE: For other ceramics and glassware, see appropriate section in HOUSEWARES.

STAR WARS (ORIGINAL SERIES)

Hamilton Collection, 1986–1989

Plates are 8¼″ in diameter, numbered limited editions, designed by the Hamilton Collection, with artwork by Thomas Blackshear. They went out of production very suddenly and values rose accordingly. As with most numbered series, lower numbers are considered more desirable.

NOTE: A series of mugs was done to go along with the collector's plates with identical artwork. Originally mugs were only sold in sets but were later made available individually in some outlets. Price each: $10–15.

Crew in Cockpit of Millennium Falcon..............$200–$250
Darth and Luke..$200–$250
Han Solo...$150–$200
Imperial Walkers..$175–$225

Hamilton Collection, original plate series and tenth anniversary plate *(bottom row, center)*

Two plates from Hamilton's Star Wars Trilogy Series

Luke and Yoda ....$100–$125
Princess Leia ....$175–$225
R2-D2 and Wicket ....$100–$125
Space Battle ....$350–$450
Star Wars 10th Anniversary Plate, 1988. Designed by Hamilton, artwork by Thomas Blackshear. 10¼″ numbered, limited edition ....$200–$250

STAR WARS TRILOGY SERIES

Hamilton Collection, 1993

9¼″ plates with artwork by Morgan Weistling. Plates depict a collage of their respective films.
Star Wars ....$125–$150
Empire Strikes Back ....$150–$175
Return of the Jedi ....$100–$125

STAR WARS SPACE VEHICLES SERIES

Hamilton Collection, 1995

Series of 8″ plates with artwork by Sonia Helios. Still in manufacture as of this writing.

B-Wing ....$30–$40
Imperial Shuttle ....$30–$40
Jabba's Sail Barge ....$30–$40
Slave I ....$30–$40
Snow Speeder ....$30–$40
Star Destroyer ....$30–$40
TIE Fighter ....$30–$40
X-Wing ....$30–$40

STAR WARS HEROES AND VILLAINS SERIES

Hamilton Collection, 1997

8″ plates with color artwork and gold border.
Luke Skywalker, artwork by Keith Birdsong....................$30–$40

COMICS

ANNUALS

These are British oversized hardcover books containing articles and comic reprints.

Star Wars Annual #1, 1978. Brown Watson ....$35–$50
Star Wars Annual, 1979. Grandreams.....................$30–$45
The Empire Strikes Back Annual, 1980. Grandreams ....
....$25–$35
The Empire Strikes Back Annual #2, 1981. Grandreams ....
....$25–$35
Star Wars Annual, Featuring Droid World, 1982. Marvel/Grandreams ....$20–$25
Return of the Jedi, Movie Adaptation, 1983. Marvel/Grandreams ....$20–$25
Return of the Jedi Annual, 1984. Marvel/Grandreams ....
....$20–$25
Star Wars, Featuring Ewoks Annual, 1985. Marvel/Grandreams ....$10–$15

BLACKTHORNE 3-D SERIES

Star Wars in 3-D
#1–3 ....$5–$10

DARK HORSE COMICS

Starting in 1992, Dark Horse Comics began a long and still continuing relationship with LucasFilms. Dozens of different Star Wars titles have been released. They have tended toward the shorter (often four issues) mini-series that completes a storyline instead of the ongoing series. These comics were not well received at first by the local comic book shops, so shortages occurred on many of the early issues, resulting in prices escalating significantly and the need for second printings on these books.

A highly informative book, *The Guide to Dark Horse Comics by* Chuck Rozanski, has an in-depth listing of all Dark Horse comics, including their Star Wars line, and was used for compiling these listings. Special thanks to Chuck for permission. Each issue is covered in-depth and dozens of covers are reprinted in color. This book is highly recommended for Star Wars comics collectors. It is available from Mile High Comics at (303) 455-2659.

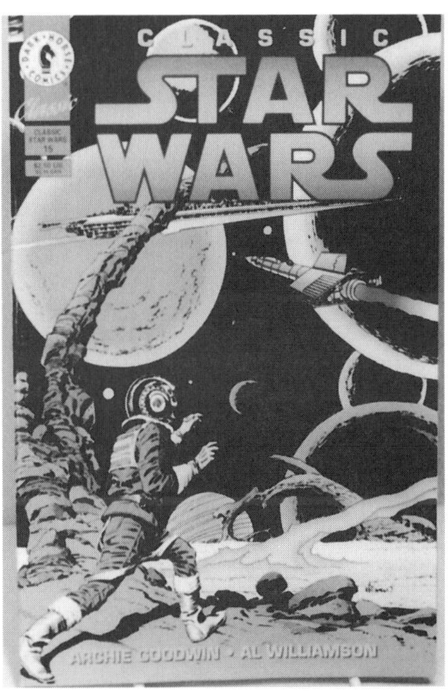

Dark Horse, Classic Star Wars comic

Classic Star Wars (Trade paperbacks)
Volume One, 1994...$15–$20

Volume Two .... $16–$18

Classic Star Wars: A New Hope, Etc. Two-issue series, 1994. Reprints Marvel comic adaptation from 1978–1983.

A New Hope, #1, 2 .... $5–$6
Empire Strikes Back, #1, 2 .... $4–$5
Return of the Jedi, #1, 2 .... $3–$4

Classic Star Wars: The Early Adventures Nine-issue series, 1994. Thirty-two pages reprinting the earliest Star Wars newspaper strips.

#1–5, 7–8 .... $3–$4
#3, with promo card .... $5–$6
#6, 9 .... $5–$6

Classic Star Wars: The Vandelhelm Mission One-shot, 1995.

#1, reprints Marvel #98 .... $3–$4

Dark Horse Comics and Dark Horse Presents Ongoing series, 1992–present. Anthology series presenting samples of upcoming books and prequel stories. Many issues had Star Wars stories.

Any issue .... $3–$4

Star Wars UK Editions English reprints of American Dark Horse Star Wars and Indiana Jones comics.

#1–3 .... $6–$10
#4–7 .... $4–$6

Star Wars: Battle of the Bounty Hunters One-shot, 1996.

Pop-Up book .... $18–$20

Star Wars: Boba Fett One-shot, 1995. Forty-eight pages.

#1 .... $4–$5

Star Wars: Dark Empire Six-issue series, 1992. Thirty-two pages.

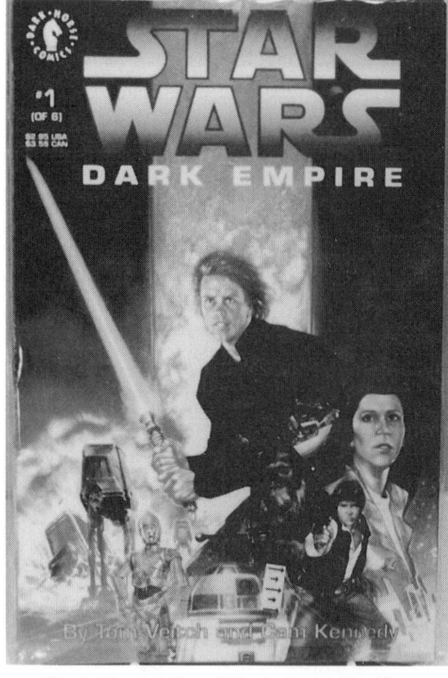

Dark Horse, Star Wars: Dark Empire

#1, first printing .... $25–$35
#1, platinum edition .... $60–$75
#1, later printings .... $4–$5
#2, first printing .... $25–$35
#2, platinum edition .... $60–$75
#2, later printing .... $4–$5
#3, first printing .... $10–$15
#3, platinum edition .... $25–$35
#3, later printings .... $4–$5
#4–6, first printings .... $8–$12
#4–6, platinum editions .... $20–$30

Star Wars: Dark Empire (Trade Paperback), 1993. 182 pages, reprints all six issues above.

First printing .... $12–$25
Later printings .... $16–$18

Star Wars: Dark Empire II Six-issue series, 1994. Thirty-two pages.

#1–6 .... $4–$5
Trade Paperback .... $16–$18

Star Wars: Droids Six-issue series, 1994.

#1 .... $3–$5
#2–6 .... $3–$4
Trade Paperback, 1995 .... $16–$18

Star Wars: Droids Vol. 2 Ongoing series, 1995. Thirty-two pages.

#1–5 .... $3–$4

Star Wars: Empire's End Two-issue series, 1995. Thirty-two pages.

#1, 2 .... $3–$4

Star Wars: Golden Age of the Sith Five-issue series, 1996.

#1–5 .... $3–$4

Star Wars: Heir to the Empire Six-issue series, 1995. Thirty-two pages.

#1–6 .... $3–$4

Star Wars: Jabba the Hutt One-shots, 1995–1996.

The Betrayal .... $3–$4
The Dynasty Trap .... $3–$4
The Garr Supoon Hit .... $4–$5
The Hunger of Princess Nampi .... $4–$5

Star Wars: The Mixed-Up Droid Ashcan One-shot, 1995. Twelve pages.

#1, Cheerios giveaway .... $4–$5

Star Wars: River of Chaos Four-issue series, 1995. Thirty-two pages.

#1–4 .... $3–$4

Star Wars: Shadows of the Empire Ongoing series, 1996–97. Thirty-two pages.

#1-present .... $3–$4

Star Wars: Splinter of the Mind's Eye Four-issue series, 1995. Thirty-two pages.

#1–4 .... $3–$4

Star Wars: Tales from Mos Eisley One-shot, 1996. Thirty-two pages.

#1 .... $3–$4

Star Wars: Tales of the Jedi Five-issue series, 1993. Thirty-two pages.

#1 .... $5–$6
#2–4 .... $3–$4

Dark Horse, Star Wars: Tales of the Jedi

#5 .... $5–$6
Trade Paperback .... $15–$16

Star Wars: Tales of the Jedi—Dark Lords of the Sith Five-issue series, 1993. Thirty-two pages.

#1 .... $5–$6
#1, ashcan edition, sold with Star Wars Galaxy magazine #1 .... $3–$4
#2–6 .... $4–$5
Trade paperback .... $16–$18

Star Wars: Tales of the Jedi—The Freedon Nadd Uprising Two-issue series, 1994. Thirty-two pages.

#1, 2 .... $3–$4

Star Wars: Tales of the Jedi—The Sith War Six-issue series, 1995. Thirty-two pages.

#1–6 .... $3–$4

Star Wars: X-Wing Rogue Squadron Ongoing series, 1995. Thirty-two pages.

#1–4 .... $4–$5
#5 to present .... $3–$4

Star Wars: X-Wing Rogue Squadron Special One-shot, 1995. Fourteen pages, cereal send-away.

#1 .... $5–$6

MARVEL COMICS GROUP

1977–1986. Marvel Comics first started their long-running series of Star Wars comics with an adaptation of the first movie. This appeared in several different formats, starting with the first six issues of the comic series. The Empire Strikes Back adaptation took place with issues #38–44, and the Return of the Jedi adaptation was done as a separate miniseries. Interest in these comics has grown exponentially over the past few years, and values are up as much as 1000 percent since the last edition of this guide.

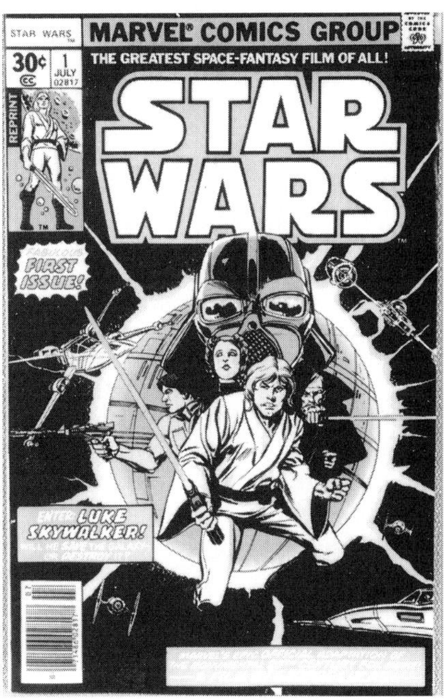

Marvel Comics, Star Wars #1

Star Wars

#1, 30 cents cover price .... $25–$50
#2, 35 cents cover price .... $50–$300
#3–4 .... $15–$50
#5–10 .... $12–$40
#11–37 .... $10–$20
#38–44, Empire Strikes Back .... $12–$30
#45–70 .... $10–$20
#71–99 .... $12–$25
#100–106 .... $15–$30
#107, last issue .... $35–$75
Star Wars Annual #1, 1979 .... $15–$30
Star Wars Annual #2, 1980 .... $10–$20
Star Wars Annual #3, 1981 .... $8–$15

Star Wars: Return of the Jedi

#1–4 .... $6–$12

MARVEL COMICS (BRITISH)

Long-running series published first on a weekly, then on a monthly basis.

Any issue .... $6–$10

MARVEL ILLUSTRATED BOOKS

Star Wars, 1981. Four original adventures.
- **Way of the Wookiee** .... $4–$8
- **The Day After the Death Star** .... $4–$8
- **Weapons Master** .... $4–$8
- **War on Ice** .... $4–$8

Star Wars Treasury, 1977. 11″ × 14″. Story of Episode IV (A New Hope). Reprints issues #1–6 of Marvel comic.
- **Issue #1** .... $5–$10
- **Issue #2** .... $5–$10
- **Issue #3,** combines #1 and #2 above .... $8–$12

Star Wars 2, 1982.
- **World of Fire** .... $4–$8

Empire Strikes Back (Marvel Super Special #2), 1980. 8½″ × 11″ magazine format. Reprints issues #38–44 of Marvel comic.
- **#2** .... $6–$12

Star Wars: Return of the Jedi, 1983. 8½″ × 11″ magazine format (Marvel Super Special). Reprints comic mini-series.
- **Each** .... $5–$10

STAR COMICS

(Juvenile division of Marvel).

Droids Based on the animated TV series.
- **#1–8** .... $5–$10

Ewoks Based on the animated TV series.
- **#1–15** .... $5–$10

COSMETICS

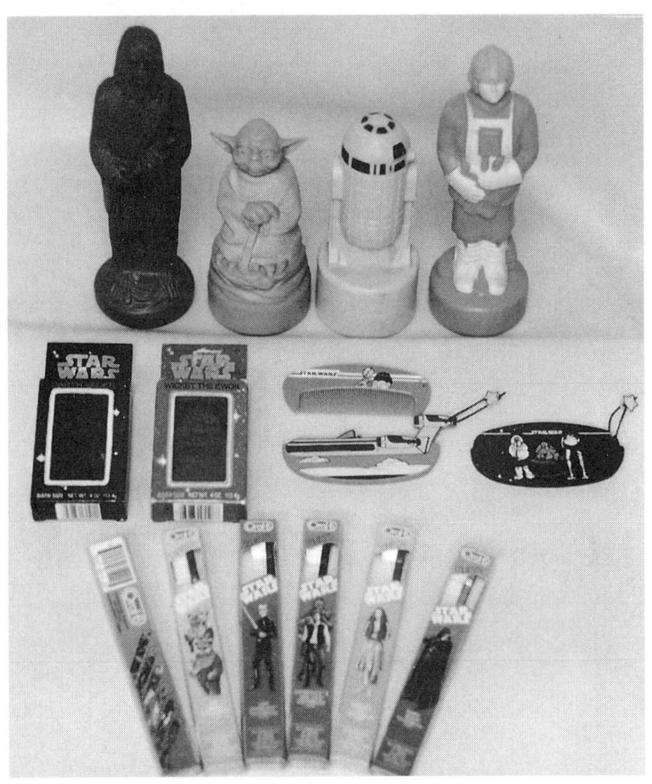

The section is organized alphabetically by item.

Beauty Bag

Omni, 1981. Contains two-ounce shampoo, cream rinse and cologne in regular-shaped plastic bottles decorated with Star Wars logo and line drawing of Leia. Also contains Leia character soap and comb. Comes in clear plastic carry bag with handles, decorated with Star Wars logo and "Princess Leia Beauty Bag" on front.

Princess Leia Beauty Bag ....$50–$70

Belt Kit

Luke Skywalker Belt Kit Omni, 1981. Contains 2 oz. bottles of shampoo, cream rinse and cologne in regular-shaped plastic bottles decorated with Star Wars logo and line drawing of Luke. Also includes Luke character soap, comb and toothbrush. Comes in clear plastic snap-shut pouch with Star Wars logo and "Luke Skywalker Belt Kit" on front ....$60–$85

Bubble Bath

Bubble Bath Refueling Station Omni, 1981. Regular-shaped plastic bottle, 6½″ tall, decorated with ships in space and Star Wars logo.

Per item ....$10–$15

Character Bubble Bath Addis (British), 1983. Packaged in tapering cylindrical bottles with artwork of character.

Ben Kenobi ....$25–$35
Chewbacca...$25–$35
C-3PO ....$25–$35
Darth Vader ....$25–$35
Gamorrean Guard...$25–$35
Han Solo ....$25–$35
Leia...$25–$35
Luke ....$25–$35
R2-D2 ....$25–$35

Character Bubble Bath Omni, 1981/83. Containers were colored plastic shaped like characters from Star Wars. 4½″ to 9½″ tall. Most were introduced in 1981, but Wicket and Jabba were added after Return of the Jedi in 1983.

NOTE: Omni used these same containers to hold their line of shampoo, which was being marketed at the same time as the bubble bath.

Chewbacca ....$20–$25
Darth Vader...$20–$25
Jabba the Hutt..$20–$25

Omni Cosmetics, Star Wars bubble bath and shampoo containers

Adam Joseph, pop-up comb

Luke Skywalker, X-Wing pilot outfit .... $20–$25
Princess Leia .... $20–$25
R2-D2 .... $20–$25
Wicket .... $20–$25
Yoda .... $20–$25

Gift Set Addis (British), 1985. Boxed bubble bath gift set includes two oval bar soaps and one bottle of liquid bath soap.

Darth Vader and Luke soaps, Luke liquid, Darth sponge .... $40–$50
Ewoks bar soaps and liquid .... $30–$40
R2-D2 and C-3PO soaps, C-3PO liquid .... $35–$45

Combs

Comb-N-Keepers Adam Joseph, 1983. Colorful plastic combs fit into base (keeper). Small plastic star is attached by string to one end.

Speeder-R2-D2 and C-3P0 on comb, keeper is shaped like a landspeeder .... $15–$25
Rebo Band, band is shown on keeper .... $15–$25
Wicket the Ewok, Ewok on keeper .... $10–$15

Pop-Up Combs Adam Joseph, 1983. Combs come with flip-up mirror that looks closed when comb is inserted. Three different.

C-3PO and R2-D2, Star Wars logo .... $15–$25
Darth Vader, Jedi logo .... $15–$25
Leia, Jedi logo .... $15–$25

Personal Care Kit

Ewok Personal Care Bag Adam Joseph, 1983. Zippered bag with silk-screened picture of Princess Kneesa. Includes comb and mirror.

Per bag .... $25–$35

Shampoo

Character Shampoo Omni, 1981. See BUBBLE BATH. The same containers were used for both. Prices are comparable.

Shampoo Refueling Station Omni, 1981. Regular-shaped plastic bottle 6½″ tall, decorated with spaceships and Star Wars logo.

Per item .... $10–$15

Soap

Character Soaps Omni, 1981/83. Individual soaps were bath size in assorted colors, with character in relief on one side and Star Wars logo on the other. Came packaged in window box with header displaying Star Wars logo and character's name. Short description of character on back of box.

C-3PO .... $10–$15
Chewbacca .... $10–$15
Darth Vader .... $10–$15
Gamorrean Guard .... $10–$15
Lando Calrissian .... $10–$15

Leia .... $10–$15
Luke .... $10–$15
R2-D2 .... $10–$15
Wicket .... $10–$15
Yoda .... $10–$15

Soap Collections Omni, 1981. Four different character soaps packaged together in window box with header saying "Star Wars Soap Collection" and picturing space ships. Two different.
#1, Leia, Luke, Yoda and Chewbacca .... $25–$35
#2, R2-D2, C-3PO, Darth and Lando .... $25–$35

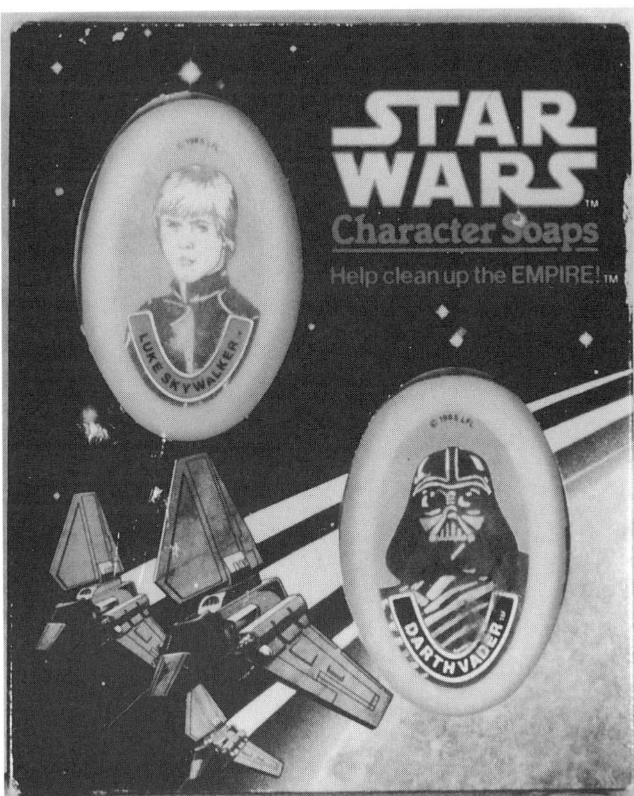

Addis (British), Star Wars character soaps

Character Soap Addis (British), 1984. Oval character soaps. Sold as two-packs in illustrated square window boxes.
Luke and Darth Vader .... $20–$35
R2-D2 and C-3PO .... $20–$35
Wicket and Baby Ewoks .... $20–$35

Character Soaps Cliro (British), 1977. 4″ high plastic figural bottles. Packaged in illustrated box.
C-3PO .... $25–$35
Darth Vader .... $25–$35
R2-D2 .... $25–$35

Sponge

Addis (British), 1983. Picture of Darth Vader on one side.
Per sponge .... $10–$15

Toothbrushes

Electric Kenner. Logo and characters on handle. Came blister-packed on header with color photos. Includes two toothbrushes.
Star Wars, 1978 .... $250–$325
Empire, 1980 .... $225–$300
Jedi, 1983 .... $220–$275

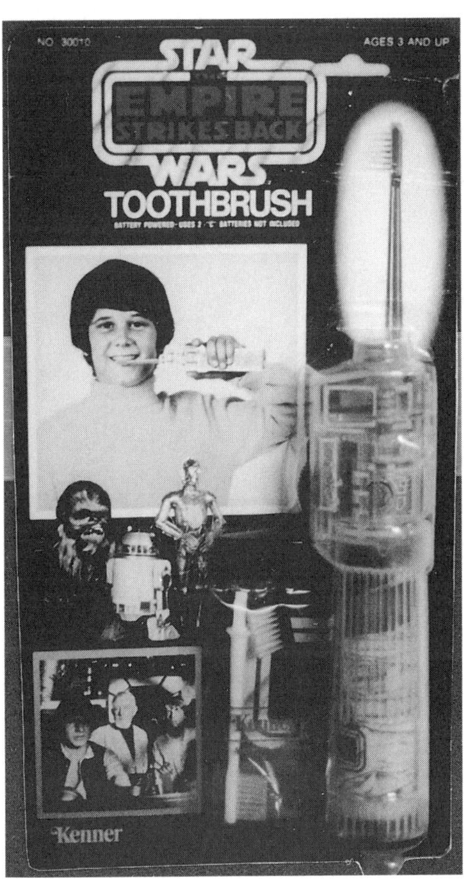

Kenner, Empire Strikes Back electric toothbrush

Electric Kenner Preschool, 1984. Handle molded in shape of Ewok on tree trunk with words "Wicket the Ewok." Green box with side flap with photo of toothbrush.
Per brush .... $75–$125

Regular Oral-B, 1983. Decal of character and Jedi logo on handle. Box displayed character and had windows to show brush. Box was either shrink-wrapped or blister-packed on header card showing X-Wing.
Chewbacca and Han Solo .... $10–$15
C-3PO and R2-D2 .... $10–$15
Darth Vader .... $10–$15
Ewoks .... $10–$15
Leia .... $10–$15
Luke .... $10–$15
Two-Pack, Yoda and Obi-Wan .... $25–$35

Toothbrush Holder Sigma, 1981. Ceramic. Shaped like Snowspeeder. Toothbrushes slide in sides. Shiny white glaze. 7″ long.
Per holder .... $75–$125

COSTUMES

This section is *organized* alphabetically by *manufacturer*.

ACAMAS

(British), 1983. Sets include mask and plastic outfit in illustrated box.

C-3PO .... $30–$40
Chewbacca .... $30–$40
Darth Vader .... $30–$40
Gamorrean Guard .... $30–$40
Klaatu .... $30–$40
Luke .... $30–$40
Princess Leia .... $30–$40
Stormtrooper .... $30–$40
Wicket .... $30–$40
Yoda .... $30–$40

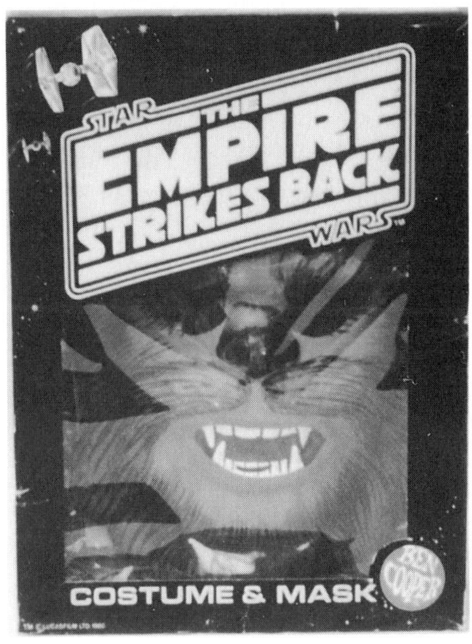

Ben Cooper, child's Halloween costume and mask

BEN COOPER

1977/83. Manufacturer of traditional Halloween-type costumes in children's sizes. Costume generally consisted of a one- or two-piece vinyl suit and a thin plastic mask. Packaging was in an 8½″ × 11″ thin cardboard window box with color artwork and logo from most current movie. Characters were added and box logos updated with each new film. Boxes displaying logos of earlier movies are slightly more valuable. Values assume costume and box are intact.

NOTE: A few characters were packaged for a short time in "Revenge of the Jedi" boxes. Values for these are approximately 50 percent above those of the same costume packaged in a "Return" package.

Admiral Ackbar .... $30–$45
Boba Fett .... $40–$65
Darth Vader .... $30–$45
C-3PO .... $30–$45
Chewbacca .... $30–$45
Gamorrean Guard .... $30–$45
Klaatu .... $30–$45
Luke Skywalker .... $30–$45
Luke X-Wing Pilot .... $30–$45
Obi-Wan Kenobi .... $30–$45
Princess Leia .... $30–$45
R2-D2 .... $30–$45
Stormtrooper .... $40–$65
Wicket .... $25–$40
Yoda .... $30–$45

Ben Cooper, child's Fun Poncho

FUN PONCHOS, 1977

Waterproof yellow vinyl poncho with printed design and matching mask. Packaged in plastic bag with paper logo header.

C-3PO....................$50–$75
Darth Vader....................$50–$75

MASKS, 1977

Ben Cooper also sold individual masks without costumes in both child and adult styles. Child's masks were the same thin plastic type as sold in the boxed costume set. Adult masks were better quality, soft plastic pullovers.

Child's Mask, any....................$5–$10
Adult Mask, any....................$25–$30

CESAR

(French), 1978. Five different masks.

C-3PO....................$15–$25
Chewbacca....................$15–$25
Darth Vader....................$15–$25
Stormtrooper....................$15–$25
Tusken Raider....................$15–$25

DON POST (PARTY PROFESSIONALS)

1980 to present. Manufacturer of quality adult masks. Sturdy, hard plastic is used for several masks and real fiber hair is employed in others. This attention to detail (which requires great variation in the cost of manufacture) is responsible as much as popularity for the variation in price of the current line of masks. Don Post's original series of Star Wars character masks came packaged in square blue boxes with movie logo. Subsequent releases were merely packed in plastic bags. New characters have been added at intervals over the years, and alterations have been made periodically to existing masks. Significant variations will be noted.

Admiral Ackbar....................$45–$55

Don Post, adult Admiral Ackbar mask

Boba Fett....................$70–$80
C-3PO....................$50–$60
Cantina band member....................$45–$55
Chewbacca, closed mouth....................$70–$80
Chewbacca, open mouth....................$300–$400
Darth Vader, rounded points either side of breathing grid..........$100–$150
Darth Vader, indentations either side of breathing grid..........$60–$70
Emperor....................$50–$60
Emperor's Royal Guard....................$70–$80
Gamorrean Guard....................$50–$70
Klaatu....................$50–$70
Nien Nunb....................$50–$60
Prince Xizor, Shadows of the Empire....................$40–$50
Prince Xizor, matching Xizor hands....................$30–$35
Stormtrooper, hard plastic, solid eye pieces....................$80–$90
Stormtrooper, soft plastic, grid eye pieces....................$55–$65
Tusken Raider....................$50–$75
Ugnaught....................$50–$75
Weequay....................$50–$60
Wicket....................$45–$55
Yoda....................$40–$50

DELUXE COLLECTOR'S HELMET, 1996/97
Professional quality limited edition helmets.
Boba Fett .... $1000–$1100
Darth Vader .... $1100–$1200

MCCALL'S

Patterns to make children's costumes. Small, medium and large size patterns were available. Came packaged in standard pattern envelope with color photo of completed outfit.
1981, included patterns for Chewbacca, Leia, Yoda, Jabba and Darth Vader .... $15–$25
1983, pattern for Ewok costume .... $10–$15

RUBIES

1994 to present. Costumes and masks produced in several grades of quality for both children and adults.
Adult Costumes Similar to children's deluxe costumes, with separate accessories and full head masks, but in adult sizes.
- **C-3PO** .... $55–$65
- **Chewbacca** .... $70–$80
- **Darth Vader** .... $60–$70
- **Princess Leia** .... $45–$55
- **Stormtrooper** .... $55–$65
- **Yoda** .... $50–$60

Children's Economy Costumes Jumpsuits with PVC masks.
- **C-3PO** .... $10–$15
- **Chewbacca** .... $10–$15
- **Darth Vader** .... $10–$15
- **Stormtrooper** .... $10–$15

Children's Deluxe Costumes Better material quality with separate accessories (belts, holsters, boot tops, etc.) and full head masks.
- **C-3PO** .... $40–$50
- **Chewbacca** .... $40–$50
- **Darth Vader** .... $40–$50
- **Jabba** .... $30–$40
- **Princess Leia** .... $25–$35
- **Stormtrooper** .... $40–$50
- **Tusken Raider** .... $35–$45
- **Yoda** .... $30–$40

Economy PVC Masks
- **C-3PO** .... $2–$5
- **Chewbacca** .... $2–$5
- **Darth Vader** .... $2–$5

Flexible Rubber Adult Full Head Masks
- **Boba Fett** .... $20–$25
- **C-3PO** .... $20–$25
- **Chewbacca** .... $20–$25
- **Darth Vader** .... $20–$25
- **Darth Vader,** two-piece molded plastic mask .... $15–$20
- **Stormtrooper** .... $20–$25
- **Tusken Raider** .... $20–$25
- **Yoda** .... $20–$25

FILMS, FILM CLIPS AND VIDEO

FILMS

All Star Wars saga movies do, of course, exist on professional-size film, primarily 70mm. It should be noted, however, that except for film clips (individual frames) and trailers designed for theatrical previews, none of this footage is available to the ordinary collector, and to own a complete copy of a film would be heavily frowned upon (especially by Lucasfilm) and could even be considered a crime.

8mm Films

Usually came boxed with color photo and logo of film

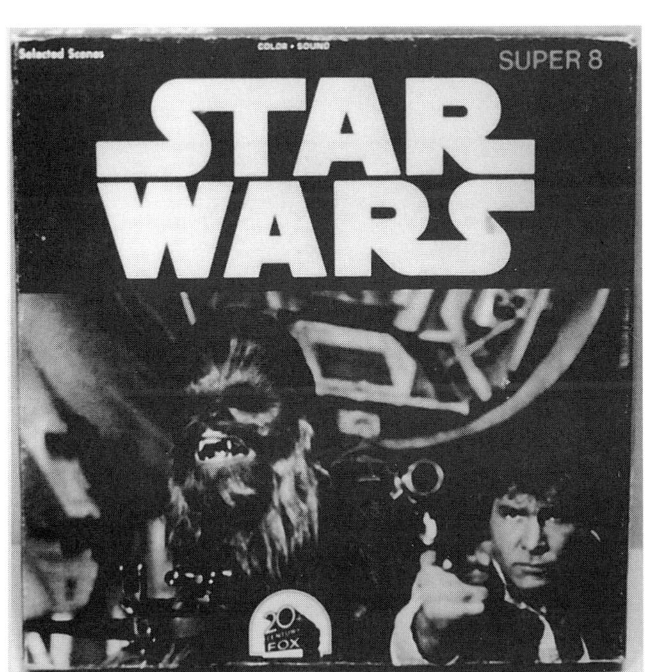

Ken Films, boxed 8mm film

KEN FILMS

Star Wars, 1977. 4 min. excerpts ....$10–$15
Star Wars, 1977. 8 min. excerpts..............................$15–$20
Star Wars, 1977. 17 min. excerpts ....$20–$25
Empire Strikes Back, 1980. 4 min. excerpts............$10–$15
Empire Strikes Back, 1980. 8 min. excerpts............$15–$20
Empire Strikes Back, 1980. 17 min. excerpts..........$20–$25

JEF FILMS

Commercial releases of theatrical film trailers (teasers for up-coming movies) for the public.
Star Wars..$10–$15
Empire Strikes Back..$10–$15
Revenge of the Jedi..$10–$15

FILM CLIPS

Most film clips available from the Star Wars saga are the result of cutting up a movie trailer, either an original or a copy, and mounting the individual frame of film. Others are either original studio promotional slides or copies of originals. Because they are so easy to reproduce, no individual clip, either unmounted or mounted in a simple cardboard slide mount, should sell for more than three or four dollars. Other, commercially available film clips are listed below, but it should be noted that though highly touted as "unique," most of the value of these items is the result of the presentation and packaging, not the clip itself.

WILLITTS DESIGNS, 1995

70mm film clips mounted in 7½″ × 2¾″ lucite block with color photo insert. Continuing series with numerous general categories (Darth Vader edition, Han Solo edition, etc.).

NOTE: Willitts also incorporated film clips into a series of Ralph McQuarrie art prints. See PRINTS section of this book.

Price for any ....$20–$25

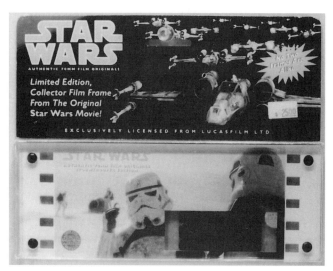

Willitts Design, Limited Edition Collector film frame

VIDEOTAPE AND DISKS

NOTE: All the Star Wars saga movies and several Ewok and Droids cartoons were released in Europe and the Pacific market on videotape as they were in the United States. It should be noted, however, that U.S. and foreign video systems are incompatible and tapes from one system cannot be viewed on the other.

CBS FOX VIDEO

Star Wars ....$20–$30
Empire Strikes Back ....$20–$30
Return of the Jedi..$20–$30
Star Wars Trilogy, boxed gift set............................$50–$75
Making of Star Wars ....$20–$30
Making of Empire Strikes Back.............................$15–$25
From Star Wars to Jedi: The Making of a Saga.......$15–$25
Ewoks: The Battle for Endor ....$15–$25
Ewok or Droids Cartoon, any.................................$10–$15

GAMES

This section is organized alphabetically by type of item and then alphabetically by manufacturer within these categories.

NOTE: See TRADING CARD section for Star Wars Customizable Card Game.

ARCADE GAMES

Atari

The large electronic games found in commercial video arcades.

Star Wars, stand-up version ....$1500–$2000
Star Wars, sitting (cock-pit) version ....$2000–$3000
The Empire Strikes Back ....$1500–$2000
Return of the Jedi...$1000–$1500

Sega

Star Wars Trilogy Special Edition Arcade Pinball Machine, 1997. Regular Star Wars-themed arcade pinball machine with electronic effects..............................$4000–$5000

BOARD GAMES

Danbury Mint

Star Wars: The Official Pewter Chess Set, 1994. Various characters from the Star Wars saga constitute the pewter playing pieces. Matching board is included in the set ....$650–$750

Kenner

Adventures of R2-D2, (Palitoy in Britain), 1977. Color-coded game for small children. Includes color game board, spinner and four R2-D2 game pieces ....$25–$35

Kenner, Adventures of R2-D2 board game

Destroy Death Star, 1979. Game includes game board, spinner, twelve X-Wing tokens and four bases ....$30–$40
Ewoks Save the Trees, 1984. Three-dimensional board and stand-up playing pieces ....$30–$35
Escape from the Death Star, (Palitoy in Britain), 1979. Game includes game board, eight playing tokens, spinner and move cards...$35–$45
Hoth Ice Planet Adventure, 1980. Game includes playing board, four Millennium Falcon tokens, spinner and move cards ....$35–$50
Yoda the Jedi Master, 1981. Includes game board, four Luke Skywalker tokens with stands, spinner and move cards. ....$35–$50

Parker Brothers

Monopoly—Star Wars Limited Collector's Edition, 1996. All game components are modified to fit Star Wars scenario. Numbered board. Star Wars box art.........................$75–$125
Star Wars, 1982. Game includes game board, four X-Wing puzzle/markers, one TIE marker, one Force card and two spinners..$25–$35

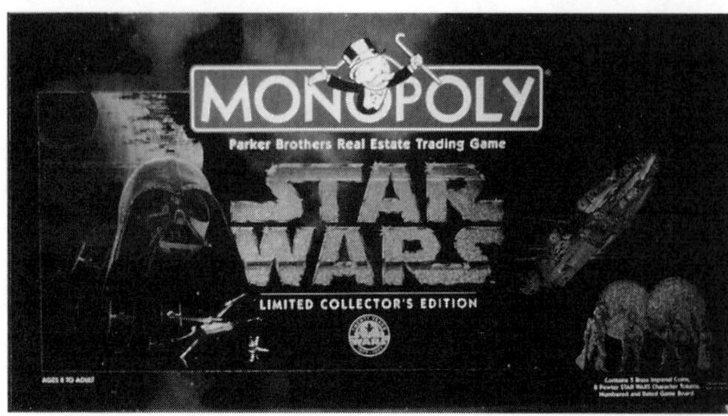

Parker Brothers, Star Wars Limited Collector's Edition Monopoly

Wicket the Ewok, 1983. Includes game board, four Ewok tokens with stands, five transportation cards and 25 food chips . ...$20–$30

COMPUTER AND VIDEO GAMES AND ACCESSORIES

Domark (British)

Computer Games 1988 Software for home computer. Tape or disk. Several brands available.
- **Star Wars** ....$15–$20
- **Empire Strikes Back**...$15–$20
- **Return of the Jedi** ....$15–$20

Lucasarts

Computer Games All book items published by Prima unless otherwise noted.
- **Dark Forces**..$40–$50
- **TIE** ....$25–$35
  - **TIE Enhancement—Defender of the Empire** ....$20–$25
- **Rebel Assault**..$25–$35
- **Rebel Assault II** ....$40–$50
- **X-Wing**..$25–$35
  - **X-Wing Enhancements—B-Wing** ....$20–$25
  - **X-Wing Enhancements—Imperial Pursuit**.....$20–$25
- **Hint Books—Dark Forces** (Prima) ....$15–$20
- **Hint Books—X-Wing** (Prima) ....$15–$20
- **Hint Books—Rebel Assault II** (Prima)..............$20–$25
- **Hint Books—TIE** (Prima)....................................$15–$20
- **Hint Books—TIE Strategy Guide,** Brady (Prima)........... ....$12–$15

Lucasarts Archives Vol. II

NOTE: Rebel Assault and Star Wars Screen Entertainment were elements of Lucasarts Archives Vol. I. However, the other four components of the set were non-Star Wars related.

Star Wars, 1996. Five CD-ROM set includes TIE Fighter, Rebel Assault, Rebel Assault II, Dark Forces and Behind the Scenes Making of the Trilogy disk ....$35–$50

Lucasarts Screen Entertainment, 1996. Screen savers, screen posters and animation.
- **Per item**...$25–$30

Nintendo, 1995

Cartridges for game systems.
- **Star Wars** ....$25–$35
  - **Star Wars Official Game Secrets,** book ....$10–$15
- **Empire** ....$25–$35
  - **Empire Official Game Secrets,** book.................$10–$15
- **Return of the Jedi**...$25–$35
  - **Return of the Jedi Player's Guide,** book ....$10–$15
- **Shadows of the Empire** ....$25–$35
  - **Shadows of the Empire Player's Guide,** book......$12–$15

Game Boy, 1995

- **Star Wars** ....$20–$30
- **Empire**...$20–$30
- **Return of the Jedi**..$20–$30

Mastertronic (British), 1988

Droids Cartoon Game for home computers ....$15–$20

Parker Brothers

Home Video Game Cartridges for Atari (or Sears) home video systems. Came packaged in $7^1/_2'' \times 5^1/_2''$ boxes with color artwork from movies.
- **Star Wars,** 1983 ....$10–$20
- **The Empire Strikes Back,** 1982.........................$10–$20
- **Jedi Arena,** 1983 ....$10–$20
- **Return of the Jedi,** 1984....................................$10–$20

Star Wars: The Interactive Board Game Three-dimensional board, 60-minute video, 80 cards and 58 assorted game pieces.
- **Game**...$35–$50

Presage

Star Wars Screen Saver..$15–$20

Sound Source, 1996

Computer Audio Clips
- **Star Wars** ....$15–$20
- **Empire Strikes Back**..$15–$20
- **Return of the Jedi** ....$15–$20
- **Star Wars Trilogy Limited Edition Entertainment Utility** Audio and video clips from all three movies.
- **Each** ....$35–$50

ELECTRONIC GAMES

Kenner

Electronic Battle Command Game, (Palitoy in Britain), 1977. Battery-powered tactical combat game. White plastic console with control console and vertical LED display. 9½″ × 7″ box shows color photo of game ....$60–$75

Kenner, Electronic Battle Command game

Electronic Laser Battle Game, 1977. Electronic reaction game. Black plastic with control panels for two players. Includes AC adaptor. Decorated with paper decals of X-Wings. 20″ × 6½″ box shows color photo of game...$75–$95

Kenner, X-Wing Aces Target game

X-Wings Aces Target Game, 1978. Large white plastic game. Gun is mounted on top of controls at one end. Screen displays TIE Fighter targets with Death Star as backdrop. Star Wars logo on side. Box shows color photo of game ....$1500–$2000

Micro Games of America

Hand-Held Electronic Games, 1992. White plastic rectangular games with movie logo above screen. Came carded; three different.

Micro Games of America, Empire Strikes Back hand-held game

Star Wars ....$15–$20
Empire Strikes Back..$15–$20
Return of the Jedi ....$15–$20

Palitoy (British), 1978

Destroy Death Star, battery-powered game board has controls for range finding and firing on enemy TIE Fighters. 17″ × 25″ box has color artwork of X-Wing and TIE fighting. Not to be confused with Kenner board game ....$125–$175

Tiger Electronics

Death Star Escape, 1997. Electronic reflex game. Four different games ....$10–$15

Galactic Battle, 1997. Electronic Star Wars-themed "battleship" game. Playing pieces are Star Wars ships. Sound effects .... $25–$35

Imperial Assault, 1997. Hand-held LCD game with removable Darth Vader figure "joystick" .... $10–$15

Quiz Whiz, 1997. Talking electronic trivia game. Includes three question booklets .... $10–$20

Millennium Falcon Challenge, 1997. Hand-held electronic LCD game with sound effects in Millennium Falcon-shaped cabinet .... $15–$20

Rebel Forces Laser Game, 1997. Target game. "Shoot the bounty hunters." Electronic target pistol with Rebel symbol. LCD target screen inside Darth Vader bust-shaped cabinet..... .... $25–$35

R2-D2 Ditto Droid, 1997. Pattern replication game (Simon Says) with R2-D2 theme .... $10–$20

Sounds of the Force Electronic Memory Game, 1997. Millennium Falcon-shaped electronic game. Includes authentic voices and sound effects .... $15–$20

Shakin' Pinball, 1996. Hand-held battery-powered Star Wars pinball game .... $25–$35

Stormtrooper Room Alarm with Laser Target Game, 1997. 13½″ high Stormtrooper "target" and red electronic target "blaster." Figure has sound effects and can also act as proximity sensor .... $25–$35

X.P.G. (Xtreme Pocket Game) Cartridges, 1997.

- **Jedi Adventure** .... $15–$20
- **Millennium Falcon Challenge** .... $15–$20

MISCELLANEOUS

Parker Brothers

Battle at Sarlacc's Pit, 1983. Includes 3-D cardboard diorama of Sail Barge and Sarlacc's Pit, plus sixteen plastic playing figures and deck of movie cards; 12″-square box has artwork of characters battling over pit.

- **Game** .... $40–$60

Ewok Card Games, 1984. Several different. Box art shows animated Ewoks.

- **Favorite Five** .... $10–$15
- **Paw Pals** .... $10–$15
- **Say "Cheese"** .... $10–$15

Return of the Jedi Card Game, 1983. Play-for-Power. Two decks, five different games. Came boxed in 3½″ × 4½″ silver box decorated with color art of Jedi characters.

- **Each** .... $10–$15

ROLE-PLAYING GAMES

West End Games, 1987 to present

West End has produced an extensive line of boxed games, game supplements, game books, playing pieces and other accessories. While all West End Star Wars products are, strictly speaking, associated with their role-playing games (which is what West End's license specifies), many would just as easily fit into other categories, such as reference books, metal figurines, etc.

Boxed Games West End Star Wars board games all come in 9″ × 11½″ boxes with color art or photos.

Assorted West End Games role-playing games

Star Warriors—Starfighter Combat, 1987. Includes color map, 80 ship counters, 100 game markers, asteroid and Star Destroyer sheets, record sheet, stand-up charts and tables screen, rules booklet, counter storage tray and six disks .... $20–$25

Assault on Hoth, 1988. Adventure board game. Two-person battle game. Includes terrain map, over 55 stand-up playing pieces, two decks of move cards, eight picture dice and rules book .... $25–$30

Battle for Endor, 1989. Solitaire adventure board game. Includes terrain map, 62 playing pieces, two decks of move cards, six picture dice and rules book .... $25–$30

Escape Death Star, 1990. Solitaire or multiplayer adventure board game. Includes Death Star schematic, four stand-up character cards, deck of sector cards, four score pads, three dice and rules book .... $25–$30

Books All are 8½″ × 11″. Basic rules books were originally printed in hardcover format. Later printings are softcover. Most older books still in print have been updated in second printings.

Star Wars: The Roleplaying Game, primary rules book .... $18–$22

Rules Companion, supplemental rules for basic role playing game .... $15–$20

Campaign Pack, includes supplemental guidelines and adventures, floor plans and gamemaster screen. Packaged like adventures modules .... $12–$15

Gamemasters Screen, instructions, charts, quick start scenarios and other useful information for conducting a game .... $12–$15

Gamemasters Kit, updated screen and rules plus scenario .... $12–$15

Gamemasters Handbook, hints and information helpful in running a successful and interesting game .... $15–$20

Books—Sourcebooks Supplemental background information and rules on various game functions.

Dark Empire Sourcebook .... $15–$20
Dark Force Rising Sourcebook .... $15–$20
Han Solo and the Corporate Sector Sourcebook .... $15–$20
Heir to Empire Sourcebook .... $15–$20
Imperial Sourcebook .... $15–$20
Last Command Sourcebook .... $15–$20
Movie Trilogy Sourcebook .... $15–$20
Rebel Alliance Sourcebook .... $15–$20
Star Wars Sourcebook .... $15–$20
Shadows of the Empire .... $20–$25

Books—Galaxy Guides These are supplemental background books on assorted subjects. Most older ones have updated, second editions.

#1 A New Hope .... $14–$16
#2 Yavin and Bespin .... $14–$16
#3 The Empire Strikes Back .... $14–$16
#4 Alien Races .... $14–$16
#5 Return of the Jedi .... $14–$16
#6 Tramp Freighters .... $14–$16
#7 Mos Eisley .... $14–$16
#8 Scouts .... $14–$16
#9 Fragments from the Rim .... $14–$16
#10 Bounty Hunters .... $14–$16
#11 Criminal Organizations .... $14–$16
#12 Aliens .... $14–$16

Books—Other Background Information Books

Cracken's Rebel Field Guide .... $15–$20
Cracken's Rebel Operatives .... $15–$20
Creatures of the Galaxy .... $15–$20
Death Star Technical Companion .... $15–$20
Galladinium's Fantastic Technology .... $15–$20
Pirates and Privateers .... $15–$20
Planets of the Galaxy Vol. I .... $15–$20
Planets of the Galaxy Vol. II .... $15–$20
Planets of the Galaxy Vol. III .... $15–$20
Platt's Starpost Guide .... $20–$25
Shadows of the Empire Planet Guide .... $15–$20
Star Wars Planet Collection .... $20–$25
Wanted by Cracken .... $15–$20

Books—Adventure Supplements Scenarios for different adventures using the rules of the basic role-playing game. Earlier "modules" typically contain booklet with adventure script and other supplemental information, pertinent maps and/or charts and gamemaster notes. Later supplements are fully contained in book form.

The Abduction .... $12–$15
Battle for the Golden Sun .... $10–$12
Black Ice .... $10–$12
Classic Adventures .... $15–$20
Classic Adventures II .... $15–$20
Classic Adventures III .... $15–$20
Crisis on Cloud City .... $10–$12
Darkstryder Campaign .... $15–$20
Darkstryder Campaign: Endgame .... $15–$20
Darkstryder Supplement: Kathol Rift .... $15–$20
Death in the Undercity .... $10–$12
Domain of Evil .... $10–$12
Flashpoint: Brak Sector .... $12–$15
The Game Chambers of Questal .... $10–$12
Goroth .... $12–$15
Graveyard of Alderan .... $10–$12
Isis Coordinates .... $10–$12
Live Action Adventures .... $15–$20
Mission to Lianna .... $12–$15
No Disintegrations .... $15–$20
Otherspace .... $10–$12
Otherspace II: Invasion .... $10–$12
Planet of the Mists .... $10–$12
Riders of the Maelstrom .... $10–$12
Scavenger Hunt .... $10–$12
Starfall .... $10–$12
Strike Force: Shantipole .... $10–$12
Supernova .... $12–$15
Tatooine Manhunt .... $10–$12
Twin Stars of Kira .... $12–$15

Books—Plot Your Own Adventure Books

Jedi's Honor, solitaire plot your own adventure game book. Player takes the part of Luke .... $13–$15

Scoundrel's Luck, solitaire plot your own adventure game book. Player takes the part of Han Solo....... $13–$15

Lightsaber Dueling Pack Two-player game utilizing two "flip" books and two score cards to play. Comes shrink-wrapped in color folder.

Each .... $12–$15

Starfighter Battle Book Flip book game similar to Lightsaber Dueling Pack. Two books come in slipcase with color artwork of X-Wing and TIE Fighter.

Each .... $12–$15

Star Wars Adventure Journals Original adventure stories and background information based on the Star Wars saga and the Star Wars role-playing universe.

#1 .... $12–$15
#2 .... $12–$15
#3 .... $12–$15
#4 .... $12–$15
#5 .... $12–$15
#6 .... $12–$15
#7 .... $12–$15
#8 .... $12–$15

#9 .... $12–$15
#10 .... $15–$20
#11 .... $15–$20
#12 .... $15–$20

Starter Sets Include figures, books and other game material.
Miniature Battles Starter Set .... $30–$35
Mos Eisley Starter Set .... $30–$35
Vehicle Starter Set .... $30–$35

West End Games, metal figure sets

Metal Figure Sets, 25mm sculpted metal miniature gaming pieces. Come unpainted in 4″ × 8″ boxes with color artwork or photos on lid. Number of figures per set varies with size of figures.
Bounty Hunters .... $12–$15
The Empire Strikes Back .... $12–$15
Heroes of the Rebellion .... $12–$15
Imperial Forces .... $12–$15
Imperial Troopers .... $12–$15
Jabba's Palace .... $12–$15
Mos Eisley Cantina .... $12–$15
A New Hope .... $12–$15
Rancor Pit .... $12–$15
Rebel Characters .... $12–$15
Rebel Troopers .... $12–$15
Return of the Jedi .... $12–$15
Stormtroopers .... $12–$15
Zero G Assault Troopers .... $12–$15

Blister-Packed Figure Sets Smaller sets of miniatures blister-packed on color header cards.
Aliens of the Galaxy #1 .... $6–$8
AT-AT .... $9–$12
Bantha and Rider .... $6–$8
Bounty Hunters #1 .... $6–$8
Bounty Hunters #2 .... $6–$8
Bounty Hunters #3 .... $6–$8
Cloud City .... $6–$8
Darkstryder #1 .... $9–$12
Darkstryder #2 .... $9–$12
Darkstryder #3 .... $9–$12
Denizens of Tatooine .... $6–$8
Droids #1 .... $6–$8
Emperor .... $6–$8
Encounter on Hoth .... $9–$12
Ewoks .... $6–$8
Gamorrean Guards .... $9–$12
Heir to Empire Villains .... $6–$8
Heroes #1 .... $6–$8
Heroes #2 .... $6–$8
Hoth Rebels .... $6–$8
Imperial Army Troopers #1 .... $6–$8
Imperial Army Troopers #2 .... $6–$8
Imperial Crew with Heavy Blaster .... $6–$8
Imperial Navy Troopers #1 .... $6–$8
Imperial Navy Troopers #2 .... $6–$8
Imperial Officers .... $6–$8
Imperial Speeder Bikes .... $9–$12
Imperial Troop Pack .... $9–$12
Jabba's Servants .... $9–$12
Jabba the Hutt .... $9–$12
Jedi Knights .... $6–$8
Landspeeder .... $9–$12
Mon Calamari .... $6–$8
Mos Eisley Cantina .... $9–$12
Mos Eisley Space Station .... $9–$12
Nogri .... $6–$8
Pilots and Gunners .... $6–$8
Pirates .... $9–$12
Rebel Commanders #1 .... $6–$8
Rebel Commanders #2 .... $6–$8
Rebel Operatives .... $6–$8
Rebel Speeder Bikes .... $9–$12
Rebel Troopers #1 .... $6–$8
Rebel Troopers #2 .... $6–$8
Rebel Troopers #3 .... $6–$8
Rebel Troopers #4 .... $6–$8
Rebel Troop Pack .... $9–$12
Sand Troopers .... $6–$8
Scout Troopers .... $6–$8
Skywalkers .... $6–$8
Snowspeeder .... $9–$12
Snowtroopers .... $6–$8
Storm Skimmers .... $9–$12
Stormtroopers #1 .... $6–$8
Stormtroopers #2 .... $6–$8
Stormtroopers #3 .... $6–$8
Stormtroopers #4 .... $6–$8
Taun-Taun and Rider .... $6–$8
Users of the Force .... $6–$8
Wookiees .... $6–$8
Zero G Troopers .... $6–$8

Miniature Guide Books
Star Wars Miniatures Battles, assembling miniatures for tabletop battles .... $15–$20
Star Wars Miniatures Battle Companion, supplement to Star Wars Miniatures Battles .... $15–$20

GREETING CARDS

This section is divided chronologically by movie, and then alphabetically by manufacturer.

STAR WARS

Drawing Board

Birthday and Everyday Cards, 1977. Full-color photos from Star Wars with text on front and inside.

C-3PO, "Sorry I Haven't Written . . . But I'm Only Human!" ....$3–$5

C-3PO, "Feeling Kinda Rusty? How About a Warm Lubrication Bath? Get Well Soon!" ....$3–$5

C-3PO and Luke, "They Don't Make Them Like You Anymore!" ....$3–$5

C-3PO in desert, ". . . Lost Without You!" ....$3–$5

Chewbacca, "You're Weird . . . But Wonderful!" ...$3–$5

Chewbacca, "Not Feeling Well? May You Soon Have the Strength of a Wookiee!" ....$3–$5

Darth Vader, "When I Say Have a Nice Day, I Mean Have a Nice Day!" ....$3–$5

Darth Vader, "Happy Birthday, Earthling!" ....$3–$5

Darth Vader, "Don't Play Games With Me . . . WRITE!!!" . ...$3–$5

Luke, "Hold It Right There! . . . and have a Happy Birthday" ....$3–$5

Luke in trash compactor, "There's No Escaping . . . Another Birthday!" ....$3–$5

Millennium Falcon, "Greetings from Tatooine!" ....$3–$5

Obi-Wan, "May the Force Be With You" ....$3–$5

R2-D2, "From your faithful Droid; . . . within me is a message expressly beamed to you from one of your fellow humanoids, Happy Birthday!" ....$3–$5

R2-D2 and C-3PO, "29 Again? . . . It boggles the memory bank! Oh well, Happy Birthday!" ....$3–$5

Space Battle, "Would Have Written Sooner . . . But I Just Haven't Had a Minute!" ....$3–$5

Die-Cut Birthday and Everyday Cards, 1977. Full-color artwork.

C-3PO, "Happy birthday from your Friendly Droid!" ....$4–$6

Chewbacca, "That's Wookiee Talk for Happy Birthday".. ....$4–$6

Darth Vader, "The Empire Commands You to Have a Happy Birthday" ....$4–$6

Luke, Leia and Han, "Happy birthday from the Alliance!" ....$4–$6

Obi-Wan, "Happy Birthday and May the Force Be With You!" ....$4–$6

R2-D2, "That's Droid Talk for Happy Birthday!" ....$4–$6

R2-D2 and C-3PO, "Sorry to hear about your malfunction! Hope all systems are functioning soon!" ....$4–$6

Stormtrooper, "Have a Happy Birthday! Darth Vader Wants It That Way!" ....$4–$6

Juvenile Birthday Cards, 1977. Color artwork.

C-3PO, "You're 12 . . . Hope it's the best day on Earth since you were born!" ....$3–$4

Chewbacca, "Now that you're 7 . . . Wishing you 7 gronks and one to grow on"......................................$3–$4

Darth Vader, "I've uncovered information that says you are 11 . . . And I will see to it that it's celebrated throughout the far reaches of the galaxy!"............................$3–$4

Obi-Wan, "Honored One, now that you are 10 . . . May the Force Be With You on your birthday and for many years to come" ....$3–$4

R2-D2, "Earthling, my calculations confirm that you are 9 . . . Hope it's your finest day on the planet yet" ....$3–$4

Stormtrooper, "You're 8 . . . So join the troops and have the best birthday in the universe!"............................$3–$4

Christmas Cards, 1977. 5½″ × 8″. Color photo or artwork covers.

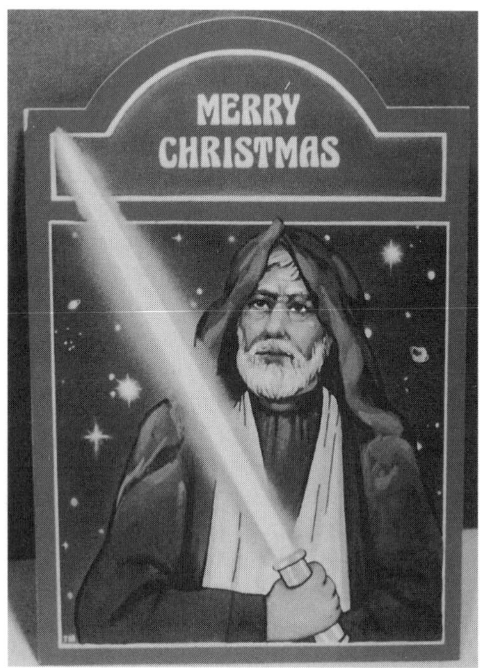

Drawing Board, Merry Christmas ". . . and May the Force Be With You"

C-3PO, "For an out-of-this-world Grandson . . . from our galaxy to your galaxy, Happy Holidays!" ....$3–$5

Chewbacca, "Merry Christmas Earthling"..............$3–$5

Chewbacca, "Happy Holidays . . . To a favorite bipedal earthling!" ....$3–$5

Luke, Han and Chewbacca, "From the Alliance . . . Happy Holidays" ....$3–$5

Obi-Wan, "MERRY CHRISTMAS . . . and May the Force Be With You" ....$3–$5

R2-D2, "VREEP ADOOT BLEEP . . . That's Droid talk for Happy Holidays!" ....$3–$5

R2-D2, projecting image of Leia, "For an out-of-this-world granddaughter . . . The code is broken and the message is clear—Have a Merry Christmas and a Happy New Year"...$3–$5

R2-D2 and C-3PO, "PEACE and GOODWILL toward all mankind . . . and to their faithful androids!" ....$3–$5

X-Wings, "Intergalactic Greetings . . . for a fantastic Holiday Season" ....$3–$5

X-Wings, "To an out-of-this-world boy . . . Intergalactic Greetings and May the Force Be With You" ....$3–$5

Halloween Cards, 1977. Color photos or artwork on cover.

C-3PO, "Trick or Treat, Earthling" ....$3–$5

Chewbacca, "Do Not Fear . . . Your Wookiee friend is here" ....$3–$5

Darth Vader, "This is MY kind of holiday! Happy Halloween"..$3–$5

Han, Luke and Chewbacca, "From the Alliance . . . Happy Halloween" ....$3–$5

Leia, "For an out-of-this-world daughter . . . Intergalactic wishes for a Happy Halloween!"..............................$3–$5

Luke, "For an out-of-this-world son . . . May your deflector shields protect you this Halloween!" ....$3–$5

Millennium Falcon, "For an Earthling girl . . . All Hallows Eve greetings from Tatooine!"..........................$3–$5

Obi-Wan, "Happy Halloween . . . and May the Force Be With You" ....$3–$5

X-Wing and TIE Fighter, "For an Earthling boy . . . Intergalactic greetings for a Happy Halloween!"......$3–$5

THE EMPIRE STRIKES BACK

Drawing Board

Die-Cut Birthday Cards, 1980. Color artwork covers.

Boba Fett, "May you get your share of bounty on your birthday" ....$5–$8

Luke on Tauntaun, "Wishing you the happiest birthday in the galaxy!" ....$5–$8

Yoda, "Happy Birthday . . . and may you live to be 800" .. ..$5–$8

RETURN OF THE JEDI

Drawing Board

Greeting and Birthday Cards, 1983. Die-cut with color artwork on cover.

C-3PO and Ewoks, "Hope you have a Royal time! Happy Birthday!"...$4–$6

Darth Vader, "I want you to have a Happy Birthday" ....$4–$6

Darth Vader and Imperial Guards, "May the Force Be With You" ....$4–$6

Ewoks, "Have a Birthday filled with happy surprises!" ....$4–$6

Ewoks and R2-D2, "Happy Birthday to a wonderful friend!" ....$4–$6

Ewok and Leia, "It's so special having a friend like you!" .... $4–$6

Leia and Luke on Speeder Bike, "It's your birthday—have a thrilling day" .... $4–$6

Rebo Band, "Droopy, Sy, Max and I hope your birthday strikes a happy note!" .... $4–$6

Valentine Cards, 1983. Boxed sets of thirty-two "classroom" valentines. Eight perforated sheets (seven regular and one teacher) of four small (3″ × 4″) cards plus envelopes.

Ewok set .... $10–$15

Star Wars set .... $15–$20

Patti M. Productions

Color-Me-Cards, 1987. Eight cards and envelopes plus four markers. Line drawings of Ewoks. Come packaged in clear plastic box. Three different assortments.

Per assortment .... $7–$10

Westbrook (British)

Greeting Cards, 1983.

#1 Lightsaber, (poster design) "May the Force Be With You" .... $4–$6

#2 Luke in Bespin fatigues, "Happy Birthday Rebel" .... $4–$6

#3 Stormtroopers, "If the Universe Is Immeasurably Vast, Why Are You So Close to Me?" .... $4–$6

#4 Luke (Jedi Knight), "Happy Birthday to the Universe's Blue Eyed Boy" .... $4–$6

#5 Han Solo, "Happy Birthday Rebel" .... $4–$6

#6 Wicket and R2-D2, "You're the Right Height, Why Aren't You Furry?" .... $4–$6

#7 Revenge of the Jedi, "May the Force Be With You" .... $4–$6

#8 Vader in the Stars, "You're the Embodiment of All That Is Mean, Nasty, Malevolent and Evil in the Universe. I Guess That's What Makes You So Lovable" .... $4–$6

#9 Princess Leia, "Happy Birthday Princess" .... $4–$6

#10 Darth Vader, "So It's Your Birthday. What Do You Expect Me to Do, Blow Up a Planet?" .... $4–$6

#11 Yoda, "I Like You, You've Got Cute Ears" .... $4–$6

#12 Vader and Boba Fett on Cloud City, "Right, I'll Have the Sauna Now and the Manicure Afterwards" .... $4–$6

#13 Han Solo, "Happy Birthday, hero" .... $4–$6

#14 Luke and Vader, "Don't Jump, It's Only Another Birthday" .... $4–$6

#15 R2-D2 and C-3PO, (with broken leg) "You Think You've Got Problems" .... $4–$6

#16 R2-D2 and C-3PO approaching Jabba's palace, "Are You Sure This Is the Right Way to the Party?" .... $4–$6

#17 C-3PO, Jabba, Leia and Bibb Fortuna, "It's Your Birthday, Bring on the Dancing Girls" .... $4–$6

#18 Luke, Han and Leia, "I could Travel the Universe and Not Find Friends Like You" .... $4–$6

#19 Baby Ewok, "Here's to the Cutest Thing in Four Galaxies" .... $4–$6

#20 B-Wing Fighter, "Hope Your Birthday Is a Blast!" .... $4–$6

#21 Han and Chewie shoot it out, "We Have This Trouble Every Time You Come to the Barbers" .... $4–$6

#22 Millennium Falcon in the Asteroid Field, "Even at Light Speed Your Birthday's Got to Catch Up With You Sometime" .... $4–$6

#23 Gamorrean Guard, "If You Had My Dentist's Bills, You Wouldn't Smile Either" .... $4–$6

#24 Luke and Vader, "Is This Your First Lesson in How to Use Chopsticks?" .... $4–$6

HOUSEWARES

This section is organized alphabetically first by item and then by manufacturer.

BANKS

ADAM JOSEPH, 1983

Plastic

Return of the Jedi Banks In the shape of characters. Came in red and black window boxes with Jedi logo.

- **Darth Vader,** 9″ tall...$30–$45
- **Emperor's Royal Guard,** 9″ tall..........................$30–$45
- **Gamorrean Guard,** 9″ tall; rare.......................$150–$250
- **R2-D2,** 6″ tall ....$40–$60

Wicket the Ewok Character banks came in blue window boxes with cartoon illustrations of Ewoks. 6″ tall.

- **Princess Kneesaa,** playing tambourine ....$20–$35
- **Wicket,** playing drum ....$20–$35

LEONARD SILVER MFG. (UNDER LICENSE FROM TOWLE SIGMA), 1981

Darth Vader figure, 6″ high; metal.......................$125–$150

Adam Joseph, Wicket the Ewok bank

Metal Box Co., Darth Vader combination bank

METAL BOX CO., 1980

Tin Combination Banks Color photo fronts with two combinations on face and slot at top for coins. Two different.

Darth Vader ....$50–$75

Yoda ....$50–$75

Tin Octagonal Bank Has photos of characters on side panels and removable lid with slot for coins. Lid has Empire logo and word "Bank."

Each ....$45–$60

Roman, R2-D2 ceramic bank

ROMAN, 1977

Ceramic Approximately 8″ tall. Plug-in bottom for removal of coins. All use shiny glazes.

C-3PO, waist up, metallic gold.........................$100–$150

Darth Vader, head only ....$100–$150

R2-D2, entire figure ....$100–$150

SIGMA, 1982/83

Ceramic Store packaging was silver box with color photo of bank on front. Many were sold in plain white mail boxes. All use shiny glazes.

Chewbacca, 10½″ tall; kneeling with gun ....$60–$75

Jabba the Hutt, 6″ tall...$60–$75

Yoda, 8″ tall ....$60–$75

THINK WAY, 1995

Plastic Character Busts Packaged in tray boxes.

C-3PO ....$15–$25

Darth Vader ....$15–$25

Electronic Banks, 1995/96. Banks move and have light and sound functions when coin is deposited or bank is activated manually. Packaged in vertical format window boxes.

Darth Vader ....$35–$50

Droids ....$35–$50

COIN SORTER

MERIT (BRITISH), 1984

Plastic mechanical sorter, for British coins. Backdrop is color action artwork collage of scenes from Return of the Jedi and logo. Packaged open blue frame tray box ....$125–$150

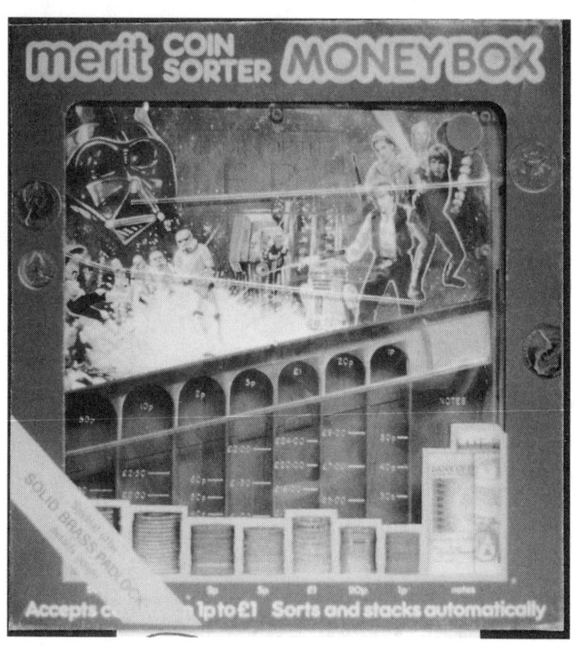

Merit (British), mechanical sorter for British coins

CLOCKS

BRADLEY TIME

This company made several table clocks with three-dimensional figures designed primarily for children. Clocks came packaged in window boxes.

Clock/Radio, 1984. R2-D2 and C-3PO on face of quartz clock with built-in AM/FM radio..........................$100–$150

Talking Alarm Clock, 1980. Clock, R2-D2 and C-3PO stand on base with speaker on bottom. Voice is battery operated.

Each, 9″ tall ....$75–$100

3-D Sceni-Clock Free-standing R2-D2 and C-3PO in front of backdrop with space scene. 8″ tall. Clock is in middle of TIE Fighter. Battery operated...$75–$90

George Lucas's Super Live Adventure Clock Promotional, 1994. Plastic digital table clock with three-dimensional statues of R2-D2 and C-3PO in the foreground. Souvenir item from the Japanese show.

Each ....$45–$60

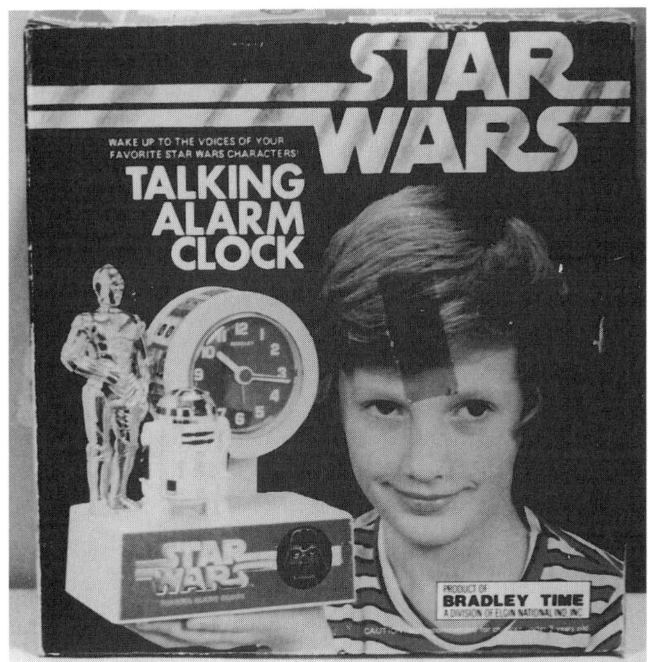

Bradley Time, Star Wars talking alarm clock

Clock-Wise, 1992. Clock hands on photo of space battle scene with second Death Star mounted under glass. Black rectangular frame.

Each .... $35–$45

MICRO GAMES OF AMERICA, 1995

Darth Vader Head Clock Radio Tabletop style approx. 5″ high with digital clock in base. Packaged in open window box with low header.

Each .... $25–$35

TIGER ELECTRONICS, 1996

Darth Vader Head Clock Radio Tabletop style approximately 5″ high with digital clock in base.

Each .... $25–$35

WELBY ELGIN, 1981

Wall Clocks Two different styles, round and square. Both models have blue plastic cases and come either as cord or battery operated.

Star Wars, R2-D2 and C-3PO .... $50–$75

Empire Strikes Back, Darth Vader, Stormtroopers and Empire logo .... $50–$75

DISPLAY ITEMS

NOTE: For other items that could be considered decorative figurines, see PEWTER, TOYS and ACTION FIGURE sections.

Figurines

APPLAUSE, 1996

Cast resin in metallic colors. Limited to 5000 pieces.

NOTE: Though sold separately, the Luke and Darth figurines were designed to be displayed together in a fighting pose.

Applause, Bounty Hunters cast resin figurines

Bounty Hunters .... $60–$75
Darth Vader .... $50–$75
Emperor .... $60–$75
Jabba the Hutt .... $60–$75
Luke .... $50–$75
Sandtrooper and Dewback .... $60–$75

ILLUSIVE ORIGINALS

Maquettes. Limited edition, hand-detailed sculptures limited to 10,000 pieces. Mounted with numbered plaques.

Admiral Ackbar, bust; 11″ tall .... $100–$150
Boba Fett, bust; 15″ tall .... $200–$350
Chewbacca .... $200–$300
Jabba the Hutt, full figure; 25″ long .... $250–$300
Yoda, full figure .... $400–$500

KENNER, 1995

"CinemaCast" 14″-tall resin figure of Darth Vader on three-tiered base with lightsaber raised over his head. Limited to 10,000 pieces.

Each .... $160–$200

LEGENDS IN THREE DIMENSIONS, 1997

Cold-cast porcelain bust of Emperor Palpatine. 10″ high; with certificate of authenticity.

Each .... $140–$165

SIGMA, 1983

Ceramic. Figures are hand-painted porcelain bisque and range in height from $3^1/_2$″ to 5″. Figurines come in silver-colored boxes with photo of item and Jedi logo on front.

Sigma, Return of the Jedi porcelain figurines

Bib Fortuna .... $35–$50
Boba Fett .... $50–$75
C-3PO and R2-D2 .... $35–$50
Darth Vader .... $40–$60
Galactic Emperor, seated .... $40–$60
Gamorrean Guard .... $35–$50
Han Solo .... $45–$65
Klaatu .... $35–$50
Lando Calrissian .... $35–$50
Luke Skywalker, Jedi Knight .... $45–$65
Princess Leia, Boush disguise .... $35–$50
Wicket W. Warrick .... $25–$35

Holographic Stands

A.H. PRISMATIC, 1994

Holographic foil stickers approximately 2″ square affixed to black display stand.

C-3PO and R2-D2 .... $6–$8
Darth Vader .... $6–$8
Millennium Falcon .... $6–$8
X-Wing .... $6–$8

Ingot

Gold-plated steel ingot picturing Star Wars Trilogy Special Edition logo encased in $5^1/_4$″ × $3^1/_2$″ block. Comes boxed with certificate of authenticity.

Each .... $65–$75

Miniature Collectors Helmets

RIDDELL, 1997

One-fourth to one-half scale exact replicas of character helmets with electronic functions. Come with stands.

Riddell, C-3PO miniature collectors' helmet

Boba Fett .... $70–$80
C-3PO .... $60–$70
Darth Vader .... $85–$95
Stormtrooper .... $70–$80
X-Wing Pilot .... $70–$80

Musical Figurines

SIGMA

Ceramic. All turn and play Star Wars Theme. Display packaging was silver box with color photo of item. Many came in plain white shipping boxes.

Hoth Turret, 1981; C-3PO on top. 8″ tall .... $75–$125
Ewoks, 1983; 6″ high .... $60–$95
Max Rebo Band, 1983 .... $125–$150

Prop Reproductions

ICONS, 1996

High-quality reproductions of equipment and ships. Come mounted in Plexiglas display cases.

Lightsaber, three different planned .... $350–$450
TIE Fighter .... $1500–$1700
X-Wing .... $1500–$1700

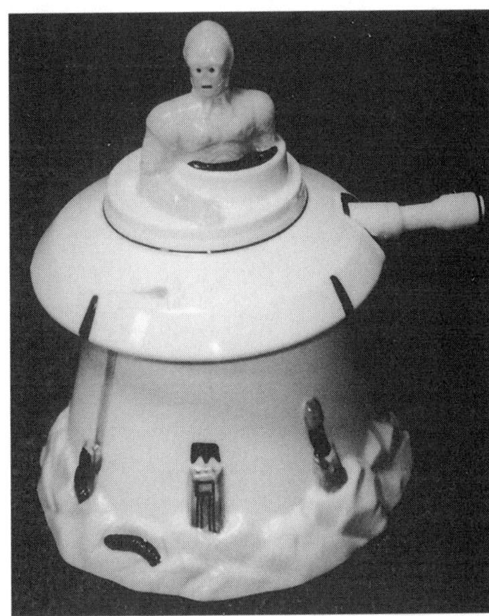

Sigma, Hoth Turret musical figurine

Prop Statuettes

DON POST, 1997

Full-size (6′ tall) Stormtrooper. Fiberglass statue posed with blaster.

Each .... $4500–$5000

ILLUSIVE ORIGINALS, 1997

Han in Carbonite, 83″ high fiberglass replica .... $1000–$1200

Signs

CUI, 1996

Color replicas of movie poster art reproduced onto tin backings. Two sizes: large (15″ × 25″) and small (12″ × 17″).

Star Wars, large .... $20–$25
Empire Strikes Back, large .... $20–$25
Return of the Jedi, large .... $20–$25
Star Wars, small; two different .... $12–$18
Empire Strikes Back, small .... $12–$18
Return of the Jedi, small .... $12–$18

FURNITURE

BOOKCASE

American Toy and Furniture Co., 1983. Wood and fiberboard with scenes from Return of the Jedi on back panel. 20″ × 18″ × 41″.

Each .... $150–$200

BOOKCASE/TOY CHEST

American Toy and Furniture Co., 1983. Shelves above, toy chest below, with slanted chalkboard sliding cover. Decorated with Ewoks and Droids. 32″ × 18″ × 41″.

Each .... $175–$225

CHALKBOARD

American Toy and Furniture Co., 1983. Free swinging on pedestal decorated with Ewok scenes. Shelf below.

Each .... $125–$150

COAT RACK

American Toy and Furniture Co., 1983. Base decorated with picture of Darth Vader and Jedi logo. Pegs above. Approximately 47″ tall.

Each .... $150–$200

DESK

American Toy and Furniture Co., 1983.

Child's chalkboard top, with attached bench. Sides have Ewok designs .... $150–$225

Double chalkboard top children's desk, with two benches. Sides decorated with Ewok artwork ... $175–$250

DESK AND CHAIR

American Toy and Furniture Co., 1983.

Child's desk, with shelf above. Movie scenes on back and sides. Approximately 32″ high .... $200–$300

NIGHTSTAND

American Toy and Furniture Co., 1983. Scalloped edges with scenes from Return of the Jedi. 20″ × 16½″ × 25″.

Each .... $150–$225

PICNIC TABLE

American Toy and Furniture Co., 1983. Pedestal table with benches on either side attached to base. Ewok scenes on top. Approximately 36″ long.

Each .... $150–$225

American Toy and Furniture Co., Return of the Jedi table and chairs set

TABLE AND CHAIRS SETS

American Toy and Furniture Co., 1983.

Set, 25 1/2″ round table with scenes and character portraits from Jedi. Two chairs with Jedi logo ....$200–$275

Set, 25 1/2″ round table with Ewoks cartoon scenes on top. Two chairs with Ewoks logo ....$150–$200

TOY BIN

American Toy and Furniture Co., 1983. Open-topped rectangular box on wheels. Decorated on sides with Ewoks.

Each ....$125–$200

TOY CHEST

American Toy and Furniture Co., 1983. Shaped like R2-D2. Wooden base on wheels with plastic lid. 28″ tall.

American Toy and Furniture Co., R2-D2 toy chest

Each ....$325–$400

GLASSES (DRINKING)

Star Wars Promotional

BURGER KING/COCA-COLA, 1977

Four different with color silk-screened artwork. Designs were: Luke Skywalker, Han Solo, Darth Vader and R2-D2/C-3PO. Burger King also issued a set of matching promotional posters.

Per glass ....$10–$15
Set of all four ....$50–$60

Burger King/Coca-Cola Star Wars glasses

The Empire Strikes Back Promotional

BURGER KING/COCA-COLA, 1980

Four different silk-screened artwork scenes from Empire. Scenes include Luke, Lando, R2-D2 and C-3PO and Darth Vader. Descriptions appear on back of glass.

Burger King/Coca-Cola Empire Strikes Back glasses

Per glass ....$8–$12
Set of all four ....$40–$50

Return of the Jedi Promotional

BURGER KING/COCA-COLA, 1983

Four different silk-screened artwork scenes: Sand Barge fight scene, Jabba's Palace scene, Ewok Village and Luke and Darth Vader fighting.

Per glass ....$5–$10
Set of all four ....$30–$40

BURGER KING/COCA-COLA, 1983

Set of three glasses with color artwork of characters made for the European market.

Per set ....$35–$50

LINENS

Star Wars

BIBB, 1977

Matching bedroom accessories. Star Wars characters in action poses. At least three background color variations for most if not all pieces, light blue being the most common.

Bibb, Star Wars linen

Bedspread, quilted twin, bunk or full sizes..............$45–$65
Blanket..$45–$60
Coverlet...$45–$65
Drapes, assorted sizes..$20–$40
Pillow cases...$10–$15
Sheets..$15–$25
Sleeping bag...$40–$60
Towels, bath, Luke, Leia and Droids.......................$25–$35
Towels, bath, Darth Vader......................................$25–$35
Towels, face cloth, R2-D2 and C-3PO......................$10–$15

Bibb, Empire Strikes Back linen

Empire Strikes Back

BIBB, 1980

Empire Strikes Back matching bedroom accessories. Several motifs: Darth Vader's chamber, Darth and Boba Fett, Darth and Yoda and character collages. Variations may exist.

Bedspread, twin and full, quilted.............................$40–$60
Blanket..$40–$60
Coverlet...$40–$60
Drapes, assorted sizes..$20–$40
Pillow cases...$10–$15
Sheets...$15–$25
Sleeping Bag...$40–$60

BLACK FALCON (BRITISH), 1979

Bed set, shows characters. Includes pillow case and duvet..$35–$50
Bedspread, blue background with characters from the movie. Several sizes..$45–$65

BIBB—REVERSIBLE PILLOW CASES, 1980

Character designs.

Chewbacca and Yoda...$15–$25
Darth Vader and Boba Fett....................................$15–$25
R2-D2 and C-3PO..$15–$25

BIBB—TOWELS, 1979/80

Beach towel, Yoda..$25–$35
Beach towel, Darth Vader.......................................$25–$35
Bath towel, Darth Vader..$20–$30
Hand towel, Darth Vader and boba Fett........................$10–$15
Face cloth, Darth Vader..$10–$15
Face cloth, Tauntauns..$10–$15
Face cloth, Yoda...$10–$15

Return of the Jedi

BIBB, 1983

Jedi matching bedroom accessories. Character collage on tan or (different character art) white backgrounds.

Bibb, Return of the Jedi linen

Bedspread, twin or full, quilted..............................$35–$50
Blanket...$35–$50
Drapes, assorted sizes...$20–$40
Pillow cases ....$10–$15
Sheets ....$15–$25
Sleeping bag ....$40–$60
Towels, beach, Darth Vader....................................$20–$30
Towels, beach, character montage; several variations ....$20–$30
Towels, hand ....$10–$15
Towels, face cloth..$5–$10
Towles, wash mitt ....$5–$10

HAY JAX (BRITISH), 1983

Bed set, duvet and pillow case. Brown or white background.. ....$35–$40

MARIMEKKO, 1983

Sheet set, characters from the movie, twin size.........$40–$60
Sleeping bag, Luke and Leia....................................$60–$95
Sleeping bag, characters from Empire ....$60–$95

Combined Logo

BIBB, 1983

Bedroom accessories with logos from all three Star Wars Trilogy movies. Packaging has Jedi logos.

Bibb, combined logo linen

Bedspread, twin or full, quilted..............................$35–$50
Drapes, assorted sizes...$20–$40
Pillow cases ....$10–$15
Sheets ....$15–$25

Trilogy

FRANCO, 1997

Beach towels. 30″ × 60″ color designs.
Darth Vader, two different ....$15–$20
Droids ....$15–$20
Stormtrooper ....$15–$20

LUNCH BOXES

All lunch boxes in this section were produced by King Seeley-Thermos unless noted. Prices listed are for boxes complete with Thermos bottle.

Star Wars, metal. 1977. Color silk-screened artwork shows space battle on cover and Tatooine scene on reverse. Plastic Thermos has silk-screened design of Droids ....$50–$60

King Seely (Canadian) Return of the Jedi lunch box

Star Wars, plastic. 1977. Red box with paper decal. Color artwork shows Darth Vader, R2-D2 and C-3PO. Picture on one side only. Plastic thermos has silk-screened artwork of Droids...$40–$50
Star Wars, Spearmark Int. (British). Plastic. 1996. Blue with color decals based on movie poster art on box and flask ....$0–$0
Empire Strikes Back, metal. 1980. Color silk-screened artwork shows scene in Millennium Falcon on lid, Luke, Yoda and R2-D2 on back. Plastic thermos has silk-screened artwork of Yoda ....$50–$60
Empire Strikes Back, metal. 1980. Color photo shows Dagobah scene on lid, Hoth battle on back. Plastic thermos has silk-screened artwork of Yoda. ....$65–$85

Empire Strikes Back, plastic. 1980. Red with color photo silk-screened on lid only. Shows Chewbacca, Han, Leia and Luke. Thermos has silk-screened artwork of Yoda .... $35–$45

Empire Strikes Back, plastic. 1980. Silk-screened photo cover has logo and small hexagonal inset pictures. Plastic thermos has silk-screened picture of Droids and logo .... $35–$45

Return of the Jedi, metal. 1983. Color silk-screened artwork shows Luke in Jabba's Palace on lid, space scene on reverse. Plastic thermos has silk-screened artwork of Ewok ...... $35–$45

Return of the Jedi, plastic. 1983. Red with cartoon-style artwork of Wicket and R2-D2 on lid only. Plastic thermos has silk-screened artwork of Ewok .... $25–$40

Return of the Jedi, King-Seeley Canadian division. Plastic. 1983. Vertical design with paper sticker on front side of lid depicting Luke and characters from Jabba's Palace. Plain plastic thermos .... $40–$50

Droids, plastic. 1983. Blue with cartoon Droids artwork on lid only. Plastic thermos has silk-screened cartoon Droids artwork. .... $25–$40

Ewoks, plastic. 1983. Red with cartoon Ewoks artwork on lid only. Plastic thermos has silk-screened cartoon Ewok .... $25–$40

LUGGAGE AND TOTE BAGS

BACKPACKS

Adam Joseph, 1983. Canvas pack with color artwork.

- **Darth Vader and Imperial Guards,** red pack .... $35–$50
- **R2-D2 and C-3PO,** blue pack .... $35–$50
- **Yoda,** red pack .... $35–$50

Adam Joseph, 1983. Nylon pack with line artwork.

- **AT-AT** .... $30–$45
- **Darth Vader** .... $30–$45
- **R2-D2 and C-3PO** .... $30–$45
- **Wicket,** cartoon series .... $25–$35
- **Yoda** .... $30–$45

Bags of Character Blue canvas with small outside pocket. Darth Vader and two Stormtroopers on flap, Luke, Leia, C-3PO and R2-D2 on front, along with Jedi logo.

- **Each** .... $40–$60

Pyramid—Dark Side Collection Vinyl/nylon with embossed rubber artwork

- **Boba Fett** .... $15–$25
- **Darth Vader** .... $15–$25
- **Luke** .... $15–$25
- **Stormtrooper** .... $15–$25

Pyramid—Destroyer Collection Vinyl with metallic trim and inset artwork.

- **Boba Fett** .... $15–$25
- **Darth Vader** .... $15–$25
- **Luke** .... $15–$25
- **Stormtrooper** .... $15–$25

Pyramid—Hi-Tech Collection Nylon with all-over artwork.

- **Boba Fett** .... $20–$30
- **Darth Vader** .... $20–$30
- **Stormtrooper** .... $20–$30
- **Yoda** .... $20–$30

Pyramid—Imperial Collection, 1996. Nylon with rubber patch. *NOTE: Artwork varies slightly with design; variations in pack design occur in various collections.*

- **Boba Fett** .... $15–$25
- **Darth Vader** .... $15–$25
- **Stormtrooper** .... $15–$25

Pyramid—Pilot Collection Vinyl with all-over schematic artwork.

Pyramid, Pilot Collection vinyl backpack

- **Darth Vader/TIE** .... $10–$15
- **Luke/X-Wing** .... $10–$15

Pyramid—Star Class Collection Vinyl with inset artwork.

- **Boba Fett** .... $15–$25
- **C-3PO** .... $15–$25
- **Darth Vader** .... $15–$25
- **Stormtrooper** .... $15–$25

Pyramid—Zoom Collection Vinyl with all-over artwork.

- **Boba Fett** .... $12–$20
- **Darth Vader** .... $12–$20
- **Luke** .... $12–$20

Star Tours Black with blue and silver "Star Tours" logo.

- **Each** .... $25–$30

BACKPACKS (INTERACTIVE)

Pyramid, 1997. Equipped with sound and/or light functions.

- **Darth,** breathing sound .... $15–$20
- **Darth/TIE,** lights/battle sounds .... $15–$20
- **Luke/X-Wing,** lights/battle sounds .... $15–$20

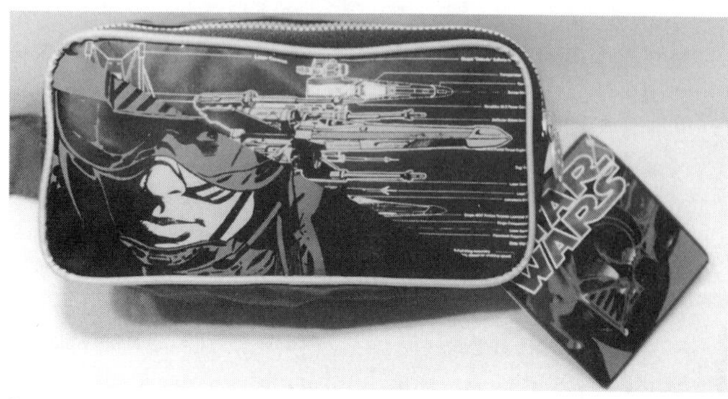

Pyramid, Pilot Collection vinyl belt pack

BELT PACKS

Pyramid—Dark Side Collection Vinyl/nylon with embossed rubber artwork.

Boba Fett .... $10–$15
Darth Vader .... $10–$15
Luke .... $10–$15
Stormtrooper .... $10–$15

Pyramid—Destroyer Collection Vinyl with metallic trim and inset artwork.

Boba Fett .... $5–$10
Darth Vader .... $5–$10
Luke .... $5–$10
Stormtrooper .... $5–$10

Pyramid—Hi Tech Collection Nylon with all-over artwork.

Boba Fett .... $10–$15
Darth Vader .... $10–$15
Stormtrooper .... $10–$15
Yoda .... $10–$15

Pyramid—Imperial Collection, 1996. Nylon with rubber patch. *NOTE: Artwork varies slightly with design; variations in pack design occur in various collections.*

Boba Fett .... $7–$10
Darth Vader .... $7–$10
Stormtrooper .... $7–$10

Pyramid—Pilot Collection Vinyl with all-over schematic artwork.

Darth Vader/TIE .... $7–$10
Luke X-Wing .... $7–$10

Pyramid—Star Class Collection Vinyl with inset artwork.

Boba Fett .... $9–$12
C-3PO .... $9–$12
Darth Vader .... $9–$12
Stormtrooper .... $9–$12

Pyramid—Zoom Collection Vinyl with all-over artwork.

Boba Fett .... $7–$10
Darth Vader .... $7–$10
Luke .... $7–$10

Star Tours Black with blue and silver "Star Tours" logo.

Each .... $10–$15

BOOK BAGS

Adam Joseph, 1983. Color artwork on canvas bags with fold-over flaps and buckle closures.

Darth and Imperial Guards .... $30–$45
R2-D2 and C-3PO .... $30–$45
Wicket, cartoon series .... $25–$35
Yoda .... $30–$45

DUFFEL BAGS

Adam Joseph Plastic drawstring bags with color artwork of characters.

Biker Scout .... $30–$45
Jabba's Sail Barge .... $30–$45
R2-D2 and C-3PO .... $30–$45
Yoda .... $30–$45

GYM BAGS

Adam Joseph, 1983. Zipper-topped, barrel-shaped, with artwork on ends.

Darth Vader .... $35–$50
Millennium Falcon .... $35–$50
R2-D2 and C-3PO .... $35–$50
Wicket, cartoon series .... $30–$45
Yoda .... $35–$50

Star Tours Horizontal design with blue and silver "Star Tours" logo.

Each .... $25–$30

OVERNIGHT CASE

Adam Joseph, 1983. Soft-sided, zippered case with cartoon scenes.

Ewok .... $30–$45

SHOULDER TOTES

Adam Joseph, 1983. Ewoks cartoon series. Color artwork on zippered tote with shoulder strap. Assorted designs.

Price for any .... $30–$35

SUITCASES

Adam Joseph, 1983. Three different-sized suitcases with Jedi logo and scenes. Came as set packaged one inside another.

Per set .... $85–$150

TOILETTE CASE

Star Tours Black with blue and silver "Star Tours" logo.

Each .... $10–$15

TOTE BAGS

Adam Joseph, 1983. Canvas with handles and snap closure.

Darth Vader and Imperial Guards, red bag .... $25–$40
R2-D2 and C-3PO, blue bag .... $25–$40
Yoda and "May the Force Be With You," all-over design on red bag .... $25–$40

Adam Joseph, canvas tote bags

Pyramid—Dark Side Collection Vinyl/nylon with embossed rubber artwork.

Boba Fett .... $20–$25
Darth Vader .... $20–$25
Luke .... $20–$25
Stormtrooper .... $20–$25

Pyramid, Destroyer Collection vinyl tote bag

Pyramid—Destroyer Collection Vinyl with metallic trim and inset artwork.

Boba Fett .... $20–$25
Darth Vader .... $20–$25
Luke .... $20–$25
Stormtrooper .... $20–$25

Pyramid—Hi Tech Collection Nylon with all-over artwork.

Boba Fett .... $30–$35
Darth Vader .... $30–$35
Stormtrooper .... $30–$35
Yoda .... $30–$35

Pyramid—Imperial Collection Nylon with rubber patch.

NOTE: Artwork varies slightly with design; variations in bag design vary with collection.

Boba Fett .... $20–$25
Darth Vader .... $20–$25
Stormtrooper .... $20–$25

Pyramid—Star Class Collection Vinyl with inset artwork.

Boba Fett .... $25–$30
C-3PO .... $25–$30
Darth Vader .... $25–$30
Stormtrooper .... $25–$30

Pyramid—Zoom Collection Vinyl with all-over artwork.

Boba Fett .... $12–$20
Darth Vader .... $12–$20
Luke .... $12–$20

Star Tours Black open design with blue and silver "Star Tours" logo.

Each .... $15–$20

WHEELED CARRY-ON

Pyramid, 1996. With pull-up handle. Padded plastic with line artwork.

Pyramid, carry-on bag

Boba Fett .... $25–$30
Darth Vader .... $25–$30
Luke as X-Wing Pilot .... $25–$30

MAGNETS

A.H. PRISMATIC (BRITISH), 1994

Holographic foil magnets approximately 2″ square

AT-AT .... $3–$4

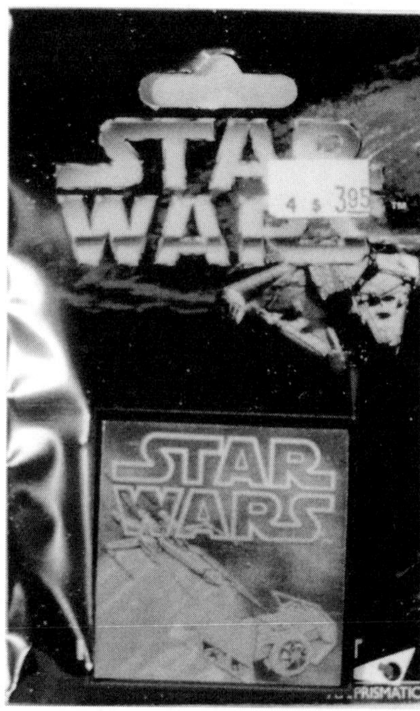

A.H. Prismatic (British), holographic magnet

B-Wing .... $3–$4
Darth Vader .... $3–$4
Darth TIE Fighter .... $3–$4
Millennium Falcon .... $3–$4
Millennium Falcon w/logo .... $3–$4
TIE Interceptor .... $3–$4
X-Wing .... $3–$4

ADAM JOSEPH

Jedi Logo, 1983. Four 1″ color plastic magnets of Darth Vader, Chewbacca, R2-D2 and Yoda. Came blister-packed as set on cardboard header with Jedi logo.

Per set .... $10–$15

Ewok Logo, 1983. Two 1″ color plastic magnets of Ewoks. Came blister-packed on cardboard header with Wicket the Ewok logo.

Per set .... $5–$10

HOWARD ELDON, 1987

Flexible plastic $1^1/_2$″ × 2″ rectangular. Color movie logo art on white background. No packaging.

Star Wars, triangular "A New Hope" logo .... $5–$8
The Empire Strikes Back, Vader head in flames .... $5–$8
Return of the Jedi, Yoda head in circle .... $5–$8

ATA-BOY, 1995/96

Rectangular, color photo magnets. No individual packaging.

B-Wing .... $4–$5
C-3PO .... $4–$5
Chewbacca and Han .... $4–$5
Darth Vader, close-up .... $4–$5
Darth Vader with lightsaber, two variations .... $4–$5
Empire poster art .... $4–$5
Han .... $4–$5
Jedi poster art .... $4–$5
Leia and Luke .... $4–$5
Leia and Luke, close-up .... $4–$5
Leia and R2-D2 .... $4–$5
Luke in garage .... $4–$5
Luke, Leia and Han .... $4–$5
Luke (lightsaber) .... $4–$5
Luke (Tauntaun) .... $4–$5
Luke and Yoda .... $4–$5
Millennium Falcon .... $4–$5
Millennium Falcon in asteroid field .... $4–$5
Obi-Wan .... $4–$5
Obi-Wan (lightsaber) .... $4–$5
R2-D2 .... $4–$5
R2-D2 and C-3PO, two variations .... $4–$5
Stormtrooper on Dewback .... $4–$5
Stormtroopers .... $4–$5
TIE Interceptor .... $4–$5
X-Wing .... $4–$5
X-Wing and Darth TIE .... $4–$5
Yoda .... $4–$5

STAR TOURS

Disney.

"Star Tours" logo .... $2–$4
R2-D2, picture and name. Cut-out design .... $2–$4
C-3PO, picture and name. Cut-out design .... $2–$4

MISCELLANEOUS HOUSEWARES

CANDLEHOLDER

Sigma, 1981. Ceramic. Yoda standing by tree stump (which holds candle). $4^1/_2$″ tall.

Each .... $45–$65

CASSETTE PLAYER

Tiger Electronics, 1997. Shaped like flattened version of R2-D2. Headphones, belt clip.

Each .... $25–$30

CHRISTMAS ORNAMENTS

Hallmark, 1996. Limited editions. Box displays photo of product.

Millennium Falcon .... $75–$100

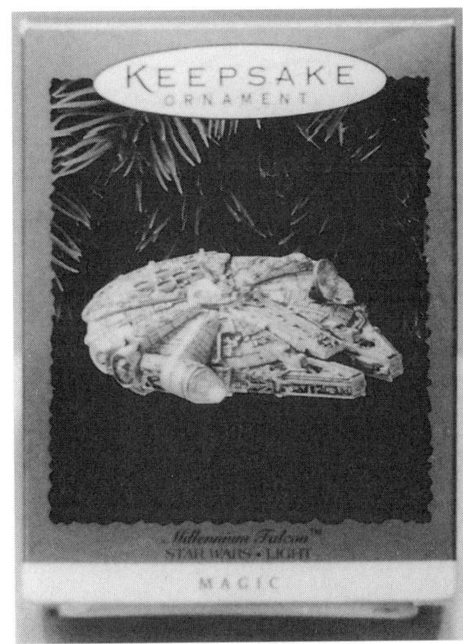

Hallmark, Millennium Falcon Christmas ornament

Vehicles of Star Wars Three-Ornament Set, X-Wing, TIE Fighter and AT-AT .... $50–$75

COOLER

Pepsi Promotional, 1997. R2-D2-shaped cooler approximately 4′ high on wheels. Removable dome and adjustable interior shelf.

Each .... $400–$500

DOORKNOB HANGERS

Antioch, 1996. 4″ × 9″ with color photo on one side and "Do Not Disturb" on the other.

Great Scott, Hang Ups Star Wars Trilogy flag

C-3PO .... $2–$4
Darth Vader .... $2–$4

FLASHLIGHT

General Mills, 1977. Promotional. Black plastic with foil decal with color artwork of Luke and Leia, logo with words "Light Saber."

Each .... $10–$15

HANG-UPS

Great Scott, 1996. Color nylon banners with plastic poles and string for hanging. Smaller size come bagged with color cardboard insert showing product. Larger size is boxed.

Darth Vader, 28″ × 40″ color artwork .... $15–$20
Empire (Stormtrooper), 20″ × 36″ half-face trilogy banner .... $15–$20
Jedi (Yoda), 20″ × 36″ half-face trilogy banner ...... $15–$20
Star Wars (Darth Vader), 20″ × 36″ half-face trilogy banner .... $15–$20
X-Wing, 28″ × 40″ color artwork .... $15–$20

LAMPS

Windmill Ceramics, 1979. Unlicensed ceramic accent lamps containing blinking color lights. Three different.

Chewbacca, 9½″ tall .... $40–$60
Darth Vader, 12″ tall .... $50–$75
R2-D2, 8½″ tall .... $40–$60

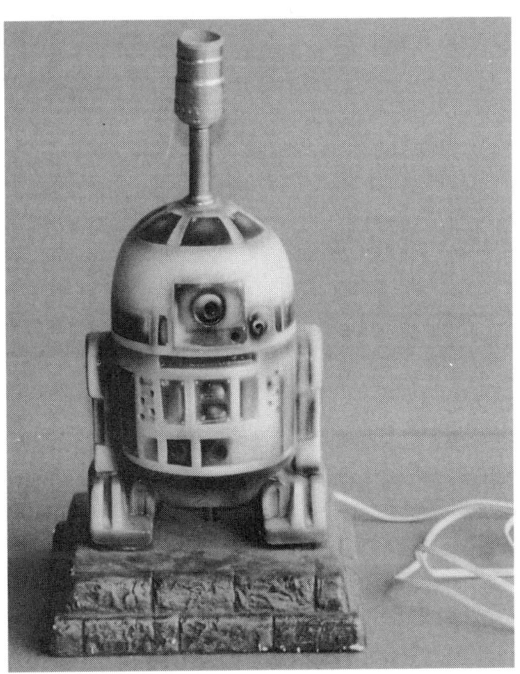
Windmill Ceramics, R2-D2 lamp

LAMPSHADES

Hay Jax (British), 1983. Main characters from Return of the Jedi on brown background. For ceiling light.

Each .... $40–$60

LAUNDRY BAGS

Adam Joseph, 1983. Designed to hang. Pictured characters on front.

- **C-3PO and R2-D2**..$35–$50
- **Darth Vader and Emperor's Guards**...............$35–$50
- **Wicket,** cartoon..$30–$40
- **Wicket and Kneesa,** cartoon.............................$30–$40

LIGHT SWITCH COVERS (SWITCHEROOS)

Kenner, 1979. Snap-on covers in shapes of characters with eyes that glow in the dark. Come blister-packed on header cards with movie logo. Three different.

- **C-3PO,** head only...$15–$25
- **Darth Vader,** head only.....................................$15–$25
- **R2-D2,** full figure...$15–$25

MAT

Recticel Sutcliffe Ltd. (British), 1983.

- **Play mat,** 24½″ × 39″ color artwork of scenes from all three movies...$125–$175

Reticel Sutcliffe Ltd. (British), Star Wars play mat

MIRROR

Lightline Industries, 1977. 20″ × 30″ in silver frame.

- **C-3PO and R2-D2**...$45–$60
- **Darth Vader**..$45–$60
- **Han and Chewbacca**...$45–$60

Sigma, 1981.

- **Table mirror,** 10″ tall in black ceramic Darth Vader frame..$50–$75

NIGHTLIGHTS (DIMENSIONAL)

Adam Joseph, 1983. Three different flat nightlights in colored plastic. Come carded. Cards display Return of the Jedi logo.

- **C-3PO,** head in circle...$10–$15
- **R2-D2,** full figure..$10–$15
- **Yoda,** full figure..$10–$15

NIGHTLIGHTS (DOMED)

Adam Joseph, 1983. Three different domed plastic lights in the shapes of figures' heads. Come carded. Cards display Return of the Jedi logo.

Adam Joseph, Darth Vader domed and R2-D2 dimensional nightlights

- **C-3PO**..$15–$20
- **Darth Vader**...$15–$20
- **Yoda**..$15–$25

NIGHTLIGHTS

Adam Joseph, 1983. Ewok cartoon. Comes carded.

- **Kneesa**..$5–$10
- **Wicket**..$5–$10

PENNANT

Tenth Anniversary Pennant, 1987. Color artwork of Darth Vader head and Jedi Death Star with 10th Anniversary logo on cloth pennant. Approximately 2′ long.

- **Each**..$10–$15

Star Tours Disney. Color artwork of "Star Tours" and Disney-MGM logos with R2-D2, C-3PO and Star Tours Droid and vehicle.

- **Each**..$5–$10

PICTURE FRAMES

Sigma, 1981. Ceramic. Three different.

- **C-3PO,** 5″ × 7″. Head in bottom righthand corner, arms and legs around sides, word "help" at top.............$40–$65
- **R2-D2,** 7″ × 10″. Full figure of R2-D2 in bottom right corner...$40–$65

PILLOWS (THROW)

Adam Joseph, 1983. Small die-cut accent pillows. Two different.

- **Darth Vader,** black figure on red background.....$25–$45
- **R2-D2,** white figure on blue background decorated with Return of the Jedi logo..$25–$45

Bibb, 15″ square, quilted cover. R2-D2 and C-3PO on one side, Darth Vader on the other. Star Wars logo on both sides. Matches Star Wars linens.

- **Each**..$20–$30

RADIO

Kenner, 1978.

Luke Skywalker head-set radio, uses 9V battery. Earpiece has Star Wars logo, mouthpiece extends from right side. Rare ....$950–$1200

Kenner, Luke Skywalker AM headset radio

R2-D2, uses 9V battery. Shaped like R2-D2. Hand strap on back. 6½″ tall ....$225–$275

RADIO/CASSETTE PLAYER

Tiger Electronics, 1997.

R2-D2 Data Droid, shaped like R2-D2. Pop-up handle. DC and earphone jacks. Tape storage. Sound effects ....$25–$35

RECORD TOTE

Disneyland—Vista, 1982. Lacquered cardboard box with plastic handle for 45s. Scenes from Empire Strikes Back on side panels.

Each ....$30–$45

SOAPDISH

Sigma, 1981. Ceramic. Shaped like Landspeeder. Shiny glaze. 7″ long.

NOTE: See COSMETICS for soap, shampoo, etc.

Each ....$50–$75

TAPE (AUDIO) CARRIER

Disneyland—Vista, 1983.

"Take-A-Tape-Along," holds six tapes. Decorated with photos from Return of the Jedi ....$20–$25

TELEPHONE

American Telecommunications, 1983.

Sigma, ceramic Yoda vase

Darth Vader Speakerphone, Darth Vader statuette on touchtone base. 14″ high. Comes in box with photo of phone and Darth Vader artwork on front panel. Plastic handle at top. Limited edition collectible..........$150–$200

American Telecommunications, Darth Vader speakerphone

TISSUES (FACIAL)

Puffs (Procter & Gamble), 1980. Color photo on front of box, cut-out on bottom. Six different.

Each ....$10–$15

TRAY

Chein, 1983. Metal. 12″ × 14½″.

Return of the Jedi, color artwork montage of characters and logo from Return of the Jedi .... $25–$35

Ewoks, color Ewoks cartoon artwork and logo .... $25–$35

Disney Metal Star Tours souvenir has logo and artwork from Star Wars and the park attraction.

Each .... $10–$15

VASE

Sigma, 1981. Ceramic. Shaped like Yoda standing by tree. Shiny glaze. 9″ high.

Each .... $50–$75

WALLPAPER

Characters, scenes and ships from their respective movies. Prices are per roll.

Star Wars .... $75–$100

Empire Strikes Back .... $50–$75

Return of the Jedi .... $50–$75

WALLPAPER (TRIM)

For room borders. Color photos of characters set in ovals of various sizes.

Per roll .... $35–$50

WASTEBASKET

Chein, 1983. Metal.

Return of the Jedi, montage of characters and Return of the Jedi logo in color on black background .... $45–$65

Ewoks, cartoon artwork .... $40–$50

Chein, Return of the Jedi waste basket

WINDOW DECALS

Image Marketing, 5½″ (approximately) plastic squares with color photos that adhere to smooth surfaces through static cling. Packaged in open front envelopes designed for hanging.

C-3PO and R2-D2 .... $3–$5

Darth Vader .... $3–$5

Millennium Falcon .... $3–$5

Yoda .... $3–$5

MISCELLANEOUS KITCHENWARE

CAKE CANDLES

Wilton, 1980. 3½″-high character candles with paper inset at base with character's name. Comes blister-packed on color cardboard header.

Chewbacca .... $5–$10

Darth Vader .... $5–$10

R2-D2 .... $5–$10

Wilton, Star Wars character cake candles

CAKE DECORATING KITS

Wilton, 1983. Includes molded aluminum pan in the shape of the character, plus tools for decorating. Comes boxed. Box shows photo of decorated cake.

Darth Vader .... $25–$35

R2-D2 .... $25–$35

CAKE PANS

Wilton, 1980. Molded reusable aluminum in shape of character. Paper sticker affixed to bottom of pan showed photo of finished, decorated cake.

Boba Fett .... $40–$50

C-3PO .... $30–$40

Wilton, Star Wars character cake pans

Darth Vader .... $30–$40
R2-D2 .... $30–$40

CAKE PUT-ONS

Wilton, 1980. Plastic figures of characters for decorating cakes. Come packaged with header describing item and photo of product on front.

C-3PO and R2-D2 .... $15–$20
Darth Vader and Stormtrooper .... $15–$20

CANDY MOLD

Wilton, 1980. 8″ × 7½″ plastic sheets.

Roman Ceramics, C-3PO cookie jar

Star Wars I, Darth Vader, Boba Fett and Stormtrooper .... $35–$50
Star Wars II, C-3PO/R2-D2, Yoda, Chewbacca .... $35–$50
Lollipop sheet, C-3PO, Chewbacca, Darth Vader, R2-D2, Stormtrooper, Ewok, Yoda .... $45–$65

COOKIE JARS

Roman Ceramics, 1977.

C-3PO, gold glazed ceramic. Head and shoulders lift off .... $250–$350
R2-D2, blue and white glazed ceramic. Head lifts off .... $225–$300

Sigma, 1981. Ceramic hexagonal design shows Darth Vader on one side and R2-D2 and C-3PO on the other.

Each .... $125–$175

PLACE SETTINGS

Sigma, 1981. Ceramic plate, bowl and mug set. Plate has color artwork of Chewbacca, R2-D2 and C-3PO. Bowl has color artwork of R2-D2. Mug has same color artwork as Droid mug from 1981 Sigma mug set (see MUGS, below) but with rounded rather than square handle. Came boxed; box art shows color picture of plate.

"The World of Star Wars Fantasy Childset" .... $125–$150

PLATES (DECORATIVE)

See COLLECTOR PLATES.

SALT AND PEPPER SHAKERS

Sigma, 1981. Ceramic.

R2-D2 and R5-D4 .... $75–$115
Yoda, both shakers the same .... $75–$95

Sigma, Yoda salt and pepper shakers

SQUEEZE BOTTLE

Star Tours Disney. Translucent white with black and silver "Star Tours" logo on front.

Each .... $3–$5

TEAPOT

Sigma, 1981. Ceramic. Luke riding Tauntaun. Luke's body comes off to add water. Tauntaun's tail is the handle and its head and neck are the spout. Approximately 10½″ tall.

Each .... $250–$350

MUGS AND STEINS (CERAMIC)

APPLAUSE, 1995/96

Figural Mugs Come packaged in box with color artwork and checklist on side to indicate which mug is in box.

- **Bib Fortuna** .... $14–$18
- **Boba Fett** .... $14–$18
- **C-3PO** .... $14–$18
- **Darth Vader** .... $14–$18
- **Darth Vader,** silver .... $14–$18
- **Emperor Palpatine** .... $14–$18
- **Gamorrean Guard** .... $14–$18
- **Han Solo** .... $14–$18
- **Stormtrooper** .... $14–$18
- **Tusken Raider** .... $14–$18

CALIFORNIA ORIGINALS, 1977

Steins Three different large steins in the shape of character heads from Star Wars. All are approximately 7½″ tall.

NOTE: Bootleg versions of these steins (especially the Darth Vader) are common.

Ben Kenobi, matte brown glaze outside; shiny blue glaze lining .... $125–$150

California Originals, Chewbacca character stein

Chewbacca, matte brown glaze outside; shiny blue glaze lining .... $125–$150

Darth Vader, shiny black glaze inside and out ... $100–$125

CUI, 1996

Color silk-screened artwork designs. No display packaging.

Regular Steins Open-topped. Approximately 6″ tall with circular area for artwork with "Star Wars" below in relief.

- **Star Wars** .... $20–$25
- **Empire** .... $20–$25
- **Jedi** .... $20–$25

Lidded Steins Shiny white glaze with artwork around entire stein. Hinged, flip-up pewter lids.

- **Star Wars** .... $20–$25
- **Empire** .... $20–$25
- **Jedi** .... $20–$25

Deluxe Darth Vader Stein Approximately 11″ tall with artwork over entire area of stein and hinged pewter lid topped with pewter figure of Darth Vader.

Each .... $125–$135

EARNST/HAMILTON

See COLLECTOR PLATES

RAWCLIFFE, 1996

Mugs The flat pewter insignias used in this company's keychain line are affixed to the front of mug. (See JEWELRY for different designs.)

Price for any .... $10–$15

SIGMA, 1981

Mugs Set of four standard size and shape mugs with color silk-screened artwork scenes.

- **Chewbacca and Boba Fett** .... $15–$20
- **C-3PO and R2-D2** .... $15–$20

Sigma, ceramic Tauntaun teapot

Darth Vader, Leia and Stormtroopers ....$15–$20
Yoda and Luke...$15–$20

Character Mugs, 1982/83. Mugs molded in the shape of figure's head. Shiny full-color glaze. Came boxed for stores in silver box with color photo of mug, though many not intended for store sales are in simple white mailing boxes.

Sigma *(left)* and Roman Darth Vader mugs

Biker Scout...$25–$35
C-3PO ....$20–$25
Chewbacca ....$20–$25
Gamorrean Guard...$20–$25
Han Solo, Hoth gear ....$20–$25
Klaatu ....$20–$25
Lando, Skiff Guard outfit ....$20–$25
Leia ....$20–$25
Luke, X-Wing Pilot gear ....$20–$25
Wicket...$20–$25
Yoda..$20–$25

STAR TOURS

Disney.

Glass Mug, 1986. Silver metallic finish and glitter Star Tours logo. 6″ tall.
Each ....$5–$10

Star Tours Logo Logo and character. Two different.
C-3PO and Star Tours logo ....$5–$10
R2-D2 and Star Tours logo...................................$5–$10

STAR WARS FAN CLUB, 1987

10th Anniversary Logo Gold on black.
Each ....$5–$10

PAPER CUPS

NOTE: See PARTY GOODS for more paper cups.

Dixie cups with Star Wars, Empire Strikes Back, and Return of the Jedi artwork

DIXIE

1980

Box of 100 five-ounce cups. Forty different scenes on cups. Color box art of characters and Star Wars logo. Prices are per box.
Darth Vader ....$15–$20
Han and Chewbacca..$15–$20
Leia ....$15–$20
Luke ....$15–$20
Obi-Wan ....$15–$20
R2-D2 and C-3PO..$15–$20
Stormtrooper ....$15–$20
X-Wing and TIE Fighter ....$15–$20

1981

Box of 100 five-ounce cups with Empire artwork. Box art of Empire subject and logo. Prices are per box.
AT-AT ....$10–$15
Bespin and Cloud Car...$10–$15

Darth Vader .... $10–$15
Luke on Tauntaun .... $10–$15
Millennium Falcon .... $10–$15
Star Cruiser .... $10–$15
X-Wing on Dagobah .... $10–$15
Yoda .... $10–$15

1983

Box of 100 five-ounce cups with Jedi artwork. Box art of Jedi characters and logo. Prices are per box.
Ewoks .... $10–$15
Emperor and Darth Vader .... $10–$15
Leia and Jabba .... $10–$15
Luke and Yoda .... $10–$15

1984

Box of 100 five-ounce cups with photos from movies and Star Wars Saga logo. Prices are per box.
Darth Vader .... $10–$15
Droids .... $10–$15
Han and Leia .... $10–$15
Luke and Yoda .... $10–$15

PLACEMATS

NOTE: See PARTY GOODS for paper placemats.

DIXIE, 1980

Plastic. Set of four: AT-AT, Luke and Darth Vader, space scene and Yoda.
Price per set .... $30–$40

ICARUS (BRITISH)
1982

Set of three 9″ × 10″ laminated placemats. Two different sets.
Set 1, R2-D2/C-3PO, Lando, Han and Chewie, Bounty Hunters .... $30–$40
Set 2, Yoda, Darth and Stormtroopers, Luke on Tauntaun .... $30–$40

1983

Illustrations by Andrew Skilleter. Two different, with story summaries.
Luke, Vader helmet, Guards and Speeder bikes .... $25–$30
Leia, Lando, Jabba and Wicket .... $25–$30

SIGMA, 1981

Vinyl. 11″ × 17″. Set of four color artwork scenes from The Empire Strikes Back. Luke and Yoda, R2-D2 and C-3PO, Darth and Leia and Chewbacca and Boba Fett.
Price per set .... $35–$50

PLASTIC TABLEWARE

APPLAUSE, 1997

Plastic figural mugs. Approximately 3″ high.
C-3PO .... $6–$8
Darth Vader .... $6–$8
Ewok .... $6–$8
Stormtrooper .... $6–$8

DEKA

This company produced an extensive line of plastic tableware for all three movies in the Star Wars Saga. Pieces are heavy-duty plastic with full-color photo scenes in the case of Star Wars and Empire and color artwork for Return of the Jedi. Pieces included six-ounce, eleven-ounce and seventeen-ounce tumblers, soup bowls, cereal bowls, mugs, plates and pitchers.
Star Wars, 1977. Items depicted major characters with labels identifying each. One design throughout.

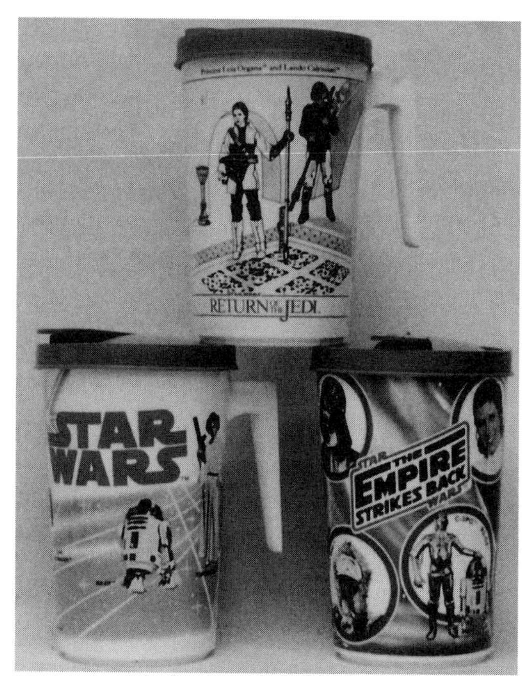

Deka produced plastic tableware for all three Star Wars saga movies

Bowl, soup or cereal .... $10–$15
Compartment plate .... $10–$15
Mug .... $10–$15
Pitcher .... $25–$35
Tumbler, any size .... $5–$10

The Empire Strikes Back, 1980. Items depict major characters set in circles.
Bowl, soup or cereal .... $10–$15
Compartment plate .... $10–$15
Mugs, four different styles .... $10–$15

Left: **This Cloud City Playset by Kenner was a Sears promotional item in 1981. *Right:* Hoth Wampa (Kenner, 1981) is 6" tall and has movable arms and legs.**

Left: **The original large Star Wars action figures produced by Kenner from 1977 to 1980. *Right:* Original Stormtrooper figures; from *left* to *right*, Kenner's large action figure (12"), Takara's Stormtrooper (7"), Kenner's small action figure (approximately 4 1/2") and Galoob's Micro Machine die-cast figure (approximately 1").**

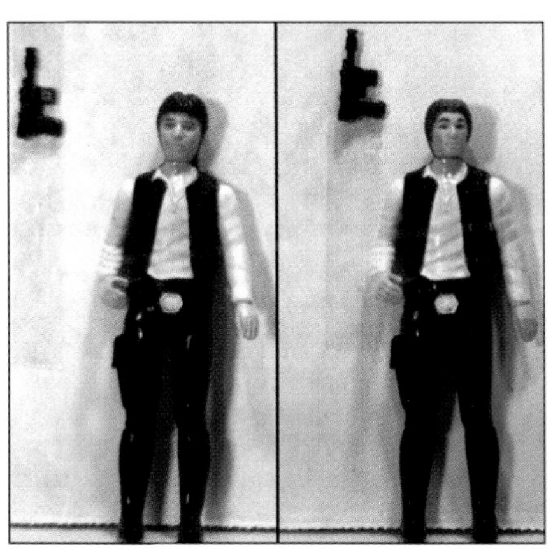

Kenner produced two different versions of the Han Solo action figure: the large head (*left*) and the small (*right*).

Kenner's Droids and Ewoks action figures, based on the animated TV series, were similar in size and construction to their movie line.

Ballantine Books has published many Star Wars–related books.

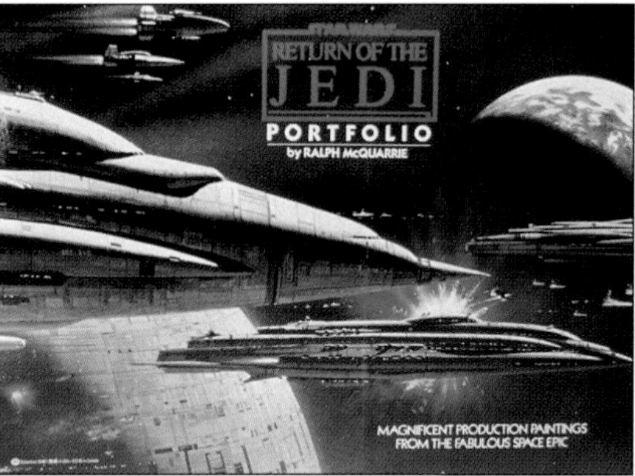

Left: Star Wars Book of Days, published by Antioch in 1994. *Center: Luke Skywalker's Activity Book* (Random House, 1979). *Right: Return of the Jedi Portfolio* by Ralph McQuarrie, published by Ballantine Books in 1983.

Left: Thinking Cap Co.'s Yoda Ear Cap was produced at the time of the release of *The Empire Strikes Back*. *Right:* Child's baseball cap from Sales Corporation of America (1983).

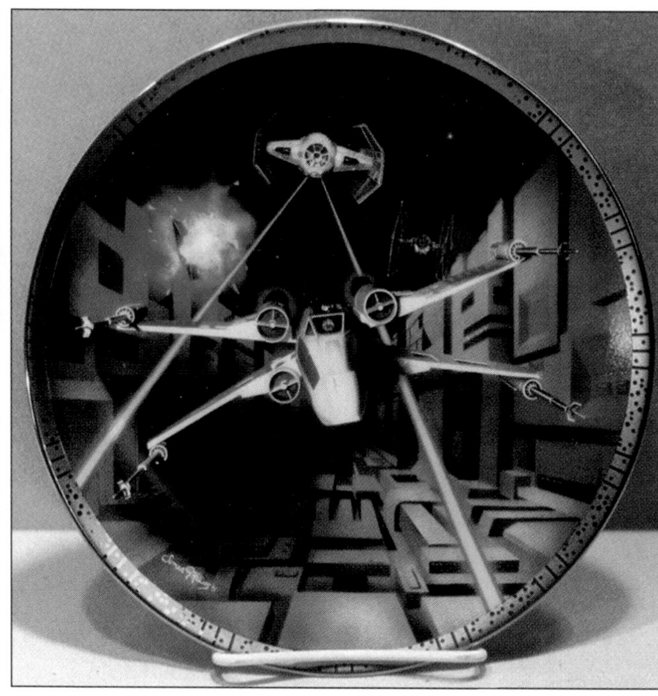

Left: Return of the Jedi collector plate from the Star Wars Trilogy Series by Hamilton Collection (1993). *Right:* X-Wing collector plate from Hamilton Collection's Star Wars Space Vehicles Series (1995).

From 1980, the Hoth Ice Planet Adventure Game and from 1981, the Yoda the Jedi Master Game, both from Kenner.

Star Wars 3-D #3, comic by Blackthorne.

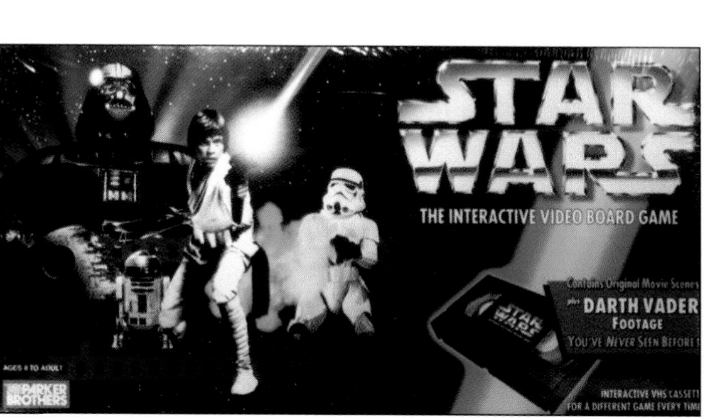

Star Wars: The Interactive Video Board Game by Parker Brothers.

Left: Sigma's Chewbacca ceramic bank.
Center: Yoda Decal Magic Window Art by Image Marketing.
Right: Antioch's C-3PO Doorknob Hanger (1996) says "Do Not Disturb" on the back.

Left: Spearmark Int. (U.K.) produced this Star Wars Special Edition lunch box in 1996. *Right:* R2-D2–shaped cooler was a Pepsi promotion in 1997.

Sigma's four-piece mug set (1981).

Left: Gamorrean Guard figural mugs: *left*, from Applause (1995/96) and *right*, Sigma (1982/83).
Right: C-3PO and Stormtrooper plastic mugs by Applause (1997).

Left: Vinyl place mat by Sigma (1981). *Right:* Hope packaged character watches inside Millennium Falcon watch cases in 1996/97.

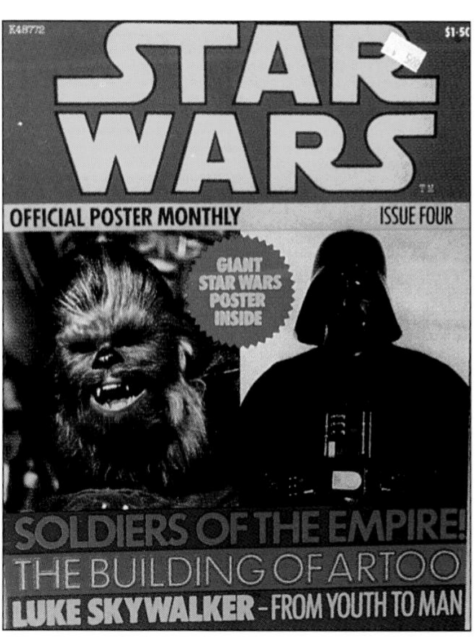

Left: Cinefex #3.
Right: Star Wars Official Poster Monthly, Issue Four.

Left: **MPC Encounter with Yoda on Dagobah model kit (1982).** ***Right:*** **Drawing Board Empire Strikes Back party blowouts, paper plates, and party hats.**

Left: **This Return of the Jedi promotional poster was free with the purchase of four cans of Hi-C in 1983.** ***Right:*** **Sales Corporation of America's 1983 Darth Vader montage mini poster.**

Left: **The Empire Strikes Back and Return of the Jedi crew patches.** ***Right:*** **The Empire Strikes Back 550-piece puzzle by Rose Art (1996).**

Left: Planet of the Hoojibs book and record set from Buena Vista Records (1983). *Right: The Story of Return of the Jedi* Special Edition picture disc (RSO).

Left: Antioch's Star Wars die-cut and tasseled bookmarks. *Right*: Return of the Jedi construction paper by Stuart Hall (1983).

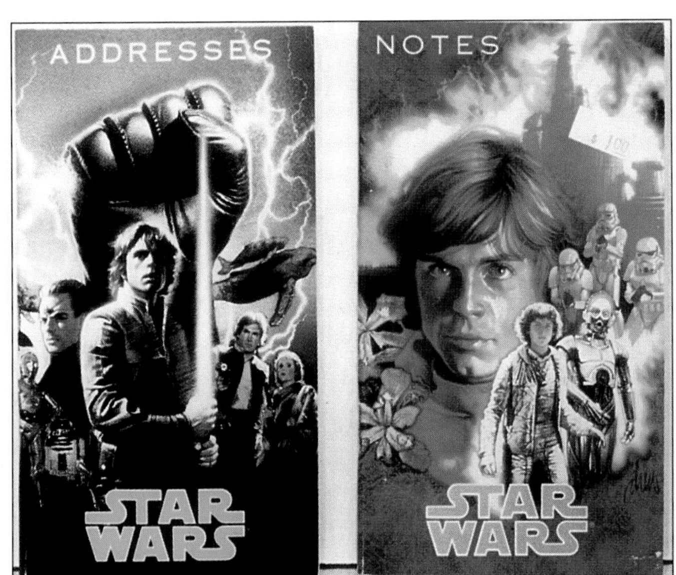

Left: Star Wars Addresses and Notes booklets from Antioch (1992). *Right:* Die-cast R2-D2 and C-3PO by Takara (1977/78).

Left: Galoob's Planet Tattooine (#4) Micro Machine Playset. *Right:* Action Fleet Death Star Playset by Galoob.

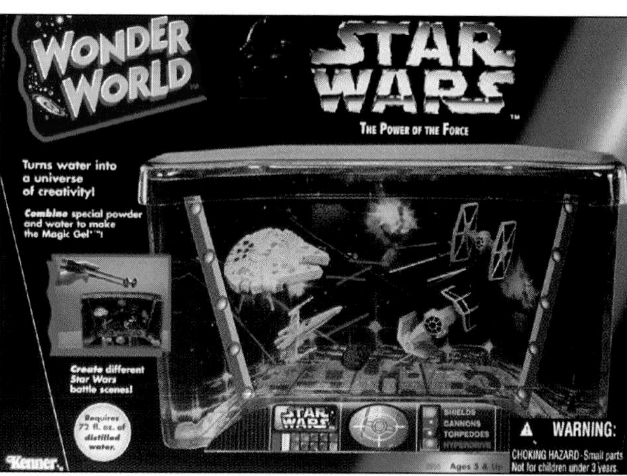

Left: Return of the Jedi child's roller skates by Brookfield Athletic Shoe. *Right:* Kenner's Star Wars The Power of the Force Wonder World (1995), "Turns water into a universe of creativity!"

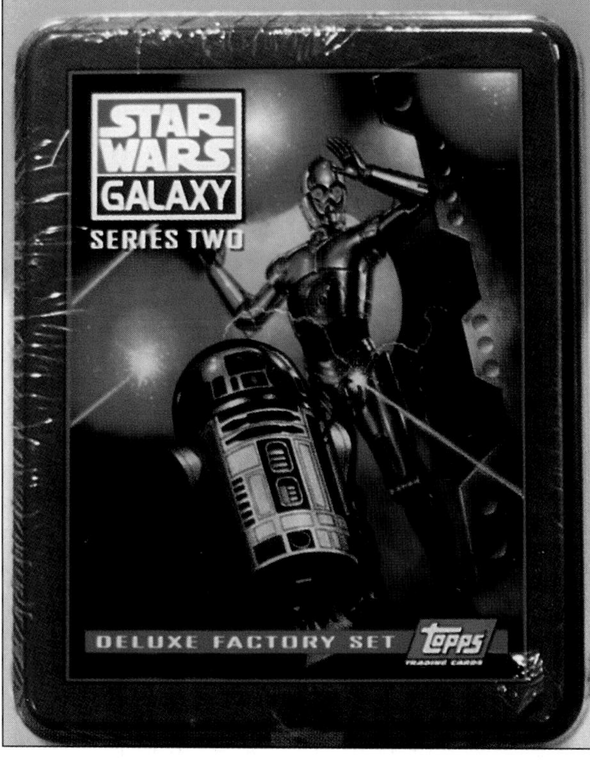

Left: Star Wars Galaxy Series One (1993) by Topps, set of 140 cards. *Right:* Star Wars Galaxy Series Two trading cards (1994) by Topps in a limited-edition, factory-sealed set.

Pitcher ..... $25–$35
Tumbler, any size ..... $5–$10

Return of the Jedi, 1983. Items show artwork of scenes from the movie.

Bowl, soup or cereal ..... $5–$10
Compartment plate ..... $5–$10
Mugs, two different styles ..... $5–$10
Pitcher ..... $15–$25
Tumbler, any size ..... $3–$5

Wicket the Ewok Three-Piece Set, 1983. Boxed set has mug, plate and bowl with color artwork of Ewok scenes and Return of the Jedi logo.

Per set ..... $25–$35

PROMOTIONAL PLASTIC WARE

Coca-Cola, 1977. Large (eighteen-ounce) plastic tumblers with color artwork scenes from Star Wars. Eight different.

Price each ..... $3–$5

Coca-Cola, 1977. Small (twelve-ounce) tumblers with color artwork scenes from Star Wars. Twenty different.

Price each ..... $3–$5

Coca-Cola, 1979. Large (eighteen-ounce) tumblers with color artwork of characters and scenes primarily from Star Wars, though Boba Fett is shown on one.

Price each ..... $3–$5

Coca-Cola, 1982. Pitcher. Logo and characters from Empire Strikes Back.

Price each ..... $5–$10

Pepperidge Farm, Return of the Jedi promotional tumblers

Coca-Cola, 1983. Large (eighteen-ounce) tumbler with scenes from Return of the Jedi.

Price each ..... $3–$5

Coca-Cola, 1983. Pitcher with scenes from Return of the Jedi (matches tumbler above).

Price each ..... $5–$10

Pepperidge Farm, 1983. Small tumblers with scenes from Return of the Jedi. Four different.

Price each ..... $2–$5

Pepsi/Kentucky Fried Chicken, 1996. 3-D Cups. Plastic tumblers with waist-up plastic character figurines for lids. C-3PO, Darth Vader, R2-D2 or Stormtrooper.

Pepsi/Kentucky Fried Chicken 3-D cups

Price each ..... $20–$25

Star Tours Disney.

Thermal mug, with "Star Tours" logo, 1986 ..... $5–$10
Thermal mug, with "Star Tours" logo and R2-D2, C-3PO and Star Tours Droid. Color artwork ..... $5–$10

STORAGE CONTAINERS

A.H. PRISMATIC, 1994

Plastic boxes approximately 2″ square. Lids are decorated with foil hologram. Nine different.

Price each ..... $4–$8

CHEIN (CHEINCO), 1983

Metal. This company made an assortment of tin containers featuring characters and scenes from Return of the Jedi. All feature a black background with color artwork and Jedi logo.

Trinket Tins, 3½″ round, 1″ deep. Artwork on lid. Six different.

Darth Vader ..... $8–$15

Metal Box Co. *(top)* and Chein metal storage containers

Droids ... $8–$15
Ewoks ... $8–$15
Jabba ... $8–$15
Luke, Leia and Han ... $8–$15
Max Rebo Band ... $8–$15

Mini-Tins, 3½″ round, 3½″ deep. Artwork on lid and sides. Six different (same subjects as on trinket tins).
Price each ... $10–$20

Cookie Tin, 6″ round, 4″ deep. Artwork on lid and sides shows montage of characters and scenes.
Price each ... $20–$30

Carry-All Tin, 6″ × 5″ rectangular, 4½″ deep. Two hinged metal handles. Artwork on lid and sides shows montage of characters and scenes.
Price each ... $25–$40

Metal Box Co. (British), 1980. This company made an assortment of storage tins in various sizes. All are decorated with color photos of characters and other subjects from The Empire Strikes Back.

Macro Tins Shallow, 3½″ square tins with photos on hinged lids. Eight different.
Chewbacca ... $8–$15
Darth Vader ... $8–$15
Han Solo ... $8–$15
Imperial Cruiser ... $8–$15
Leia ... $8–$15
Luke ... $8–$15
Probe Droid ... $8–$15
Yoda ... $8–$15

Micro Tins Small (2¼″ × 1¾″), shallow rectangular boxes with photos on lids. Reverse had Empire logo. Six different.
AT-ATs ... $5–$10
Boba Fett ... $5–$10
Lando Calrissian ... $5–$10
Luke fighting Darth Vader ... $5–$10
Luke on Tauntaun ... $5–$10
Yoda ... $5–$10

Oval Storage Tin, 4½″ tall. Front and back panels show Cloud City (Bespin). Hinged lid with logo.
Price each ... $25–$35

Space Trunks, 6½″ high hinged container tins. Lid has Empire logo and words "Space Trunk." Side panels have character photos. Two different.
Droids on front panel ... $45–$75
Luke on front panel ... $45–$75

Tall Square Storage Tin, 4″ high. Logo on hinged lid, photos of R2-D2, Darth Vader, Yoda and Probot on side panels.
Price each ... $15–$25

SIGMA, 1982

Ceramic. Shiny glazes. Came packaged for stores in silver boxes with color photo of product, though many were sold in plain white mail boxes.
Stormtrooper box, head only ... $40–$60
Yoda backpack box, Yoda is lid ... $35–$50

WRAPPERS AND PRODUCT CONTAINERS

Values on food products are for empty containers. For obvious aesthetic reasons elderly edibles have limited appeal to most collectors.

CANDY BOX

Kinnerton Confectionery (U.K.), 1996. Black box approximately 5″ × 5″ × 7″ with Space Battle scenes on sides, cutout bookmark on back and 3-D window scene of Darth and Obi-Wan in foreground with Millennium Falcon in background behind clear plastic window. Box held hollow chocolate egg filled with Star Wars jelly shapes.
Price each ... $15–$20

CANDY HEADS, TOPPS, 1980

Empire Strikes Back.

NOTE: Candy heads have a tendency to become very brittle with age.

First Series Red box contains candy dispensers in shapes of Stormtrooper, Boba Fett, Chewbacca, C-3PO or Darth Vader.
Individual head ... $1–$2
Box ... $15–$25

Second Series Yellow box contains candy dispensers in shape of 2-1B, Bossk, Tauntaun or Yoda.
Individual head ... $1–$2
Box ... $15–$20

Topps, Empire Strikes Back First Series candy heads

CANDY HEADS, TOPPS, 1983

Return of the Jedi. Contains candy dispensers in shapes of Admiral Ackbar, Jabba, Ewok, Darth Vader or Sy Snoodles.

Individual head .... $1–$2
Box .... $15–$20

CEREAL BOXES

Kellogg's, 1984. C-3PO Cereal. Picture of C-3PO on front; back has six different cut-out masks or promotion for stickers included in box. Masks were of C-3PO, Chewbacca, Darth Vader, Luke, Stormtrooper or Yoda.

Per box .... $25–$45

Kellogg's (Canadian), cereal boxes with hologram cards

Kellogg's (Canada), 1997. Boxes feature removable hologram cards on front of box and 3-D illusion picture on back.

Star Wars, Frosted Flakes .... $15–$25
Empire Strikes Back, Corn Flakes .... $15–$25
Return of the Jedi, Corn Pops .... $15–$25
Tri-Pack, one of each .... $45–$75

Nabisco, 1978. Star Wars Shreddies (British). Back has scenes from movie. Includes sheets of transfers as prize.

Price each .... $25–$45

CEREAL BOXES WITH MAIL-AWAY OFFERS

Ads printed on boxes offering a variety of mail-in offers for merchandise. Over the years such offers have appeared on General Mills, Kellogg's and Post cereals.

Boxes from the 1970s, any .... $25–$35
Boxes from the 1980s, any .... $15–$25
Boxes from the 1990s, any .... $5–$10

CEREAL BOXES WITH PREMIUMS

General Mills, 1978. Cereals aimed at the children's market had box ads for prizes contained in the cereal (usually stickers or cards).

NOTE: Individual premiums contained in the cereals are of minimal value (no more than $2 or $3). Sets, though small (usually four), are slightly more desirable.

Boo Berry .... $45–$70
Cocoa Puffs .... $25–$35
Count Chocula .... $45–$70
Crazy Cow .... $45–$70
Franken Berry .... $45–$70
Lucky Charms .... $25–$35
Trix .... $25–$35

CONTAINERS (CHEESE SPREAD)

Dairylea (British), 1988. Plastic illustrated with Droids and Ewok characters.

Price each .... $10–$15

CONTAINERS (YOGURT)

Dairylea (British), 1983/88. Plastic illustrated with different characters for different flavors.

Admiral Ackbar, pineapple .... $10–$15
Chewbacca, fudge .... $10–$15
Darth Vader, black cherry .... $10–$15
Ewoks, banana .... $10–$15
Jabba the Hutt, peach melba .... $10–$15
Luke Skywalker, raspberry .... $10–$15
Princess Leia, strawberry .... $10–$15
Yoda, gooseberry .... $10–$15

COOKIE BOXES

Pepperidge Farm, 1983. Eight-ounce boxes of molded cookies in three different shapes and flavors.

The Imperial Forces (chocolate), Darth Vader, Gamorean Guard, Jabba, Emperor's Royal Guard .... $15–$25
The Rebel Alliance I (vanilla), Luke, Leia, Han and Yoda .... $15–$25
The Rebel Alliance II (peanut butter), Admiral Ackbar, Chewbacca, R2-D2, Max Rebo .... $15–$25

KID'S MEAL BOXES

Taco Bell, 1997. Carry-out boxes decorated with photos from the movies and punch-out characters and ships to "create your own scene." Three different.

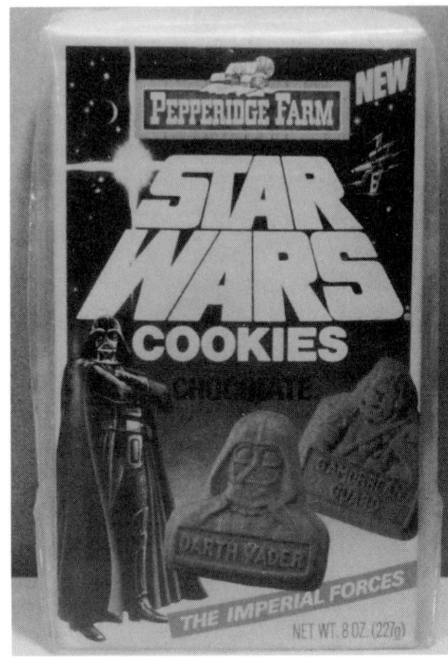

Pepperidge Farm, Star Wars cookies

NOTE: Taco Bell also had several different take-out bags decorated with Star Wars themes that have as yet to attain any appreciable collectible value.

Star Wars .... $5–$10
Empire .... $5–$10
Jedi .... $5–$10

PEPSI PRODUCT BOXES, 1997

Promotional artwork on boxes and individual drink containers for Pepsi products (regular, diet and caffeine-free versions of Pepsi, Mountain Dew and 7-Up). Three different basic styles: Yoda, C-3PO and Darth Vader.

Box, 12 or 24 pack .... $5–$10
Bottle .... $2–$5

PIZZA BOXES

Pizza Hut, 1997. Covers have line artwork of characters designed to be colored. Three different.

- **C-3PO** .... $5–$10
- **Darth Vader** .... $5–$10
- **Stormtrooper** .... $5–$10

SNACK BAGS

Tostitos, 1997. Bags had promotional offer for lenticular cards or disks included in product.

- **Large bag** .... $2–$3
- **Snack size bag** .... $1–$2

VITAMINS

Natural Balance, 1992. Sixty-tablet-count box pictures logo with R2-D2 and C-3PO. Tablets are shaped like the characters.

- **Star Wars Multivitamins** .... $10–$20

WRAPPERS

Burtons (British), 1984. Plastic. Illustrated with artwork of Vader on one side and Luke on the other.

- **Star Wars Biscuits (Cookies)** .... $10–$15

Dairylea (British), 1988. Cheese wedges. Paper. Twelve different Droids and Ewoks characters.

- **Baga** .... $5–$10
- **C-3PO** .... $5–$10
- **Chirpa** .... $5–$10
- **Kneesa** .... $5–$10
- **Latara** .... $5–$10
- **Logray** .... $5–$10
- **Malani** .... $5–$10
- **R2-D2** .... $5–$10
- **Shodu** .... $5–$10
- **Teebo** .... $5–$10
- **Wicket** .... $5–$10
- **Winda** .... $5–$10

JEWELRY

When Star Wars first came out in 1977 the costume jewelry industry was by nature somewhat informal. As a result, many of the pieces of jewelry are either unlicensed or are indistinguishable copies of licensed products. This section is

organized alphabetically by type of item and then alphabetically by manufacturer within these categories.

BARRETTES

FACTORS ETC., 1977

Plated or painted character charms affixed to small oval hair barrette. Originally came individually carded.

C-3PO .... $25–$35
Darth Vader .... $25–$35
R2-D2 .... $25–$35

BELT BUCKLES

See CLOTHING AND ACCESSORIES.

BRACELETS

FACTORS ETC., 1977

Gold Link Bracelet With character charms. Several different combinations.

Each .... $35–$50

Metal Band Bracelet, 1/2″ figures in metal affixed to metal-band-type bracelet.

C-3PO, gold-plated head .... $30–$40
Darth Vader, black-painted head .... $30–$40
R2-D2, full-figure unplated metal .... $30–$40
Stormtrooper, white-painted head .... $30–$40
X-Wing, unplated metal .... $30–$40

EARRINGS

FACTORS ETC., 1977

1/2″ figure earrings in metal. Earrings were either pierced or clip-on and were sold on padded earring mounts with Star Wars logo usually from open displays.

C-3PO, gold-plated heads .... $25–$35
Darth Vader, black-painted head .... $25–$35
R2-D2, full figure in unfinished metal .... $25–$35

3/4″ metal full-figure earrings with moving arms and/or legs.

C-3PO, gold plated .... $30–$35
Chewbacca, brown painted .... $30–$35
R2-D2, unfinished metal .... $30–$35

Adam Joseph, Ewok key ring

KEY RINGS

ADAM JOSEPH, 1983

Heavy brass. 2″ high. Figure is in relief.

Darth Vader .... $25–$30
Millennium Falcon .... $25–$30
R2-D2 .... $25–$30
Yoda .... $25–$30

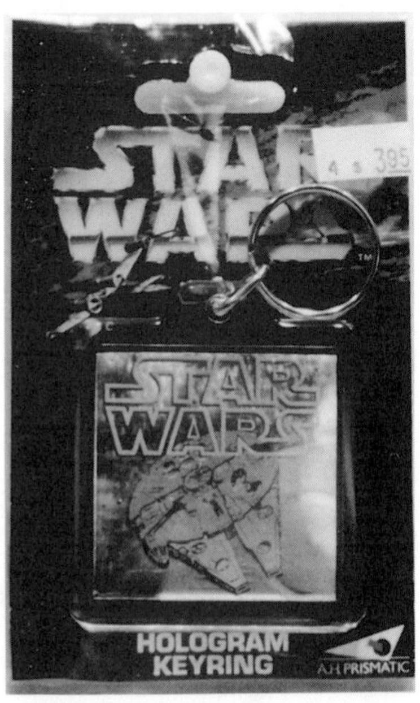

A.H. Prismatic, hologram key ring

ADAM JOSEPH, 1983

Ewok key rings. Three-dimensional. 2″ high. Hard plastic. Molded in color and painted.

Boy Ewok .... $5–$8
Girl Ewok .... $5–$8

A.H. PRISMATIC, 1994

3-D key rings. Foil holograms encased in 2″ lucite square.

C-3PO and R2-D2 .... $4–$6
Darth Vader bust .... $4–$6
Millennium Falcon .... $4–$6
X-Wing .... $4–$6

FACTORS ETC., 1977

Darth Vader head, 1 1/4″ black painted metal .... $15–$20
Stormtrooper head, 1″ white painted metal .... $15–$20
X-Wing, 2″ unpainted metal .... $15–$20

HOLLYWOOD COMMEMORATIVE PIN, 1996

Metal key rings with color cloisonne designs.

Darth Vader, head and Star Wars logo .... $5–$10
Millennium Falcon .... $5–$10
Rebel Alliance symbol, with Star Wars logo .... $5–$10
R2-D2 .... $5–$10
Yoda, head with Star Wars logo .... $5–$10

HOWARD ELDON, 1987

Flexible plastic magnetic 1 1/2″ × 2″ rectangles. Color movie logo art on white backgrounds.

Star Wars, triangular "A New Hope" design .... $5–$10
Empire Strikes Back, Vader head in flames .... $5–$10
Return of the Jedi, Yoda in circle .... $5–$10

Rawcliffe *(left)* and Hollywood Pin key rings

RAWCLIFFE, 1996

Solid pewter keychains, some with enamel backgrounds. Designs are flat unless otherwise noted.

AT-AT .... $5–$10
AT-ST .... $5–$10
Blaster Pistol, three-dimensional .... $5–$10
Blaster Rifle, three-dimensional .... $5–$10
Darth Vader .... $5–$10
Death Star, three-dimensional .... $5–$10
Empire Strikes Back logo .... $5–$10
Imperial symbol .... $5–$10
Obi-Wan Kenobi .... $5–$10
R2-D2, three-dimensional .... $5–$10
Rebel Alliance symbol .... $5–$10
Return of the Jedi logo .... $5–$10
Sand Skiff .... $5–$10
Shadows of the Empire logo .... $5–$10
Shuttle Tydirium .... $5–$10
Star Wars logo .... $5–$10
TIE Fighter .... $5–$10
Yoda .... $5–$10

STAR TREK GALORE

See PEWTER section

TENTH ANNIVERSARY LOGO, 1987

1 1/2″ square plastic. Promotional.

Each .... $10–$15

TIGER ELECTRONICS, 1997

Each is plastic with various electronic functions. Came blister-packed on header cards. Two different assortments.

Assortment 88-019 (manufacturer's number).
- **Darth head,** sound (one phrase) .... $4–$7
- **Death Star,** voice record and playback .... $4–$7
- **Millennium Falcon,** sound .... $4–$7
- **Stormtrooper head,** sound (one phrase) .... $4–$7

Assortment 88-020
- **C-3PO,** flashlight .... $4–$7
- **Lightsaber,** light and sound; retractable .... $4–$7

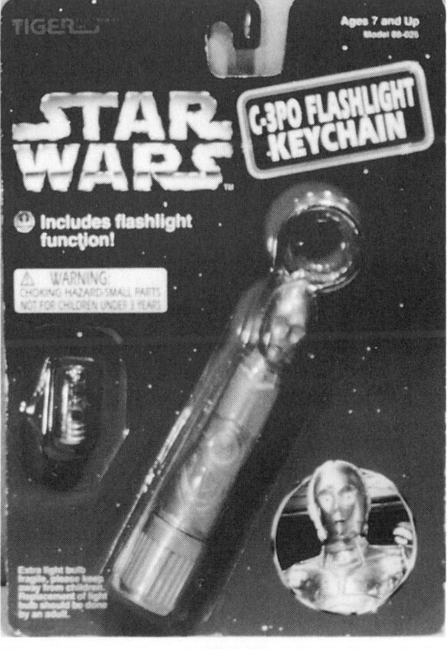

Tiger Electronics, C-3PO Flashlight key chain

R2-D2, digital clock .... $4–$7
Star Destroyer, lights and sound .... $4–$7

MEDALS

WALLACE BERRIE, 1980

Color enamel two-piece jewelry items. Top portion is pinned to the wearer, the bottom is attached to the top by a jump ring and dangles freely. Between 1″ and 1½″ total length. Pins came affixed to blue backing with Empire logo in blue box with clear lid. Six different.

Boba Fett, figure above, name below .... $25–$35
Chewbacca, figure above, name below .... $25–$35
Darth Vader, Empire logo above, Darth head below .... $25–$35

Wallace Berrie, Empire Strikes Back Millennium Falcon medal

Millennium Falcon Pilot, words above, ship below .... $25–$35
X-Wing Fighter Pilot, words above, ship below ...... $25–$35
Yoda, "May the Force Be With You" above, figure below .... $25–$35

PENDANTS

ADAM JOSEPH, 1983

Photo-etched black and gold colored. Die-cut. Came mounted on black plastic jewelry card with Jedi logo for display on rack. Included chain.

May the Force Be With You, words. 1½″ .... $10–$15
Return of the Jedi, logo. 1½″ .... $10–$15
X-Wing Pilot, round Rebel logo from movies .... $10–$15
Figure Pendants Gold color characters in relief. Came carded like photo-etched pendants. Included chain.

- **C-3PO,** bust. 1″ .... $15–$20
- **Emperor's Royal Guard,** 1¼″ .... $15–$20
- **Ewok,** 1″ .... $15–$20
- **R2-D2,** 1″ .... $15–$20

Adam Joseph, figure pendant

- **Salacious Crumb,** 1¼″ .... $15–$20
- **Yoda,** 1″ .... $15–$20

Full-Figure Pendants, 1983. Painted metal. 1½″ high. Came blister-packed on red header card with Jedi logo. Includes chain.

- **Darth Vader** .... $15–$25
- **R2-D2** .... $15–$25
- **Yoda** .... $15–$25

FACTORS ETC., 1977

Darth Vader head, 1¼″. Black painted metal.......... $15–$25
Darth Vader head, ¾″. Black painted metal .... $10–$20
Stormtrooper head, 1″. Painted metal .... $15–$25

Factors Etc., C-3PO articulated figure pendant

X-Wing, 2″. Unpainted metal .... $20–$30
Articulated Figure Pendants Arms and/or legs move. Two sizes.

- **C-3PO,** large; 2″. Gold plated .... $30–$35
- **Chewbacca,** large; 2″. Painted .... $30–$35
- **R2-D2,** large; 1 1/2″. Unplated metal .... $30–$35
- **C-3PO,** small; 1 1/2″. Gold plated .... $25–$35
- **Chewbacca,** small; 1 1/2″. Painted .... $25–$30
- **R2-D2,** small; 1″. Unplated metal. .... $25–$30

HOWARD ELDON, 1987

Magnetic plastic rectangles with color logo art. Leather neck cord.

Star Wars .... $5–$10
Empire Strikes Back .... $5–$10
Return of the Jedi .... $5–$10

MISCELLANEOUS

Manufacturers and dates unknown.

C-3PO, 1 1/4″ enamel .... $15–$25
R2-D2, 3/4″ enamel .... $15–$25
Millennium Falcon, small .... $15–$25
TIE Fighter, small .... $15–$25
Star Wars, logo. Flat, trapezoidal design .... $15–$25
Star Wars, logo and stars. Cut-out .... $15–$25

WALLACE BERRIE, 1980

Color enamel pendants came affixed to blue backing with Empire logo packaged in 3″ × 2 1/4″ blue box with clear plastic lid. Chain included.

Chewbacca, 1″ octagonal design .... $20–$30
Darth Vader, 1″ outline of head .... $20–$30
R2-D2, 1″ full-figure cut-out .... $20–$30
R2-D2 and C-3PO, 1″ on circular background .... $20–$30

PINS

ADAM JOSEPH, 1983

Photo Etched Gold and black. Came affixed to black plastic header card with red Jedi logo.

- **May the Force Be With You,** 1 1/2″ .... $10–$15
- **Return of the Jedi,** logo. 1 1/2″ .... $10–$15
- **Star Wars,** 1 1/2″ .... $10–$15
- **The Force,** 1 1/2″ .... $10–$15
- **X-Wing Fighter Pilot,** 1″ round. Rebel symbol .... $10–$15

Character Pins Gold plate. In relief. Came packaged similarly to photo-etched pins. Between 1″ and 1 1/2″.

- **C-3PO,** bust .... $15–$25
- **Emperor's Royal Guard** .... $15–$25
- **Ewok** .... $15–$25
- **R2-D2** .... $15–$25
- **Salacious Crumb** .... $15–$25
- **Yoda** .... $15–$25

Ewok Pins Painted plastic. 1 1/4″. Came blister-packed on blue header card with color artwork of Ewok.

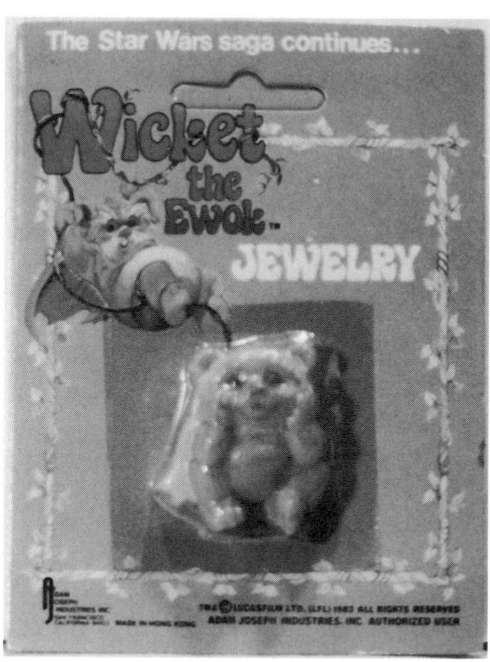

Adam Joseph, plastic Ewok pin

- **Boy Ewok** .... $5–$8
- **Girl Ewok** .... $5–$8

A.H. PRISMATIC

See BUTTONS.

ATARI

Promotional Pins Metal. Black and silver.

- **C-3PO** .... $15–$25
- **Darth Vader** .... $15–$25
- **R2-D2** .... $15–$25

FACTORS ETC., 1977

Scatter Pins, 1/2″ metal. Several combinations. Sold as set of three on padded backing with Star Wars logo. Designed to be sold in open display.

- **Price per set** .... $25–$35

Stick Pins Approximately 2 1/2″ long. Packaged on paper backing with Star Wars logo at bottom. Designed to be sold from open displays.

- **C-3PO** .... $20–$25
- **Chewbacca** .... $20–$25
- **Darth Vader** .... $20–$25
- **R2-D2** .... $20–$25
- **Stormtrooper** .... $20–$25
- **X-Wing** .... $20–$25

Hollywood commemorative pin, cloisonné pin

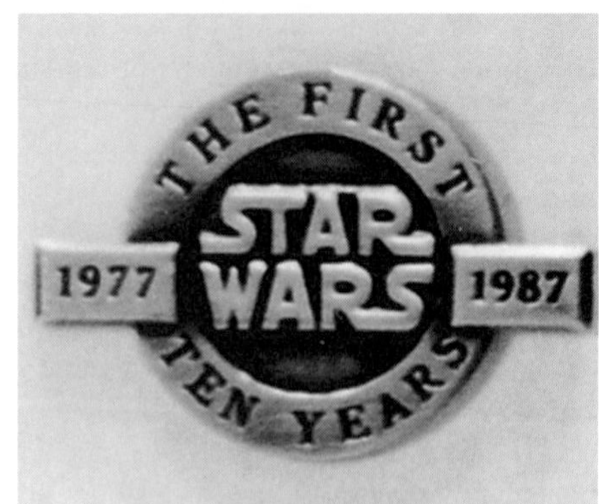

Howard Eldon, tenth anniversary pin

HOLLYWOOD COMMEMORATIVE PIN, 1996

Full-color cloisonne pins. All pins below are current. Price primarily reflects size of pin.

AT-AT .... $10–$12
Boba Fett .... $10–$12
C-3PO .... $6–$8
C-3PO, Oh Dear! We're Doomed .... $6–$8
Chewbacca .... $10–$12
Darth Vader, figural .... $10–$12
Darth Vader, three-dimensional head .... $5–$8
Emperor .... $8–$10
Emperor's Guard .... $6–$8
Empire Strikes Back, with Darth and Yoda .... $12–$15
Ewok .... $10–$12
Imperial Symbol .... $6–$8
Jabba the Hutt .... $7–$10
May the Force Be With You, with hands holding lightsaber .... $10–$12
Max Rebo Band .... $10–$12
Millennium Falcon .... $8–$10
Obi-Wan Kenobi .... $8–$10
Princess Leia .... $8–$10
Rebel Alliance symbol, large gold .... $8–$10
Rebel Alliance symbol, large red .... $8–$10
Rebel Alliance symbol, small gold .... $4–$6
Rebel Alliance symbol, small red .... $4–$6
Return of the Jedi, with Death Star .... $12–$15
Star Wars, with crossed lightsabers .... $8–$10
Star Wars, with ships .... $12–$15
Stormtrooper .... $8–$10
TIE Fighter .... $8–$10
X-Wing, front view .... $6–$8
X-Wing, side view .... $6–$8
Yoda .... $8–$10
Yoda, Try Not. Do or Do Not. There is no Try. .... $6–$10

HOWARD ELDON, 1987

Color Polycoat Figure Pins

C-3PO, 1½″ high .... $8–$12
Darth Vader, 1½″ high .... $8–$12
R2-D2, 1¼″ high .... $8–$12

Color Polycoat Logo Pins

Star Wars, black and silver .... $8–$12
The Empire Strikes Back, blue and silver .... $8–$12
Return of the Jedi, red and silver .... $8–$12

Pewter 10th Anniversary Pins

Original design, round with dates set inside circle .... $15–$20
Later design, dates set outside circle .... $10–$15

STAR TOURS (DISNEY)

Triangular "Star Tours" logo .... $10–$15

Factors Etc., three-piece ring set

RINGS

ADAM JOSEPH, 1983

X-Wing Fighter Pilot Photo etched. Gold-plated adjustable. Circular design featuring Rebel symbol with words around it.

Ring .... $15–$25

FACTORS ETC., 1977

Set of three different (Darth, C-3PO and R2-D2) in box with Star Wars logo.

Set .... $45–$60

WALLACE BERRIE, 1980

Color enamel designs on adjustable ring. Came affixed to blue card with Empire logo inside blue box with clear lid.

Darth Vader, head on blue circular background ...... $25–$30
May the Force Be With You, words on blue square background .... $25–$30
R2-D2, on blue circular background .... $25–$30
R2-D2 and C-3PO, on blue circular background...... $25–$30
X-Wing, on blue circular background .... $25–$30
Yoda, on orange circular background, name below head .... $25–$30

WATCHES

A.H. PRISMATIC (BRITISH), 1995

3-D Darth Vader Watch True hologram on face. Black watch casing band with "Star Wars" and "Darth Vader" on sides. Packaged in flat clear plastic case.

Each .... $25–$35

BRADLEY

Darth Vader Analog Watch, 1977. Full figure on gray background. Came in cylindrical blue case with decals of Vader and Star Wars logo.

Per watch .... $75–$100

BRADLEY, 1982

R2-D2 and C-3PO, digital with rectangular face. Star Wars logo below .... $40–$60
R2-D2 and C-3PO, analog. Round stainless steel case. Black strap. At least one minor case variation exists for this watch .... $40–$60
R2-D2 and C-3PO, blue face with two ships and Star Wars logo. Black case and band. Musical alarm .... $50–$70
Darth Vader double image, Star Wars logo alternates with picture of Darth when watch is moved. Digital .... $50–$70

BRADLEY

Radio Watches Digital watch/radio set came complete with headphones. Packaged in window box showing headphones and character artwork.

Star Wars logo, R2-D2 artwork .... $150–$200
Jedi logo, Ewok artwork .... $125–$175

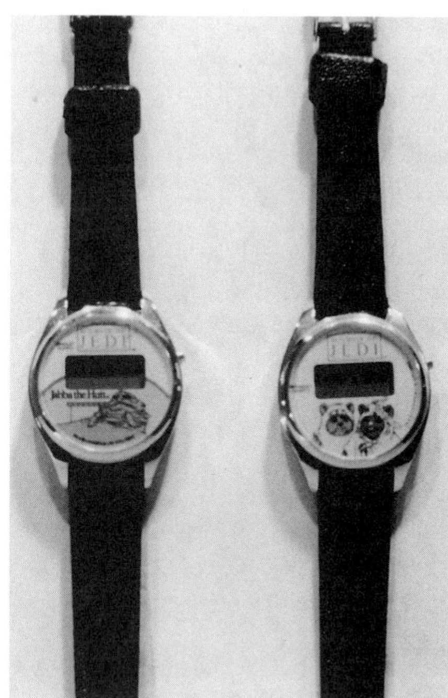

Bradley, Return of the Jedi watches

BRADLEY, 1982/83

Extensive series of watches with round or oval faces and plastic or stainless steel cases. Watches displayed color artwork and movie logo on face. Black vinyl bands. Watches were either blister-packed on card with movie logo or in some cases just bagged in clear plastic envelopes. Watches were either battery-digital style or wind-up analog with minor variations in artwork to accommodate watch face. Many minor variations in watch size and casing style may occur.

C-3PO and R2-D2, black background with Star Wars logo .... $25–$50
Darth Vader, head and name on gray .... $25–$50
Darth Vader, figure with lightsaber .... $25–$50
Ewoks, with Jedi logo .... $25–$50
Jabba the Hutt .... $25–$50
Star Wars, logo .... $25–$50
Yoda, head and name on gray .... $25–$50

BRADLEY, 1983

Analog Watches Series of analog watches with round faces show artwork of character and stars around rim.

Darth Vader .... $30–$50
Ewok .... $30–$50
Yoda .... $30–$50

Droids Watch, 1983. Digital watch with Droids logo and animated R2-D2 and C-3PO on face. Black band.

Each .... $30–$50

Stopwatch/Timer With cord. Stormtroopers on Speeder Bikes. Came boxed.

Per watch..........$150–$200

FANTASMA, 1993

Darth Vader Watch Black watch casing with bust of Darth on face. Instead of second hand, TIE Interceptor chases X-Wing on clear disk. A few were packaged in padded display box. Most only had velveteen watch covers. Included certificate of authenticity.

Per watch..........$30–$65

Millennium Falcon Watch Watch casing is shaped like ship and opens to reveal color artwork of Millennium Falcon on face. Packaged in round plastic ball inside blue open window box. Includes certificate of authenticity.

Per watch..........$50–$100

FOSSIL, 1996

Limited Edition Collector's Watch Star Wars logo with Rebel and Imperial symbols on face. Silvertone metal band. Packaging is designed to resemble Death Star.

Per watch..........$90–$150

HOPE, 1996/97

Character Watches Color plastic with matching decorated bands. Comes packaged on blister card with plastic Millennium Falcon watch case.

Boba Fett..........$10–$15
C-3PO..........$10–$15
Darth Vader..........$10–$15
R2-D2..........$10–$15
Stormtrooper..........$10–$15
Yoda..........$10–$15

LUCASFILM (THX DIVISION), 1996

Watch, Half face of Darth Vader with THX logo below. Black case and band..........$50–$60

STAR TOURS (DISNEY)

Darth Vader head, outline in gold on black-faced analog watch. No numerals..........$100–$125

TEXAS INSTRUMENTS, 1977

Digital Star Wars Logo Watch, logo above and below face of watch..........$75–$100

Digital Watch Gray band and decals of Star Wars scenes and characters around face. Red faceplate. Came packaged in clear plastic vertical display box that fit into slipcase with color artwork. Included strip of ten extra artwork stickers that could be applied to watch.

Each..........$125–$150

THIRD DIMENSION ARTS, 1990

3-D Watches True hologram face with black watch casing and band. Packaged in cylindrical clear plastic display boxes. Some casing variations may occur.

Boba Fett..........$35–$45
Darth Vader..........$35–$45
X-Wing..........$35–$45
Yoda..........$35–$45

ZEON (BRITISH)

Alarm, Date, Time, Calendar, C-3PO, R2-D2, X-Wing and TIE fighter on face. Came boxed..........$75–$100

Logo with R2-D2 and C-3PO, 1982. Promotion with British Star Wars/Empire weekly and monthly comic magazines..........$75–$100

MAGAZINES

Magazines are organized alphabetically by title. For comics, see COMICS section of this book; for gaming supplements, see GAMES.

Amazing Heroes

#13, "Star Wars in Comics," cover ....$5–$8

American Cinematographer

Star Wars issue, cover ....$75–$100

Empire Strikes Back issue, June 1980, cover .....$35–$45

R2-D2 and C3PO on cover, profiles Return of the Jedi inside...$25–$30

American Film

April 1977, "George Lucas Goes Far Out"............$5–$10

June 1983, Lucas cover, Jedi special effects articles ....$5–$8

Bantha Tracks See "Star Wars Fan Club."

Best of Starlog, The

Vol. 1, Luke Skywalker with blaster in photographs from Empire Strikes Back on cover, assorted articles ....$6–$8

Vol. 2, Yoda on cover, assorted articles....................$6–$8

Vol. 4, Jabba on cover..$6–$8

Vol. 5, Luke and Vader fighting scene on cover.......$6–$8

British Star Wars Poster Magazine Galaxy Press, 1978. Ran at least five issues.

Price each ....$15–$20

Chicago Tribune

May 4, 1980, Empire Strikes Back ....$5–$10

Cinefantastique F.S. Clark Publishers. The magazine with a "sense of wonder."

Vol. 6, No. 4, Vol. 7, No. 1, double issue, "Making Star Wars," 23 interviews with the actors, technicians and artists...$25–$35

American Cinematographer, **Star Wars issue (July 1977)**

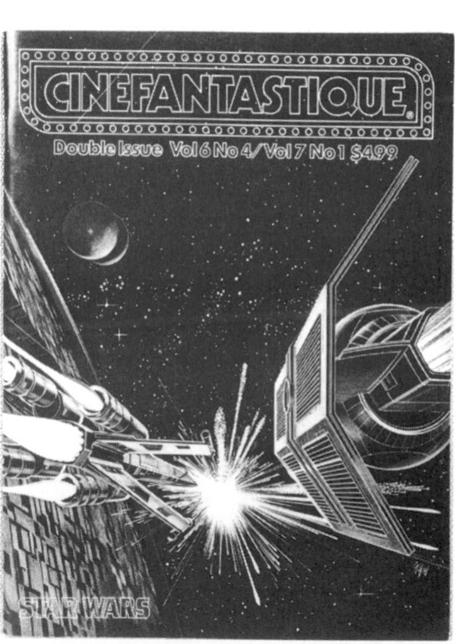

Cinefantastique, **Star Wars double issue**

Vol. 10, No. 2, review of Empire ....$5–$10
Vol. 12, No. 5 and 6, July/August 1982, "Star Trek II" and "The Revenge of the Jedi" ....$15–$25
Vol. 13, No. 4, Jedi plot revealed ....$7–$10

Cinefex
No. 2, August 1980, special effects articles ....$50–$75
No. 3, Empire cover ....$50–$75
No. 13, Jedi film production ....$35–$50
No. 65, ILM 20th Anniversary Issue, Millennium Falcon cover ....$10–$15

Comic Collector's Magazine
No. 139, October 1977, this issue devoted to Star Wars, interviews, behind the scenes and comic art ....$5–$10

Comics Journal
#2, Empire issue ....$5–$8
#37, articles on SW comics and movie ....$5–$8

Comics Scene
Vader cover and article on Jedi comic ....$5–$10

Commodore User Magazine Dutch computer magazine.
No. 3, 1988, Star Wars cover art and game information ....$5–$8

Cracked
No. 146, November 1977, R2-D2/C-3PO cover, Star Wars spoof ....$15–$20
No. 173, November 1980, "The Empire Strikes It Out" ....$10–$15
No. 174, December 1980, "The Empire Strikes It Rich" ....$10–$15
No. 199, November 1983, "Returns of the Jedi Eye" ....$10–$15

Crash British computer magazine.
No. 54, July 1988, cover and article on Empire computer game ....$5–$8

Crazy
Vol. 1, No. 32, December 1977, cover and Star Wars spoof ....$10–$15

Creative Computing
Vol. 8, No. 8, August 1982, cover photograph of Darth Vader ....$5–$8

Delap's F and SF Review A review of fantasy and science fiction, Fredric Pattern Publisher.
Vol. 3, No. 7, July 1977, cover story on Star Wars plus reviews of the movie ....$10–$15

Der Nederlandse Mad Dutch version of Mad.
No. 87, March 1978, Star Wars spoof ....$15–$20

Die Ruckkehr Der Jedi-Ritter Das Offizielle Magazin Zum Film. German version of the ROTJ collectors magazine.
Each ....$15–$25

Die Sprechblase German comic fan magazine.
October 1981, Star Wars cover and articles ....$5–$10
December 1981, Star Wars cover and articles ....$5–$10

Discover
Vol. 5, No. 8, August 1984, Lucas, C-3PO and R2-D2 on cover, contains article entitled "Computerizing the Movies" ....$15–$20

Dreamwatch (British).
April 1997, Star Wars/Star Trek issue. Interior article and partial cover ....$7–$10

Dynamite
No. 41, 1977, article on Star Wars ....$5–$10
No. 63, preview of Empire; cover ....$5–$10
No. 76, 1980, Scholastic Magazines, Luke with saber on cover, article on The Empire Strikes Back ....$5–$10
No. 114, 1983, Luke and Leia on cover ....$5–$10

Electric Company, The
April/May 1983, Yoda on cover, Star Wars articles ....$5–$10

Empire Strikes Back Official Collector's Edition
Each ....$10–$15

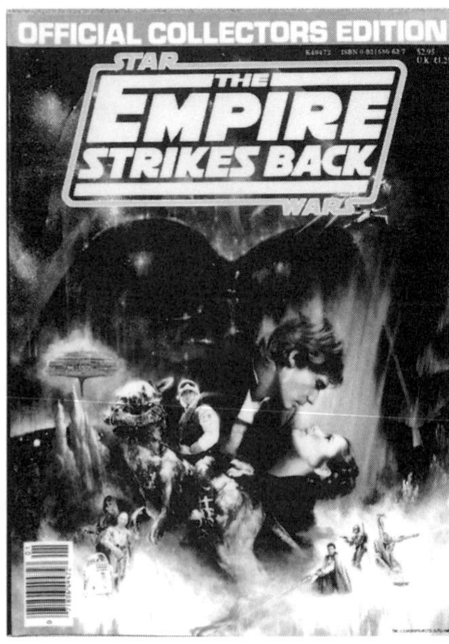

The Empire Strikes Back Official Collectors Edition **magazine**

Empire Strikes Back Poster Album Bantha Tracks, an official Star Wars fan club publication, featuring all the characters.
Each ....$10–$20

Empire Strikes Back Poster Book Giant poster with editorials and information on back.
Issue One, "Back in Action," Princess Leia, Han Solo and Chewbacca on bridge ....$5–$10
Issue Two, "The Dark Lord, The Forces of the Empire," Darth Vader ....$5–$10
Issue Three, "The mysteries of Yoda, the indignities of Artoo Detoo" ....$5–$10
Issue Four, "AT-AT attack, the magic factory" ....$5–$10
Issue Five, "Han Solo—Hero and Scoundrel," laser weapons ....$10–$15

Enterprise Spotlight
#4, Star Wars special ....$3–$5

Entertainment Weekly
January 10, 1997, Remaking Star Wars, Luke Skywalker cover ....$5–$10

Eppo Dutch comic fan magazine.

No. 11, 1983, Star Wars cover art and comics..........$5–$8

No. 22, 1983, Jedi cover and comics......................$5–$10

No. 32, 1983, Jedi cover art and comics.................$5–$10

Famous Monsters

No. 137, September 1977, Star Wars special issue...$15–$25

No. 138, Star Wars cover....................................$10–$15

No. 140, Star Wars article.....................................$5–$10

No. 142, Darth Vader cover................................$10–$15

No. 145, Empire article...$5–$8

No. 147, Star Wars cover....................................$10–$15

No. 148, Darth Vader cover................................$10–$15

No. 153, David Prowse interview............................$5–$8

No. 156, Empire cover...$10–$15

No. 165, Empire Strikes Back special issue..........$15–$20

No. 166, Empire cover...$10–$15

No. 167, Empire cover...$10–$15

No. 174, Star Wars cover....................................$10–$15

No. 177, Yoda cover...$10–$15

No. 190, Empire cover...$10–$15

Movie Aliens, special reprints Famous Monsters articles. Darth Vader cover..$10–$15

Fantascene Fantascene Productions.

No. 3, 1977, "The Star Wars," an article on the technical aspects of the film..$10–$15

Fantastic Films Blake Publishing.

Vol. 1, No. 1, April 1978, Star Wars, "Let the Wookiee Win," "The Ships of Star Wars," "Interview with Rick Baker" and "Animating the Death Star Trench"...$15–$20

Vol. 1, No. 3, May 1978, the latest on behind the scenes during the making of Star Wars.............................$6–$10

Vol. 1, No. 8, April 1979, "Star Wars Strikes Back," news on sequel..$5–$8

Vol. 2, No. 2, June 1979, Star Wars: "One last time down the death trench" with never before seen photos.......$5–$8

Vol. 3, No. 2, July 1980, "An interview with Larry Kasdan, the screenwriter for Empire Strikes Back," "An interview with special effects photographer Dennis Muren"...$5–$8

Vol. 3, No. 3, September 1980, "Gary Kurtz Interviewed," the producer of Star Wars and Empire Strikes Back, a Wookiee on the cover.................................$5–$8

Vol. 3, No. 4, October 1980, "The Empire Talks Back," "Painting the Empire," Yoda on the cover.............$5–$10

Vol. 3, No. 5, December 1980, "Speculation concerning the future history of the Star Wars saga," clone wars explained..$5–$8

Vol. 3, No. 7, February 1981, "From Star Wars to Empire," "The Weapons of Star Wars," "Rich Baker," "Animating the Death Star Trench," "The Best of Fantastic Films"..$5–$8

Vol. 3, No. 8, April 1981, part two of "From Star Wars to Empire," "The mystery behind Darth Vader's prothetic armor"...$5–$8

Vol. 3, No. 9, June 1981, "Star Wars comes to radio," illustrated cover of characters making radio program.........$5–$8

Vol. 4, No. 1, August 1981, "The Voice of Vader," "Nevana Limited," "From Star Wars to Empire"......$5–$8

Vol. 4, No. 4, April 1982, "From Star Wars to Empire to Revenge of the Jedi"..$5–$8

Vol. 5, No. 2, "Revenge of the Jedi." Partial cover...$5–$8

Vol. 5, No. 3, Return of the Jedi. Cover................$5–$10

Vol. 6, No. 4, Return article and cover...................$5–$10

Vol. 6, No. 5, Return of the Jedi. Cover.................$5–$10

Fantasy Film Preview

1977, special effects...$5–$6

Fantasy Modeling

#6, Star Wars miniature models...............................$4–$6

Film Review (British).

June 1980, "Star Wars Rage Again Against the Empire." Cover...$4–$8

July 1980, "More Photos From the Empire Strikes Back." 1/4 cover..$4–$8

August 1980, "Carrie Fisher and Mark Hamill Talk About Their Roles in Empire"..$4–$8

July 1983, "Star Wars—The Final Force Filled Phase"...$4–$8

Films and Filming Hansom books, London.

Vol. 23, No. 11, August 1977, preview of Star Wars...$6–$10

Finescale Modeler

No. 43, Summer 1983, Jedi diorama cover.............$4–$5

Fortune

October 6, 1980, The Empire pays off..................$5–$10

Future The magazine of science adventure, Future Magazine, Inc., New York.

No. 1, April 1978, advertising posters of Star Wars...$4–$8

No. 19, Empire preview...$4–$8

No. 20, Empire cover and article...............................$4–$8

Gateways

#6, Star Wars role-playing game...............................$3–$5

Hollywood Studio Magazine D. Denny Publisher.

Vol. 12, No. 5, June 1978, "New 15 million Star Trek movie," "Star Wars, a sequel"................................$6–$10

Hot Dog

#17, 1983, article on Star Wars action figures...........$3–$4

House of Hammer (British).

#13, article..$4–$8

#16, articles plus poster..$5–$10

Kuifje (Belgian).

Vol. 38, No. 5, Return of the Jedi issue....................$4–$8

LA Times

June 14, 1977, George Lucas on Opening Night......$5–$8

Ladies Home Journal

September 1983, contains article entitled "Jedimania: Why We Love Those Star Warriors".......................$4–$6

L'ecran Fantastique (French).

No. 13, Empire Strikes Back issue.......................$10–$15

No. 31, Jedi cover....................................$10–$15
No. 33, Empire Strikes Back cover (special effects)..........
....$10–$15
No. 37, Return of the Jedi cover...........................$10–$15
No. 38, Return of the Jedi cover...........................$10–$15
No. 86, 10th Anniversary article ....$5–$10

L'Express (French).
No. 1519, August 23, 1980, cover story, "La Guerre Pour Rire," Star Wars II..$10–$15

Life
Vol. 4, No. 1, January 1981, features Yoda on cover, title: "The Year in Pictures" ....$25–$35
Vol. 6, No. 6, June 1983, article: "George Lucas: A Man and His Empire" ....$5–$10

Look-In (British).
The Junior TV Times, June 4, 1983, Return of the Jedi. Cover, articles, poster...$4–$8

Mad
No. 196, January 1978, "Star Bores," Mad plot synopsis
....$10–$15
No. 197, March 1979, "A 'Mad' Look at Star Wars"........
....$10–$15
No. 203, December 1979, "The Mad Star Wars Musical"
....$15–$20
No. 220, January 1981, "The Empire Strikes Out"..........
....$10–$15
No. 230, April 1982, "The Star Wars Log—Mad's version of Lucas's personal log"...$5–$10
Mad Superspecial, Summer 1983, Star Wars spoofs ....
....$5–$10
No. 242, October 1983, "Star Bores—Rehash of the Jedi"
....$5–$10

Mad Movies (French).
No. 20, 1980, Empire Strikes Back cover ....$5–$10

Mediascene Preview Supergraphics.
Vol. 1, No. 22, November 1976, the first Star Wars feature news, color cover and center spread art ....$15–$20
Vol. 2, No. 4, August 1980, The Empire Strikes Back, an interview with Mark Hamill, a profile of Harrison Ellenshaw, creator of unknown worlds...........................$8–$12
Vol. 2, No. 11, "Darth Vader returns with a new ally, Boba Fett" and new costume designs ....$6–$10
Vol. 3, No. 2, Star Wars interview with Brian Johnson, special effects ....$4–$8

Midnight Marquee
#29, Yoda cover, Empire review ....$5–$10

Military Modeler
Vol. 7, No. 11, November 1980, cover photograph of Millennium Falcon, "Han Solo's Millennium Falcon"......$4–$6

Modesto Bee
June 5, 1977, Star Wars ....$5–$10

Movie Monsters
Vol. 1, No. 3, Fall 1981, Darth and Bounty Hunters on cover, article entitled "Star Wars: The Legend of Darth Vader"..$5–$10

Muppet Magazine
Vol. 1, No. 3, Summer 1983, cover features Kermit as Luke, Gonzo as Darth, Piggy as Leia. Article: "Super Star War: Battle of the Space Heroes" ....$4–$6

National Enquirer
June 21, 1983, cover photograph of stolen shuttle scene from Return of the Jedi; contains article, "Top Psychiatrists Explain the Amazing Appeal of Return of the Jedi"
....$4–$6

Newsweek Newsweek, Inc.
Vol. 89, No. 22, May 30, 1977, "Fun in space," a review of Star Wars...$30–$40

New Voyager (British).
No. 4, Summer 1983, Jedi articles...........................$3–$5

New Yorker
January 6, 1997, Why the Force is still with us. Lucas interview. Interior article ....$3–$6

NY Times
December 20, 1980, The saga beyond Star Wars.....$3–$5

Official 20th Anniversary Commemorative Magazine Topps, 1997.
Newsstand version, flat ink "Star Wars" logo ....$6–$10
Collector's version, gold foil "Star Wars" logo. Originally came bagged with three trading cards ....$15–$25
Special collector's version, same as collector's version but with blue foil "Star Wars." One per case ....$50–$60

Official 20th Anniversary Poster Magazine Topps, 1997.
Star Wars Heroes ....$4–$6
Star Wars Villains ....$4–$6

Orbit (Dutch).
No. 13, Winter 1981, Empire cover and articles....$5–$10

Orbit and SF Terra Presenteren Return of the Jedi. Dutch collaboration between two magazines to publish a Return of the Jedi special issue.
Each ....$5–$10

People

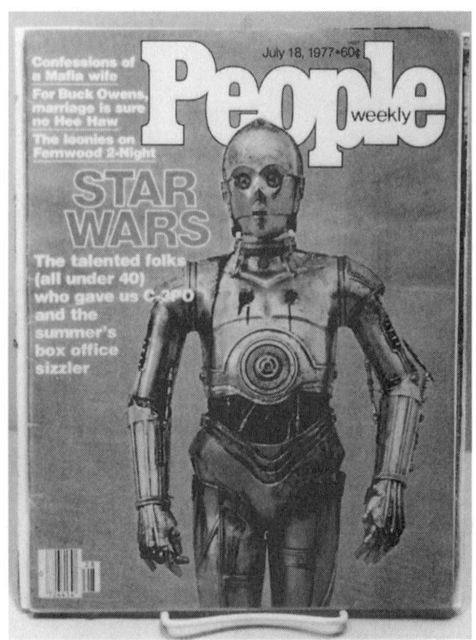

***People,* July 18, 1977, issue**

July 18, 1977, contains article entitled "The Talented Folks Who Gave Us C-3PO and the Summer's Box Office Sizzler," with photographs ....$5–$10

Vol. 8, No. 26, "The 25 Most Intriguing People of 1977," R2-D2 on cover, "The Shyest Guy in Hollywood Creates 'Star Wars' " ....$5–$10

July 7, 1980, Empire cover and article ....$10–$15

June 6, 1983, cover shows Carrie Fisher from Return of the Jedi..$10–$15

Vol. 19, No. 24, June 20, 1983, Darth Vader on cover, "Match Wits with the Jedi Quiz Kid" ....$10–$15

Vol. 16, No. 9, August 31, 1981, Mark Hamill and Yoda on cover, story on Mark Hamill ....$10–$15

August 14, 1978, contains article about Carrie Fisher entitled "Star Wars Strikes Again," cover photo shows Carrie and Darth Vader ....$10–$15

June 9, 1980, contains article entitled "Star Wars Strikes Back," cover shows Yoda.......................................$5–$10

February 3, 1997, "The Force Goes On," Star Wars and its stars after 20 years, interior article ....$5–$8

Photoplay (British).

January 1978, Star Wars cover...........................$10–$15

February 1978, Star Wars cover..........................$10–$15

June 1980, Empire Strikes Back cover................$10–$15

Pizzaz

#1, R2-D2 and C-3PO on cover ....$5–$10

Poster Monthlies—Star Wars Paradise Press. Magazine folded into poster. Interviews, stories, inside looks at production and special effects.

No. 1, R2-D2 and C-3PO, plus the stories of the stars........ ....$5–$10

No. 2, Darth Vader, plus how the dogfights were made...... ....$5–$10

No. 3, R2-D2 and C-3PO in the Death Star, plus Han Solo, rogue space pilot..$5–$10

No. 4, Chewbacca, plus soldiers of the Empire and the building of R2-D2...$5–$10

No. 5, Darth Vader, portrait of evil, plus inside stories of Chewbacca and Tarkin ....$5–$10

No. 6, C-3PO, plus the secrets of Artoo Detoo and the spaceships ....$5–$10

No. 7, R2-D2, plus the Droids of Star Wars...........$5–$10

No. 8, Imperial Stormtrooper, plus Ben Kenobi, man or legend, also space travel secrets ....$5–$10

No. 9, the Dark Lord, plus the brains of the Droids ....$5–$10

No. 10, Star Wars montage, plus what it takes to be a space pilot and the return of evil ....$5–$10

No. 11, R2-D2, plus the men behind the masks ....$6–$12

No. 12, space dogfight, plus the Cantina aliens and the Soundmaster ....$6–$12

No. 13, Luke and C-3PO, plus the shooting of Star Wars and the model squad..$6–$12

No. 14, attacking the Death Star, plus the machines that made the lines move ....$6–$12

No. 15, C-3PO, plus "Empires latest" and the Orbiter 102 Space Freighter..$10–$15

No. 16, R2-D2 with C-3PO, plus the Star Wars quiz and fan club facts...$15–$20

Premiere

February 1997, Star Wars Anniversary Special; article ....$3–$5

Questar William Wilson Publisher.

No. 1 (c. 1978), "The Triumph of Star Wars," "Close Encounters with Star Wars"......................................$10–$15

No. 8, August 1980, cover story, "The Making of an Empire: Star Wars Returns" ....$10–$15

***Questar,* August 1980, issue**

Reel Fantasy

#1, Star Wars issue ....$5–$10

Return of the Jedi Giant Collector's Compendium Magazine with poster and stories on production and the actors.

Each ....$5–$10

Return of the Jedi Poster Book Paradise Press.

#1 ....$5–$10

#2 ....$5–$10

#3 ....$5–$10

#4 ....$5–$10

Review

Vol. 2, No. 14, interview with Billy Dee Williams, Rogue's eye view of Star Wars Adventure ....$4–$8

Vol. 2, No. 12, double-length interview with Richard Marquand, Luke and Leia on cover ....$5–$10

Rolling Stone

August 25, 1977, The Force Behind George Lucas........... ....$10–$15

August 12, 1980, The Empire Strikes Back ....$10–$15

No. 322, July 24, 1980, cover features Luke, Leia, Han and Lando in street clothes, article entitled, "Slaves to (of) the Empire" ....$10–$15

No. 400/401, Darth Vader, Jedi monsters and Princess Leia on cover, "George Lucas: The Rolling Stone Interview," "Space Cadet: A Few Words with Carrie Fisher" .... $15–$25

Science and Fantasy R. Finton, publisher.

No date, interviews with the stars of Star Wars and an article on the music .... $4–$6

Science Fiction, Horror and Fantasy Douglas Wright Publishing, Los Angeles, CA.

Vol. 1, No. 1, Star Wars collector edition, Fall 1977, the making of Star Wars: the secrets behind the special effects, official blueprints, discussions with all the main characters .... $5–$10

Sci-Fi Entertainment

February 1997, Star Wars cover .... $5–$10

Sci-Fi Universe

July 1994, The Next Star Wars Trilogy; cover story for premiere issue .... $6–$10

November 1995, Star Wars Lives cover .... $5–$8

Scintillation The magazine of science fiction people, Carl Bennet, publisher.

No. 13, June 1977, "George Lucas brings the excitement back" .... $6–$10

Screen Superstars

#8, 1977, Star Wars issue .... $5–$10

Seventeen

March 19, 1983, interview on location .... $4–$6

SFTV

#7, Star Wars costume article .... $3–$5

Space Wars

October 1977, Star Wars .... $5–$8

June 1978, Star Wars, Close Encounters comparison .... $4–$6

Star Blaster

Vol. 1, #2, article on Droids; Darth cover .... $5–$8

Starblazer

December 1986, special issue; Vader cover .... $5–$8

Starburst (British).

#1, February 1978, Star Wars cover .... $20–$25

#2, "3PO Unmasked" article .... $10–$15

#3, Star Wars article .... $10–$15

#8, Empire Strikes Back .... $15–$20

#22, Empire .... $10–$15

#23, Empire articles plus poster .... $8–$10

#24, Star Wars interviews .... $8–$10

#25, Empire interview .... $8–$10

#26, Empire special effects .... $8–$10

#43, Star Wars article .... $8–$10

#58, Jedi articles .... $8–$10

#59, Jedi articles .... $8–$10

#60, C-3PO .... $8–$10

#61, Carrie Fisher interview .... $8–$10

#93, Return of the Jedi video .... $5–$8

#208, Stormtrooper cover .... $5–$8

#223, Lucas interview, Darth Vader cover .... $5–$8

#225, Present and future of Star Wars article .... $5–$8

Winter Special 1987, Star Tours and 10th Anniversary articles .... $10–$15

Classic Sci-Fi Special, 1993, Star Wars cover .... $8–$10

Outer Space Special, 1996, Special Edition article, partial cover .... $8–$10

Star Encounters

Vol. 1, #1, April 1978, Making of Star Wars article .... $5–$10

Starfix (French).

1980, Return of the Jedi special issue .... $5–$10

Star Force

Vol. 1, No. 2, October 1980, features Star Wars, Empire Strikes Back and other creepy crawlies .... $5–$8

***Starburst* (British), February 1978 issue**

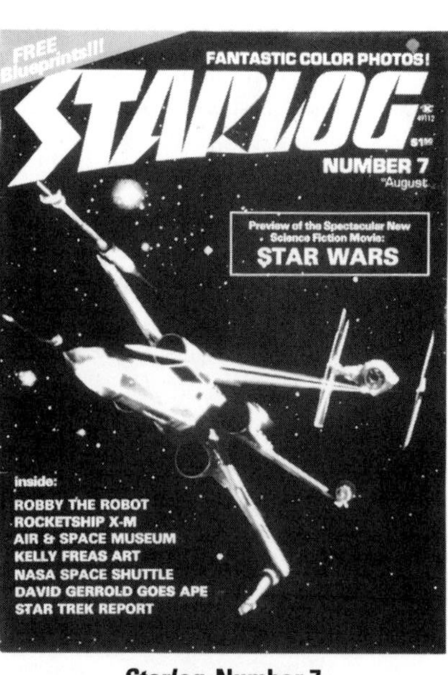

***Starlog*, Number 7**

Vol. 2, No. 3, August 1981, Darth Vader, Lando and scenes from Empire Strikes Back on cover, contains article "Star Wars III: The Sci-Fi Success Story Continues" ... .$5–$10

October 1981, Revenge of the Jedi ....$5–$10

Starlog

#7, features an X-Wing fighter and a TIE fighter on cover. ....$25–$35

#16, 1978, "Invisible Visions of Star Wars" article ....$5–$10

#17, Miniature explosion and R. McQuarrie articles ....$5–$10

#19, 1979, Star Wars TV special ....$5–$10

#19, Cantina creatures on cover, Star Wars TV special ....$5–$10

#31, ESB on cover, report on movie inside ....$5–$10

#35, Darth Vader on cover ....$5–$10

#36, Vader and Boba Fett on cover ....$5–$10

#37, Millennium Falcon on cover ....$5–$10

#40, features Luke Skywalker and Yoda on cover ....$5–$10

#41, cover photograph of Luke and Yoda on Dagobah, interview with Mark Hamill ....$5–$10

#48, features Luke Skywalker and Yoda on cover ..$5–$10

#50, features Boba Fett on cover ....$5–$10

#51, features Luke Skywalker on cover ....$5–$10

#56, features Darth Vader on cover ....$5–$10

#65, cover photograph of Luke with lightsaber; interview with Mark Hamill, "I Was Mark Hamill's Stand-In" ....$5–$10

#69, features Return of the Jedi cast on cover ....$5–$10

#71, June 1983, assorted articles on Return of the Jedi, interviews with Carrie Fisher and Richard Marquand, cover photograph of Han, Luke and Leia ....$5–$10

#72, Mark Hamill interview ....$5–$8

#74, Jedi creature manufacture ....$5–$8

#76, preview of Jedi ....$5–$8

#80, Jedi special effects, cover ....$5–$10

#82, Jedi effects, Emperor interview ....$5–$8

#84, Frank Oz on Yoda ....$5–$8

#86, Jedi special effects ....$5–$8

#90, Ewok Adventure ....$5–$8

#93, Jedi bike special effects ....$5–$8

#94, Jedi special effects ....$5–$8

#96, Peter Cushing interview ....$5–$8

#99, C-3PO cover ....$5–$8

#100, Lucas interview ....$5–$8

#104, Peter Mayhew article, Chewbacca cover ....$5–$10

#115, Star Tours ....$5–$8

#118, Lucas/Star Tours cover ....$5–$8

#120, Star Wars 10th Anniversary Special, cover ....$10–$15

#127, Lucas interview ....$5–$8

Starlog Poster Magazine

Vol. 2, 1984, contains ten 16″ × 21″ color posters, includes close-up of Darth Vader ....$5–$8

Starlog Star Wars Technical Journals, 1996. 1997 reprints contained updated information from the Special Edition movie releases. No difference in value.

Vol. 1 ....$10–$12

Vol. 2 ....$10–$12

Vol. 3 ....$10–$12

Star Warp

April 1978, includes posters ....$4–$5

Star Wars Compendium

World of "Star Wars"—A Compendium of Fact and Fantasy from Star Wars and The Empire Strikes Back, Paradise Press, 1981 ....$6–$10

Vol. II, June 1981, compilation of information on the Star Wars poster book (minus the posters) ....$6–$10

Vol. III, June 1982, reset of the poster book on The Empire Strikes Back ....$5–$8

Star Wars Fan Club Magazines—Original Bantha Tracks, 1977–1987. Most were simple flyer formats of four to eight pages.

Issues 1–35, (except 34) ....$5–$10

Issue 34, included soundtrack record ....$10–$15

Star Wars Fan Club Magazines—Current Fan Clubs, Inc. Thin magazine with authorized articles. Early issues were rag paper with slick covers. Later issues have slick interior pages.

Lucasfilm Fan Club (original name) issues 1–22, Star Wars covers (each) ....$8–$15

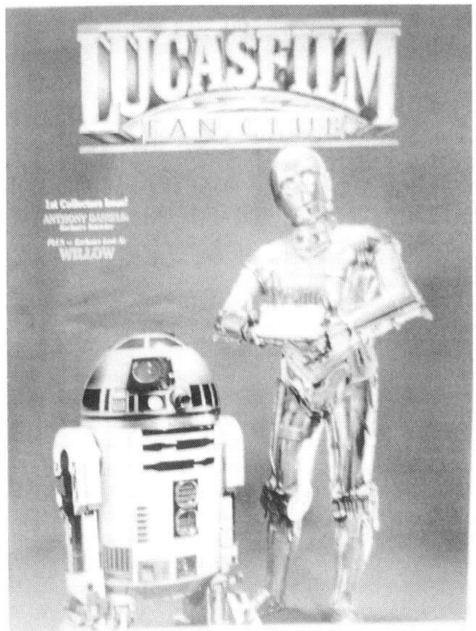

Lucasfilm Fan Club **magazine**

Lucasfilm Fan Club, other covers (each) ....$4–$6

Star Wars Insider issues 23 to present, (each) ....$5–$10

Star Wars Galaxy Magazine Topps, 1994 to present. Articles on the movies and collecting, plus original stories and comics.

#1 ....$25–$35

#2 ....$20–$25

#3 .... $20–$25
#4 .... $10–$15
#5 .... $10–$15
#6 .... $10–$15
#7 .... $10–$15
#8 .... $10–$15
#9 .... $5–$10
#10 .... $5–$10
#11 .... $5–$10

Star Wars Newspaper Starfleet Productions, Inc., publisher.
1977 .... $5–$10

Star Wars Spectacular A Warren Magazine, special edition, issue devoted to the motion picture, articles on robots, special effects, a tribute to George Lucas.
Each .... $10–$15

Star Wars, The Making of the World's Greatest Movie Paradise Press, Inc., 1977, an entire magazine devoted to the making of Star Wars, with special effects, who's who in Star Wars.
Each .... $10–$15

Time, **May 19, 1983, issue**

Stripschrift (Dutch).
No. 142, December 1980, Empire cover and article on McQuarrie artwork .... $5–$10

Time Magazine R. Davidson Publishing.
Vol. 109, No. 22, May 30, 1977, "The Year's Best Movie-Star Wars," profile of the movie and stars .... $20–$30
Vol. 115, No. 20, May 19, 1980, "The Empire Strikes Back" profiles of the movie, behind-the-scenes production and George Lucas .... $6–$12
Vol. 121, No. 21, May 23, 1983, "Star Wars III: The Return of the Jedi," profiles of the movie and its stars, a second article profiles George Lucas .... $6–$12
February 10, 1997, The Return of Star Wars cover .... $6–$10

True—UFOs and Outer Space Quarterly
No. 19, Fall 1980, AT-ATs on cover, story: "The Empire Strikes Back . . . But Not Out!" .... $4–$5

US
Vol. 4, No. 7, July 22, 1980, cover story: "The Good Guys of Star Wars" .... $10–$15
Vol. 8, No. 13, June 20, 1983, cover photograph and articles on Return of the Jedi .... $10–$15

Variety
February 3, 1997, "Star Wars in Outer Space" lead article .... $10–$15

Videofilmmagazine (Dutch).
No. 3, 1986, Return of the Jedi cover art and article .... $5–$10

Video Games
Vol. 2, No. 2 .... $4–$5

Videogaming Illustrated
February 1983, cover illustration of Darth Vader. Articles: "Star Wars Spectacular: First Look at the Jedi Arena Videogame," "Revenge of the Jedi Film and Videogame," "Darth Vader Interviewed" .... $4–$5

Weird Worlds
#6, 1980, Scholastic Magazine. Vader cover. Empire article .... $5–$8

MODELS

All of the models in this section are regular mass-produced kits made by companies for mass-market sale. Not included are homemade (garage) resin kits or enhancement kits for regular models, both of which can be produced in very small quantities. Models are in truly collectible condition only unbuilt, in the original box with all small pieces, instructions and unapplied decals. While there are a few collectors who appreciate a well-built kit enough to pay a premium for it, they are few and far between, and the detailing involved in turning a model into a truly desirable piece could easily put the piece into the category of artwork rather than models. For finished ship and figural representations designed for display (as opposed to kits), see ACTION FIGURES, HOUSEWARES and PEWTER sections of this book.

This section is organized alphabetically by manufacturer.

Assorted Star Wars models

ESTES

Flying Models, 1977. These were actual flying rocket kits built in the shape of the ship or character. Models were originally packaged in plastic bags with color headers and a color cover sheet.

R2-D2 .... $30–$40

Estes, flying models

TIE Fighter...$35–$50
X-Wing...$35–$50

Deluxe Flying Models, 1977. Included not only rocket but complete launching kit. Came boxed.

Proton Torpedo ....$40–$50
R2-D2...$40–$50
X-Wing, starter set..$50–$65
X-Wing...$75–$85

Flying Models, 1993 to present. Reissues of some of this company's original models plus some new editions.

Darth Vader TIE ....$17–$28
Death Star...$17–$28
R2-D2, two different ....$17–$28
TIE Fighter...$17–$28
X-Wing...$17–$28

Deluxe Kits, 1993 to present.

A-Wing...$35–$40
Death Star...$35–$40
Y-Wing...$35–$40
X-Wing...$35–$40
X-Wing, advanced kit......................................$90–$100

Gliders, 1997.

A-Wing ....$10–$12
Star Destroyer...$10–$12
X-Wing ....$10–$12
Y-Wing ....$10–$12

Propeller Driven Models, 1997 (Estes/Cox).

Darth TIE...$50–$60
Snowspeeder ....$50–$60
X-Wing ....$20–$30
X-Wing, deluxe..$50–$60
X-Wing and TIE set ....$90–$100
X-Wing and Death Star set...........................$125–$150

MPC

1977–1984. MPC was originally the major model licensee for the Star Wars saga. Box art showed color picture of the subject and movie logo. Movie logos were often updated to depict the most recent film. Models in earlier boxes tend to be slightly more valuable, though in all cases except the Millennium Falcon (whose original production run had lights), the model remained the same. At one time many of these models were worth considerably more than their present value, but reissues made by Ertl (see below) after they purchased MPC have caused devaluation of the originals. Essentially identical kits were issued in foreign countries by Kenner and its affiliates, notably Airfix, Denys Fisher, Lily Ledy and Meccano. Values on these in the United States are generally slightly higher than their U.S. counterparts.

AT-AT, 1982 ....$20–$30
Battle on Ice Planet Hoth, 1982; diorama ....$20–$30
C-3PO, 1977; two box sizes ....$35–$50
Darth Vader Action Model, 1978; bust with lights and sound ....$75–$100
Darth Vader's TIE Fighter, 1977; two box sizes.......$20–$30
Darth Vader, 1979; full figure.................................$20–$30
Darth Vader Van, 1979...$30–$45
Encounter with Yoda on Dagobah, 1982; diorama ....$20–$30
Jabba the Hutt Throne Room, 1983; diorama........$20–$30
Luke Skywalker Van, 1977 ....$30–$45
Millennium Falcon, 1977; lighted version ....$100–$125
Millennium Falcon, 1982; no lights ....$20–$30
R2-D2, 1977; two box sizes....................................$35–$50
R2-D2 Van, 1977 ....$30–$45
Shuttle Tyderium, 1983 ....$20–$30
Slave I, 1982 ....$20–$30

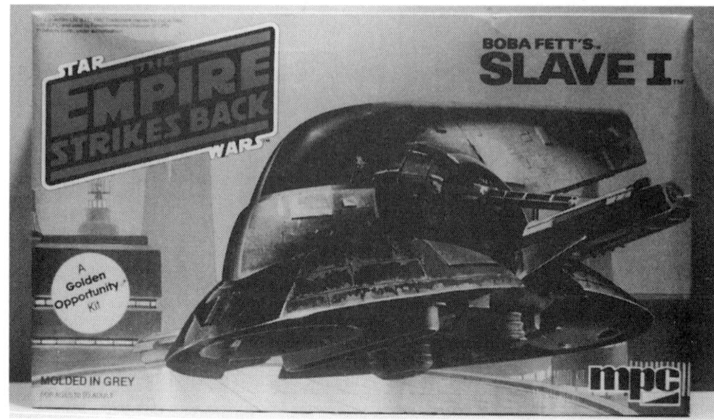

Original MPC Slave I kit

Snowspeeder, 1980 ....$20–$30
Speeder Bike Vehicle, 1983....................................$25–$35
Star Destroyer, 1980 ....$20–$30

MPC, Speeder Bike Mirr-A-Kit

X-Wing Fighter, 1982 .... $20–$30

Mirr-A-Kits, 1984. Small, easy snap-kits where half a vehicle is affixed to a mirror surface to give the illusion of a whole ship. Came in 4½″ × 5½″ header boxes showing color artwork of subject.

- **AT-ST** .... $15–$25
- **Shuttle Tyderium** .... $15–$25
- **Speeder Bike** .... $15–$25
- **TIE Interceptor** .... $15–$25
- **Y-Wing** .... $15–$25
- **X-Wing** .... $15–$25

Snap-Kits, 1983. Small, easily built kits requiring no glue. These come in 7″ × 9½″ boxes with box art similar to the larger models.

- **AT-ST,** 6″ high (Scout Walker) .... $15–$25
- **A-Wing Fighter** .... $15–$25
- **B-Wing Fighter** .... $20–$30
- **TIE Interceptor** .... $15–$25
- **X-Wing Fighter** .... $15–$25
- **Y-Wing** .... $15–$25
- **Space Vehicle set (Airfix, U.K. only),** combined set of A-Wing, B-Wing, TIE Interceptor and X-Wing Snap-Kits .... $75–$85

Structor Walkers, 1984. Simple snap-kits included wind-up motor. Completed model "walked." Came in 5½″ × 8″ header boxes showing color artwork of subject in action pose.

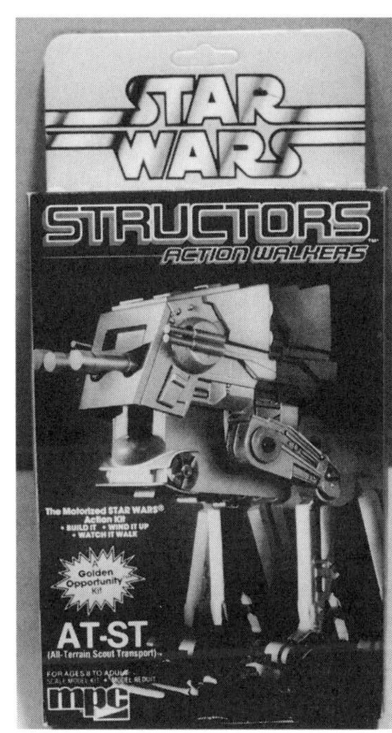

MPC, AT-ST Structors Action Walker

- **AT-AT,** 4½″ high .... $25–$35
- **AT-ST,** 4½″ high .... $25–$35
- **C-3PO,** 4¾″ tall .... $25–$35

MPC/ERTL (OR) AMC/ERTL

1989 to present. Both of these companies' logos have been used on recent kits. Reissues of older MPC kits are noted. Early reissue packaging was identical to old MPC Jedi packaging, but with new company logo. Later original package art was created for both reissue and new models. It should be noted that even the "new" models in this line utilize the molds from the originals.

AT-AT, reissue .... $15–$20
Battle on Hoth, diorama; reissue .... $10–$15
Darth Vader, full figure; reissue .... $15–$20
Darth Vader TIE Fighter .... $10–$15
Darth Vader TIE Fighter Flight Display .... $15–$20
Encounter with Yoda, diorama; reissue .... $10–$15
Jabba's Throne Room, diorama; reissue .... $10–$15
Millennium Falcon, no lights; reissue .... $15–$20
Millennium Falcon Cut-Away .... $25–$30

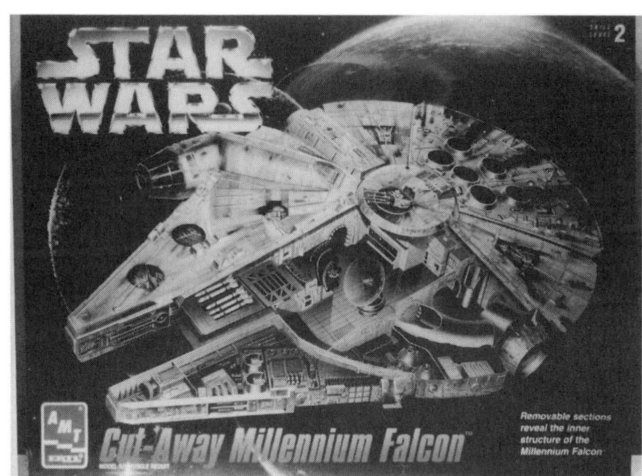

MPC/Ertl, Cut-Away Millennium Falcon model kit

Rebel Base, diorama; reissue .... $10–$15
Shuttle Tydirium, reissue .... $10–$15
Slave I, reissue .... $10–$15
Snowspeeder, reissue .... $15–$20
Speeder Bike, reissue .... $15–$20
Star Destroyer, reissue .... $10–$15
Star Destroyer with Fiber Optics .... $40–$50
X-Wing, reissue .... $10–$15
X-Wing Flight Display .... $15–$20
Snap Kits

- **AT-ST,** reissue .... $10–$15
- **A-Wing,** reissue .... $10–$15
- **Gold B-Wing** .... $30–$35
- **Gold TIE Interceptor** .... $30–$35
- **Gold X-Wing** .... $30–$35
- **TIE Interceptor,** reissue .... $10–$15
- **X-Wing,** reissue .... $10–$15

MPC/Ertl, X-Wing Flight Display model kit

Y-Wing, reissue ....$10–$15
Three-Ship set, B-Wing, TIE Interceptor and X-Wing...... ....$20–$25

Vinyl Kits These are models aimed at the more advanced modeler. Though vinyl kits typically have far fewer parts than the more familiar injection-molded kits, vinyl kits require more advanced skills in the form of trimming and painting. Because vinyl shows detail especially well, figural kits are often done in this material. Models come in boxes with photo of completed kit. All include bases.

Darth Vader ....$25–$30
Emperor....................$25–$30
Han Solo ....$25–$30

MPC/Ertl, Han Solo vinyl kit

Luke Skywalker....................$25–$30
Xizor....................$25–$30

POLYDATA

1995 to present. Pre-painted vinyl kits. Box has photo of completed model on one side and artwork of character on other. Window in side of box displays figure's head.

Emperor ....$20–$25
Luke....................$20–$25
Obi-Wan....................$20–$25
Princess Leia....................$20–$25

Polydata, Obi-Wan Kenobi vinyl kit

SCREAMIN'

1992 to present. Vinyl kits come in boxes with picture of completed kit on lid. Two different lines.

1/4 Scale Kits

Boba Fett ....$65–$75
C-3PO ....$65–$75

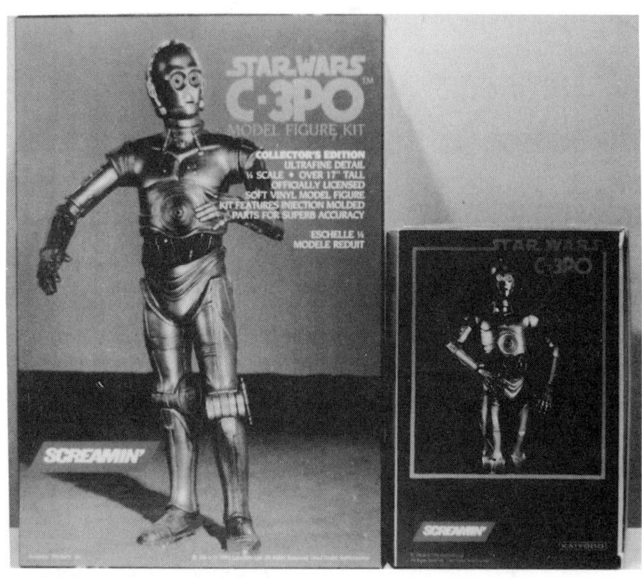

Screamin', C-3PO vinyl kit

Chewbacca .... $65–$75
Darth Vader .... $65–$75
Han Solo .... $65–$75
Luke Skywalker .... $65–$75
Stormtrooper .... $65–$75
Tusken Raider .... $65–$75
Yoda .... $65–$75

1/6 Scale Kits
Boba Fett .... $45–$55
C-3PO .... $45–$55
Darth Vader .... $45–$55
Han Solo .... $45–$55
Stormtrooper .... $45–$55

STEEL TEC (REMCO)

1995. Kits include over 1000 parts, mostly metal and tools. Box shows photo of completed kit.

Millennium Falcon .... $55–$60
X-Wing .... $35–$40

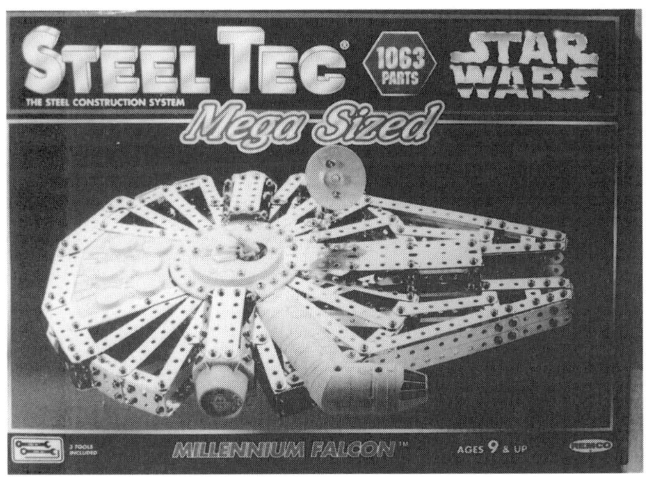

Steel Tec (Remco), Millennium Falcon kit

TAKARA

(Japan), 1977.

Model Kits Made of Cut-out Wood
Landspeeder .... $225–$350
R2-D2 .... $225–$350
TIE Fighter .... $225–$350
X-Wing .... $225–$350

Plastic Kits These are similar to MPC kits but sell for a premium in Takara packaging.
C-3PO .... $100–$150
Darth TIE .... $100–$150
R2-D2 .... $100–$150
X-Wing .... $100–$150

TSUKUDA

(Japan), 1982. Very small scale metal model kits. Most are two-vehicle sets. Box art depicts action scenes with vehicles and Empire logo.

NOTE: Unlicensed versions of these kits have been made in Europe, but counterfeit kits do not come boxed.

Tsukuda, small-scale metal kit

AT-AT and Snowspeeder .... $100–$225
AT-ST and Snowspeeder .... $100–$225
Millennium Falcon and Slave I .... $100–$225
Star Destroyer, with very tiny Millennium Falcon and Rebel ship .... $100–$225
TIE Fighter and X-Wing .... $100–$225

MUSIC

MUSIC BOOKS

FOX FANFARE MUSIC (JOHN WILLIAMS)

Star Wars, 1977. Includes "Main Title" piano solo and sketch score, "Princess Leia's Theme" and "Cantina Band." Numerous pictures with extensive outlines.

Per book..$15–$20

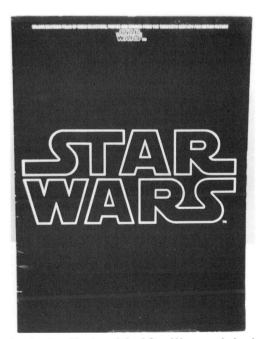

Fox Fanfare Music, original Star Wars music book

Star Wars Picture Book Twenty-six pages, color cover.

Per book ....$10–$15

The Empire Strikes Back, 1980. "Star Wars" (main theme), "The Imperial March" (Darth Vader's theme), "Yoda's Theme," "Han Solo and the Princess," "May the Force Be With You" and "Finale." Numerous photos.

Per book ....$10–$15

Star Wars Saga Book One hundred pages, black cover, black-and-white interior photos.

Per book..$15–$20

WARNER BROTHERS MUSIC

Star Wars Trilogy Special Edition, 1997. Special Edition trilogy logo on front. Includes trilogy collage poster.

Per book..$15–$17

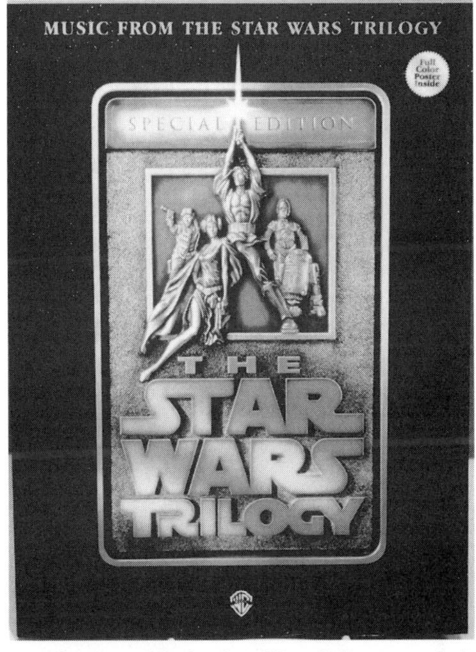

Warner Brothers Music, Star Wars Trilogy music book

SHEET MUSIC

FOX FANFARE MUSIC (JOHN WILLIAMS)

Star Wars, 1977. Main theme from movie. ....$3–$5

Princess Leia's Theme, 1977 ....$3–$5

Empire Strikes Back Medley, 1980. Darth Vader/Yoda's themes..$3–$5

Han Solo and the Princess, 1980 ....$3–$5

PARTY GOODS

Prices on party goods assume a complete package, if applicable, since the price on individual paper goods is negligible. Packaging is generally very basic, usually shrink-wrapping with either a sticker or simple header describing the product.

The section is organized alphabetically by type of item. For other paper products and plasticware, see HOUSEWARES section.

BALLOONS

ARIEL (BRITISH), 1979/83

Assorted characters and colors.

C-3PO .... $3–$6
R2-D2 .... $3–$6
Stormtrooper .... $3–$6
Darth Vader .... $3–$6
Millennium Falcon .... $3–$6
AT-AT .... $3–$6
Chewbacca .... $3–$6

DRAWING BOARD

1980, package of 10 character balloons packaged in plastic bag with color Empire logo and artwork .... $10–$15

1983, package of 10 character balloons in plastic bag with color Jedi logo and artwork .... $10–$15

1983, Ewok balloons, packages of 5 or 6. Packaged in plastic bag with Ewoks animated logo. Assorted colors .... $5–$10

BANNERS

DRAWING BOARD, 1981

"Happy Birthday," with characters off to sides. Small Empire logo below .... $10–$15

BLOWOUTS

DRAWING BOARD

1980/83 Darth Vader head at mouthpiece end, star design on streamer. Packaged in fours.

Empire packaging .... $10–$15
Jedi packaging .... $10–$15

1983 Packaged in fours.

Ewok animated packaging, Ewok on glider on mouthpiece .... $5–$10

CAKE DECORATING ACCESSORIES

See HOUSEWARES section.

CENTERPIECES

DRAWING BOARD

1980, die-cut color cardboard. Shows characters in Cloud City scene. 14″ tall. Packaged in paper envelope with color photo of product and Empire logo..............................$15–$20

Drawing Board, Empire Strikes Back table centerpiece

1983, die-cut color cardboard scene of Luke and Darth dueling. Jedi packaging..$10–$15

1983, die-cut color cardboard scene featuring Ewok animated characters. Packaging displays both Ewok and Jedi logos....... ....$10–$15

GIFT TAGS

DRAWING BOARD

1978, R2-D2 and C-3PO. Package of 5 self-sticking ....$3–$5

1978, 4 different Star Wars scenes on fold-over cards: Space Battle, Luke, Leia and Han with Star Wars logo, R2-D2 and C-3PO artwork, "A Gift for You," R2-D2 and C-3PO artwork, "Happy Birthday"; each ....$2–$4

1980, Cloud City with Empire characters on fold-over note card...$2–$4

1983, Luke and Darth dueling on fold-over card ....$2–$4

1983, Ewok (animated) on fold-over card ....$1–$3

HATS

DRAWING BOARD

1978, package of 8 open-top paper party hats with pointed front and back flange to resemble Darth Vader's helmet......... ....$20–$25

1981, package of 8 pointed paper party hats with color artwork of characters and Empire logo ....$15–$20

1983, package of 8 pointed paper party hats with color artwork of Luke and Vader dueling...............................$15–$20

1983, package of 8 pointed paper party hats with color artwork of animated Ewok with glider..........................$10–$15

INVITATIONS

DRAWING BOARD

1978, package of 8 die-cut cards shaped like R2-D2 ....$15–$20

Drawing Board, R2-D2 party invitations

1978, package of 8 greeting-card-style invitations picturing R2-D2 and C-3PO ....$15–$20

1978, package of 16 postcard-style invitations with R2-D2, C-3PO and Darth head ....$10–$15

1981, package of 8 greeting-card-style invitations with artwork of characters and Empire logo ....$10–$15
1981, package of 8 fold-out-style invitations with artwork of characters and Empire logo ....$10–$15
1983, package of 8 greeting-card-style invitations with artwork of Luke and Darth dueling ....$10–$15
1983, package of 8 greeting-card-style invitations with animated Ewok with glider ....$5–$10

HALLMARK (PARTY EXPRESS)
1997, package of 8 fold-out open invitations with die-cut photo of R2-D2 on cover and C-3PO inside ....$4–$10

NAME BADGES

DRAWING BOARD
1978, package of 16 with Darth Vader head on left-hand side ....$5–$10
1978, package of 16 with Star Wars logo in lower left-hand corner...$5–$10

Drawing Board, Star Wars napkins and cups

NAPKINS

DRAWING BOARD
1978 Package of 16. Artwork of R2-D2 and C-3PO.
Beverage size..$10–$15
Dinner size..$10–$15
1981 Package of 16. Artwork of Empire characters and logo.
Beverage size..$10–$15
Dinner size..$10–$15
1983 Package of 16. Artwork of Luke and Vader dueling.
Beverage size..$10–$15
Dinner size..$10–$15
1983 Package of 16. Artwork of Ewok.
Each ....$5–$10

HALLMARK (PARTY EXPRESS), 1997
Package of 16. White color artwork of Space Battle and Star Wars logo.
Beverage size..$2–$4
Dinner size..$3–$5

PACKAGE DECORATIONS

DRAWING BOARD, 1981
R2-D2...$5–$8
Yoda...$5–$8

HALLMARK (PARTY EXPRESS), 1997
Each package, 4 sheets of paper with 8 stickers each. Color photos of ships and Star Wars logo ....$2–$4

PAPER CUPS

NOTE: See also HOUSEWARES section for kitchen/bathroom style paper cups.

DEEKO (BRITISH), 1977
Package of 8, illustrated with Star Wars scenes ....$10–$15

DRAWING BOARD
1978, package of 8 with Star Wars motif and logo....$15–$20
1981, package of 8 with Empire characters and logo $10–$20
1983, package of 8 with Luke and Darth Vader dueling ....$10–$15
1983, package of 8 with animated Ewok ....$5–$10

HALLMARK (PARTY EXPRESS), 1997
Package of eight 7-ounce cups. Color artwork of Space Battle ....$3–$5

PAPER PLATES

DEEKO (BRITISH), 1997
Package of 8 with characters, ships and logo ....$20–$25

DRAWING BOARD, 1978
1978, package of 8, luncheon size (7″). Artwork of Darth Vader and Star Wars logo ....$15–$20
1978, package of 8, dinner size (9″). Artwork of R2-D2 and C-3PO with Star Wars logo.....................................$15–$20
1981, package of 8, luncheon size (7″). Artwork of Chewbacca and Empire logo ....$10–$15
1981, package of 8, dinner size (9″). Artwork of Chewbacca and Empire logo ....$10–$15

Drawing Board, Return of the Jedi paper plates and napkins

1983, package of 8, luncheon size (7″) and dinner size (9″). Artwork of Luke and Darth dueling. Each................$10–$15
1983, package of 8, luncheon size (7″) and dinner size (9″). Artwork from Ewok animated series ....$5–$10

HALLMARK (PARTY EXPRESS), 1997

Packages of 8. Color artwork of Space Battle with Vader head in background.
Luncheon size, 6¾″..$3–$6
Dinner size, 8¾″..$3–$6

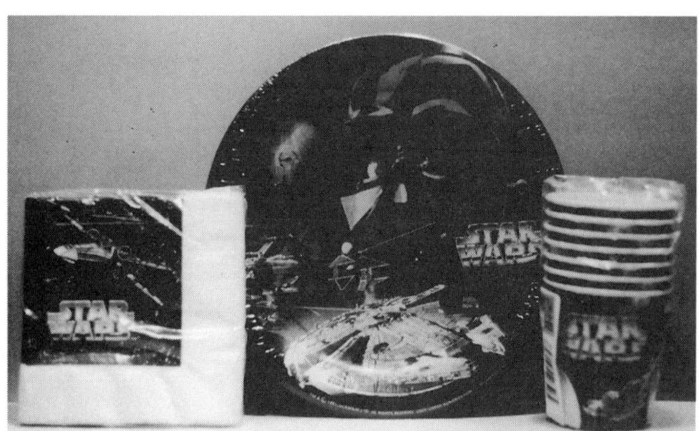

Hallmark (Party Express), Star Wars party goods

PARTY BAGS

DRAWING BOARD, 1983

Packages of eight
With artwork of Luke and Darth Vader dueling.....$10–$15
With artwork of animated Ewoks............................$5–$10

PLACE CARDS

DRAWING BOARD, 1978

Packages of eight.
With artwork of R2-D2 and C-3PO on left-hand side........ ....$5–$10

PAPER PLACE MATS

NOTE: See HOUSEWARES section for plastic mats.

DRAWING BOARD, 1978

Packages of eight.
Designed as maze decorated with Star Wars characters ....$15–$20

TABLE COVERS

DEEKO (BRITISH), 1978

Star Wars Space Battle design. Sold in packages of 3 ....$20–$25

DRAWING BOARD

1978, 60″ × 96″ paper with color artwork of C-3PO and R2-D2 with Star Wars logo.......................................$15–$20
1981, 60″ × 96″ paper with color artwork of characters in front of Cloud City scene..$10–$20
1983, 54″ × 96″ paper with color artwork of Luke and Darth Vader dueling...$10–$15
1983, 54″ × 96″ paper with color artwork of animated Ewoks with gliders...$5–$10

HALLMARK (PARTY EXPRESS)

1997, 54″ × 89¼″. White with blue and black ship artwork... ....$5–$10

THANK-YOU NOTES

DRAWING BOARD

1981, package of 8 pictures R2-D2 and says “Thanks” on cover, “From the bottom of my circuits” inside.........$15–$20

WRAPPING PAPER

DRAWING BOARD

1978, color artwork of Space Battle scenes. Rolls or sheets.... ....$15–$25

Drawing Board, assorted Star Wars wrapping paper

1978, color artwork of R2-D2 and C-3PO. Rolls or sheets..$15–$25

1978, color artwork of assorted characters. Rolls or sheets...$15–$25

1978, color photos of assorted scenes and logo. Rolls or sheets ....$15–$25

1981, color artwork of characters and city scene. Rolls or sheets ....$15–$20

1983, color artwork of Luke and Darth Vader. Rolls or sheets ....$10–$15

1983, set—2 sheets, tag, ribbon and bow ....$10–$15

1983, color artwork of animated Ewoks with gliders. Rolls or sheets ....$5–$10

PATCHES

As with several other categories of merchandise, patches are too easy to reproduce for them to accumulate much collectors' value. Though Lucasfilm has been diligent in the protection of its licensees, a well-made counterfeit patch is virtually indistinguishable from the original since virtually all mass-produced patches have minor variations in color and detail. This section is organized by manufacturer.

NOTE: Not included in this section are peripherally Star Wars-related patches that have been manufactured over the years, including Star Tours and Fan Club patches and those intended for internal promotions by licensees. Values on these follow the same general guidelines as all patches. Larger, more colorful, irregularly shaped and fully embroidered patches are more difficult to manufacture and are therefore more costly.

FACTORS ETC.

1977. Embroidered patches with iron-on backing. Patches were originally sold either blister-carded or loose, depending on the needs of the particular retailer.

"Brotherhood of Jedi Knights," 2″ × 3″ rectangular. Words and stylized lightsaber. Blue on white ....$4–$6

"Darth Vader Lives," 3″ circle. Words and Darth's head. White on black background. (Early versions of this patch had a spelling variation, Vadar instead of Vader. Neither version is appreciably more valuable.) ....$4–$6

"May the Force Be With You," 2″ × 3″ rectangular. Words only. White on black ....$4–$6

Star Wars, 2″ × 3″ rectangular. Outline logo. White on black ....$4–$6

Star Wars, 2″ × 3″ rectangular. Logo. Red, yellow, black and blue ....$4–$6

LUCASFILM FAN CLUB

1987.

Tenth Anniversary Star Wars, 4″ wide. "Star Wars" in yellow on shades of blue in center of circle. "The First Ten Years" on purple border around outside of circle. Side bars with "1977" and "1987" ....$6–$8

STAR WARS FAN CLUB

These embroidered patches were first made by the original Fan Club. Though this club disbanded, the current Lucasfilm Fan Club and others continued to produce the patches. All are embroidered and have iron-on backings.

NOTE: The "crew patches" are copies of the patches originally worn by the film crew of the movies. Though theoretically an original would be considerably more valuable, it would be difficult to authenticate. A "Revenge" crew patch similar to the "Return" patch was made and would be worth more still. However, all crew patches have been extensively duplicated.

Empire Strikes Back, 2″ × 3″ rectangular. White and red on black ....$4–$6

Factors Etc. Star Wars *(left)* and Fan Club Empire patches

Empire Strikes Back, "Crew patch." Darth Vader head surrounded by flames with logo on shield-shaped patch. Seven colors. 4 1/2" high. ....$9–$15
Return of the Jedi, logo. 2 1/2" × 4 1/4" rectangular. Red on black ....$4–$6
Return of the Jedi, "Crew patch." Yoda in circle surrounded by logo on rectangular background. Ten colors. 5 1/4" high...... ....$9–$15
Star Wars, logo. 2" × 3 3/4" rectangle. White on black ....$4–$6
Star Wars—A New Hope, figure in front of orange planet on light blue background. Triangular. 4 3/4" high............$6–$8

THINKING CAP COMPANY

Empire Strikes Back, Logo. 2 1/2" × 4" rectangular. White and red on black. Iron-on backing. Though designed to be applied to hats, this patch was also sold separately ....$4–$6
Star Wars/Rebel Forces, 2 3/4" round. Red with blue and gold embroidery. Designed for application to hats ....$4–$6

PEWTER

The figurines in this section were all designed strictly for display. For metal figurines designed for other purposes, see GAMES and TOYS AND CRAFTS. This section is organized alphabetically by manufacturer and then alphabetically by item.

FRANKLIN MINT

Vehicles all have separate black wood bases and have gold plate and colored glass crystal accents.

AT-AT .... $200–$225
Millennium Falcon .... $200–$225

HERITAGE/STAR TREK GALORE

1977/78. Figures are 1″ to 2″ in height. All but one of the figurines (Han Solo) was originally produced by Heritage. Star Trek Galore re-did all of the original Heritage figures and added the Han Solo figure. In addition to selling them strictly as figures, Star Trek Galore adapted a number of the pieces to different types of jewelry—key chains, charms, etc. Neither company was licensed, and when Twentieth Century Fox forced manufacturing to cease, most were destroyed. Figures were sold either painted or unpainted. No packaging.

Bantha Set, Bantha ridden by two Sand People. Sand People were removable but wouldn't stand alone .... $35–$45
C-3PO .... $10–$15
Chewbacca .... $15–$20
Darth Vader .... $15–$20
Han Solo .... $10–$15
Jawa .... $10–$15
Luke Skywalker .... $15–$20

(Left) **Rawcliffe and *(right)* smaller Heritage/Star Trek Galore pewter figures**

Obi-Wan Kenobi .... $15–$20
Princess Leia .... $15–$20
R2-D2 .... $10–$15
Sand Person, (not the same as in Bantha set) .... $10–$15
Snitch .... $10–$15
Stormtrooper .... $15–$20

RAWCLIFFE

1994 to present. Rawcliffe also manufactures a line of pewter Star Wars key chains and also uses these pieces in a line of ceramic mugs. For these items, see JEWELRY and HOUSEWARES.

Deluxe Ships Limited to 15,000 pieces. Each comes with a detachable black wooden stand with metal name and plaque. Pieces are approximately 5″ to 6″ high with stand.

- **Darth Vader TIE** .... $130–$140
- **Millennium Falcon** .... $120–$130
- **X-Wing** .... $100–$110

Regular *(left)* and deluxe Millennium Falcon pewter figures, both by Rawcliffe

Regular Ships Approximately 2½″ to 4″ high with attached stands. Many have movable parts and gold-plated accents.

A-Wing Fighter...$40–$45
B-Wing Fighter...$40–$45
Imperial Star Destroyer...$70–$80
Millennium Falcon...$35–$40
Outrider...$45–$50
Sail Barge...$45–$50
Shuttle Tydirium...$45–$50
Slave I...$35–$40
Snowspeeder...$45–$50
TIE Fighter...$40–$45
X-Wing...$45–$50
Y-Wing...$45–$50

Character Figurines Approximately 1½″ to 3″ high with attached bases.

Admiral Ackbar...$20–$25
Bib Fortuna...$20–$25
Boba Fett...$20–$25
C-3PO...$17–$22
Chewbacca...$27–$32
Darth Vader...$30–$35
Emperor...$20–$25
Ewok...$12–$17
Gamorrean Guard...$20–$25
Han Solo...$17–$22
Lando Calrissian...$20–$25
Luke Skywalker...$17–$22
Obi-Wan Kenobi...$27–$32
Princess Leia...$17–$22
R2-D2...$17–$22
Stormtrooper...$20–$25
Yoda...$12–$17

POSTAGE STAMPS

This is a relatively new collectible field for media products and to date there has only been one manufacturer, SSCA. Their products are listed below.

SSCA

1995. All products are actual official issue postage stamps from St. Vincent and the Grenadines. Designs are variations on half-face color character artwork (Vader, Yoda and Stormtrooper) used extensively on other licensed products. All items come with a certificate of authenticity.

First Day Cover Collection One of each $1 stamp design on three different envelope designs (Star Wars, Empire and Jedi). Packaged in silver embossed black cardboard box.

Per collection .... $15–$20

SSCA, first-day cover collection

Stamp Collection Silver embossed black cardboard folder containing a sheet of nine (three each design) $1 stamps and a sheet of three (one each design) of the triangular $2 stamps.

Per collection .... $25–$30

Stamp Wallets Silver embossed black plastic fold-over wallets. Each contains a first day issue postcard with a $1 stamp and a large (2″ × 3½″) $30 stamp with a relief background of either gold or silver.

SSCA, Star Wars stamp collection

Star Wars Darth Vader design.

Gold .... $50–$55

Silver .... $40–$45

Empire Strikes Back Stormtrooper design.

Gold .... $50–$55

Silver .... $40–$45

Return of the Jedi Yoda design.

Gold .... $50–$55

Silver .... $40–$45

SSCA, Star Wars stamp wallet

POSTERS

There are two main categories in this section: Promotional Posters and General Public Posters. They are organized slightly differently. See category heads for explanation.

PROMOTIONAL POSTERS

Many of these posters are relatively rare. Limited or regional distribution adds to their desirability and value and often they were only available for a short period of time. Posters are listed chronologically by movie, and then alphabetically by manufacturer.

STAR WARS

Burger Chef/Coca-Cola Promotional Posters Set of four full-color posters (Luke Skywalker, Darth Vader, C-3PO and R2-D2, Chewbacca and Han Solo). 20th Century Fox, 1977, 18″ × 24″.

Each .... $10–$15
Set of four .... $35–$50

Burger King/Coca-Cola Promotional Posters Set of four with same art as above but with white borders. 20th Century Fox, 1977, 18″ × 24″.

Each .... $10–$15
Set of four .... $35–$50

Concert Promotional Star Wars Poster Illustrated by John Alum. Sold only at Hollywood Bowl on November 30, 1978, 24″ × 37″.

Rolled .... $200–$400
Folded .... $150–$300

General Mills Two-sided, set of four (Star Destroyer, R2-D2 and C-3PO, Space Battle, Hildebrandt art), 1978, 9″ × 14½″.

Each .... $8–$12
Set .... $30–$35

Immunization Poster From U.S. Department of Health, Education and Welfare/Public Health Service, promotes immunization of children. Features R2-D2 and C-3PO, 1979.

Each .... $30–$35

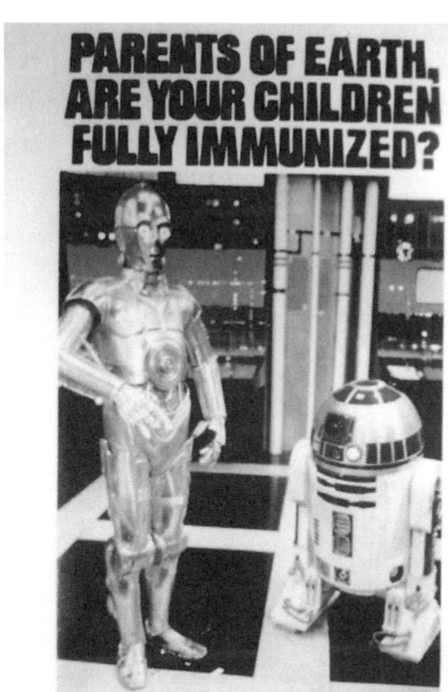

U.S. Public Health Service Star Wars immunization poster

Kenner Promotional Poster Captioned "Star Wars is forever," montage on one side and Star Wars toys advertised on the back.

Each .... $20–$25

National Public Radio Star Wars Radio Drama Poster Illustration by Celia Strain. Sent only to National Public Radio stations for promotion. Lucasfilms Ltd., 1979, 17″ × 29″.

Rolled .... $75–$125
Folded .... $50–$75

National Public Radio Star Wars poster

Procter & Gamble Promotional Posters Set of three (Ben Kenobi and Vader fighting, C-3PO and R2-D2, Leia, Han, Chewbacca and Luke collage). 20th Century Fox, 1978, 17½″ × 23″.

Each .... $10–$15
Set of three .... $25–$30

Procter & Gamble, Darth Vader Empire poster

Record Promotional Star Wars Poster Tom Jung, artist. Design is basically the same as style "A" Star Wars one-sheet poster with the rearranging of the credits at the bottom and the enlargement of the phrase, "Original Motion Picture Soundtrack on 20th Century Record and Tapes," 1977, 27″ × 41″.

Rolled .... $50–$100
Folded .... $40–$60

Record Promotional Star Wars-Style Poster Drew Struzan and Charles White III, artists. Similar to style "D" Star Wars theater poster with record promo added, 1978, 27″ × 41″.

Rolled .... $60–$100
Folded .... $40–$75

Star Wars Record Mylar Poster Included in Star Wars Soundtrack album. Darth Vader's helmet in mylar, black background.

Rolled .... $10–$15
Folded .... $5–$10

Studio Promotional Luke Skywalker Poster Howard Chaykin, artist. Star Wars in red letters on lower right. Images of Luke, Leia and others superimposed over aqua and orange circle, black background. First promotional poster, distributed at the World Science Convention in Kansas City. Star Wars Corporation, 1976, 20″ × 29″.

Rolled .... $150–$250
Folded .... $40–$100

Topps Bubble Gum Press Sheets Often the gum card art is printed first on paper to test it. Sometimes offered as a promotion on gum wrappers, often 22″ × 28″.

Star Wars .... $40–$60
Empire Strikes Back .... $30–$45
Return of the Jedi .... $25–$40

Coca-Cola, Boris Vallejo Empire Strikes Back promotional poster

EMPIRE STRIKES BACK

American Library Association Promotional Poster Captioned "Read and the Force is with you." Features Yoda, 22″ × 34″.

Per poster .... $20–$25

Coca-Cola Boris Poster Art by Boris Valejo. Sold in theaters, Lucasfilm Ltd., 1980, 24″ × 33″.

Per poster .... $15–$25

Coca-Cola Promotional Posters Set of three by famous artist Boris Valejo (Darth Vader, Luke of Dagobah, Luke and Han on Hoth). Lucasfilm Ltd., 1980, 17″ × 23″.

Each .... $10–$15

Set of three .... $25–$40

National Public Radio Empire Strikes Back Radio Drama Poster Illustration by Ralph McQuarrie. Sent only to National Public Radio stations for publicity. Much more rare than Star Wars version. Lucasfilm Ltd., 1982, 17″ × 28″.

Rolled .... $75–$125

Folded .... $50–$75

Palitoy (British), 1981.

Poster, two-sided. Toy AT-AT on front. Information on reverse .... $25–$30

Poster, two-sided. Shows product line (toys) on both sides .... $30–$35

Procter & Gamble Promotional Posters Set of four (Luke, Darth Vader, C-3PO and R2-D2, Han and Leia in Bespin freeze chamber). Photographic, Lucasfilm Ltd., 1980, 17″ × 23″.

Each .... $8–$12

Set of four .... $20–$30

Star Wars Fan Club Empire Issue. Kissing scene. Membership kit. 22″ × 28″.

Each .... $15–$25

Video Promotion Main characters and AT-AT battle scene, given to video shops to promote cassette.

Each .... $15–$25

Weekly Reader Book Club Montage of characters, 1980, 14½″ × 20½″.

Each .... $10–$15

RETURN OF THE JEDI

Marvel Comics, Jedi Promotional Poster Issued to promote Marvel Super Special #27, 1983.

Rolled .... $10–$15

Folded .... $5–$10

Oral-B Toothbrush Jedi Poster Free with purchase of two Oral-B adult toothbrushes.

Each .... $10–$15

Palitoy (British).

Poster, 1983. Only given away with ten pounds or more toy purchase .... $25–$35

Poster, 1984. Advertises upcoming toy line. Only available from manufacturer .... $30–$35

Procter & Gamble Jedi Posters Set of four (Leia and Jabba, Lando and Skiff Guard, Luke with blaster at Jabba's, R2 and Teebo the Ewok). 1983, 18″ × 22″.

Each .... $10–$15

Set .... $35–$50

Return of the Jedi Hi-C Promotional Poster Front: painted Jedi montage. Back: selection of photographs from the film. Free with purchase of four cans of Hi-C. 1983, 17″ × 22″.

Each .... $10–$15

Scholastic Inc.

Mother and baby Ewok, 1983. 22″ × 15″ .... $10–$15

Star Wars Fan Club Jedi issue. Death Star, B-Wing and other vehicles. In membership kit. 22″ × 28″.

Each .... $10–$15

Video Poster, 24″ × 14½″ horizontal poster. 3-D effect has tapes appearing to fly out of forest.

Each .... $25–$30

Weekly Reader Book Club

Montage of characters, 1983, 14½″ × 20½″ .... $15–$20

Wicket the Ewok, 1983, 14½″ × 20½″ .... $10–$15

Star Wars Special Edition Trilogy

Pepsi Product Promotional Posters, 1997. Mail-in offer originally required $9.99 and original order form from product package.

C-3PO .... $10–$15

Darth Vader .... $10–$15

Yoda .... $10–$15

Pizza Hut Promotional Posters, 1997. 19½″ × 35″ two-sided posters. Came in plastic tubes.

Star Wars, R2-D2 and C-3PO .... $10–$15

Empire, Yoda .... $10–$15

Jedi, Ewok .... $10–$15

Pizza Hut Star Wars Special Edition poster

GENERAL PUBLIC POSTERS

Listed alphabetically by manufacturer.

ANABAS (BRITISH)

Return of the Jedi, 1983.

- **The Team of Endor** .... $10–$15
- **Lord Darth Vader** .... $10–$15
- **Darth Vader** .... $10–$15
- **Luke and Leia** .... $10–$15
- **Wicket the Ewok** .... $5–$10

FACTORS, ETC

The first Star Wars poster licensee, full-color, 20″ × 28.″

Star Wars

- **Hildebrandt artwork** .... $10–$15
- **Cantina Band poster,** limited distribution .... $10–$15
- **Ship Battle scene,** limited distribution .... $15–$20
- **Darth Vader** .... $10–$15

Factors Etc. Darth Vader poster

- **Princess Leia** .... $10–$15
- **Luke Skywalker** .... $10–$15
- **C-3PO and R2-D2** .... $10–$15

Empire Strikes Back

- **Darth Vader and Stormtroopers** .... $10–$15
- **Boba Fett** .... $10–$15
- **Montage of characters** .... $10–$15
- **R2-D2, C-3PO, w/Empire logo** .... $10–$15
- **Yoda** .... $10–$15

FAN CLUB INC.

Empire 15th Anniversary Mylar Poster, Boba Fett artwork on 27″ × 41″ gold mylar .... $100–$125

Tsuneo Sanda Artwork Series of 24″ × 36″ color posters.

- **Cantina Star Wars 20th Anniversary** .... $10–$15
- **George Lucas** .... $10–$15
- **Millennium Falcon** .... $10–$15
- **Slave One** .... $10–$15
- **Yoda** .... $10–$15

L'AFFICHE

Star Wars Saga Poster, two-sided, full-color poster/guide shows theater poster from the Star Wars Trilogy. One-sheet size. .... $10–$15

PORTAL PUBLICATIONS

Full color, 24″ × 36″.

Theater Poster Reproductions

- **Star Wars,** Style C .... $8–$10
- **Empire Strikes Back,** advance .... $8–$10
- **Return of the Jedi,** advance .... $8–$10

Theater Poster Mini-Poster Reproductions

- **Star Wars,** Style C .... $4–$6
- **Empire Strikes Back,** advance .... $4–$6
- **Return of the Jedi,** advance .... $4–$6

Other Posters

- **All I Need to Know About Life I Learned From Star Wars** .... $5–$10
- **Art of Star Wars,** Luke battles Darth (McQuarrie art) .... $5–$10
- **Jabba's Palace** .... $5–$10
- **Rancor Monster** .... $5–$10
- **Space Battle** .... $5–$10
- **Star Destroyer** .... $5–$10
- **Trilogy** .... $5–$10
- **X-Wing Fighters** .... $5–$10
- **Yoda** .... $5–$10

SALES CORPORATION OF AMERICA

Animated TV Posters Each is full color, 17″ × 22″.

- **Droids,** The Adventures of R2-D2 and C-3PO .... $10–$15
- **Ewoks,** Friends Come in All Shapes and Sizes .... $10–$15

Darth Vader Door Poster Color, 24″ × 72″.

- **Each** .... $20–$30

Return of the Jedi Poster Art Mini-Posters, 1983. Full color, 11″ × 14″.

- **#0021,** Jabba and Friends .... $5–$10
- **#0023,** vehicle battle scene .... $5–$10
- **#0025,** Jedi teaser .... $5–$10
- **#0027,** vehicle shuttle landing .... $5–$10
- **#0029,** laser, one-sheet .... $5–$10
- **#0031,** Ewok montage .... $5–$10
- **#0033,** Darth Vader montage .... $5–$10
- **#0035,** Luke Skywalker .... $5–$10
- **#0037,** Emperor montage .... $5–$10
- **#0039,** Creature M montage .... $5–$10

#0041, Speeder Bike .... $5–$10
#0043, montage, one sheet .... $5–$10

Other Posters, 22″ × 34″.

Star Wars, Style D .... $5–$10
Empire Strikes Back, advance .... $5–$10
Return of the Jedi, teaser .... $5–$10
Return of the Jedi, Style A .... $5–$10
Darth Vader, montage .... $5–$10
Space Battle .... $5–$10
Vehicle battle scene .... $5–$10
Ewok, montage .... $5–$10

Sales Corporation of America, Ewok montage poster

Endor, portrait .... $5–$10
Return of the Jedi, Style B .... $5–$10

SCANLITE (BRITISH)

The Empire Strikes Back

Snowspeeder Model .... $10–$15
Imperial Star Destroyer Model .... $10–$15
Luke Skywalker .... $10–$15
Yoda on Dagobah .... $10–$15

SCI PUB TECH

24″ × 36″ color schematic posters.

Vehicles of the Galactic Empire .... $12–$16
Vehicles of the Rebel Alliance .... $12–$16

STAR TOURS TRAVEL POSTERS

All have a small "Star Tours" logo at the bottom center. Each depicts color artwork of the planet to be visited.

Yavin, landscape below a red planet .... $5–$10
Dagobah, view of a swamp .... $5–$10
Endor, view of Ewok village .... $5–$10
Tatooine, Jabba's Palace .... $5–$10
Hoth, Luke on Taun-Taun .... $5–$10
Star Tours Promotional Poster, Star Tours ship chased by TIE Fighters over Magic Kingdom .... $10–$15

WESTERN GRAPHICS

Darth Vader, half-face .... $5–$10
Stormtrooper, half-face .... $5–$10
Yoda, half-face .... $5–$10

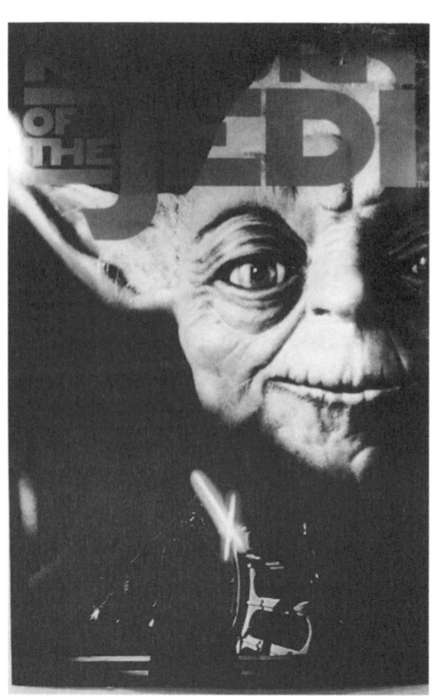

Western Graphics, Special Edition Yoda poster

Darth on red background theater poster art .... $5–$10
Cantina artwork .... $5–$10
Empire Strikes Back collage, Boris artwork .... $5–$10
3-D (with B-wings) artwork .... $5–$10
W-Wings and TIE Fighters in Death Star trench .... $5–$10

PUZZLES

Jigsaw puzzles in collectible condition should be complete and in a box which is also complete and in good condition. Puzzles in this section are assumed to be in unopened, basically new condition. The section is organized alphabetically by manufacturer.

Applause, Star Wars puzzle cube

APPLAUSE

Puzzle Cube, 1995. Plastic 2¾″ cube which rearranges to display nine different Star Wars saga photos.

Each .... $7–$10

CAPIEPA (FRENCH), 1977

150 pieces, 17″ × 11″. Puzzles also appeared in France under Waddington name.

Entre Dans LaVille .... $25–$30
Dans Le Millenium Condor .... $25–$30
Yan Solo et Chiquetaba .... $25–$30
C-3PO et D2-R2 .... $25–$30

CRAFT-MASTER (FUNDIMENSIONS), 1983

Match Block Puzzles, 1983. Nine blocks and tray.

- **Ewoks,** cartoon..$10–$15
- **Jedi characters**..$10–$15

170 Pieces, 16″ × 20″

- **Battle of Endor** ....$20–$25
- **B-Wings**..$20–$25
- **Ewok Leaders** ....$20–$25

70 Pieces, 12″ × 18″

- **Jabba's Friends** ....$10–$15
- **Jabba's Throne Room**...$10–$15
- **Death Star** ....$10–$15

Frame Tray Puzzles, 1983. Fifteen pieces, 8″ × 11″.

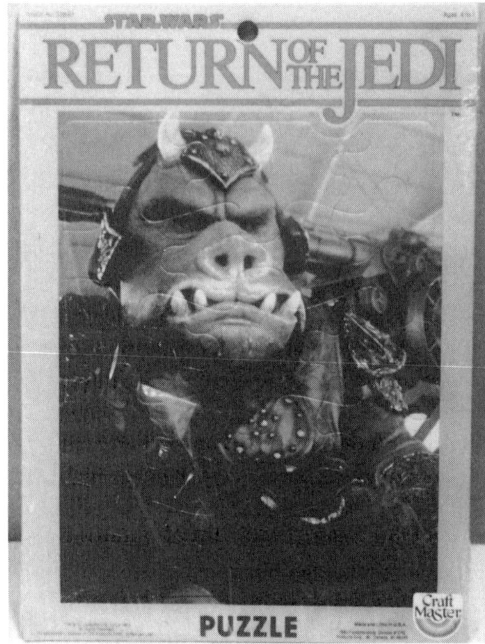

Craft Master, Frame Tray puzzle

- **Darth Vader** ....$5–$10
- **Ewoks on Hang Gliders**..$5–$10
- **Ewok Village** ....$5–$10
- **Gamorrean Guard**...$5–$10
- **Kneesa**...$5–$10
- **Leia and Wicket**..$5–$10
- **R2-D2 and Wicket** ....$5–$10
- **Wicket**...$5–$10

KENNER, 1977

Color photo puzzles in 140-, 500-, 1000- and 1500-piece sizes. Earlier packaging was blue or purplish star border around photo of puzzle. Later packaging had black star border. Though 140- and 500-piece black border puzzles have series numbers, they were probably released at or near the same time. The same puzzles and box styles were released in Canada under the Parker brand name. Series number (if any) is in parentheses.

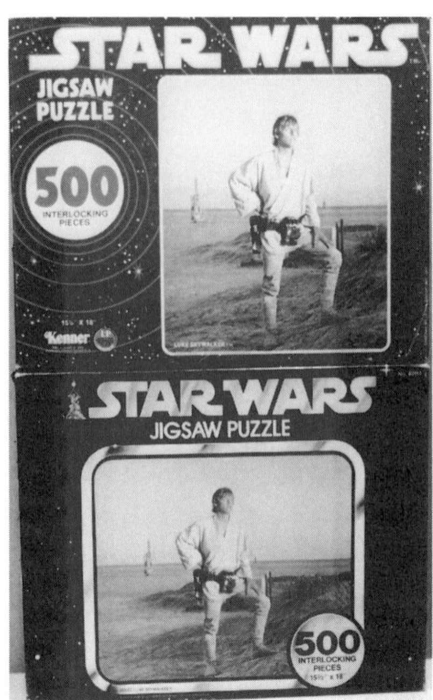

Kenner, 500-piece Luke Skywalker puzzle, early *(top)* and later box styles

NOTE: Pictures on four Kenner puzzles, Han and Chewbacca, Aboard the Millennium Falcon, C-3PO and R2-D2 and Stormtroopers and Landspeeder, were used on 150-piece puzzles by Waddington in England (value: $30 to $35 each).

140-Piece Puzzles, 14″ × 18″.

- **Bantha (IV)**...$15–$20
- **C-3PO and R2-D2 (I),** early box style.................$20–$25
- **C-3PO and R2-D2 (I),** later box style..................$15–$20
- **Han Solo and Chewbacca (I),** early box style ....$20–$25
- **Han Solo and Chewbacca (I),** later box style......$15–$20
- **Jawas Capture R2-D2 (IV)** ....$15–$20
- **Luke Meets R2-D2 (II)** ....$15–$20
- **Trash Compactor (II)**..$15–$20
- **Attack of Sand People (III)**...............................$15–$20
- **Stormtroopers Stop Landspeeder (III)**.............$15–$20

500-Piece Puzzles, 15½″ × 18″.

- **Ben Kenobi and Darth Vader Duel (II)**.............$20–$25
- **Cantina Band (IV)**..$20–$25
- **Luke and Leia (II)** ....$20–$25
- **Luke (I),** early box style ....$25–$30
- **Luke (I),** later box style ....$20–$25
- **Selling Droids (IV)**..$20–$25
- **Space Battle (I),** early box style ....$25–$30
- **Space Battle (I),** later box style...........................$20–$25
- **Victory Celebration (III)** ....$20–$25
- **X-Wing Fighter in Hangar (III)**.........................$20–$25

1000-Piece Puzzles, 21½″ × 27½″.

- **Crew Aboard the Millennium Falcon**................$25–$30
- **Star Wars Adventure,** movie poster art ....$25–$30

1500-Piece Puzzles, 27″ × 33″.

Corridor of Light .... $30–$40
Millennium Falcon in Space .... $30–$40

MILTON BRADLEY

Foil Highlight Puzzles, 1995. 550-piece, 18″ × 24″ artwork.

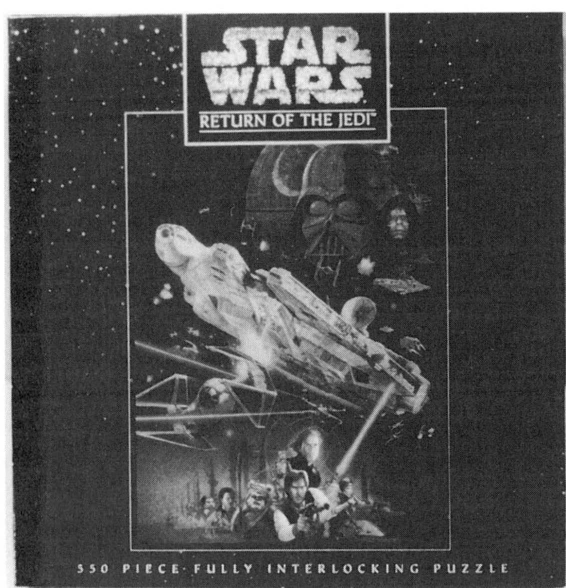

Milton Bradley, Return of the Jedi foil highlights puzzle

Star Wars .... $10–$15
Empire Strikes Back .... $10–$15
Return of the Jedi .... $10–$15

3-D Puzzles, 1996. 857 foam-backed pieces. Includes stands.
Imperial Cruiser .... $30–$35
Millennium Falcon .... $30–$35

ROSE ART, 1996

100-piece, 11″ × 12½″ artwork puzzles
Luke and Leia .... $5–$10
Star Wars, poster art .... $5–$10

550-piece, 18″ × 24″ artwork puzzles
Star Wars .... $6–$10
Empire Strikes Back .... $6–$10
Return of the Jedi .... $6–$10

SCHMID (GERMANY)

Puzzle, 1983. Two-in-one Return of the Jedi jigsaw puzzle. Jabba the Hutt and Luke in Jabba's Court .... $25–$35

SPRINGBOK (HALLMARK)

Star Wars art puzzle, 1995. 1000 pieces .... $15–$20

TAKARA (JAPAN)

Photo Jigsaw Puzzles, 1977. Six different varieties.
60 pieces, price each .... $20–$25
100 pieces, price each .... $25–$35
500 pieces, price each .... $35–$50
700 pieces, price each .... $50–$75
Frame Tray .... $20–$30
Plastic Frame Tray .... $30–$35

T. Theophanides & Son (Greek), mini puzzle

T. THEOPHANIDES & SON (GREECE)

Color Photo Mini-Puzzles, 1984. 63 pieces, 14 × 18 cm. Boxed with photo on front and Jedi logo on side. Eight different.
Price each .... $20–$25

WADDINGTON (BRITISH)

150 pieces, 17″ × 11″, 1977.
R2-D2 and C-3PO .... $25–$30
Han and Chewie .... $25–$30
Entering the City .... $25–$30
Inside the Millennium Falcon .... $25–$30

Toy Puzzles, 350 pieces, 14″ × 19″.
Small Action Figures and Landspeeder .... $40–$50

Waddington (British), small action figures puzzle

Small Action Figures, Landspeeder, X-Wing and TIE Fighter .... $40–$50

150-piece, 17″ × 11″, 1983.

Darth Vader .... $15–$20

Crew of Millennium Falcon .... $15–$20

Jabba's Throne Room .... $15–$20

Luke with Blaster .... $15–$20

Ewoks (animated), 1983. 150 pieces, 17″ × 11″.

Home Scene .... $10–$15

Sled .... $10–$15

Swimming .... $10–$15

Woods Scene .... $10–$15

RECORDS, TAPES AND COMPACT DISCS

The recordings in this chapter are divided into two sections: (1) soundtracks and music, and (2) story recordings. Organization is then alphabetically by title except in cases where there are several titles in one series (audio novels are example). Values all assume that the item has all packaging (such as slipcases) and inserts (posters, booklets, etc.) it was originally sold with.

STAR WARS SOUNDTRACKS AND MUSIC

Bienvenide, E. T. Arranged and directed by Rafael Acosta. Contains theme from Star Wars. Orfeon Records, Spanish album.
12-inch LP album ....$15–$20

Big Daddy Contains theme from Star Wars. Rhino Records.
12-inch LP album ....$10–$15
Cassette ....$9–$12

Chewie, The Rookie Wookiee From the album Living in These Star Wars, performed by The Rebel Force Band. Bonwhit Records.
7-inch 45rpm ....$5–$10

Cinema Gala—Star Wars/Close Encounters John Williams and the Los Angeles Philharmonic Orchestra. Decca, 1987.
Cassette only ....$9–$12

Classic Space Themes Includes music from The Empire Strikes Back, performed by the Birchwood Pops Orchestra. Contains Star Wars, main theme from The Empire Stikes Back, The Imperial March (Darth Vader's Theme) and Yoda's Theme. Pickwick Records, 1980.
12-inch LP album ....$10–$15

Classic Space Themes Includes Star Wars Theme (disco version). Pickwick Records, 1980.
12-inch LP album ....$10–$15

Close Encounters of the Third Kind and Star Wars Composed by John Williams, performed by the National Philharmonic Orchestra, conducted by Charles Gerhardt. Contains main title, The Little People Work, Here They Come!, Princess Leia Theme, The Final Battle, The Throne Room and End Title. RCA Red Seal Record, 1978.
12-inch LP album ....$10–$15

Disco Excitement Performed by Enoch Light and His Light Brigade. Contains disco version of theme from Star Wars. Lakeshore Music, 1978.
12-inch LP album ....$10–$15
8-track tape ....$5–$8
Cassette ....$8–$12

Dune Arranged by David Matthews. Contains Princess Leia's Theme and the main theme from Star Wars. CTI Records, 1977.
12-inch LP album ....$15–$20
8-track tape ....$5–$10
Cassette ....$10–$15

Empire Jazz Produced and arranged by Ron Carter from the original soundtrack from the motion picture Star Wars/The Empire Strikes Back. Composed by John Williams. Contains The Imperial March (Darth Vader's Theme), The Asteroid Field, Han Solo and the Princess (Love Theme), Lando's Palace, Yoda's Theme. RSO Records, 1980.
12-inch LP album ....$15–$20
8-track tape ....$5–$8
Cassette ....$10–$15

The Empire Strikes Back The original soundtrack from the motion picture, composed and conducted by John Williams with the London Symphony Orchestra. RSO Records, 1980.
Two 12-inch LP albums ....$30–$35
8-track tape ....$8–$10
Cassette ....$10–$15

The Empire Strikes Back (Medley) Performed by Meco. Contains Darth Vader's Theme, Yoda's Theme and The Force Theme. RSO Records, 1980.

7-inch 45rpm ....$10–$15

The Empire Strikes Back Performed by Boris Midney and His Orchestra. Contains Yoda's Theme, The Imperial March (Darth Vader's Theme), Han Solo and the Princess (Love Theme) and Star Wars (Main Theme). RSO Records.

12-inch LP album ....$10–$15

8-track tape ....$5–$8

Cassette ....$5–$10

The Empire Strikes Back (Meco Plays Music From) Contains The Empire Strikes Back (Medley), Darth Vader/ Yoda's Themes, The Battle in the Snow, The Force Theme, The Asteroid Field/Finale. RSO Records, 1980.

10-inch LP album ....$10–$15

E.T. and Star Wars: The Best 12 Arts of John Williams Victor Musical Industries, 1987.

12-inch LP album ....$15–$20

Ewoks: Original Soundtrack Original soundtracks from "Caravan of Courage" and "Battle for Endor." Varese Sarabande Records, 1986.

12-inch LP album ....$15–$20

The Empire Strikes Back Special Edition Soundtrack Laser-engraved picture CD. Newly released tracks and previously unreleased material. Includes 20-page booklet of notes. Fox Records, 1997.

CD ....$35–$40

The Empire Strikes Back Symphonic suite from the original motion picture soundtrack. Performed by the National Philharmonic Orchestra. Conducted by Charles Gerhardt. Chalfont Digital Records, 1980 (pressed in Japan).

12-inch LP album ....$20–$25

The Empire Strikes Back Music from the original soundtrack of the motion picture. Music composed and conducted by John Williams, performed by the London Symphony Orchestra. RSO Records, 1980 (British pressing).

12-inch LP album ....$25–$30

Flip Side of Red Seal Performed by Tomita. Contains theme from Star Wars. Victor (S) Records.

12-inch LP album ....$10–$15

Greatest Science Fiction Hits II Conducted by Neil Norman and His Cosmic Orchestra. Contains Star Wars: The Empire Strikes Back (Medley). GNP Crescendo Records, 1980.

12-inch LP album ....$10–$15

Cassette ....$9–$12

Great Movies—There's Something Going On Out There Contains main title from Star Wars. Performed by the National Philharmonic Orchestra. His Masters Voice Records.

12-inch LP album ....$10–$15

Horspiel Nach Dem Gleichnamigen Film Mit Den Orginalsprechern Kreig Der Sterne (The Story of Star Wars in German). With music and sound effects from the original soundtrack from the motion picture. Full color, eight-page photo booklet. Fontana Records.

12-inch LP album ....$20–$25

The Imperial March (Darth Vader's Theme) and The Battle in the Snow. Performed by the London Symphony Orchestra, conducted by John Williams. From the original soundtrack of the motion picture The Empire Strikes Back. RSO Records.

12-inch LP album ....$20–$25

John Williams Symphonic Suites E.T. the Extraterrestrial, Close Encounters of the Third Kind, and Star Wars. Performed by the London Symphony Orchestra and the National Philharmonic Orchestra. Conducted by Frank Barber. EMI-Angel Records (British recording).

12-inch LP album ....$20–$25

Cassette ....$10–$15

La Guerre Des Etoiles Star Wars in French. Buena Vista Records.

7-inch 33 1/3 rpm ....$10–$15

Living in These Star Wars Country-western version of Star Wars. Performed by the Rebel Force Band. Bonwhit Records.

12-inch LP album ....$15–$20

Main Theme—Star Wars Performed by David Matthews. From the album Dune. CTI Records, 1977.

7-inch 45rpm ....$5–$10

Main Title Themes From The Empire Strikes Back, Star Wars, 2001: A Space Odyssey and Close Encounters. Peter Pan Records.

12-inch LP album ....$10–$15

Meco—Ewok Celebration Contains themes from Star Wars: The Motion Picture. Arista Records.

12-inch LP album ....$10–$15

Music from John Williams Close Encounters of the Third Kind and Star Wars. Performed by the National Philharmonic Orchestra. Conducted by Charles Gerhardt. RCA Records.

12-inch LP album ....$15–$20

Music from Other Galaxies and Planets Featuring the Main Theme and Princess Leia's Theme from Star Wars. Performed by Don Ellis and Survival. Atlantic Records, 1977.

12-inch LP album ....$10–$15

Music from Star Wars Performed by the Electric Moog Orchestra. Arranged and conducted by Jimmy Wisner. Musicor Records

12-inch LP album ....$15–$25

Music from the Galaxies Music from Star Wars and other science fiction movies. Performed by the London Symphony Orchestra. CBS Masterworks, 1980.

12-inch LP album ....$10–$15

1084—A Space Odyssey Performed by John Williams conducting the Boston Pops Orchestra. Includes Parade of the Ewoks from Return of the Jedi, Star Wars Main Theme, The Empire Strikes Back, The Asteroid Field, The Forest Battle from Return of the Jedi, Star Trek, The Main Theme from TV, and the Main Theme from Star Trek: The Motion Picture. J & B Records.

12-inch LP album ....$20–$25

Pops in Space Performed by the Boston Pops Orchestra, conducted by John Williams. Contains The Asteroid Field, Yoda's Theme, and The Imperial March from The Empire Strikes Back. Philips Digital Record, 1980.

12-inch LP album ....$15–$20

Pops in Space Performed by the Boston Pops Orchestra.

Conducted by John Williams. Contains Star Wars Main Theme and The Princess Leia Theme. Philips Digital Record, 1980.

12-inch LP album ....$15–$20

Princess Leia's Theme from Star Wars Performed by David Matthews. From the album Dune. CTI Records, 1977.

7-inch 45rpm ....$5–$10

Return of the Jedi Soundtrack. RSO Records, 1983.

12-inch LP album ....$15–$25

Return of the Jedi Symphonic rendition. National Philharmonic Orchestra. RCA Red seal.

12-inch LP album ....$15–$20

Return of the Jedi Special Edition Soundtrack Laser-engraved picture CD. Newly recorded tracks and previously unreleased material. Includes 20-page booklet of notes. 1997.

CD ....$35–$40

Shadows of the Empire Enhanced Soundtrack CD Fifty minutes of music inspired by the novel. Includes interactive CD-ROM with Nintendo screen shots. Varese, 1997.

CD ....$15–$20

Sounds of Star Wars Performed by the Sonic All-Stars. Synthesizer. Pickwick (British), 1977.

12-inch LP album ....$10–$15

Space Organ Performed by Jonas Nordwall. Contains medley from Star Wars: Main Title, Princess Leia's Theme, Cantina Band. Crystal Clear Records, 1979.

12-inch LP album ....$10–$15

Spaced Out Disco Fever Contains theme from Star Wars, Star Trek Theme, Bionic Woman Theme, Six Million Dollar Man Theme, Theme from 2001: A Space Odyssey, Beyond the Outer Limits, Rocket Man, Space Race, and Star Light. Wonderland Records.

12-inch LP album ....$10–$15

Spectacular Space Hits Performed by the Odyssey Orchestra. Includes themes from 2001, Star Trek, Star Wars, Superman, Close Encounters, and The Empire Strikes Back. Sina Qua Non Records.

12-inch LP album ....$10–$15

Star Tracks Performed by Erich Kunzel and the Cincinnati Pops Orchestra. Includes Main Title from Star Wars, The Imperial March from The Empire Strikes Back, Luke and Leia (Love Theme) from Return of the Jedi and Main Theme from Star Trek TV. Telarc Digital Record.

12-inch LP album ....$10–$15

Star Trek—Main Theme from the Motion Picture Performed by the Now Sound Orchestra. Contains Theme from Star Wars, Part I, and Theme from Star Wars, Part II. Synthetic Plastic Records.

12-inch LP album ....$10–$15

Star Trek—21 Space Hits Contains theme from Star Wars. Music World Ltd. Record (New Zealand), 1979.

12-inch LP album ....$15–$20

Star Wars Selections from the film. Performed by Patrick Gleeson on the world's most advanced synthesizer. Contains Star Wars Theme, Luke's Theme, The Tatooine Desert, Death Star, Star Wars Cantina Music, Princess Leia's Theme, Droids, and Ben Kenobi's Theme. Mercury Records, 1977.

12-inch LP album ....$15–$20

8-track tape ....$5–$8

Cassette..$10–$15

Star Wars John Rose playing the Great Pipe Organ at the Cathedral of St. Joseph in Hartford, CT. Delos Records.

12-inch LP album ....$10–$15

Star Wars Music from the film. Composed by John Williams, performed by the London Philharmonic Orchestra. Conducted by Colin Frechter. Contains Main Titles, Imperial Attack, Princess Leia's Theme, Fighter Attack, Land of the Sand People, The Return Home. Damil Records.

NOTE: Also manufactured in the United Kingdom by Damont Records, Ltd., Hayes, Middlesex.

12-inch LP album ....$20–$25

Cassette, Ahed Records.......................................$10–$15

12-ınch LP album, Damont Records ....$20–$25

Star Wars Performed on two pianos by Ferrante & Teicher. Contains Main Title from Star Wars. United Artists Record.

12-inch LP album ....$20–$25

Cassette, 20th Century Records...........................$10–$15

Star Wars Main Title and Cantina Band, from the original soundtrack performed by the London Symphony Orchestra, conducted by John Williams. 20th Century Records, 1977.

7-inch 45rpm, short version (2:20)........................$5–$10

7-inch 45rpm, longer version (5:20) ....$10–$15

Star Wars and Close Encounters of the Third Kind Suite conducted by Zubin Mehta and the Los Angeles Philharmonic Orchestra. Star Wars Suite contains Main Title, Princess Leia's Theme, The Little People, Cantina Band, The Battle, Throne Room, and End Title. London Records, 1978.

12-inch LP album ....$20–$25

Star Wars and Other Galactic Funk Performed by Meco. Casablanca Records (Meco Millennium Record Co., Inc.), 1977.

12-inch LP album ....$10–$15

Star Wars and Other Space Themes Music for Pleasure. Performed by Geoff Love and Orchestra. 1978.

12-inch LP album ....$10–$15

Star Wars/Close Encounters Performed by Richard "Groove" Holmes. Contains theme from Star Wars. Versatile Records, 1977.

12-inch LP album ....$10–$15

Star Wars Dub British recording, Burning Sounds Record.

12-inch LP album ....$15–$20

Star Wars, Empire Strikes Back, Return of the Jedi Three-CD Special Edition Set. All three of the Special Edition release CDs in one set. 1997.

Per set ....$105–$110

Star Wars Main Theme From the album Not of This Earth by Neil Norman and His Cosmic Orchestra. GNP Crescendo Records, 1977.

7-inch 45rpm ....$5–$10

Star Wars, Main Title From the 20th Century Fox film, Star Wars, performed by Maynard Ferguson. Columbia Records.

7-inch 45rpm ....$5–$10

Star Wars—Main Title From the original soundtrack of the motion picture. Performed by the London Symphony Orchestra. Conducted by John Williams. 20th Century Records, 1977.

7-inch 45rpm .... $10–$15

Star Wars Special Edition Soundtrack Laser-engraved picture CD. Newly recorded tracks and previously unreleased material. Includes 20-page booklet of notes. 1997.

CD .... $35–$40

Star Wars/The Empire Strikes Back Special in-store play disc. Featuring excerpts from Star Wars/The Empire Strikes Back. Promotion copy; not for sale. RSO Records.

12-inch LP album .... $40–$50

The Star Wars Stars Lifesong Records.

7-inch 45rpm .... $5–$10

The Star Wars Trilogy Return of the Jedi, The Empire Strikes Back and Star Wars. Music by John Williams from the original motion picture scores. Varuan Kojian, conducting the Utah Symphony Orchestra. Contains Darth Vader's Death and Fight With the TIE Fighters. Varese Sarabande Digital Record, 1983.

12-inch LP album .... $35–$45

Themes from the Movies Contains Main Theme from Star Wars and The Princess Theme. Peter Pan Records.

12-inch LP album .... $10–$15

Themes from Star Wars New York, New York, The Deep, Black Sunday, The Greatest, A Bridge Too Far, Annie Hall, Exorcist II The Heretic and Roller Coaster. Performed by the Birchwood Pops Orchestra. Contains Main Theme from Star Wars. Pickwick Record.

12-inch LP album .... $10–$15

STAR WARS STORY RECORDS AND TAPES

The Adventures of Luke Skywalker From The Empire Strikes Back. Featuring the voices of Mark Hamill, Carrie Fisher, Billy Dee Williams, Anthony Daniels, James Earl Jones and Frank Oz. Music performed by the London Symphony Orchestra. Conducted by John Williams. RSO Records, 1980.

12-inch LP album .... $30–$35

8-track tape .... $10–$15

Cassette .... $10–$15

Christmas in the Stars Star Wars Christmas album. Featuring the original cast: R2-D2 and C-3PO (Anthony Daniels). Album concept by Meco Monardo. RSO Records.

12-inch LP album .... $25–$30

Droid World—The Further Adventures of Star Wars Adapted from Marvel Comics. Story by Archie Goodwin, illustrated by Dick Foes. Includes 24-page full-color illustrated booklet. Buena Vista Records.

7-inch LP album .... $5–$10

The Empire Strikes Back Original Radio Drama From the National Public Radio broadcast. Ten episodes. Highbridge, 1993.

5-cassette boxed set .... $35–$38

5-CD boxed set .... $55–$60

The Empire Strikes Back Read-along book and record. Story, music, sound effects, and photos from the original motion picture. Includes 24-page full-color illustrated book. Buena Vista Records, 1979.

7-inch LP album .... $10–$15

Cassette .... $5–$10

Ewoks Join the Fight Book and Record Set Buena Vista Records, 1983.

7-inch LP album .... $5–$10

L'Empire Contre-Attaque The Empire Strikes Back in French. Buena Vista Records.

7-inch LP album .... $10–$15

La Guerre des Etoiles, L'Empire Contre-Attaque Raconte par Dominique Paturel, livre-disque, 24 pages du film. (Star Wars—The Empire Strikes Back. Narrated by Dominique Paturel. Book and record, 24-pages of photos from the original motion picture.) Buena Vista Records.

12-inch LP album .... $10–$15

La Guerra de las Galaxias Star Wars, story, music and sound effects from the original motion picture (in Spanish). Includes 24-page full-color illustrated booklet. Buena Vista Records, 1979.

7-inch LP album .... $10–$15

Cassette .... $5–$10

La Guerra de las Galaxias Read-along book and record (in Spanish), story, music and sound effects from the original motion picture. Includes 24-page full-color illustrated booklet. Buena Vista Records.

7-inch LP album .... $10–$15

cassette .... $5–$10

L'Histoire de la Guerre Des Etoiles Raconte par Dominique Paturel. Bande originale de la musique et des effets sonores du film. (The Story of Star Wars, narrated by Dominique Paturel. Music and sound effects from the original soundtrack of the motion picture, in French.) Buena Vista Records.

12-inch LP album .... $10–$15

Cassette .... $5–$10

Planet of the Hoogibs—The Further Adventures of Star Wars Adapted from Marvel Comics, story by David Micheline, illustrated by Greg Winters. Includes 24-page full-color illustrated booklet. Buena Vista Records, 1983.

7-inch LP album .... $10–$15

Cassette .... $5–$10

Read-Along Audio Tape and Storybook Sets TW Kids, 1994.

Star Wars, includes Image cling stickers .... $9–$12

Empire, includes Snow Speeder Micro Machine .... $9–$12

Jedi, includes Millennium Falcon Micro Machine .... $9–$12

Rebel Mission to Ord Mantel, A Story from the Star Wars Saga Script by Brian Daley, author of Star Wars and The Empire Strikes Back radio series. Buena Vista Records, 1983.

Record .... $10–$15

Cassette .... $5–$10

Return of the Jedi Picture disk, story record. RSO Records.

Record .... $25–$35

Return of the Jedi Story record. RSO Records.

Record ....$20–$25

Return of the Jedi, Read-Along Book and Record Music and photos. Buena Vista Records, 1983.

33⅓ rpm ....$5–$10

Return of the Jedi Dialogue and Music Includes 16-page souvenir book. Buena Vista Records, 1983.

Record ....$20–$25

Return of the Jedi Original Radio Drama From the National Public Radio broadcast. Six episodes. Highbridge, 1996.

3-cassette boxed set ....$24–$28

3-CD boxed set ....$34–$38

Star Wars Read-along adventure series. Story, music and photos from the original motion picture. Includes 24-page full-color illustrated booklet. Buena Vista Records, 1979.

7-inch LP album ....$10–$15

Cassette ....$5–$10

Star Wars Adventures in ABC Buena Vista Records

7-inch LP album ....$10–$15

Cassette ....$5–$10

Star Wars Adventures in Colors and Shapes Buena Vista Records.

7-inch LP album ....$5–$10

Star Wars and the Story of Star Wars Two four-track reel-to-reel tapes with illustrated full-color 16-page booklet and program. This is a rare item. The record manufacturer that bought out 20th Century Records has no record of its existence. 20th Century Records.

Tapes ....$100–$125

Star Wars Cassette Storybook Book and cassette. Black Falcon Ltd.

Cassette ....$10–$15

Star Wars: Dark Empire Audio dramatization from graphic novel. Full cast. Highbridge, 1996.

Cassette ....$16–$18

Star Wars: Dark Empire II Audio dramatization from graphic novel. Full cast. Highbridge, 1996.

Cassette ....$16–$18

Star Wars Original Radio Drama From the National Public Radio broadcast. Thirteen episodes. Highbridge, 1993.

6-cassette boxed set ....$35–$38

6-CD boxed set ....$60–$65

Star Wars Saga Book/Cassette Set Books and cassettes from all three movies packaged together. Buena Vista Records.

Cassettes ....$20–$30

Star Wars Spin-Off Novelization Audio Dramatizations Two-cassette boxed sets. BDD.

Ambush at Corellia, performed by A. Heald ......$16–$18

Assault at Selonia, performed by A. Heald ......$16–$18

Bacta War ....$16–$18

Before the Storm ....$16–$18

Children of the Jedi, performed by A. Heald......$16–$18

Courtship of Princess Leia, performed by A. Heald........ ....$16–$18

Crystal Star, performed by A. Heald....................$16–$18

Dark Force Rising, performed by A. Daniels......$16–$18

Heir to the Empire, performed by D. Lawson ....$16–$18

Jedi Search, Jedi Academy Trilogy, performed by A. Heald ....$16–$18

Dark Apprentice, Jedi Academy Trilogy, performed by A. Heald ....$16–$18

Champions of the Force, Jedi Academy Trilogy, performed by A. Heald....................$16–$18

Krytos Trap, performed by Henry Thomas.........$16–$18

Last Command, performed by A. Daniels...........$16–$18

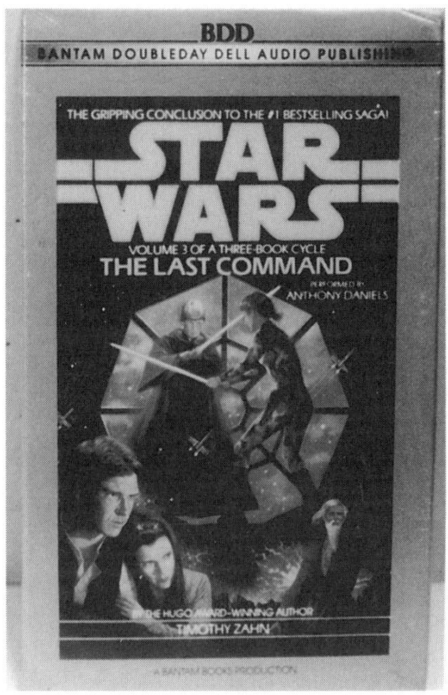

Bantam, Last Command Star Wars audio

New Rebellion, performed by A. Heald ....$16–$18

Truce at Bakura, performed by A. Heald ....$16–$18

Tyrant's Test, performed by A. Heald.................$16–$18

Star Wars Spin-Off Novelization Audio Drama Boxed Set T. Zahn novels Heir to Empire, Dark Force Rising, The Last Command and previously unreleased short story Hannertong in box decorated with Millennium Falcon in relief. BDD.

Each ....$55–$60

Star Wars: The Mixed-Up Droid Cassette and Dark Horse mini-comic. TW Kids, 1994.

Each ....$9–$12

Star Wars Trilogy Special audio Collector's Edition. Read by Tony Roberts. 1996.

Cassette boxed set ....$45–$50

CD boxed set ....$70–$75

Star Wars Trilogy Original Radio Drama CD Set From the National Public Radio broadcasts. Includes making of CD exclusive to trilogy set. Highbridge, 1996.

Each ....$190–$200

Star Wars: We Don't Do Weddings, The Band's Tale Story dramatization. BDD, 1996.

Cassette .... $10–$12

The Story of The Empire Strikes Back Dialogue, music and sound effects from the original motion picture soundtrack. Includes 16-page full-color souvenir photo booklet. Features the voices of Mark Hamill, Harrison Ford, Carrie Fisher, Billy Dee Williams, Anthony Daniels, James Earl Jones, Alec Guiness, and Frank Oz. Narration by Malachi Throne. Buena Vista Records, 1983.

12-inch LP album .... $20–$25

The Story of Star Wars From the original soundtrack. Includes 16-page full-color photo booklet. Narration by Roscoe Lee Brown. Contains voices, music and sound effects from original motion picture. 20th Century Fox Records.

12-inch LP album .... $30–$40

8-track tape .... $10–$15

Cassette .... $15–$20

Tales of the Jedi Audio dramatization from graphic novel. Full cast. Two-cassette boxed set. Time Warner, 1996.

Cassettes .... $16–$18

SCHOOL AND OFFICE SUPPLIES

This section is organized by type of item and then alphabetically by manufacturer.

BINDERS, NOTEBOOKS AND PORTFOLIOS

ANTIOCH

Booklets, 1992. 3½″ × 6¼″ vertically formated booklets with color artwork borrowed from novel series.

Addresses .... $1–$3
Notes .... $1–$3

Journals, 1996. Hardbound blank books with 160 ruled pages. Color artwork covers. Each comes shrink-wrapped with complementary tasseled bookmark.

"Star Wars" Movie Poster Art .... $8–$10
Space Battle .... $8–$10
"Truce at Bakura" Novel Art .... $8–$10
20th Anniversary Photo Collage .... $8–$10
"Crystal Star" Novel Art .... $8–$10
20th Anniversary Photo Collage, two different.... $8–$10

H.C.F. (BRITISH)

Notebooks (mini), 1983. Color cover art with Jedi logo. Several different styles.

Each .... $5–$10

Pocket Memo, 1983. Luke and Yoda, C-3PO or Han and Chewbacca.

Price each .... $5–$10

Scrap Book, 1984. Collage of character photos.

Price each .... $20–$25

Sketch Pad, 1984. Collage of character photos.

Price each .... $10–$15

LETRASET (BRITISH)

Notebooks, 1977.

Chewbacca's Space Notes .... $10–$15
Princess Leia's Rebel Jotter .... $10–$15
Stormtrooper Manual .... $10–$15
R2-D2's Memory Book .... $10–$15

Scrapbook, 1977. Character collage on cover.

Price each .... $25–$30

MEAD

Notebooks, 1977. Spiralbound, approximately 10½″ × 8″ with color photo covers.

Darth Vader .... $10–$15
Han and Chewbacca .... $10–$15

Mead, Star Wars portfolio. Stormtroopers are pictured on the back

R2-D2 and C-3PO......$10–$15
Stormtroopers......$10–$15

Portfolios, 1977. 9½″ × 12″. Different color photos front and back. Inside pocket.
Leia, Luke......$5–$10
Obi-Wan, Stormtrooper......$5–$10
Darth Vader, Stormtroopers......$5–$10
C-3PO, R2-D2, (both sides)......$5–$10

Portfolios, 1997. Color covers.
C-3PO......$2–$4
Darth Vader......$2–$4
Han Solo......$2–$4
Leia......$2–$4
May the Force Be With You......$2–$4
R2-D2......$2–$4
Ships......$2–$4
Title Crawl......$2–$4
Yoda......$2–$4

Notebooks, 1997. Spiral bound with color covers.
Darth Vader......$3–$5
Darth Vader, quotes......$3–$5
Han Solo......$3–$5
May the Force Be With You......$3–$5
Ships......$3–$5
Stormtroopers......$3–$5

File Binders, 1978.
C-3PO and R2-D2......$10–$15
Darth Vader......$10–$15
Group......$10–$15
Han and Chewbacca......$10–$15
Darth Vader......$10–$15
Ewoks......$10–$15
Luke......$10–$15
Stormtroopers......$10–$15
Yoda......$10–$15

Notebooks, 1980. 8½″ × 11″. Color photo covers with Empire logo.
Boba Fett......$10–$15
Bounty Hunter and 2-1B......$10–$15
C-3PO and R2-D2......$10–$15
Darth Vader......$10–$15
Darth Vader and Stormtroopers......$10–$15
Han, Leia and Luke......$10–$15
Hoth and Bespin scenes......$10–$15
Luke......$10–$15
Yoda......$10–$15

Pencil Tablets, 1980/83. 8″ × 10″. Fifty sheets each with color photo covers with movie logos.
C-3PO and R2-D2......$10–$15
Space scene......$10–$15
Empire montage......$10–$15
R2-D2 and Ewok......$10–$15

Pocket Memos, 1980. Spiralbound vertical 3″ × 5″ notebooks. Color photo cover.
Boba Fett......$5–$10
C-3PO and R2-D2......$5–$10
Character montage......$5–$10
Darth Vader and Stormtroopers......$5–$10
Luke......$5–$10

Pocket Memos, 1983. Return of the Jedi color artwork covers.

Stuart Hall, doodle pad

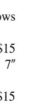

STUART HALL

Doodle Pad, 1983. 12″ × 7″ horizontal format. Cover shows Max Rebo Band and Jedi logo.
Price each......$10–$15

Learn to Letter and Write Tablets, 1980/83. 11¾″ × 7″ horizontal design. Color photo covers with movie logos.
Boba Fett......$10–$15

Stuart Hall, Jedi pocket memo

Space Battle scenes......$3–$8
Biker Scouts......$3–$8
C-3PO, R2-D2 and Wicket......$3–$8
Jabba the Hutt......$3–$8

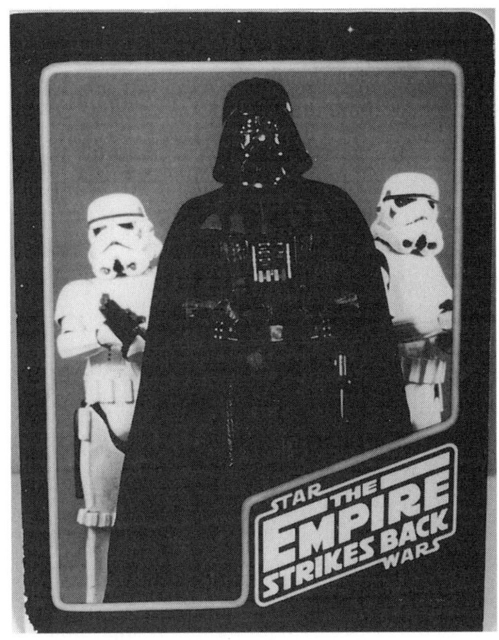

Stuart Hall, Empire Strikes Back portfolio

Stuart Hall, Empire spiral themebook

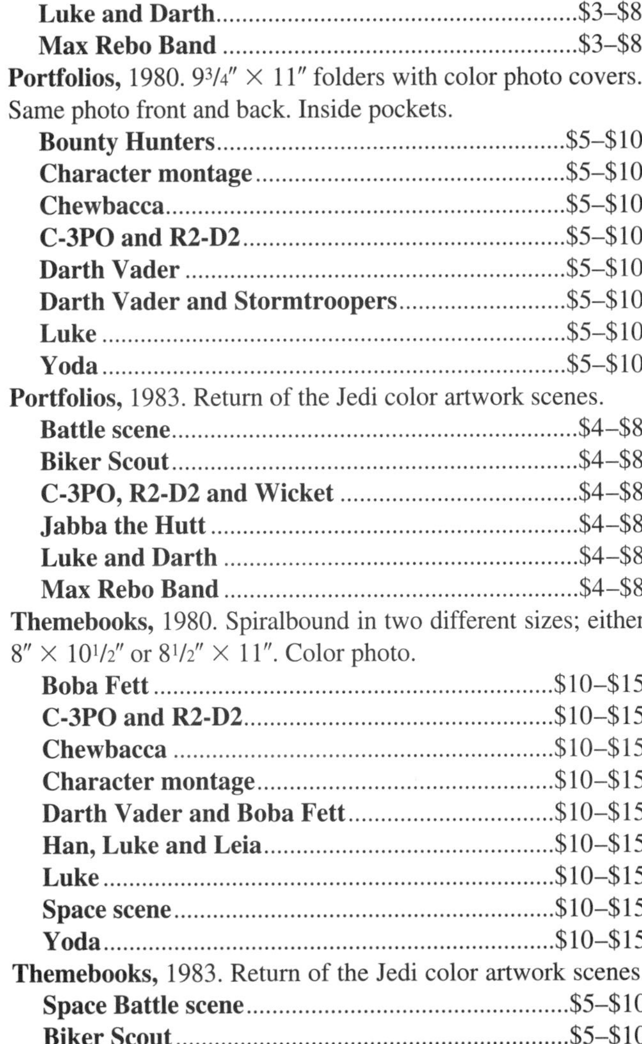

Luke and Darth .... $3–$8
Max Rebo Band .... $3–$8

Portfolios, 1980. 9³/4″ × 11″ folders with color photo covers. Same photo front and back. Inside pockets.

Bounty Hunters .... $5–$10
Character montage .... $5–$10
Chewbacca .... $5–$10
C-3PO and R2-D2 .... $5–$10
Darth Vader .... $5–$10
Darth Vader and Stormtroopers .... $5–$10
Luke .... $5–$10
Yoda .... $5–$10

Portfolios, 1983. Return of the Jedi color artwork scenes.

Battle scene .... $4–$8
Biker Scout .... $4–$8
C-3PO, R2-D2 and Wicket .... $4–$8
Jabba the Hutt .... $4–$8
Luke and Darth .... $4–$8
Max Rebo Band .... $4–$8

Themebooks, 1980. Spiralbound in two different sizes; either 8″ × 10¹/2″ or 8¹/2″ × 11″. Color photo.

Boba Fett .... $10–$15
C-3PO and R2-D2 .... $10–$15
Chewbacca .... $10–$15
Character montage .... $10–$15
Darth Vader and Boba Fett .... $10–$15
Han, Luke and Leia .... $10–$15
Luke .... $10–$15
Space scene .... $10–$15
Yoda .... $10–$15

Themebooks, 1983. Return of the Jedi color artwork scenes.

Space Battle scene .... $5–$10
Biker Scout .... $5–$10
C-3PO, R2-D2 and Wicket .... $5–$10
Jabba the Hutt .... $5–$10
Luke and Darth Vader .... $5–$10
Max Rebo Band .... $5–$10

Three-Ring Binders, 1980. Flexible plastic. Color photo covers. Five different.

C-3PO and R2-D2 .... $15–$20
Darth Vader and Stormtroopers .... $15–$20
Luke .... $15–$20
Montage .... $15–$20
Yoda .... $15–$20

BULLETIN BOARDS

MANTON CORK, 1980/83

All boards have color artwork.

First Series, Rectangular, 1980. All approximately 17″ × 23″.

Star Wars, logo with spaceships. Horizontal format .... $15–$25
Darth and Company, Darth and Stormtroopers .... $15–$25
Good Guys, Group picture .... $15–$25

First Series, Die-Cut

Darth Vader .... $15–$25
Yoda, glow-in-the-dark .... $15–$25
R2-D2 and C-3PO, two separate boards in set .... $20–$30

Second Series, 1981. Glo-Dome. Glow-in-the-dark. Arched vertical design, 11″ × 17″.

AT-AT .... $15–$20
C-3PO and R2-D2 .... $15–$20
Chewbacca .... $15–$20

Darth Vader .... $15–$20
Luke on Tauntaun .... $15–$20
Yoda .... $15–$20

Third Series, Horizontal, 1982. All are rectangular with Return of the Jedi across the top. 17″ × 23″.

Ewok Village, group with main characters .... $20–$30
Jabba's Palace, group with main characters .... $20–$30

Third Series, Vertical, 1982. All are rectangular with Return of the Jedi logo across the top; 11″ × 17″.

Darth and Luke .... $15–$20
Ewoks and Droids .... $15–$20
Jabba's Palace .... $15–$20
Max Rebo Band .... $15–$20

PENS, PENCILS, AND ACCESSORIES

PENCIL CUP

H.C.F., 1982. Metal. 4″ high with color artwork of characters on both sides.

Each .... $25–$35

Sigma, 1982. Open ceramic container with Yoda relief on the front.

Each .... $40–$50

PENCIL SHARPENER AND ERASER SET

Butterfly Originals, 1983.

Wicket the Ewok, flat die-cut Ewok eraser and sharpener with Ewok decal. Blister packed on color header with cartoon Ewok artwork .... $10–$15

PENCIL AND ERASER SET

Butterfly Originals, 1983. Flat character eraser and plastic pencil sharpener blister-packed together on Jedi header card.

Each .... $10–$15

PENCIL BOX

Helix (British), 1978. Contains pencils, eraser and sharpener.

Each .... $35–$45

PENCIL HEADS

Butterfly Originals, 1983. Colored plastic. Variously sold on pencils, separately or in sets. Four different: Emperor's Guard, Darth Vader, C-3PO or Ewok.

Each .... $5–$10

PENCIL POUCHES

Butterfly Originals, 1983. Zippered plastic pouch with artwork of Luke, Darth Vader and Jedi logo.

Each .... $15–$25

Helix (British), 1978. Zippered plastic. Eight different.

Ben Kenobi .... $20–$30
C-3PO .... $20–$30
Darth Vader .... $20–$30
Han .... $20–$30
Leia .... $20–$30
Luke .... $20–$30
R2-D2 .... $20–$30
Stormtrooper .... $20–$30

H.C.F. (British), 1983. Zippered plastic with artwork of Darth Vader, spaceships and Jedi logo.

Each .... $15–$25

PENCIL SHARPENERS

Butterfly Originals, 1983. Colored plastic figures. Came individually blister packed on header with Jedi logo. Three different.

Darth Vader .... $10–$15
R2-D2 .... $10–$15
Yoda .... $10–$15

Butterfly Originals, 1983. Round plastic with paper decal of TIE Fighter.

Each .... $5–$10

H.C.F. (British), 1982. Domed with line drawing on top. Four different.

C-3PO and R2-D2, red .... $15–$25
Darth Vader and Stormtrooper, gray .... $15–$25
Han and Chewbacca, yellow .... $15–$25
Luke and Leia, blue .... $15–$25

H.C.F. (British), 1982. Flat oval with picture of Darth Vader and X-Wing.

Each .... $10–$15

Helix (British), 1978. Shaped like the Death Star.

Each .... $25–$35

PENCIL TINS

A.H. Prismatic (British), 1994. Black metal with holographic foil sticker affixed to lid. Three slight variations.

Each .... $4–$8

Metal Box Co., 1980. Shallow-hinged rectangular tins with color photo covers and Empire logo on bottom. Four different.

C-3PO and R2-D2 .... $20–$25
Chewbacca .... $20–$25
Darth Vader .... $20–$25
Yoda .... $20–$25

PENCIL TOPS

H.C.F. (British). 1″ to 2″ color full-figure pencil decorations. Sold separately or in various sets. Two series.

Chewbacca, Series One .... $5–$10
Darth Vader, Series One .... $5–$10
Han Solo, (Hoth Gear) Series One .... $5–$10
Luke, (Flight Suit) Series One .... $5–$10
R2-D2, Series One .... $5–$10
Yoda, Series One .... $5–$10
Admiral Ackbar, Series Two .... $5–$10
Bib Fortuna, Series Two .... $5–$10
Darth Vader, Series Two .... $5–$10
Gamorrean Guard, Series Two .... $5–$10

H.C.F., Pencil Top Gift Set

Imperial Guard, Series Two .... $5–$10
Wicket, Series Two .... $5–$10

PENCIL TRAY

Sigma, 1982. White ceramic with C-3PO decoration on right side.
Each .... $20–$30

Butterfly Originals, glow-in-the-dark Erasers

ERASERS

Butterfly Originals, 1983. Colored figure erasers. Came blister packed on color artwork headers with Jedi logo.
Admiral Ackbar .... $5–$10
Baby Ewoks .... $5–$10
Bib Fortuna .... $5–$10
Darth Vader .... $5–$10
Emperor's Royal Guard .... $5–$10
Gamorrean Guard .... $5–$10
Jabba the Hutt .... $5–$10
Max Rebo Band, set of three .... $5–$10

Butterfly Originals, R2-D2 eraser

R2-D2 .... $5–$10
Wicket .... $5–$10
Yoda .... $5–$10

Butterfly Originals, 1983. Glow-in-the-Dark. Set of three. Darth head, C-3PO head and Millennium Falcon. Came blister-packed on header with Jedi logo.
Per set .... $10–$15

Butterfly Originals, 1983. Small rectangular eraser with decal of Emperor's Guard on top.
Per item .... $10–$15

Crystal Craft (Australia), 1983. Set of three (C-3PO, Darth Vader and Millennium Falcon) die-cut, glow-in-the-dark erasers. Came blister-packed.
Per set .... $10–$15

H.C.F. (British), 1982. Character erasers. Color artwork printed on flat die-cut eraser.
Per eraser .... $5–$10

H.C.F. (British), 1982. Record erasers. Shaped like record albums. 3¾″ diameter with Darth head and Jedi logo on label. Packaged in plastic wrap with paper cover art of Jedi lightsaber logo or Darth and Luke. Assorted colors.
Price each .... $5–$10

H.C.F. (British), 1982. Perfumed character erasers. Came in illustrated clear plastic cases. Six different.
Chewbacca, orange .... $4–$8
Darth Vader, grape .... $4–$8
Han Solo, apple .... $4–$8
Luke Skywalker, mint .... $4–$8
Princess Leia, strawberry .... $4–$8
R2-D2 and C-3PO, raspberry .... $4–$8

Helix (British), 1978. Carded character erasers.
Price each .... $5–$10

PENS

Butterfly Originals, 1983. White pens with drawings of characters in blue and Jedi logo in red. Blister-packed two pens per card. Card has Emperor's Guard and Jedi logo.
Per card .... $10–$15

Butterfly Originals, 1983. Felt tip. Two per package. Blue and black or red and black with Jedi logos. Blister-packed on header with artwork of C-3PO.
Per pack .... $10–$15

Fantasma, 1992. Ball point. Star Wars logo and line artwork on defractive foil background. Several minor variations.
Price each .... $3–$5

Fisher, 1994.
Rebel Fighter Pen, click ballpoint. Black rubberized grip. "Star Wars" on clip and Rebel emblem on end. Packaged in clear plastic tube. .... $15–$20
Star Wars Titanium Ballpoint Pen, dark gray metal with "Star Wars" and "May the Force Be With You" imprinted on the barrel. Packaged in generic Fisher pen case. .... $65–$75

Helix (British), 1978. Colored felt tips. Boxed sets. Two different sizes.
Large, ten different .... $40–$65
Small, five different .... $25–$35

Star Tours Disney. "Star Tours" logo and stars on black nylon-tip-type with cap.
Per pen .... $2–$5

Tiger Electronics, 1997. Ballpoints with character heads that say phrases appropriate to character and have record/playback functions.
C-3PO .... $6–$10
Darth Vader .... $6–$10
Luke X-Wing Pilot .... $6–$10

Tiger Electronics, 1997.
Lightsaber FX Pen, ballpoint with four sound effects and twelve-second record/playback capability and voice changer switch .... $10–$15

PENCILS

Butterfly Originals, 1983. Packed in sets of four on header with pictures of Darth Vader and Jedi logo. Per set.
Darth Vader .... $2–$5
C-3PO .... $2–$5
Jedi logo .... $2–$5

Fantasma, 1992. Star Wars logo and line artwork printed on diffraction foil. Two basic styles. Both have minor pattern variations.
Plain .... $1–$3
Fringe topped .... $1–$3

H.C.F. (British), 1982. Tag-Top pencils. Decorated with puffy flower-shaped tag. Four different.
Han and Chewbacca .... $5–$10
Darth Vader and Stormtroopers .... $5–$10
Luke and Leia .... $5–$10
R2-D2 and C-3PO .... $5–$10

Helix (British), 1978. With shaped tops. Four different.
C-3PO .... $2–$3
Darth Vader .... $2–$3
R2-D2 .... $2–$3
Stormtrooper .... $2–$3

Helix (British), 1978. Ten colored pencils. Packaging pictures Stormtroopers.
Per package .... $4–$8

Helix (British), 1978. Blue with "May the Force Be With You" in gold.
Per pencil .... $1–$2

Star Wars Fan Club, 1980. White and red with pictures of characters and Empire logo.
Per pencil .... $1–$2

Butterfly Originals, Pop-A-Point pencils

PENCILS, MECHANICAL

Butterfly Originals, 1983. Pop-A-Point. Red plastic sparkle embossed with "May the Force Be With You" in gold. Came blister-packed on header with picture of Darth Vader and Jedi logo. Two pencils and box of 22 points per package.
Per package .... $10–$15

MISCELLANEOUS

BOOKENDS

Sigma, 1982. Ceramic. Darth Vader and Chewbacca (kneeling) in pair.
Per pair .... $200–$300

BOOK COVERS

Butterfly Originals, 1983. Laminated. Packages of two
- **Per package** .... $5–$10

Factors Etc., 1978. 13″ × 21″. Original Fan Club logo in color.
- **Per item** .... $5–$10

BOOKMARKS

A.H. Prismatic, 1994. Holographic. Three foil holograms on each. Three slight variations.
- **Price each** .... $2–$4

Antioch, 1992 to present. Tasseled with color artwork from novels.
- **Glove of Darth Vader** .... $1–$3
- **Crystal Star** .... $1–$3
- **Lost City of the Jedi** .... $1–$3
- **Truce at Bakura** .... $1–$3
- **Zorba the Hutt's Revenge** .... $1–$3

Antioch, 1996 to Present Tasseled character bookmarks. Color photos.
- **Darth Vader** .... $1–$3
- **Han Solo** .... $1–$3
- **Lando Calrissian** .... $1–$3
- **Luke Skywalker** .... $1–$3
- **Princess Leia** .... $1–$3

Antioch, 1995 to present Die-cut color photo character bookmarks.
- **Artoo-Detoo** .... $2–$4
- **Boba Fett** .... $2–$4
- **See-Threepio** .... $2–$4
- **Stormtrooper** .... $2–$4
- **Tusken Raider** .... $2–$4
- **Yoda** .... $2–$4

Fantasma, 1992. Darth and Luke fighting and logo printed on refractive plastic bookmark.
- **Per item** .... $2–$4

Random House, 1983. Color artwork on lightweight die-cut cardboard. Sixteen different.
- **Admiral Ackbar** .... $5–$10
- **Ben Kenobi** .... $5–$10
- **Boba Fett** .... $5–$10
- **C-3PO** .... $5–$10
- **Chewbacca** .... $5–$10
- **Darth Vader** .... $5–$10
- **Emperor's Royal Guard** .... $5–$10
- **Han Solo** .... $5–$10
- **Jabba the Hutt** .... $5–$10
- **Lando,** Skiff Guard .... $5–$10
- **Leia,** Boush .... $5–$10
- **Luke** .... $5–$10
- **R2-D2** .... $5–$10
- **Stormtrooper** .... $5–$10
- **Wicket the Ewok** .... $5–$10
- **Yoda** .... $5–$10

BOOKPLATES

Random House, 1983. All are captioned, "This book belongs to . . ." Four different. Price per box.
- **Darth Vader,** black border .... $5–$10
- **C-3PO and R2-D2,** blue border .... $5–$10
- **Wicket,** brown border .... $5–$10
- **Yoda,** green border .... $5–$10

CALCULATOR

Tiger Electronics, 1997.
- **A-Wing Calculator,** shaped like A-Wing. Top slides back to reveal solar calculator. Also has three sound effects........ $15–$25

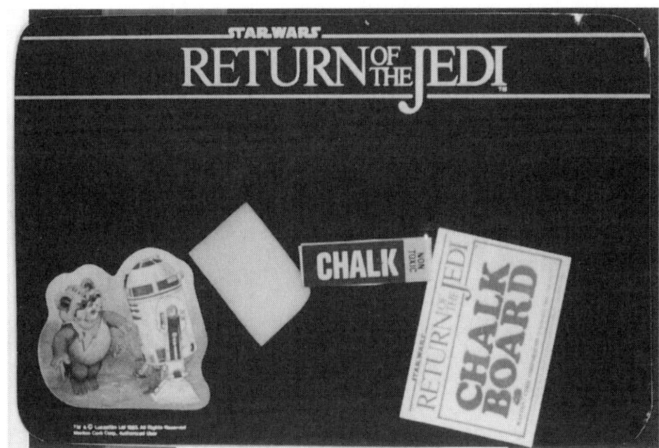

Manton, Return of the Jedi chalkboard

CHALKBOARD

Manton, 1983. 11″ × 17″ horizontal format. R2-D2 and Wicket in lower left corner. Jedi logo at top.
- **Chalkboard** .... $40–$65

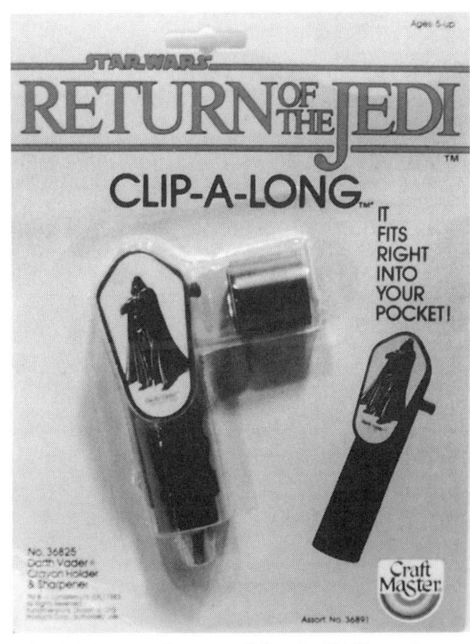

Craft Master, Return of the Jedi Clip-a-Long

CLIP-A-LONGS

Craft Master (Fundimensions), 1983. Children's desk tools designed to clip to pocket. Colored plastic with artwork paper decal of character. Came blister-packed on header with Jedi logo. Three different.

CONSTRUCTION PAPER

Stuart Hall, 1983. Forty-sheet pad of assorted colors. Horizontal format 12″ × 9″. Color artwork of Biker Scout and Jedi logo on cover.

Per pad ....$10–$15

DRAWING SET

Helix (British), 1978. Tin containing drawing instruments. Lid illustrated with photo of C-3PO and R2-D2.

Per item ....$50–$75

GLUE

Butterfly Originals, 1983. "Color Glue." Tube of blue glue with illustration of X-Wing and Jedi logo. Came blister-packed on header with X-Wing and Jedi logo.

Per tube ....$10–$15

I.D. CARDS

Antioch, 1996. Color photo wallet cards approximately 2″ × 3¼″.

Bounty Hunter ....$1–$2
Chewbacca....................$1–$2
Imperial AT-AT....................$1–$2
Imperial TIE Fighter....................$1–$2
Millennium Falcon....................$1–$2
Rebel Alliance ....$1–$2
X-Wing Starfighter....................$1–$2

LABELS

Introduct (Dutch), 1983. School labels. Sheet consisting of six labels each with a different character.

Per sheet ....$5–$10

MARKERS

Butterfly Originals, 1983. Felt tip. Shaped like Darth Vader. 3½″ tall.

Per pack....................$15–$20

MEMO BOARD

Icarus (British), 1982. 8½″ × 12″. Wipe clean with felt-tip marker.

Han, Chewbacca and Lando, in Skiff Guard outfit ....$20–$30
Darth and Stormtroopers ....$20–$30
Luke, Leia and Han....................$20–$30

MEMO HOLDER

Union, 1987. Blue or purple plastic with pocket for paper and pen. Magnetic-backed.

Tenth Anniversary logo ....$15–$25

MOUSEPADS

Moustrak, 1992/93. Padded rectangular computer mousepads with color photos on surface.

Bounty Hunters....................$15–$20
C-3PO and R2-D2....................$15–$20
Dark Forces....................$15–$20
Darth Vader ....$15–$20
Luke and Leia on Jabba's sail barge ....$15–$20
Millennium Falcon....................$15–$20
Rebel Assault....................$15–$20
Yoda ....$15–$20

PAPER CLIP

Tenth Anniversary logo, 1987. Spring-hinge-type with magnetic back....................$5–$10

PAPERWEIGHTS

3-D Arts, 1993. Holographic images in lucite paperweights.

Darth Vader ....$18–$22
Yoda ....$18–$22

RULER

Butterfly Originals, 1983.

Ruler, 6″. With changing space battle scene....................$5–$10
Ruler, 12″. Decorated with characters and Jedi logo ....$10–$15

Bradley Time, 1983. Built in LCD calculator and clock.

Ruler, decorated with characters and Jedi logo ....$25–$35

SCHOOL KIT

Butterfly Originals, 1983.

School Kit, pencil pouch, ruler, eraser, pencil and pencil sharpener in clear plastic bag with Jedi header.....$40–$50

Butterfly Originals, Return of the Jedi school kit

SCHOOL SETS

Helix (British), 1978. Padded front with illustration. Contains assorted school supplies. Two sizes.

Large School Set, pictures Han and Chewie........$60–$75
Small School Set, pictures a Star Destroyer.........$40–$50

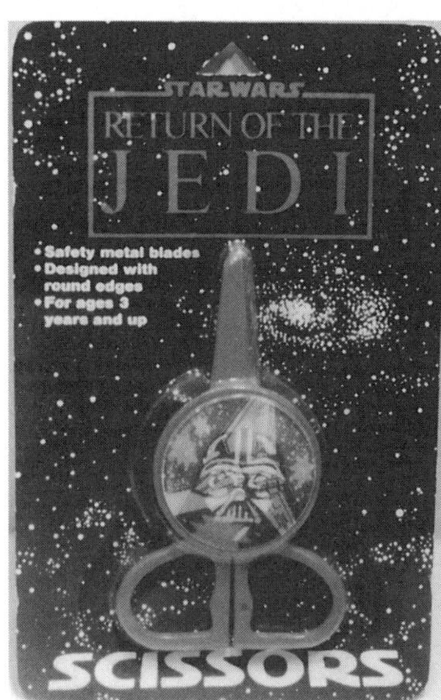

Butterfly Originals, Return of the Jedi scissors

SCISSORS

Butterfly Originals, 1983. Red plastic adorned with round medallion that changed between Darth Vader head and Shuttle Tydirium. Blister-packed on header card with Jedi logo.

Scissors...$15–$20

STATIONERY SETS

H.C.F. (British), 1983. Came with assorted H.C.F. school products. Packaged in shallow window box with color artwork. Several different assortments.

Per set ....$20–$30

STRING DISPENSER

Sigma, 1982. Ceramic. Shaped like R2-D2. Lid comes off to insert string, which is fed through hole in top.

Dispenser ....$75–$100

TAPE DISPENSER

Butterfly Originals, 1983. Red plastic. Standard size and shape. Illustrated with Darth Vader figure and Jedi logo. Came blister-packed on card with Jedi logo.

Dispenser..$10–$15

Sigma, 1982. Ceramic. In the shape of C-3PO seated with tape spool between his knees.

Dispenser ....$75–$100

REINFORCEMENTS

BUTTERFLY ORIGINALS

Stickers Foil stickers of characters and ships with punch-out holes; forty-eight per package.

Each ....$10–$15

RUBBER STAMPS

Per set ....$15–$25

STAR WARS

All Night Media Inc. Set of six in clear plastic case with color artwork of stamps.

Per set ....$15–$25

RETURN OF THE JEDI

Adam Joseph, 1983. Color plastic silhouette of character or ship is handle of stamp. Came individually blister-packed on Jedi header or in boxed counter display. Twelve different.

Admiral Ackbar..$5–$10
Biker Scout...$5–$10
C-3PO ....$5–$10
Chewbacca...$5–$10
Darth Vader ....$5–$10
Emperor's Royal Guard ....$5–$10
Gamorrean Guard..$5–$10
Millennium Falcon...$5–$10
TIE Fighter...$5–$10
Wicket..$5–$10
X-Wing...$5–$10
Yoda ....$5–$10

WICKET THE EWOK

Adam Joseph, 1983. Boy or Girl Ewok is handle of set, which includes three interchangeable stamps. Came blister-packed on header card.

Per set ....$5–$10

STATIONERY

DIE-CUT STATIONERY

Drawing Board, 1977. Shaped like R2-D2; eighteen sheets and twelve envelopes per package.

Each ....$15–$25

ENVELOPES

Letraset (British), 1977. Pack of twelve, illustrated in front corner and on reverse.

Each ....$10–$15

FOLD-OVER NOTES

Drawing Board, 1977. No envelope necessary; fold and mail. R2-D2 on cover, twelve to a package.

Each ..... $15–$20

LAP PACK

Drawing Board, 1977. Ten printed sheets, ten plain sheets and ten envelopes in folder with Hildebrandt poster art and Star Wars logo on front.

Each ..... $20–$30

NOTE PADS

Drawing Board, 1977. Two different. Both have title at top with drawing of character and Star Wars logo at bottom.

Official Duty Roster, Darth Vader ..... $10–$15
Wookiee Doodle Pad, Chewbacca ..... $10–$15

NOTES, BOXED

Drawing Board, 1977. Ten fold-over note cards with envelopes. Color artwork covers; two different. Per box.

Hildebrandt poster art ..... $15–$20
R2-D2 and C-3PO ..... $15–$20

Drawing Board, 1977. Twelve assorted fold-over note cards with envelopes. Four each of three different designs (Chewbacca, C-3PO and Darth Vader artwork).

Per box ..... $20–$25

PADDED STATIONERY

Drawing Board, 1977. Pad of twenty-five sheets. Hildebrandt poster art on cover and corners of sheets.

Each ..... $10–$15

POSTCARDS

NOTE: See also GREETING CARDS.

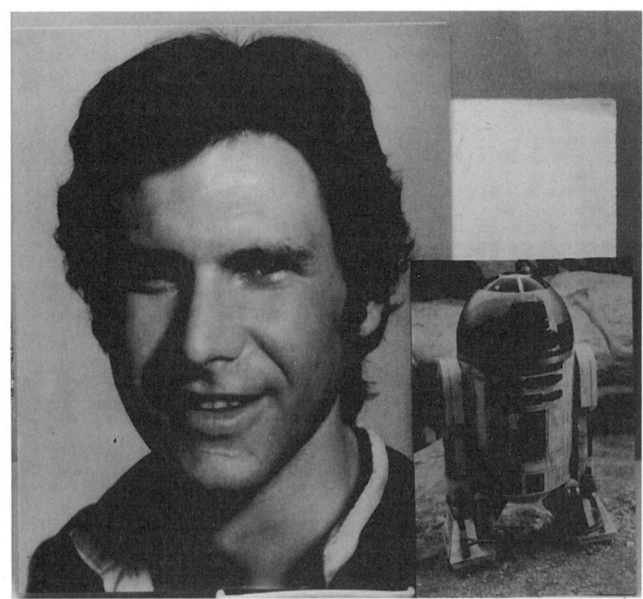

Classico, postcards in two sizes

A.H. Prismatic (Britain), 1994. Lasergrams. Regular-size postcards with holographic foil images.

Darth Vader ..... $4–$5
Millennium Falcon in Asteroid Field ..... $4–$5
Millennium Falcon with TIE Fighters ..... $4–$5

Classico, 1993 to present. Current, extensive, expanding line of postcards with color artwork from all three movies. Two sizes.

Small, approx. 4″ × 6″ ..... $1–$2
Large, approx. 8″ × 10″ ..... $2–$3

Drawing Board, 1977.

C-3PO and R2-D2, twenty to a package ..... $4–$8

Filmwelt Berlin (German), 1995 to present. Current, extensive, expanding line of postcards with color photos and poster artwork from all three movies. Approx. 4¼″ × 5¾″.

Filmwelt Berlin, Star Wars postcard

Price each ..... $1–$2

Giftworks (Chronicle Books), 1995. Sets of thirty color postcards in perforated pads with heavy plastic covers.

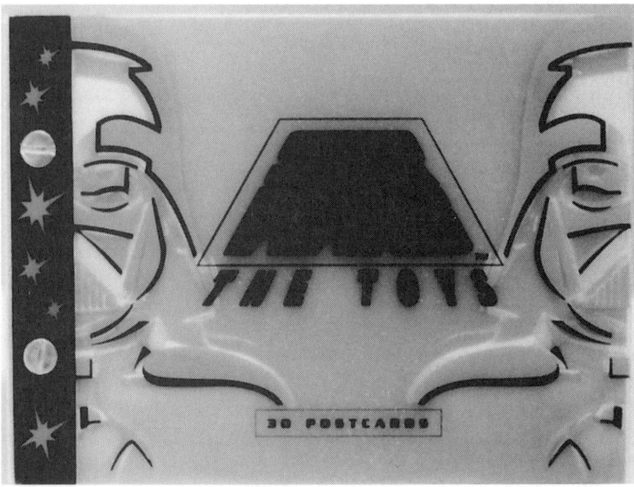

Giftworks, Star Wars postcard set

Star Wars—Aliens and Creatures ....$9–$12
Star Wars—Behind the Scenes............................$9–$12
Star Wars—The Toys...$9–$12
Oral B, 1983. Dental check-up reminders.
Ewoks...$1–$2
Heroes ....$1–$2
Luke and Darth...$1–$2
R2-D2/C-3PO ....$1–$2
Star Tours Disney. Large postcards are 8″ × 10″; small are 4″ × 6″.
C-3PO, large ....$1–$3
C-3PO and R2-D2, large...$1–$3
Han Solo, large ....$1–$3
Luke, large ....$1–$3
Stormtroopers, large ....$1–$3
Bespin, Cloud City; small ....$1–$2
"Star Tours," color artwork; small ....$1–$2
Tatooine, artwork of Jabba's Palace; small ....$1–$2

POSTCARD SET

Giftworks (Chronicle Books), 1996. Artbox #4, The Art of Ralph McQuarrie Star Wars set. Boxed set includes fifteen postcards plus forty-eight-page booklet and sheet of six Star Wars postage stamps. Fold-open box has wraparound McQuarrie artwork.
Each ....$9–$12

STATIONERY, BOXED

Drawing Board, 1977. Boxed set displays X-Wing artwork on stationery and envelope; eighteen sheets and twelve envelopes tied with blue ribbon.
Each ....$15–$20

STANDEES

A standee is simply a die-cut poster affixed to a cardboard backing with a fold-out support to keep the standee upright. All standees in this section are color photos and may be assumed to be close to life-size unless otherwise noted. This section is alphabetical by name of character.

NOTE: This section contains mass-market products. For those standees designed for use in theaters, see section on STUDIO PROMOTIONAL MATERIAL.

Advanced Graphics, 1993 to present.

Admiral Ackbar .... $25–$35
Boba Fett .... $25–$35
C-3PO .... $25–$35
Darth Vader .... $25–$35
Darth Vader, with lightsaber .... $25–$35
Emperor .... $25–$35
Han Solo .... $25–$35
Han Solo, Stormtrooper outfit .... $25–$35
Han Solo, in carbonite .... $25–$35
Imperial Guard .... $25–$35
Jawa .... $25–$35
Luke .... $25–$35
Obi-Wan Kenobi .... $25–$35
Princess Leia .... $25–$35
Princess Leia, slave outfit .... $25–$35
R2-D2 .... $25–$35
Stormtrooper .... $25–$35
Tusken Raider .... $25–$35
Yoda .... $25–$35

Factors Etc., 1978–1980.

Boba Fett .... $30–$40
Chewbacca .... $30–$40
C-3PO .... $30–$40
Darth Vader .... $30–$40
R2-D2 .... $30–$40

Sales Corporation of America, 1983. Standees are approximately 1/2 size.

Darth Vader and Imperial Guards .... $25–$35
Ewoks .... $15–$25
R2-D2 and C-3PO .... $25–$35

Sales Corporation of America, R2-D2 and C-3PO standee

STUDIO PROMOTIONAL MATERIAL

POSTERS

All movie posters are printed at contracted printing plants called National Screen Services, which are generally located near areas of distribution. These distribution points have been sending out advertising material for films from most studios since 1942. Movie posters come in five basic sizes. The most commonly used size, especially today, the one-sheet (27″ × 41″), is usually printed on a thin clay-coated paper stock. The insert size (14″ × 36″) is printed on a heavy card stock paper which lends itself to greater durability. The half-sheet or display poster is also printed on the more durable paper stock and is the only U.S. movie poster with a horizontal composition. The thirty-forty (30″ × 40″) is printed on the heavy card stock paper. In most cases the printing plates used to print the one-sheets are also used for the thirty-forty. The last of the standard movie poster sizes is the forty-by-sixty (40″ × 60″) and it, too, is printed on the heavy card stock paper. Larger sizes exist, usually for sign and billboard use. These are usually designed as a multiple of one-sheets (three-sheet or six-sheet), each being three or six times the standard size of a one-sheet.

A popular movie will often release more than one style of artwork or photograph for theater posters. When this is done they will letter the posters (A, B, C, etc.) on the lower border where the title is printed. Prices and descriptions are for U.S. posters. Foreign posters, which generally have different though similar artwork, are comparable in value. The posters listed here are the major versions of the trilogy theater posters. Some minor variations do occur.

In this section, posters are arranged chronologically by movie. You will find Star Wars first, followed by Empire Strikes Back and then Return of the Jedi. The Ewok "Caravan of Courage" movie, released theatrically in foreign markets, is also included. Examples of other studio promotional materials follow the poster section.

Star Wars First Advance Poster (First Version) This was the first one-sheet-size poster to be released for Star Wars. It was printed on silver mylar paper that has a chrome finish and is very reflective. It features the phrase, "COMING TO YOUR GALAXY THIS SUMMER—STAR WARS." The Star Wars logo featured on this poster is different than the standardized logo that was adopted a few months later.

One-sheet rolled ....$600–$900
One-sheet folded ....$400–$600

Star Wars First Advance Poster (Second Version) Similar to first version but flat silver and black on white paper with standard trademark logo.

One-sheet rolled ....$400–$600
One-sheet folded ....$200–$300

Star Wars Style "A" one-sheet

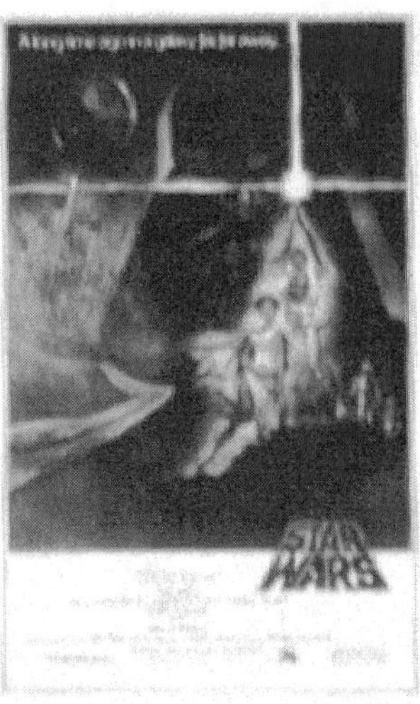

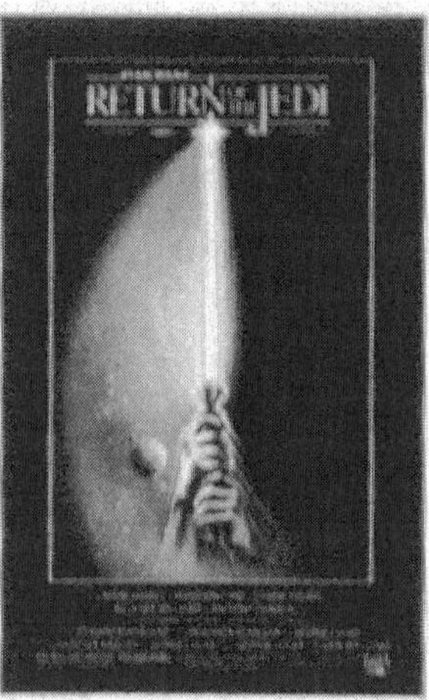

Star Wars Trilogy one-sheet movie posters

Star Wars Advance Poster (Style "B") Blue ink on white paper, "A LONG TIME AGO IN A GALAXY FAR, FAR AWAY . . . STAR WARS."

- **One-sheet rolled** .... $250–$400
- **One-sheet folded** .... $150–$300

Star Wars Style "A" Illustration by Tom Jung. Luke with lightsaber and Leia in front of large Darth Vader helmet.

- **One-sheet rolled** .... $200–$300
- **One-sheet folded** .... $150–$250
- **Insert rolled** .... $100–$200
- **Insert folded** .... $75–$175
- **30″ × 40″ rolled** .... $100–$200
- **30″ × 40″ folded** .... $75–$175
- **40″ × 60″ rolled** .... $300–$400

40″ × 60″ folded .... $200–$300
Three-sheet folded .... $400–$600
Six-sheet folded .... $600–$800
Standee .... $400–$600

Star Wars Style "A" Half-Sheet Different artwork from regular style "A."

Half-sheet rolled .... $150–$250
Half-sheet folded .... $75–$175

Star Wars Style "C" Illustrated by Tom Cantrell. Artwork used on many foreign posters.

One-sheet rolled .... $200–$300
One-sheet folded .... $150–$250

Star Wars Style "D" Illustration by Drew Struzan and Charles White III. Done in 1930s style of circus posters.

One-sheet rolled .... $200–$300
One-sheet folded .... $150–$250
30″ × 40″ rolled .... $100–$200
30″ × 40″ folded .... $75–$150
40″ × 60″ rolled .... $200–$300
40″ × 60″ folded .... $150–$250
Standee .... $300–$500

Star Wars Happy Birthday At the end of the first year of Star Wars distribution, a special birthday poster was released to theaters still playing the movie. Probably fewer than 500 were printed.

One-sheet rolled .... $500–$800
One-sheet folded .... $400–$600

Star Wars 1979 Reissue Cropped-style "A" artwork with red band across the middle containing information on new Star Wars toys.

One-sheet rolled .... $150–$300
One-sheet folded .... $100–$200

Star Wars 1981 Reissue Cropped version of style "A" artwork with banner proclaiming that "The Force will be with you for two weeks only."

One-sheet rolled .... $150–$300
One-sheet folded .... $100–$200
Half-sheet rolled .... $100–$175
Half-sheet folded .... $75–$150
Insert rolled .... $50–$125
Insert folded .... $50–$100
30″ × 40″ rolled .... $75–$150
30″ × 40″ folded .... $50–$125
40″ × 60″ rolled .... $150–$250
40″ × 60″ folded .... $100–$200
Standee .... $250–$400

Star Wars 1982 Reissue "Star Wars Is Back" with "Revenge of the Jedi" trailer advertisement.

One-sheet rolled .... $150–$300
One-sheet folded .... $100–$200
Half-sheet rolled .... $100–$175
Half-sheet folded .... $75–$150
Insert rolled .... $75–$125
Insert folded .... $60–$100
30″ × 40″ rolled .... $75–$125
30″ × 40″ folded .... $60–$100
40″ × 60″ rolled .... $150–$250
40″ × 60″ folded .... $100–$200
Standee .... $250–$400

Star Wars 10th Anniversary

One-sheet mylar .... $150–$250
One-sheet Drew art .... $100–$150
16″ × 36″ Mind's Eye Press, McQuarrie art ..... $20–$40

The Empire Strikes Back Advance Style "A" Darth Vader's helmet superimposed on a field of stars.

One-sheet rolled .... $50–$125

Star Wars 1982 reissue insert with Revenge of the Jedi ad

Empire Strikes Back Advance Style "A" one-sheet

One-sheet folded .... $40–$75

The Empire Strikes Back Style "A" Illustration by Rodger Kastel. Dubbed the "Love Story" or "Kissing Scene" poster due to the "Gone With the Wind" style artwork.

One-sheet rolled .... $125–$175
One-sheet folded .... $100–$125
Half-sheet rolled .... $75–$100
Half-sheet folded .... $50–$75
Insert rolled .... $75–$100
Insert folded .... $50–$75
30″ × 40″ rolled .... $75–$100
30″ × 40″ folded .... $50–$75
40″ × 60″ rolled .... $125–$150
40″ × 60″ folded .... $100–$150
Standee .... $200–$350

The Empire Strikes Back Style "B" Illustration by Tom Jung. Light blue background.

One-sheet rolled .... $100–$150
One-sheet folded .... $75–$125
Half-sheet rolled .... $50–$100
Half-sheet folded .... $40–$75
Insert rolled .... $50–$100
Insert folded .... $40–$75
30″ × 40″ rolled .... $50–$100
30″ × 40″ folded .... $40–$75
40″ × 60″ rolled .... $100–$150
40″ × 60″ folded .... $75–$125
Standee .... $200–$300

The Empire Strikes Back 1981 Summer Re-Release

One-sheet rolled .... $100–$150
One-sheet folded .... $75–$125
Half-sheet rolled .... $50–$100
Half-sheet folded .... $40–$75
Insert rolled .... $50–$100
Insert folded .... $40–$75
30″ × 40″ rolled .... $50–$100
30″ × 40″ folded .... $40–$75
40″ × 60″ rolled .... $100–$150
40″ × 60″ folded .... $75–$125
Standee .... $200–$300

The Empire Strikes Back 1982 Re-Release

One-sheet rolled .... $100–$150
One-sheet folded .... $75–$125
Half-sheet rolled .... $50–$100
Half-sheet folded .... $40–$75
Insert rolled .... $50–$100
Insert folded .... $40–$75
30″ × 40″ rolled .... $50–$100
30″ × 40″ folded .... $40–$75
40″ × 60″ rolled .... $100–$150
40″ × 60″ folded .... $75–$125
Standee .... $200–$300

The Empire Strikes Back 10th Anniversary

One-sheet silver mylar .... $100–$150
One-sheet gold mylar .... $200–$250
One-sheet mobile art .... $15–$25

Revenge of the Jedi Advance (First Version) No release date on bottom.

One-sheet rolled .... $100–$200
One-sheet folded .... $50–$100

Revenge of the Jedi Advance (Second Version) Release date May 25, 1983, on bottom. Most of the print run was distributed through the Star Wars Fan Club.

One-sheet rolled .... $75–$150
One-sheet rolled .... $40–$75

Return of the Jedi Style "A" Illustration by Tim Reamer. Lightsaber artwork.

One-sheet rolled .... $35–$50
One-sheet folded .... $25–$35
Half-sheet rolled .... $25–$35
Half-sheet folded .... $20–$25
Insert rolled .... $25–$35
Insert folded .... $20–$25
30″ × 40″ rolled .... $25–$35
30″ × 40″ folded .... $20–$25
40″ × 60″ rolled .... $35–$50
40″ × 60″ folded .... $25–$35
Standee .... $100–$200

Return of the Jedi Style "B" Illustration by Kazuhiko Sano.

One-sheet rolled .... $50–$75

Return of the Jedi Style "B" one-sheet

One-sheet folded .... $35–$50
Half-sheet rolled .... $35–$40
Half-sheet folded .... $25–$35
Insert rolled .... $35–$40
Insert folded .... $25–$35
30″ × 40″ rolled .... $35–$40
30″ × 40″ folded .... $25–$35

40″ × 60″ rolled $50–$75
40″ × 60″ folded $35–$50
Standee $125–$250

Return of the Jedi 1985 Reissue Illustration by Tom Jung.
One-sheet rolled $35–$50
One-sheet folded $25–$35
Half-sheet rolled $25–$35
Half-sheet folded $20–$30
Insert rolled $25–$35
Insert folded $20–$30
30″ × 40″ rolled $25–$35
30″ × 40″ folded $20–$30
40″ × 60″ rolled $35–$50
40″ × 60″ folded $25–$35
Standee $100–$200

Return of the Jedi 10th Anniversary
One-sheet Kazo Sano art $20–$25

The Caravan of Courage Style "A" Illustration by Kazuhiko Sano. Printed for foreign theatrical release.
One-sheet rolled $25–$40
One-sheet folded $20–$30

The Caravan of Courage Style "B" Illustration by Drew Struzan. Printed for foreign theatrical release.
One-sheet rolled $25–$40
One-sheet folded $20–$30

Special Edition Trilogy (1997) All three regular theater posters are Drew Struzen artwork. Foreign posters have only very minor differences.
Special Edition Trilogy Advance, logo $25–$35
Star Wars, one-sheet $20–$25
Empire, one-sheet $20–$25
Jedi, one-sheet $20–$25
Standee, die-cut cast photo $500–$700

Japanese Empire Strikes Back theater poster

Foreign Theatrical Posters Often in different sizes, sometimes with different art. This listing is not complete but should give a feeling for pricing.

Star Wars
British, Quad poster, 30″ × 40″ $250–$400
Italian, 54″ × 39″ $150–$300
German, Style "A" $150–$300
German, Style "B" $150–$300
Japanese, teaser $100–$250
Japanese, reissue $75–$200
French $75–$150

Empire Strikes Back
German, Style "A" $100–$200
Italian, 54″ × 39″ $100–$200
Japanese, Style "A" or "B" $75–$150

Return of the Jedi
British, Quad poster, 30″ × 40″ $75–$125

Triple Feature
British, Quad poster, 30″ × 40″ $100–$200

LOBBY CARDS AND STILLS

These are color 8″ × 10″ (lobby cards) or 11″ × 14″ (stills) cards with scenes from a movie designed for theater display. In the United States they generally come in sets of eight, and both size sets almost always display the same scenes. Though stills are larger, lobbies seem to be preferred by most collectors. Other theatrical promotional paper exists, including mixed-size U.S. still sets (photobustas) and a rich variety of foreign lobbies and stills that usually have different scenes from the U.S. version and are often larger sets. The vast majority of collectors, however, choose to stick with the more common U.S. material.

Star Wars
Cards $125–$225
Stills $100–$200

Empire Strikes Back
Cards $75–$125
Stills $50–$100

Return of the Jedi
Cards $50–$100
Stills $35–$75

Caravan of Courage (Ewok Movie) Released theatrically in foreign markets.
Cards $35–$50
Stills $25–$35

MISCELLANEOUS ITEMS

The following are some examples of other types of studio promotional items that have been produced.

Program Book—Star Wars Only the first movie had an

actual theater program book. Subsequent movies' licensed special magazines (see MAGAZINES) that the studio felt took the place of programs. Horizontal format with artwork of Vader and X-Wings.

First printing, slick cover ....$50–$75

Subsequent printings, pebble-tone cover............$35–$50

Star Wars program book

Promotional Book—Star Wars Black cover with early Star Wars logo. Color interior photos. Came packaged in white box. Early promotional item.

Each ....$250–$400

Star Wars Cast Flyer, 1977

Each ....$20–$35

Empire Strikes Back Art Portfolio Not available to general public. Long black cardboard outer box embossed with Darth Vader design. Black inner envelope sealed with lead Darth Vader medallion. Contains two color McQuarrie art prints.

Each ....$250–$350

Revenge of the Jedi Promotion Guide, 1982 White cover with Revenge artwork by Ralph McQuarrie

Each ....$135–$200

PRESS KITS AND PRESS BOOKS

Press kits are promotional packages sent out by the studio to theaters and media sources. They generally contain photos and/or slides, backgound information on the film and biographies of the actors and other key personnel. Press books are pages of line art sent to theaters for inclusion in newspaper ads.

Star Wars

Kit, rare ....$500–$800

Book ....$35–$75

Empire Strikes Back

Kit ....$350–$600

Book ....$25–$50

Return of the Jedi

Kit ....$200–$450

Book ....$20–$40

TOYS AND CRAFTS

Toys in general are traditionally a very strong area of collectibility, and Star Wars toys are no exception. Crafts have always been of secondary interest, but like many other categories of merchandise, are becoming more collectible for simply economic reasons. A collector who has been forced to give up on collecting the more expensive toys may turn his or her interest toward something more affordable. As with many other collectibles, the condition of packaging is almost as important as the toy itself. For maximum collectibility boxes should be in as "near new" condition as possible. Removing a blister-carded item from the package, no matter how carefully it was done, is to bring its value down nearly to the level of an unpackaged item, which is rarely greater than 50 percent of its packaged counterpart and often less. Crafts should be in their original, un-used condition with all components still with the kit. To work the kit as the manufacturer originally designed destroys nearly 100 percent of its collectible worth. Many of the products in this section, especially those manufactured by Kenner, had nearly identical toys marketed overseas by various other companies; Palitoy in Britain, Meccano in France, Clipper in Spain and Harbert in Italy are the most common ones. Prices on these items tend to be very close to their U.S. counterparts. In Japan, Takara, the primary toy licensee for Star Wars' early years, manufactured some toys distinctly different from U.S. products, and these are listed separately.

This section is organized alphabetically by type of item.

CRAFTS

Craft kits must be complete and in original packaging to have collectible value. A completed craft project is worth only a fraction of the price of one in the original package.

AMERICAN PUBLISHING

Presto Magix, 1980. Fold-out poster with color artwork scene from Empire and transfer sheets. Came folded in plastic bag.

Asteroid Storm .... $3–$5

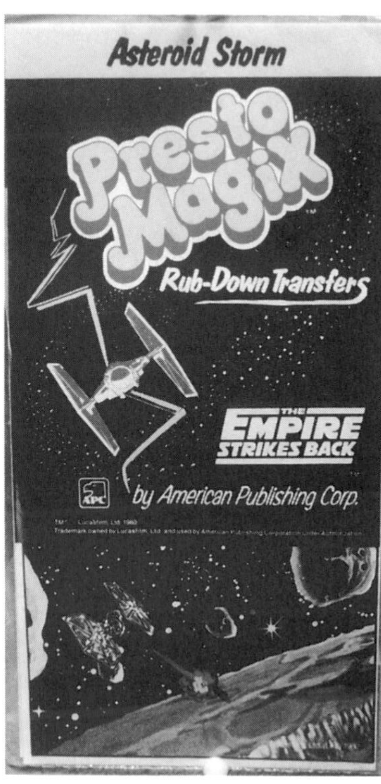

American Publishing, Presto Magix Empire Strikes Back rub-down transfers

Beneath Cloud City .... $3–$5
Dagobah Bog Planet .... $3–$5
Cloud City Battle .... $3–$5
Deck of the Star Destroyer .... $3–$5

Ice Planet Hoth .... $3–$5
Rebel Base .... $3–$5

Presto Magix, 1983. Color artwork fold-out poster of Jedi scenes and transfer sheets.

Death Star .... $2–$4
Ewok Village .... $2–$4
Jabba's Throne Room .... $2–$4
Sarlacc's Pitt .... $2–$4

Presto Magix, 1980. 18″ × 24″ folded poster and set of thirty transfers. Comes boxed.

Each .... $35–$45

Presto Magix, 16″ × 24″ fold-out color scene board plus six transfer sheets and transfer stick. Comes boxed. Box shows color photo of scene and Jedi logo.

Jabba's Throne Room .... $20–$30
Endor .... $20–$30

Presto Magix, 1984. 16″ × 24″ fold-out color board plus six transfer sheets. Comes boxed. Box art shows scenes from Ewoks TV show.

Ewoks at Home .... $15–$25
Ewok Village .... $15–$25

CRAFT HOUSE

Medallion Highlight Kits, 1996. Each kit contains two plastic medallions, display stands and stickers and paint for toning medallions. Comes blister-carded.

Craft House, medallion highlight kit

Darth Vader and C-3PO/R2-D2 .... $7–$10
Princess Leia and Han Solo .... $7–$10
Yoda and Luke Skywalker .... $7–$10

Paint-By-Number, 1996. Boxed kit contains one 16″ × 20″ panel, brush and thirty-six acrylic paints. Front of box shows completed painting.

Each .... $16–$20

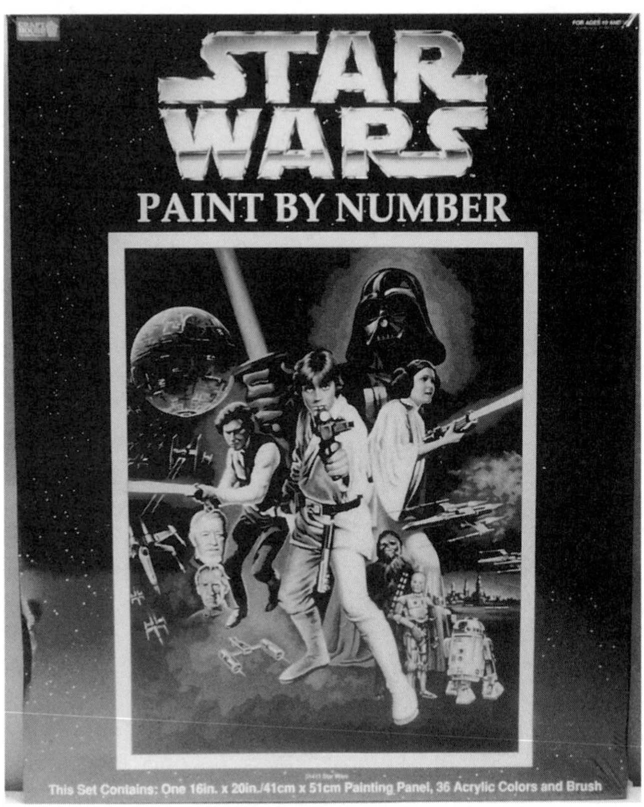

Craft House, paint by number kit

CRAFT MASTER (FUNDIMENSIONS)

Color N' Clean Machine, 1980. Box decorated with color scenes and logo from Empire frames 50″ continuous roll of reusable line-drawn scenes to color. Kit comes with four crayons and wipe cloth.

Each .... $75–$150

Figure Painting Set, 1980. Kit includes 5½″ plastic figurine, four different paints and brush. Came blister-packed on header card with photo of finished figurine and Empire logo.

Boba Fett .... $35–$50
Han Solo .... $25–$35
Leia .... $25–$35
Luke on Tauntaun .... $25–$35
Yoda .... $25–$35

Figurine Painting Set, 1983. Return of the Jedi. Plastic figures, paints and brush. Blister-packed on header card. Glow-in-the-dark accents.

Admiral Ackbar .... $20–$30
C-3PO/R2-D2 .... $20–$30
Wicket .... $20–$30

Make and Bake It, 1983. Suncatchers. Kit includes metal outline and colored plastic beads for making "stained glass" ornament. Came blister-carded with Jedi logo.

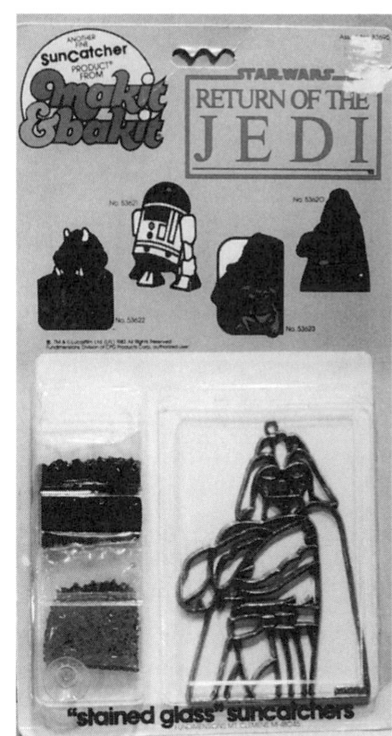

Craft Master (Fundimensions), Makit & Bakit Return of the Jedi suncatcher kit

Darth Vader .... $15–$25
Gamorrean Guard .... $15–$25
Jabba the Hutt .... $15–$25
R2-D2 .... $15–$25

Paint-By-Number, 1980. Glow-in-the-dark accents. Kit includes one 8″ × 10″ scene plus supplies. Box art shows finished artwork and Empire logo.

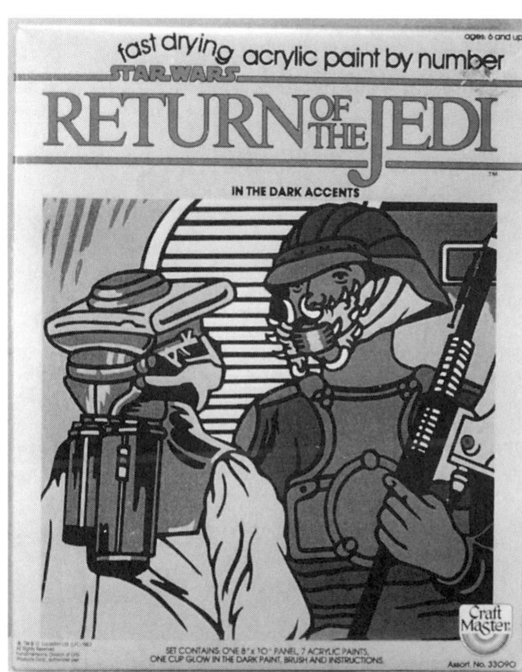

Craft Master (Fundimensions), glow-in-the-dark acrylic paint by number kit

Darth Vader .... $20–$30
Han and Leia .... $20–$30
Luke .... $20–$30
Yoda .... $20–$30

Paint-By-Number, 1983. Glow-in-the-dark accents. Kits similar to the above but with scenes from Return of the Jedi.

C-3PO and R2-D2 .... $15–$25
Jabba the Hutt .... $15–$25
Lando and Boushh .... $15–$25
Sy Snootles .... $15–$25

Paint-By-Number, 1980. "Classic Scenes" from The Empire Strikes Back. Set includes 10″ × 14″ scene plus twelve acrylic paints, brush and instructions. Two different.

The Battle on Hoth .... $25–$35
The Chase Through the Asteroids .... $25–$35

Poster Art Pen and Poster Sets, 1977/78. Each set contains two 17½″ × 22″ posters, six pens and logo insert that doubles as color guide.

Darth Vader Lives and May the Force, etc. .... $25–$35
Death Star Collage and Cantina Collage .... $25–$35
Logo Character Collage and Space Battle .... $25–$35

Poster Art Pen and Poster Set, 1982. Two 11½″ × 18″ Empire posters and eight crayons.

Each .... $20–$25

Sew 'N Show Cards, 1984. Boxed set of six Ewok cartoon cards and yarn. Wicket the Ewok cartoon logo and photo of product on front.

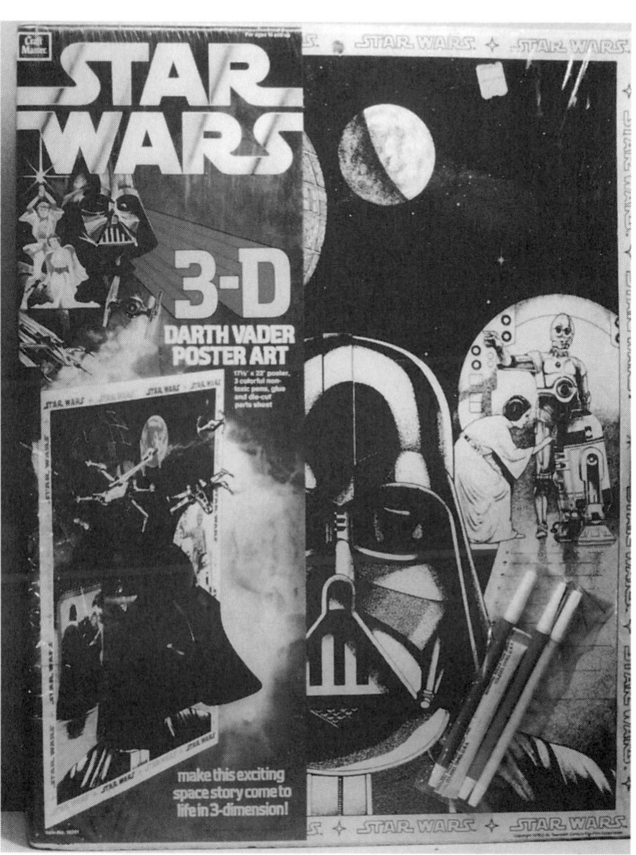

Craft Master (Fundimensions), 3-D Darth Vader poster art kit

Each .... $15–$25

3-D Darth Vader Poster Art Kit, 1978. Includes 17½″ × 22″ poster, punch-out ships and Darth Vader mask, three felt-tip pens, glue and insert that doubles as color guide.

Each .... $30–$35

FUNDIMENSIONS

Water Color Painting Set, 1983. Contains 8″ × 10″ Ewok cartoon. Eight paints, brush and instructions.

Ewok .... $15–$20
Ewok Flyer .... $15–$20
Ewok Village .... $15–$20

H. E. HARRIS

Stamp Collecting Kit, 1977. Kit includes stamp album, twenty-four Star Wars seals, thirty-five stamps, stamp hinges and magnifier. Comes boxed. Color box art shows X-Wing, TIE Fighter and Star Wars logo.

Each .... $25–$40

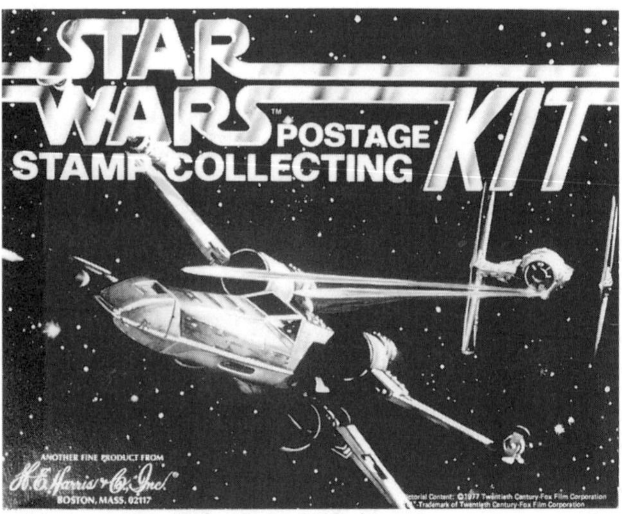

H. E. Harris, Star Wars stamp collecting kit

KENNER

Dip Dots, 1977. Water color paint set. Book of sixteen 8½″ × 11″ scenes plus tray of eight paints and brush. Box shows color photo of child painting and Star Wars logo.

Each .... $45–$65

Playnts, 1977. Set includes five different 16″ × 24″ posters to be painted, six different paints, two brushes and color guide. Came packaged with paints blister-packed on outside of color photo cover sheet.

Each .... $20–$35

Sticker Making Kit, 1995. Star Wars refill set for Kenner's Fantastic Sticker Maker. Box contains forty photos and tape refill for machine.

Each .... $15–$20

LEE WARDS

Latch Hook Pillow Kits, 1980. Printed mesh backing and yarn. Boxed with color photo of completed product and respective character below Empire logo. Two different.

Darth Vader .... $50–$75
R2-D2 .... $50–$75

Latch Hook Rug Kits, 1980. Printed mesh backing and yarn. Boxed with color photo of completed kit and photo of respective character below Empire logo. Six different.

C-3PO and R2-D2 .... $50–$75
Chewbacca .... $50–$75
Darth Vader .... $50–$75
R2-D2 .... $50–$75
Stormtrooper .... $50–$75
Yoda .... $50–$75

Suncatchers, 1980. Kits for making stained-glass ornaments. Includes metal frame and glass beads. Came blister-carded with photos of characters and Empire logo at top.

C-3PO .... $20–$30
Darth Vader, full figure .... $20–$30
Darth Vader, head .... $20–$30
IG-88 .... $20–$30
Luke .... $20–$30
Luke on Tauntaun .... $20–$30
Millennium Falcon .... $20–$30
R2-D2 and Yoda .... $20–$30
Snowspeeders .... $20–$30
Stormtrooper .... $20–$30
X-Wing .... $20–$30

LETRASET

Transfer Set (British), 1978. Included scene plus sheet of rub-off transfers. Came bagged. Two sizes.

Battle at Mos Eisley, large .... $15–$20
Escape from Death Star, large .... $15–$20
Rebel Attack, large .... $15–$20
#1 Kidnap of Princess Leia, small .... $5–$10

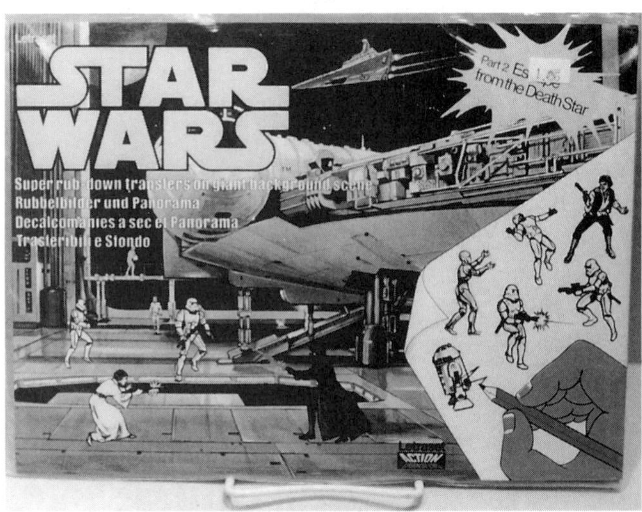

Letraset (British), Escape from Death Star rub-down transfer set

#2 Sale on Tatooine, small ....$5–$10
#3 Action at Mos Eisley, small ....$5–$10
#4 Escape from Stormtroopers, small ....$5–$10
#5 Flight to Alderaan, small ....$5–$10
#6 Inside the Death Star, small ....$5–$10
#7 Prison Break, small ....$5–$10
#8 Death Star Escape, small ....$5–$10
#9 Rebel Air Base, small ....$5–$10
#10 Last Battle, small ....$5–$10

THOMAS SALTER

Transfer Sets (British), 1983. Sets included sheet(s) of transfers and cardboard scene. Several sizes. Larger sets were boxed.

Battle on Endor, small box ....$10–$15
Ewoks, small pack ....$4–$8
Ewok Village, large pack.......................................$6–$10
Ewok Village, large box ....$15–$20
Jabba's Throne Room, small box ....$10–$15
Jabba the Hutt, small pack ....$4–$8
Sarlacc Pit, large pack ....$6–$10

DIE-CAST METAL FIGURES AND VEHICLES

Also see PEWTER and GAMING sections.

GALOOB

Die-Cast Metal Vehicles, 1997. 3″ to 4″ in length. Early packaging has toy blister-packed on round header cards. Later packaging is trapezoidal header card. Toys include stand.

Imperial Star Destroyer ....$10–$15
Jawa Sandcrawler ....$10–$15
Millennium Falcon ....$10–$15
TIE Fighter ....$10–$15
X-Wing Starfighter ....$10–$15
Y-Wing Starfighter ....$10–$15

KENNER

Action Masters Die-Cast Metal Figures, 1994. Painted metal figures range in height from approximately 1 1/4″ to 3″ high and have attached stands. Figures come blister-carded with Action Masters trading cards or (six-figure set) in shallow window box.

C-3PO, single figure ....$10–$20
Chewbacca, single figure ....$10–$20
Darth Vader, single figure ....$10–$20
Luke, single figure ....$10–$20
R2-D2, single figure ....$10–$20
Stormtrooper, single figure ....$10–$20
Four-Figure Set, R2-D2, C-3PO, Leia and Obi-Wan ....$25–$45
Six-Figure Set, Darth Vader, Chewbacca, Bob Fett, Luke, Han and Stormtrooper ....$20–$35
Special Gold-Plated C-3PO, mail-in figure ....$30–$40

Vehicles, 1978/80. Vehicles, which were not to scale with each other, are made of metal and plastic. Toys are from 4″ to 7″ in size and always had some moving parts. They come packaged two ways. Smaller vehicles were blister-packed on header cards. The four heavier ones, Star Destroyer, Y-Wing, Millennium Falcon and TIE Bomber, were blister-packed on cards that were then secured inside open 3″ deep frame boxes. Color artwork on both package styles showed craft in action. Many vehicles were made in both Star Wars and Empire logo packaging. Neither is appreciably more valuable. Unpackaged vehicles are worth approximately 50 percent of packaged counterparts.

Darth Vader TIE Fighter, pop-off side panels. Removable figure of Darth Vader....................................$60–$85
Landspeeder, rolls. Luke and C-3PO in cockpit. Windshield is often missing from unpackaged vehicle................ ....$75–$100
Millennium Falcon, swiveling cannon and antennae dish. Retractable landing gear...................................$150–$200

Kenner, die-cast TIEs; *from left to right,* TIE Fighter, TIE Bomber, and Darth Vader TIE Fighter

Slave I, retractable landing gear. Cannon and flaps swivel .... $95–$125
Snowspeeder, canopy opens, cannon swivels and landing gear retracts .... $115–$150
Star Destroyer, sliding door on underside. Compartment holds tiny removable Rebel ship .... $150–$200
TIE Bomber, pop-off side panels. This toy was only test marketed. Never generally released .... $975–$1300
TIE Fighter, pop-off side panels. Removable pilot .... $60–$85
Twin Pod Cloud Car, retractable landing gear.. $95–$135
X-Wing, wings and canopy open. Canopy is often missing from unpackaged vehicles .... $75–$125
Y-Wing, pop-off wing pods, swiveling cannon and small red bomb that is dropped with release button .... $150–$200

TAKARA (JAPAN)

Die-Cast Figures and Vehicles, 1977/78. These are larger and much more complicated toys than the Kenner die-cast series and tend to have unexpected functions. C-3PO, for instance, shoots projectiles from his stomach. Toys came packaged in boxes with color artwork of toy.

C-3PO .... $275–$350
Darth Vader .... $275–$350
R2-D2, small 3″, packaged in window box .... $125–$200
R2-D2, large 5″, packaged in solid box .... $225–$325
X-Wing .... $225–$350

Takara Zeitca Die-Cast Miniatures Ships and figures come blister-packed on color header cards.

C-3PO .... $75–$100
Landspeeder .... $75–$100
R2-D2 .... $75–$100
TIE Fighter .... $75–$100
X-Wing .... $75–$100

Kenner, die-cast X-Wing Fighter

GUNS

KENNER

Biker Scout Laser Pistol, 1983. Dark gray plastic. Approximately 9″ long. Sight on right side of pistol. Jedi logo on sight. Packaged in open frame box.

Each .... $75–$125

Blaster Rifle, 1996. Retooled version of Kenner's Electronic Laser Rifle done in white plastic instead of black. Packaged in open tray box.

Each .... $20–$25

Kenner, original Laser Pistol *(left)* and Biker Scout Pistol

Kenner, 3-Position Laser Rifle with stock extended

Electronic Laser Rifle, 1980. Essentially the same toy as 3-Position Laser Rifle, but without the stock. Came packaged in open tray box.

Each .... $175–$300

Heavy Blaster, 1996. Retooled version of Kenner's original Laser Pistol done in orange plastic instead of black. Packaged in open tray box.

Each .... $15–$20

Kenner, Heavy Blaster

Laser Pistol, 1979/83. Black plastic. Approximately 10″ long with sight above pistol. Battery sound. Movie logo sticker on side. Packaged in open frame box. This toy was produced throughout the movie trilogy with logos on the package and toy itself changing to display the most recent movie. Unpacked toys are worth considerably less than packaged ones.

Star Wars box .... $125–$175

Empire box .... $100–$150

Jedi box .... $75–$125

Pistol-Weina, 1996. Silver plastic toy with electronic sound effects. Blue Star Wars logo plaque on either side. Star Tours souvenir.

Each .... $15–$20

3-Position Laser Rifle, 1979. Black plastic. Approximately 18″ long (with stock folded). Battery sound. Movie logo sticker on side. Stock would swing from shoulder position to front handgrip or fold flat against body of gun. Came packaged in open frame tray box displayed with stick fully extended.

Each .... $400–$650

KITES

Palitoy (British), 1978. Winged shape with X-Wing and TIE Fighter. Also used as a promotional item with KP Crisps. Promotional version has "Star Wars" logo in addition to picture.

Each .... $35–$50

Spectra Star, Darth Vader head delta-wing kite

Spectra Star, 1983. Color plastic kite and framing tubes. Packaged in plastic bag picturing kite design and Jedi logo. Three different.

Darth Vader, 55″ figure kite .... $15–$25

Luke, 55″ figure kite .... $15–$25

Star Wars, 42″ delta wing kite .... $15–$25

Spectra Star, Luke Skywalker kite

Spectra Star, 1983 Eight character box kite
  Each .... $25–$35
Spectra Star, 1984 64″ streamer kites
  Darth Vader .... $20–$30
  Darth and Luke .... $20–$30
Spectra Star, 1985 Two different based on cartoon series
  Droids, 80″ streamer kite .... $20–$30
  Ewoks on Hang Glider, 80″ mylar octopus kite .... $20–$30
Spectra Star, 1994. X-Wing and Darth TIE 42″ delta wing kite. Came bagged with color photo header designed for hanging. Includes string and handle.
  Each .... $5–$10
Spectra Star, 1994. Darth Vader head 46″ delta wing kite. Came boxed with color photo of product and Darth Vader on front. Includes string and "Speed Winder."
  Each .... $10–$15
Spectra Star, 1997.
  Boba Fett, 32″ diamond kite. Head applique on black background .... $5–$10
  Darth Vader, 62″ delta wing kite. Head applique on purple and white background .... $10–$15
  Wacky Winder, black plastic string dispenser comes packaged in cardboard header with artwork of Darth Vader .... $5–$8
Worlds Apart (British), 1984. Two different standard diamond-shaped kites.
  Darth Vader .... $15–$20
  Millennium Falcon .... $15–$20

LIGHTSABERS

These are understandably very popular items. Because the simple application of a plastic tube to the end of a flashlight could produce a reasonable lightsaber facsimile, many unlicensed replicas were produced. These are essentially valueless as collectibles. For this reason only authorized lightsabers will be listed here.

KENNER, 1978

Inflatable Vinyl "blade" attached to battery-operated light source. 35″ long. Comes boxed with patch kit. Color box photo shows Darth and Obi-Wan dueling.
  Each .... $125–$175
Pop-Out, 1984. Black and silver plastic handle. Red or green plastic retractable blade. Approximately 17″ long when extended. Battery light. Attached belt clip. Droids (animated) logo on handle. Comes packaged in open tray with low header with Droids logo and photo of child with toy.
  Each .... $200–$300
Telescoping Toy, 1996. Approximately 3′ long when extended. Packaged in window box with photo of child with toy. Two styles.
  Darth Vader, red .... $20–$30

Kenner, Darth Vader telescoping lightsaber

  Luke, green .... $20–$30
"The Force" Lightsaber, 1980/83. Black plastic handle with foil decals to produce detail. Rigid red or green plastic blade. Produced howling sound when swung. No battery functions. Usually sold from store floor displays holding several lightsabers.
  Each .... $40–$60
Rubies, 1995. Light-up toy telescopes to 36″. Available in white, red, blue or green plastic. Toy comes blister carded.
  Each .... $5–$10

Rubies, light-up telescoping light saber

TIGER ELECTRONICS

Lightsaber Image Projector, 1997. Lightsaber-shaped toy can function as flashlight or has slides to project Star Wars scenes. Four authentic lightsaber sounds.
Each .... $15–$20

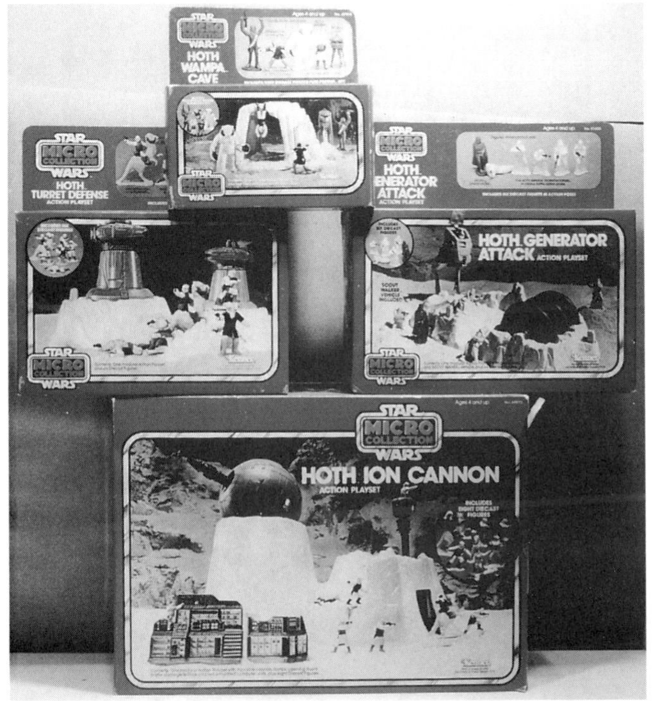

Kenner, Hoth Micro Modules. The Ion Cannon *(bottom)* was the only module not included in its respective "world"

MICRO COLLECTION TOYS

Kenner, 1982. Plastic playsets and ships designed to scale with a series of painted 1¼″ die-cast metal figures in stationary poses. Sets were comprised of several small modules with assorted manual functions that could be interconnected with other modules in the series or the complete sets could be purchased in the form of a "World." Modules and sets included figures. All sets came in boxes with color photos of product on front. The short-lived Micro series apparently could not compete successfully with Kenner's own line of 3¾″ action figures and action figure toys. As a result, Micro playsets are relatively rare.

SETS

Bespin Control Room, Breakaway window, remote lever and platform, comes with four die-cast figures .... $45–$65
Bespin Freeze Chamber, platform lowers figures into chamber, remote claw, escape hatch, four figures .... $55–$75
Bespin Gantry, remote door, rotating platform. Comes with four figures .... $45–$65
Bespin World, control room, freeze chamber and gantry sets plus sixteen figures .... $150–$185
Death Star Compactor, trash compactor, escape hatch, blast door plus eight figures .... $65–$95
Death Star Escape, bridge, exploding cannon, elevator and rope assembly. Six figures .... $65–$95
Death Star World, Death Star compactor and Death Star escape sets plus fourteen figures .... $175–$225
Hoth Generator Attack, exploding generator, scout walker and six figures .... $45–$65
Hoth Ion Cannon, cannon, observation tower with blast doors and eight figures .... $85–$115
Hoth Turret Defense, two exploding gun turrets and six figures .... $45–$65
Hoth Wampa Cave, cave and four figures .... $35–$50
Hoth World, Hoth generator attack, Hoth ion cannon and Hoth Wampa cave sets plus nineteen figures .... $100–$150

SHIPS

Millennium Falcon, top comes off to reveal compartments. Includes six figures .... $135–$200
Imperial TIE Fighter, break-apart feature, one figure ....
.... $40–$50
Rebel Armored Snowspeeder, break-apart feature. Cockpit opens and working harpoon gun, two figures .... $50–$75
X-Wing Fighter, break-apart feature, one figure ...... $40–$50

FIGURES

Set of extra figures, available only through mail-in offer ......
.... $20–$30

MICRO MACHINES

Galoob, 1993 to present.

ACTION FLEET

Though Galoob still labels them as Micro Machines, Action Fleet toys are considerably larger than the regular Micro Machine toys. Vehicles are two to four times as large as a comparable regular Micro toy and figures are about twice as large. The other major difference is that larger vehicles have moving parts and figures are jointed.

2-Pack Promotional "Exclusive" Action Fleet set consists of Luke's Landspeeder, Imperial AT-ST and four figures: Luke, Obi-Wan, Imperial Driver and Imperial Sandtrooper. Vehicles are in window boxes similar to Action Fleet vehicles.

Each .... $35–$50

Flight Controllers Action Fleet vehicles mounted on missile firing hand-held controller with lights and sound effects. Each includes two missles and two figures.

Imperial Flight Controller, Darth TIE Fighter, Darth Vader and Imperial Pilot .... $25–$35

Rebel Flight Controller, X-Wing, Luke (X-Wing Pilot) and R2-D2 .... $25–$35

Battle Packs Sets consist of one or two (if small) vehicles and four or five figures. Sets come blister-carded on backboards that are constructed so that they can either be hung or stand upright on a flat surface.

#1 Rebel Alliance, Speeder Bikes (two), Lando Calrissian, Luke (Jedi Knight), Princess Leia, Rebel Trooper, Echo Base Trooper .... $10–$15

#2 Galactic Empire, AT-ST, AT-ST Driver, Scout Trooper, Darth Vader, Sandtrooper .... $10–$15

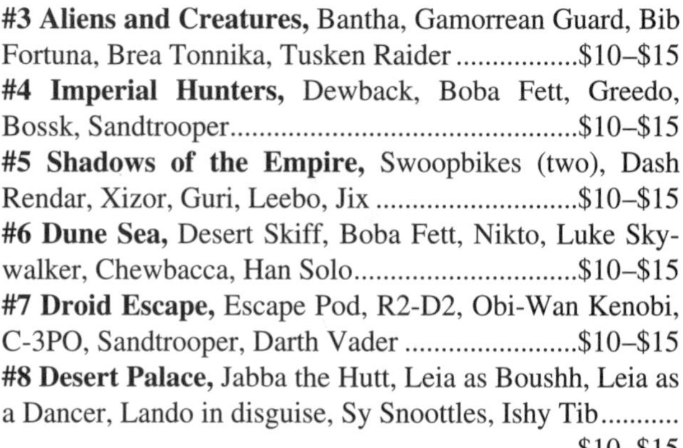

#3 Aliens and Creatures, Bantha, Gamorrean Guard, Bib Fortuna, Brea Tonnika, Tusken Raider .... $10–$15

#4 Imperial Hunters, Dewback, Boba Fett, Greedo, Bossk, Sandtrooper .... $10–$15

#5 Shadows of the Empire, Swoopbikes (two), Dash Rendar, Xizor, Guri, Leebo, Jix .... $10–$15

#6 Dune Sea, Desert Skiff, Boba Fett, Nikto, Luke Skywalker, Chewbacca, Han Solo .... $10–$15

#7 Droid Escape, Escape Pod, R2-D2, Obi-Wan Kenobi, C-3PO, Sandtrooper, Darth Vader .... $10–$15

#8 Desert Palace, Jabba the Hutt, Leia as Boushh, Leia as a Dancer, Lando in disguise, Sy Snoottles, Ishy Tib .... $10–$15

Playsets Playsets have many moving parts and accessories including vehicles and figures. All fold up and have handles for carrying. Packaging is irregularly shaped box with one sloping end. Box covers display Ralph McQuarrie artwork and have window in one corner to display vehicles and figures.

Death Star, damaged Vader TIE Fighter, Probot Capsule, Imperial Pilot, Emperor, Royal Guard, Darth Vader, Stormtrooper, Imperial Gunner .... $40–$50

Ice Planet Hoth, damaged Snowspeeder, Personnel Transport, Rebel Pilot, Luke Skywalker, Princess Leia, Tauntaun, Wampa, 2-1B .... $40–$50

Yavin Rebel Base, damaged X-Wing, R2 Unit, Luke Skywalker, Han Solo, Princess Leia, Wedge Antilles, Sentry .... $40–$50

Galoob, Action Fleet Aliens & Creatures Battle Pack #3

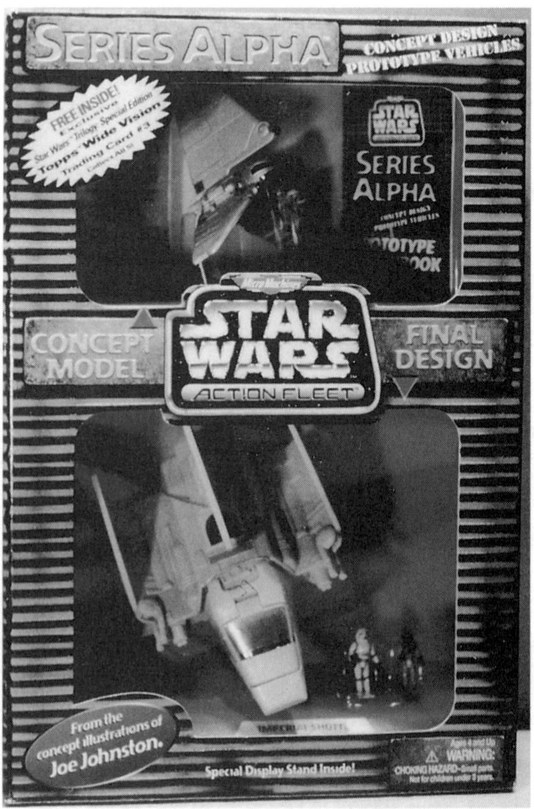

Galoob, Action Fleet Series Alpha

Series Alpha Set consists of a regular Action Fleet vehicle, the corresponding half-size Concept Model of the same vehicle and two Action Fleet figures. Packaging is an 11½″ × 8″ × 4″ box with the regular vehicle displayed in a window at the bottom of the box and the Concept Model in a window above it. Set also includes a Prototype Sketchbook and a Topps Wide Vision trading card.

AT-AT, Prototype AT-AT, AT-AT Driver, Snowtrooper .... $20–$25

Imperial Shuttle, Prototype Imperial Shuttle, Imperial Pilot, Snowtrooper .... $20–$25

X-Wing, Prototype X-Wing, Biggs Darklighter, R2-D2 .... $20–$25

Vehicles Sets consist of one vehicle and two figures. Sets are displayed in window boxes approximately 6″ × 6″ × 7″ with sloping fronts.

AT-AT, AT-AT Driver, Snowtrooper .... $15–$20

A-Wing, A-Wing Pilot, C-3PO .... $15–$20

A-Wing, Green Leader Rebel Pilot, Mon Mothma .... $15–$20

Bespin Cloud Car, Cloud Car Pilot, Lobot .... $15–$20

B-Wing, Rebel Pilot, Admiral Ackbar .... $15–$20

Darth's TIE Fighter, Darth Vader, Imperial Pilot .... $15–$20

Rancor Monster, Gamorrean Guard, Luke (Jedi) .... $15–$20

Sandcrawler, Jawa, Droid .... $15–$20

Shuttle Tydirium, Han Solo, Chewbacca .... $15–$20

Slave I, Han (carbonite), Boba Fett .... $15–$20

Snowspeeder, Rebel Pilot, Rebel Gunner .... $15–$20

TIE Bomber, Imperial Pilot, Imperial Naval Trooper .... $15–$20

TIE Interceptor, Imperial Pilot (two) .... $15–$20

TIE Fighter, Imperial Pilot, Grand Moff Tarkin .... $15–$20

Virago, Xizor, Guri .... $15–$20

Wedge's X-Wing, Wedge Antilles, Red R2 Unit .... $15–$20

X-Wing, Luke (Pilot), R2-D2 .... $15–$20

Y-Wing, Rebel Pilot, R2 Unit .... $15–$20

Y-Wing, Gold Leader Rebel Pilot, R2 Unit .... $15–$20

Remote Controlled AT-AT Action Fleet Vehicle, special promotional item available on a limited basis. Two package variations, one same as other vehicles, one same size and shape but less "window" area and set is arranged differently in box .... $30–$35

Galaxy Battle Collector's Set Twelve-piece mixed vehicle and figure set in window box. Pieces include X-Wing, Millennium Falcon, Y-Wing, Imperial Star Destroyer, TIE Fighter, Darth Vader TIE Fighter, Luke Skywalker, Rebel Pilot, Han Solo, Darth Vader, Imperial Pilot and Imperial Stormtrooper

Each .... $30–$35

LIMITED EDITION DISPLAY PIECES

Balance of Power X-Wing firing on TIE on Star Wars base. Limited to 10,000 pieces.

Each .... $20–$25

Classic Series Gold-plated ships mounted inside Plexiglas display cases. Limited to 5000 pieces each.

Classic Series I, X-Wing and Slave I (J.C. Penney exclusive) .... $100–$125

Classic Series II, Imperial Shuttle (F.A.O. Schwarz exclusive) .... $100–$125

Classic Series III, Millennium Falcon and Darth TIE Fighter .... $100–$125

Millennium Falcon Playset Large toy opens into Millennium Falcon interior/Dock playset. Designed with built-in carrying handle. Includes Lando Calrissian, C-3PO, Chewbacca, Princess Leia, Nien Nunb, Han Solo and Mynock Creature micro figures and Y-Wing micro ship. Rectangular box, approximately 13″ × 17″, shows artwork of toy and has small window in corner to display figures.

Each .... $40–$50

Galoob, Action Fleet Y-Wing Vehicle

Galoob, Micro Machines Millennium Falcon Playset

PROMOTIONAL SETS

Theater Promotional Set, made for the 1997 re-release of Star Wars. Boxed set of three tiny (less than 1″) ships. Slave I, Death Star II and Millennium Falcon ....$50–$75

Galoob, Micro Machines theater promotional set *(left)* and regular

British Promotional Set, 1995. Boxed set of three bronze-colored vehicles. AT-AT, Snowspeeder and X-Wing. Packaged in small window box. "Promotional Use, Not for Sale" on side of box ....$35–$50

Shadows of the Empire Collections Sets of mixed micro vehicles and figures from Star Wars writtten universe-based series. Sets come blister carded on color 7″ × 8½″ headers designed for hanging. Sets each come with a bonus mini comic.

#1 Stinger, IG-2000, Guri, Darth Vader, ASP ....$15–$20

#2 Virago, Swoop w/rider, Prince Xizor, Emperor ....$15–$20

#3 Outrider, Hound's Tooth, Dash Rendar, LE-BO2D9, Luke Skywalker ....$15–$20

Star Wars Adventure Gear Sets These resemble the transforming playsets in both box style and content except that when closed they form hand equipment instead of character heads.

#1 Binoculars/Yavin Base, Y-Wing, Luke Skywalker, Wedge Antilles, R5-D4 ....$10–$20

#2 Lightsaber/Death Star, X-Wing Fighter, Darth Vader, Grand Moff Tarkin, Imperial Gunner ....$10–$20

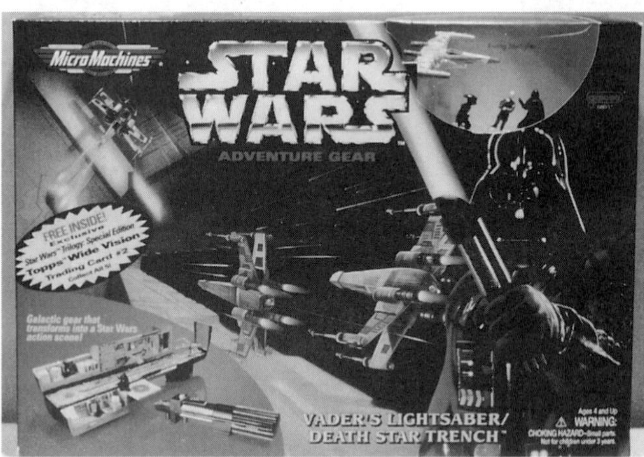

Galoob, Micro Machines Adventure Gear Set #1

Star Wars Collector's Edition Boxed Vehicle Set Set of nineteen regular micro vehicles packaged in a window box. Vehicles included X-Wing Starfighter, Millennium Falcon, Imperial Star Destroyer, Rebel Blockade Runner, Jawa Sandcrawler, Y-Wing Starfighter, TIE Starfighter, Snowspeeder, Imperial TIE Bomber, Boba Fett's Slave I, Bespin Twin-Pod Cloud Car, Imperial AT-AT, Imperial AT-ST, Jabba's Desert Sail Barge, B-Wing Starfighter, Speeder Bike, Imperial Shuttle Tyderium, A-Wing Starfighter and Super Star Destroyer Executor.

Each ....$45–$60

Star Wars Collector's Edition Boxed Vehicle Sets (Pewter Finish). Pewter-colored plastic micro vehicles packaged in window boxes.

Star Wars, X-Wing, Darth Vader's TIE Fighter, Imperial Star Destroyer, Rebel Blockade Runner, Jawa Sandcrawler, Y-Wing Starfighter, Luke's Landspeeder and TIE Starfighter ....$25–$35

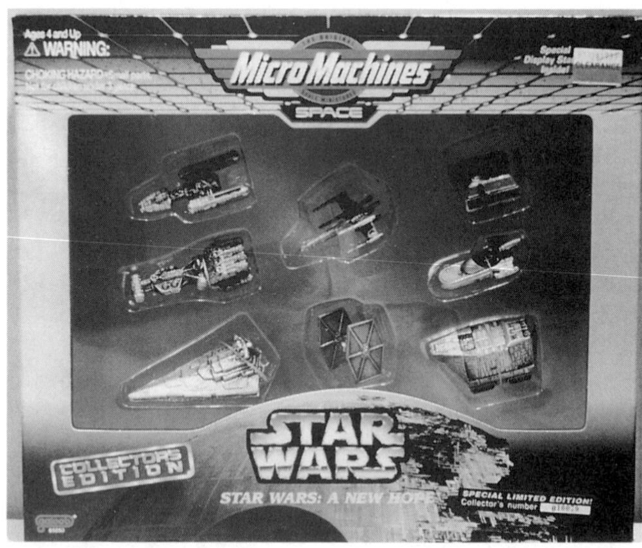

Galoob, Micro Machines Star Wars Collector's Edition pewter-finish boxed set

Empire Strikes Back, Millennium Falcon, Imperial AT-AT, Snowspeeder, Imperial Probot, Twin Pod Cloud Car, Imperial TIE Bomber, Boba Fett's Slave I and Rebel Transport ....$25–$35

Return of the Jedi, AT-ST, Jabba's Sail Barge, B-Wing Starfighter, Super Star Destroyer, Imperial Shuttle Tydirium, A-Wing Starfighter, TIE Interceptor, Mon Calamari Star Cruiser ....$20–$25

Star Wars Double/Takes Playset Full sphere model of Death Star that opens into Death Star (top) and Tatooine (bottom) double playset. Includes one micro vehicle and five micro figures.

Each ....$50–$60

Star Wars Droids Boxed Set Set of sixteen micro figures packaged in a shallow window box. Set includes B'Omarr

Monk, Interrogation Droid, Lin Demolition-mech Mining Droid, Power Droid, IG-88, FX-7, 2-1B, CZ-OR6, Mouse Droid, EV-9D9, WED-15 Treadwell, 4-LOM, R1-G4, Death Star Droid, R5-D4 and 8D8.

Each .... $15–$20

Star Wars Epic Collections Sets of mixed micro vehicles and figures from Star Wars universe-based novels. Box is designed to resemble book. "Cover" opens to reveal toys behind plastic window. Header attached to back of box for hanging.

#1 Heir to the Empire, Grand Admiral Thrawn, Mara Jade, Wedge Antilles, Lady Luck, Star Destroyer, Skipray Blastboat .... $10–$15

Galoob, Micro Machines Droids boxed set

#2 Jedi Search, Admiral Daala, Moruth Doole, Kyp Durron, Sun Crusher, TIE Interceptor, Z-95 Headhunter .... $10–$15

#3 The Truce at Bakura, Gaeriel Captison, Dev Sibwarra, Bluescale, Flurry, TIE Fighter, Shriwirr .... $10–$15

#4 Dark Apprentice, Dorsk 81, Exar Kun, Lando Calrissian, Tafanda Bay, Expanded B-Wing Fighter, Probot .... $10–$15

#5 Dark Force Rising, Garm Bel Iblis, Borsk Fey'lya, Emperor, Scimitar Assault, Coral Vanda, X-Wing .... $10–$15

#6 The Courtship of Princess Leia, Gethzerion, Prince Isolder, Princess Leia, Mon Remonda, Hapes Nova Battle Cruiser, AT-ST .... $10–$15

Star Wars Figure Sets Sets of nine figures in various poses, each approximately 1″ tall. Blister-packed on color header cards, approximately 7″ × 8½″ designed for hanging.

#1 Stormtroopers .... $8–$10
#2 Ewoks .... $8–$10
#3 Rebel Pilots .... $8–$10
#4 Imperial Pilots .... $8–$10
#5 Jawas .... $8–$10
#6 Imperial Officers .... $8–$10

Star Wars Gift Sets Sets of mixed micro vehicles and figures. Packaged in window boxes.

Imperial Forces Gift Set, eight pieces: Imperial Star Destroyer, TIE Starfighter, AT-AT, AT-ST, Darth Vader, Boba Fett, Stormtrooper and the Emperor .... $20–$25

Rebel Forces Gift Set, eight pieces: X-Wing Starfighter, Millennium Falcon, Snowspeeder, B-Wing Starfighter, Luke Skywalker, Han Solo, Princess Leia and Admiral Ackbar.. .... $20–$25

Star Wars Mini Transforming Action Sets Sets include three 1½″ to 2″ hinged character heads that open up to reveal tiny dioramas that each include one figure. Sets are blister-carded on color 7″ × 8½″ header cards designed for hanging.

#1, Admiral Ackbar, Boba Fett, Gamorrean Guard .... $8–$10
#2, Greedo, Nien Nunb, Tusken Raider .... $8–$10
#3, Jawa, Leia in Boushh helmet disguise, Yoda .... $8–$10
#4, Figrin D'an, Scout Trooper, Bib Fortuna .... $8–$10
#5, Bossk, Duros, Stormtrooper .... $8–$10
#6, Weequay, Royal Guard, 2-1B .... $8–$10
#7, Rebel Pilot, 4-LOM, Snowtrooper .... $8–$10
#8, Imperial TIE Pilot, Wampa Creature, Ewok ..... $8–$10
#9, Jabba the Hutt, Salacious Crumb, AT-AT Driver .... $8–$10

Mini Transforming Boxed Set, boxed collection of Leia in Boushh disguise, Greedo, Admiral Ackbar, Gamorrean Guard, Jawa and Nien Nunb Mini Transforming Sets plus Darth Vader Set unique to boxed collection .... $25–$30

Galoob, Micro Machines Star Wars Mini Transforming boxed set

C-3PO Mini Transforming Set, special promotional offer available only to retailers .... $20–$25

Star Wars Playsets Each set, which is considerably smaller than the Millennium Falcon set, includes one micro vehicle and five micro figures. Toys come in rectangular boxes that vary in size slightly but are approximately one-quarter the size of the Millennium Falcon set and still have small window for viewing figures.

#1 The Death Star, X-Wing, Luke Skywalker, Princess Leia, Han Solo, Darth Vader, R2-D2 .... $10–$20

#2 Ice Planet Hoth, AT-AT, Luke Skywalker, Princess Leia, C-3PO, Han Solo, Stormtrooper .... $10–$20

#3 Endor, AT-ST, Ewok, Imperial Zero G Stormtrooper, Chewbacca, Yoda, Boba Fett .... $10–$20

#4 Tattooine, Cargo Skiff, Max Rebo, Sy Snootles, Princess Leia, Boba Fett, Jabba the Hutt w/Salacious Crumb .... $10–$20

#5 Dagobah, X-Wing, Luke Skywalker, Obi-Wan Kenobi, Yoda, Darth Vader, R2-D2 .... $10–$20

Star Wars 3-Vehicle Sets Vehicles, which range in size from 1″ to approximately 2½″, are painted and detailed. Unless free-standing (such as an AT-AT), each comes with a separate stand. Sets are blister-carded to color header cards approximately 7″ × 8½″ designed for hanging. Initial series comprised only three sets. When the second series was inaugurated, the numbering system was started over.

Initial Series

#1 Star Wars, X-Wing, Millennium Falcon, Imperial Star Destroyer .... $15–$25

#2 The Empire Strikes Back, TIE Starfighter, Imperial AT-AT, Snowspeeder .... $15–$25

#3 Return of the Jedi, Imperial AT-ST, Jabba's Desert Sail Barge, B-Wing Starfighter .... $10–$20

Second Series

#1, TIE Interceptor, Imperial Star Destroyer, Rebel Blockade Runner .... $10–$20

#2, Landspeeder, Millennium Falcon, Jawa Sandcrawler .... $10–$20

#3, Darth Vader's TIE Fighter, Y-Wing Starfighter, X-Wing Starfighter .... $10–$20

#4, Imperial Probot, Imperial AT-AT, Snowspeeder .... $10–$20

#5, Rebel Transport, TIE Bomber, Imperial AT-ST .... $10–$20

#6, Escort Frigate, Boba Fett's Slave I, Twin Pod Cloud Car .... $10–$20

#7, Mon Calamari Star Cruiser, Jabba's Desert Sail Barge, Speeder Bike (Rebel Pilot) .... $10–$20

#8, Speeder Bike (Imperial Pilot), Imperial Shuttle Tyderium, TIE Starfighter .... $10–$20

#9, Super Star Destroyer Executor, B-Wing Starfighter, A-Wing Starfighter .... $10–$20

#10, Incom T-16 Skyhopper, Lars Family Landspeeder, Death Star II .... $10–$20

#11, Bespin Cloud City, Mon Calamari Rebel Cruiser, Escape Pod .... $10–$20

#12, A-Wing (battle damaged), Y-Wing (battle damaged), TIE Fighter (battle damaged) .... $10–$20

#13, Red Squadron X-Wing, Green Squadron X-Wing, Blue Squadron X-Wing .... $10–$20

Galoob, Micro Machines 3-Vehicle Set #13

Star Wars Transforming Action Sets Similar to the regular playsets. Packaging is the same and each comes with a micro vehicle and micro figures, but these form character heads when closed.

#1 C-3PO/Cantina, Millennium Falcon, Han Solo, Greedo, Gotal, Chadra-Fan, Duros, Stormtrooper .... $10–$20

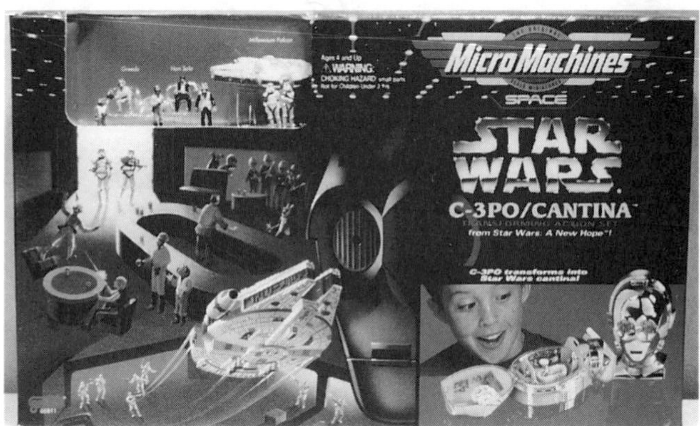

Galoob, Micro Machines C-3PO/Cantina Transforming Action Set

#2 Darth Vader/Bespin, Slave I, Darth Vader, Lando Calrissian, Luke Skywalker, Chewbacca w/C-3PO, Ugnaught .... $10–$20

#3 R2-D2/Jabba's Palace —Jabba's Desert Sail Barge, Jabba the Hutt, Rancor, Luke Skywalker, Princess Leia, Lando Calrissian .... $10–$20

#4 Stormtrooper/Death Star—Vader's TIE Fighter, Luke Skywalker, Han Solo, Chewbacca, Imperial Officer, Stormtrooper, Princess Leia .... $10–$20

#5 Chewbacca/Endor, AT-ST, Ewok (hang gliding), Chewbacca, C-3PO, Ewok, AT-ST Driver .... $10–$20

#6 Boba Fett/Cloud City, Twin Pod Cloud Car, Darth Vader, C-3PO, Han Solo, Lando Calrissian, Boba Fett, Luke Skywalker .... $10–$20

#7 Luke Skywalker/Hoth, AT-AT, Luke Skywalker, Princess Leia, Snowtrooper, Tauntaun, Wedge Antilles .... $10–$20

#8 Royal Guard/Death Star, Imperial Shuttle, Luke Skywalker, Emperor, Imperial Officer, Darth Vader, Imperial Guards (two) .... $10–$20

#9 TIE Fighter Pilot/Academy, X-Wing Fighter, TIE Interceptor, Imperial Recruit #1, TIE Fighter Pilot in Flight Simulator .... $10–$20

Trilogy Gift Set Promotional set. Set of ten X-Ray Fleet-size vehicles, all but one of which have regular, realistic-style paint schemes. Regular ships are Millennium Falcon, X-Wing, Slave I, Y-Wing, A-Wing, Darth TIE, AT-AT, Jawa Sandcrawler and Shuttle Tydirium. Tenth ship is a bonus, X-Ray Shuttle Tydirium.

Each .... $35–$45

Galoob, Micro Machines Trilogy Gift Set

X-Ray Fleet Two-piece vehicle sets with toys made of clear plastic exteriors showing multicolored interiors of vehicles. Ships are approximately twice the size of regular Micro Machines but smaller than vehicles from the Action Fleet series. Stands but not figures are included in the sets. Toys come blister-carded on 7″ × 8½″ color backings designed for hanging.

#1 Darth Vader's TIE Fighter and A-Wing Starfighter .... $10–$15

#2 X-Wing Starfighter and Imperial AT-AT .... $10–$15

#3 Millennium Falcon and Jawa Sandcrawler .... $10–$15

#4 Boba Fett's Slave I and Y-Wing Starfighter .... $10–$15

#5 TIE Bomber and B-Wing Starfighter .... $10–$15

#6 TIE Fighter and Landspeeder .... $10–$15

#7 AT-ST and Snowspeeder .... $10–$15

MISCELLANEOUS

Action Value Pack Spectra Star, 1995. Combined package of Star Wars kite, frisbee and yo-yo Spectra Star products. Toys come shrink-wrapped to a backing board with a star field and photo of Darth Vader.

Each .... $15–$20

Bob Bags Kenner, 1977. Inflatable vinyl punching bags with likeness of Star Wars character printed on toy. Came boxed with color photo of product on front.

Chewbacca, 50″ tall .... $100–$175

Darth Vader, 50″ tall .... $100–$175

Jawa, 36″ tall .... $100–$175

R2-D2, 36″ tall .... $100–$175

Danglers Applause, 1995. Small plastic ships approximately 3½″ long suspended from arm attached to suction cup designed to attach to any smooth surface. Packaged in clear plastic boxes.

Death Star .... $3–$5

Millennium Falcon .... $3–$5

Star Destroyer .... $3–$5

TIE Fighter .... $3–$5

Y-Wing .... $3–$5

Gym Set Gym-Dandy, 1983. Child's gym set includes Speeder Bike swinging ride with sound effects.

Scout Walker Command Tower .... $2000–$2500

Spectra Star, Action Value Pack

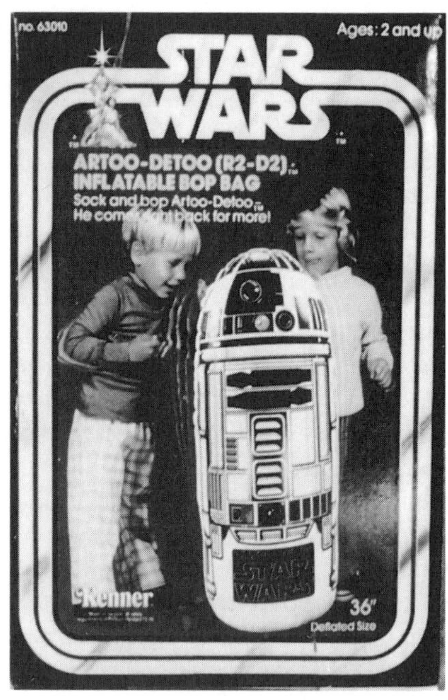

Kenner, R2-D2 Bop Bag

Ewok Family Hut Kenner Preschool, 1984. Ewoks animated series. Hut plus fifteen separate accessories including four nonposable figures. Approximately 12″ high. Kenner Preschool/Jedi box.

Each ....$95–$150

Ewok Fire Cart Kenner Preschool, 1984. From Ewoks animated series. Cart plus accessories and two nonposable figures. Kenner Preschool/Jedi box.

Each ....$95–$115

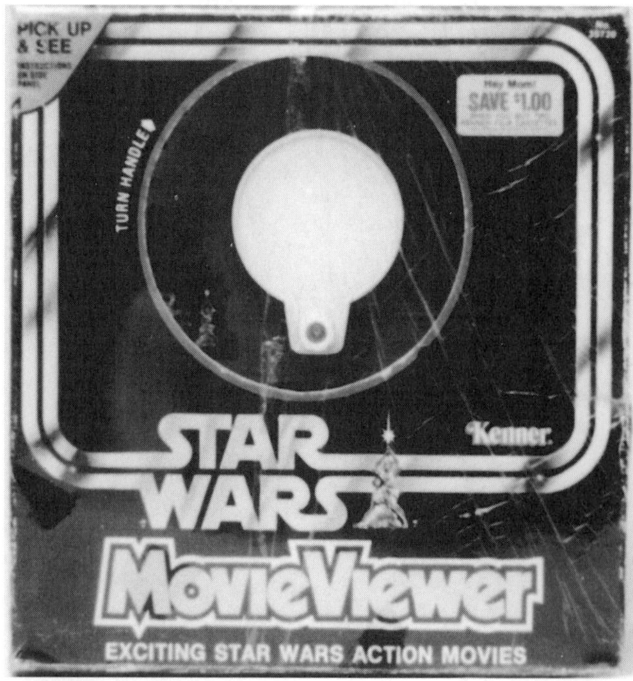

Kenner, Star Wars movie viewer

Ewok Talking Telephone Kenner Preschool, 1984. From Ewoks animated TV series. Plastic toy telephone with receiver held by Ewok figurine. Box shows color photo of toy.

Ewok Talking Telephone ....$40–$70

Ewok Teaching Clock Kenner Preschool, 1985. From Ewoks animated series. Colorful plastic shaped like Ewok village with picture of Wicket on face and pop-up counters at base. Came packaged in green window box.

Each ....$75–$100

Ewok Woodland Wagon Kenner Preschool, 1985. From Ewoks animated series. Covered two-wheel cart, horse and accessories. Kenner Preschool/Jedi box.

Each ....$65–$115

Film Projector Kenner, 1979. Blue plastic hand-held toy film projector. Hand-cranked. Star Wars logo on side. Box has windows over crank and eyepiece so toy could be used inside box. Back of box shows child using toy. Came complete with film cassette (May the Force Be With You).

Movie Viewer ....$75–$125

Film Projector Cassettes Kenner, 1979. Four different Star Wars cassettes were available for the above toy.

Assault on Death Star ....$15–$20

Battle in Hyperspace ....$15–$20

Danger at the Cantina ....$15–$20

Destroy Death Star ....$15–$20

Kenner, Give-a-show projectors, in Star Wars and Jedi boxes

Film Strip Projector Kenner, 1979. Give-A-Show Projector. Blue and red plastic toy film strip projector. Star Wars logo on front. Battery operated. Kit includes sixteen film strips. Box showed child operating toy.

Star Wars box .... $125–$175
Empire box .... $100–$150

Film Strip Projector Kenner, 1984. Similar to other Give-A-Show projector, but with Ewoks logo and film strip.

Ewoks Give-A-Show Projector .... $65–$115

Frisbee Collector Series, 1977. Line drawings of characters and Star Wars logo on silver plastic frisbee. Promotional items.

C-3PO .... $15–$20
Chewbacca .... $15–$20
Darth Vader .... $15–$20
R2-D2 .... $15–$20
Stormtrooper .... $15–$20
X-Wing .... $15–$20

Frisbee H.H. & B., 1981. Color artwork of R2-D2, C-3PO and Darth Vader with Empire logo. Promotion for Coca-Cola and Burger King.

Each .... $10–$15

Burger King/Coca-Cola Empire Strikes Back promotional Frisbee

Frisbee Spectra Star, 1994. Star Wars logo above raised images of Star Destroyer and Millennium Falcon.

Each .... $5–$10

Frisbee—Whizza Performance Disc Worlds Apart (British), 1996. Black with color sticker Star Wars logo and X-Wings. Packaged on blue cardboard header with hanger.

Each .... $15–$20

Ice Skates Brookfield Athletic Shoe, 1983. Skates had round pictures of characters on side of shoe. Box art shows Darth Vader and Jedi logo.

Darth Vader and Imperial Guard .... $125–$175
Wicket .... $95–$125

Kid's Meal Toys KFC, 1997. Offered as promotional premium. Toys and meals came in tote box with color character photos and Star Wars Special Edition trilogy and KFC logos.

NOTE: This was not an extensive promotion in the United States.

Star Wars Spinner, TIE and X-Wing .... $20–$25
Star Wars Sandcrawler .... $20–$25
Empire AT-ST .... $20–$25

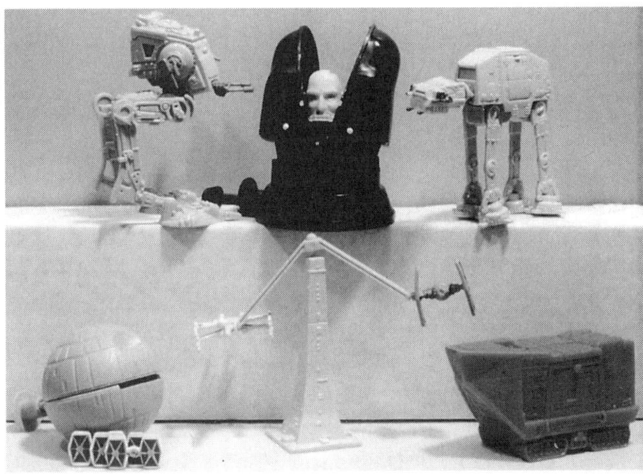

Kentucky Fried Chicken, Kid's Meal toys

Empire AT-AT .... $20–$25
Jedi Launcher, Death Star .... $20–$25
Jedi Spin Revealer, Darth head .... $20–$25

Kid's Meal Toys Taco Bell, 1997. Offered over a period of several weeks as promotional premiums.

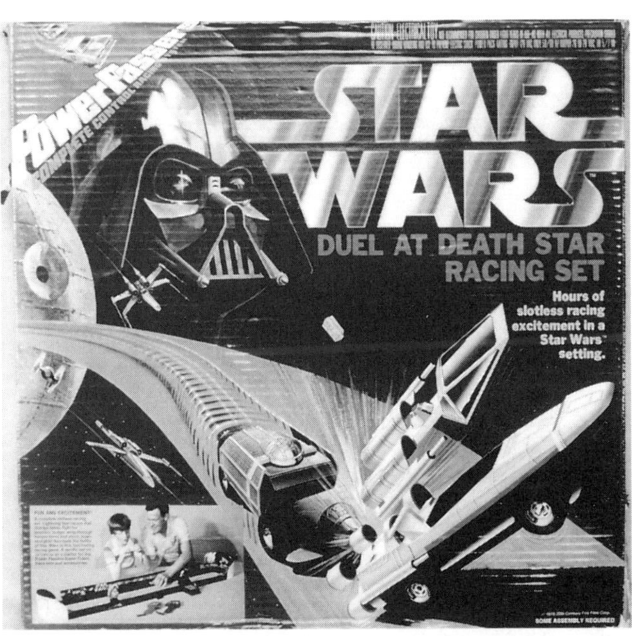

Fundimensions, Star Wars Duel at Death Star Racing Set

Balancing Boba Fett ..... $10–$15
Exploding Death Star Spinner ..... $10–$15
Floating Cloud City ..... $10–$15
Magic Cube, Darth/Yoda ..... $10–$15
Millennium Falcon Gyro ..... $10–$15
Puzzle Cube ..... $10–$15
R2-D2 Playset ..... $10–$15
Yoda Figurine, optional three-and-under toy. It was usually not listed with the other toys and was not widely advertised ..... $15–$25

Power Talker Micro Games of America, 1995. Set consists of Darth Vader mask/microphone and speaker box that attaches to belt. Toy amplifies voice. Came blister-packed inside box with die-cut cut-out around mask.
Each ..... $35–$50

Puppet Regal (Canada). Chewbacca hand puppet.
Each ..... $50–$75

Puppet Kenner, 1981. Yoda, hollow soft plastic figure. 8½″ tall. Came packaged in window box with Empire logo.
Yoda puppet ..... $50–$75

Racing Set Fundimensions, 1978. Slotless race set includes X-Wing and Darth Vader TIE Fighter "cars," track, two controllers, lap counter, power pack and decorative backdrops. 19″ × 20″ box shows color artwork of cars in foreground with Darth and Death Star behind.
Star Wars Duel at Death Star Racing Set ..... $200–$250

Radio Controlled R2-D2
NOTE: See ACTION FIGURE TOYS for other radio-controlled toys.
Kenner, 1978. Control unit with antennae directs battery-powered toy. 8″ tall. Sound and light. Color box photo shows toy with child in background and Star Wars logo ..... $150–$200

Kenner, radio-controlled R2-D2

Takara, (Japan), 1978. Approximately 8″ high. Toy fires disks and top of body turns. Box art has color picture of toy ..... $375–$600

Riding Speeder Bike Kenner, 1983. Pedal-powered metal riding toy shaped like Speeder Bike. Child sized.
Each ..... $2000–$2500

Roller Skates Brookfield Athletic Shoe, 1983. Children's shoe skates with circular design on ankle showing character and Jedi logo. Star Wars logo on tongue and wheels. Color box art of Darth Vader and Jedi logo.
Darth and Imperial Guard ..... $125–$175
Wicket ..... $95–$125

R2-D2 (Battery Powered) Takara (Japan), 1978. Approximately 6″ high. Half of box front depicts toy in motion, other half is window displaying toy.
Each ..... $325–$475

Palitoy (British), talking R2-D2

R2-D2 (Talking) Palitoy (British), 1977. Approximately 7″ high. Says four different phrases. Box art shows color photo of toy.
Each ..... $300–$400

R2-D2 (Wind-Up Walking)
Kenner, (Canadian). Came blister-packed on header card. ..... $150–$200
Takara, (Japanese). Came bagged ..... $225–$300

Sit n' Spin Kenner Preschool, 1984. Toy consists of turntable base that child sits on, with handle in center. Decorated with Ewok artwork. Color photo of toy on box. Ewok packaging.
Each ..... $75–$125

Skateboards Plan B, 1993.
Boba Fett ..... $35–$50

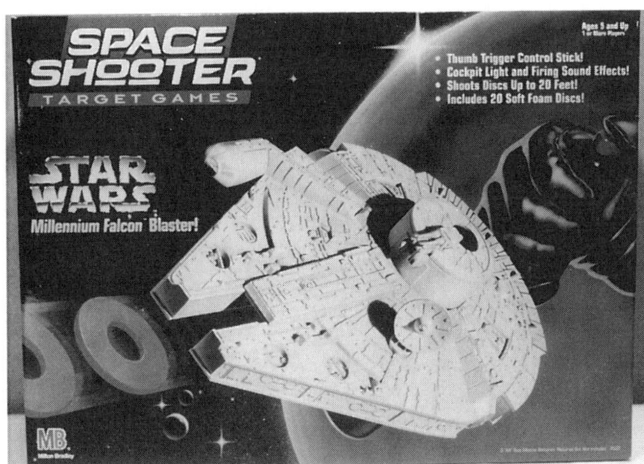

Milton Bradley, Millennium Falcon Blaster Space Shooter target game

Darth Vader .... $35–$50
Yoda .... $35–$50

Space Shooter Milton Bradley, 1996. Target game includes Millennium Falcon-shaped "Blaster," twenty foam discs and five targets. Box, which is designed as additional target, has artwork of toy on front.

Each .... $35–$50

Spinner Fantasma, 1992. 3¾″ metal disk decorated with diffractive foil printed with Star Wars logo and ships. Came bagged on header card.

Laserlight Spinner .... $6–$10

Squawk Boxes Tiger Electronics, 1997. Toys have record/playback feature which can then be slowed down or sped up, as well as authentic Star Wars phrases and sounds.

C-3PO head .... $15–$20
Darth Vader head .... $15–$20
Millennium Falcon .... $15–$20

Utility Belt Kenner (Canada), 1977. Window boxed sets all had belt and gun. Other accessories varied with character version of toy.

Any .... $750–$1000

Van Toys Kenner, 1978. Toys were approximately 7″ long and operated with T-sticks. Came packaged in window boxes with low headers and artwork of toys in action.

Black van, Darth Vader artwork .... $100–$150
White van, Heroes artwork .... $100–$150
Two-van set, both toys plus twelve barrels and two pylons .... $225–$325

Voice Changer Tiger Electronics, 1997. With bust of Darth Vader. Has original sound effects and changes speaker's voice to resemble Vader's.

Darth Vader Voice Changer .... $25–$35

Walkie-Talkies—Micro Games of America, 1994. Handheld character walkie-talkies designed to be clipped to belt. Set includes Darth Vader and Stormtrooper. Blister-packed in solid plastic header designed for hanging with paper logo insert.

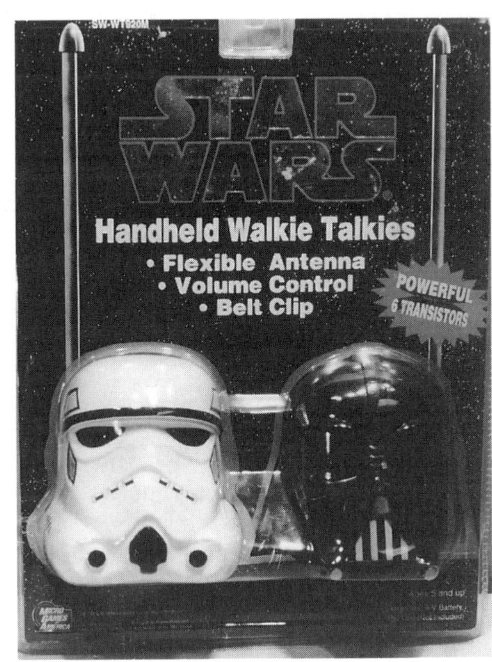

Micro Games of America, Star Wars walkie-talkies

Each set .... $25–$35

Walkie-Talkies—Tiger Electronics

Imperial Walkie-Talkie, 1997. Black with belt clips and Imperial symbol over speaker. Per pair .... $20–$30

Rebel Alliance Long-Range Walkie-Talkie, 1997. 1500

Kenner, Star Wars toy vans

feet. White with red Rebel symbol and red and yellow accents. Sound effects function. Includes replica headsets..... ....$25–$35

Darth Vader Voice Changer Walkie-Talkie, 1997. Shaped like bust of Darth Vader. Regular or Vader voice. Clips to belt. Per pair ....$25–$35

Wonder World Kenner, 1995. Kit includes tank, backdrop, chemicals for creating suspension medium, four ships, four asteroids and other props for arranging scene in gel. Box has photo of assembled kit.

Each ....$25–$40

X-Wing (Inflatable) Takara (Japanese), 1978. Inflates into torpedo-shaped toy with X-shaped fins in back. Box art has photo of child with toy.

Each ....$200–$300

X-Wing (Transforming) Takara (Japanese), 1978. Plastic toy approximately 12″ long that changes into a variety of configurations. Came boxed with artwork of toy on cover.

Each ....$425–$600

Yoda the Jedi Master Kenner, 1981. Fortune-telling toy. 5¼″ tall plastic figure of Yoda has "window" in base to allow answers to questions to be read. Toy comes packaged blister-carded inside vertical tray box.

Each ....$85–$145

Kenner, Yoda the Jedi Master fortune-telling toy

Yo-Yos Spectra Star, 1995.

R2-D2 and C-3PO ....$5–$10

Darth Vader, raised character face on both sides. Blister-packed on header card designed for hanging ....$5–$10

Stormtrooper, raised character face on both sides. Blister-packed on header card designed for hanging ....$5–$10

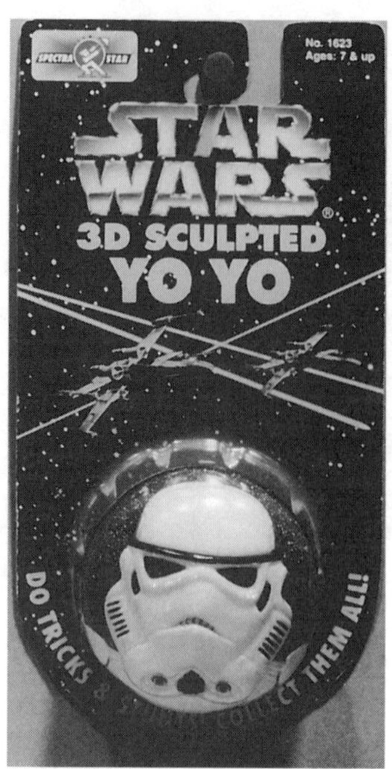

Spectra Star, Stormtrooper yo-yo

PLAY-DOH SETS

KENNER

NOTE: Palitoy's version of Star Wars Action Set in Britain was called Adventure Modelling Set.

Star Wars Action Set, 1977. Boxed set includes play mat, trim knife, X-Wing toy, three hinged molds and three cans of Play-Doh. Color box photo shows children and kit ....$50–$75

Palitoy (British), Star Wars Play-Doh Adventure Modelling Set

Empire Strikes Back Action Set, 1980. Boxed set includes play mat, trim knife, Snowspeeder toy, three hinged molds and three cans of Play-Doh. Color box photo shows children and kit ....$50–$75

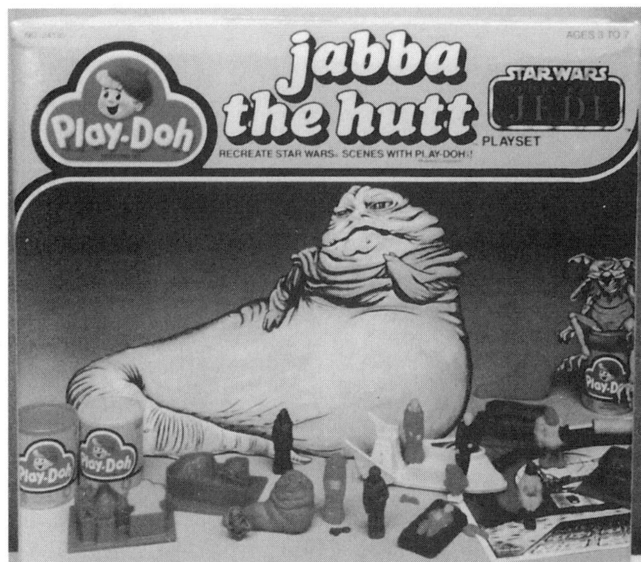

Kenner, Play-Doh Jabba the Hutt Playset

Empire Strikes Back Yoda Playset, 1982. Boxed set includes play mat, trim knife, X-Wing toy, three hinged molds and three cans of Play-Doh. Color box photo shows kit. ....$50–$75

Return of the Jedi Jabba the Hutt Playset, 1983. Boxed set includes play mat, four half-molds, rolling pin, skiff toy and three cans of Play-Doh. Color box photo shows kit ......$25–$35

Ewoks Playset, 1985. Boxed set includes play mat, trim knife, Ewok cart toy, rolling pin, three open molds and three cans of Play-Doh ....$15–$25

Kenner, Wicket the Ewok plush toy

PLUSH TOYS

DISNEY

Ewoks Sold as souvenirs at Star Tours and used as video promotions.

Large, 12″. Light brown with green cowl.............$10–$15
Small, 8″. Dark brown with pink cowl....................$8–$12

KENNER

Chewbacca, 1977. 20″ tall. Covered with brown artificial fur. Comes with bandolier containing four removable gray plastic rectangles.

Each ....$45–$65

Ewoks, 1983. 18″. Covered with artificial fur in various shades of brown and gray. Came with hood. Packaged in open cardboard trays.

Tall Adult, Zephee, comes with pouch in addition to hood ....$75–$125

Ewoks—Regular Adult, 14″. See description for “Tall Adult.”

Latara ....$45–$65
Paploo ....$45–$65
Princess Kneesaa ....$35–$50
Wicket...$35–$50

Ewoks—Baby (Wokling), 8″.

Gwig...$25–$35
Leeni..$15–$25
Malani..$25–$35
Mookiee ....$15–$25
Nippet..$15–$25
Wiley ....$15–$25

Kenner, R2-D2 stuffed toy

Takara, character plush toys

NOTE: Unpackaged Ewoks can be identified by name tag sewn in seam.

R2-D2, 1977. 10″ tall. White with silver and blue trim. Moving legs and squeaker.

Each .... $50–$75

Kenneth Feld

Yoda, 1992. Approximately 12″ tall with plastic head and tan cloth robe with brown belt. No packaging.

Each .... $115–$200

Regal (Canada).

Chewbacca Large toy approximately 3′ tall.

Each .... $750–$1000

Jawa Approximately 1′ tall with hooded outfit and bandolier.

Each .... $500–$750

Takara

Characters (Japanese), 1992. Approximately 7″ tall comic likenesses with oversized heads. Gold strings attached for hanging. Five different.

C-3PO .... $40–$65

Chewbacca .... $40–$65

Darth Vader .... $40–$65

Luke .... $40–$65

R2-D2 .... $40–$65

TRADING CARDS

Assorted trading card and sticker sets

There has been an incredible resurgence of interest in non-sports trading cards over the past few years, and Star Wars cards have been in the foreground. There have been more Star Wars trading cards issued by Topps during the 1990s than with the original releases in the 1970s and 1980s. With the popularity of these newer releases followed a renewed interest in the original issues. The original Star Wars releases are listed near the top of the top ten list every month in the Entertainment Card supplement from Krause Publications.

The introduction of randomly inserted "chase" cards in the packs has created a collector demand for these hard-to-obtain cards. These cards are inserted randomly and they vary in rarity from fairly easy to obtain to virtually impossible. In this section "chase" cards will be listed along with their ratios (example, 1:12) of insertion into individual packs.

This trading card section has been divided into three sections: American trading cards, foreign trading cards and customizable card games. Listings are first by date of issue, with continuing series grouped together. Some items may be listed in other sections, i.e., sticker albums and sticker sets in the decals and stickers section.

Topps, Series II, card #71

AMERICAN STAR WARS TRADING CARDS

STAR WARS, TOPPS, 1977–1978

With the release of the first Star Wars movie Topps began a long-lasting relationship with George Lucas that continues up to the present. The release for the first movie consisted of five individual series of sixty-six cards and eleven stickers each. The numbering was consecutive, creating a total of 330 cards and 55 stickers. As was typical of the day, stores reordered cards when they were sold out. This sometimes made obtaining one or more series somewhat difficult. If the cards did not sell out, there was no need to order more, and the last series was often missed. There were two versions of card #207. The first version (called the porno version) showed C-3PO with a metallic protuberance that could be construed to be a sexual organ. This artwork was later retouched to remove the protuberance. A fair number of these first versions were released, and most have been removed from sets to sell as curiosities, enough to make the regular version of the card hard to find.

Series I

- **Series I set,** 66 cards, blue border, #1–66 .... $75–$100
- **Series I sticker set,** 11 stickers, #1–11 .... $25–$50
- **Single cards** .... $1–$2
- **Single stickers** .... $3–$5
- **Sealed packs** .... $10–$15
- **Unopened box** .... $300–$400
- **Empty display box** .... $20–$30
- **Wrapper** .... $5–$8

Series II

- **Series II set,** 66 cards, red border, #67–132 .... $40–$80
- **Series II sticker set,** 11 stickers, #12–22 .... $25–$40
- **Single cards** .... $1–$2
- **Single stickers** .... $2–$4
- **Sealed packs** .... $6–$10
- **Unopened box** .... $75–$150
- **Empty display box** .... $15–$25
- **Wrapper** .... $4–$6

Series III

- **Series III set,** 66 cards, yellow border, #133–198 .... $40–$80
- **Series III sticker set,** 11 stickers, #23–33 .... $25–$40
- **Single cards** .... $1–$2
- **Single stickers** .... $2–$4
- **Sealed packs** .... $6–$10
- **Unopened box** .... $75–$150
- **Empty display box** .... $15–$25
- **Wrapper** .... $4–$6

Series IV

- **Series IV set,** 66 cards, green border, #199–264 .... $50–$100
- **Series IV sticker set,** 11 stickers, #34–44 .... $30–$50
- **Single cards** .... $1–$2
- **Card #207,** regular version .... $6–$10
- **Card #207,** porno version .... $25–$50
- **Single stickers** .... $2–$4
- **Sealed pack** .... $6–$10

Unopened box ..... $100–$200
Empty display box ..... $15–$25
Wrapper ..... $4–$6

Series V

Series V set, 66 cards, orange border, #265–330 ..... $75–$125
Series V sticker set, 11 stickers, #45–55 ..... $25–$40
Single cards ..... $1–$2
Single stickers ..... $2–$4
Sealed pack ..... $6–$10
Unopened box ..... $125–$200
Empty display box ..... $15–$25
Wrapper ..... $4–$6

STAR WARS GUM WRAPPERS, TOPPS, 1978

A series of sugar-free gum wrappers were issued by Topps in 1978. The set consisted of fifty-six different wrappers that when folded out showed scenes from the movie.

Set of 56 wrappers ..... $125–$250
Single wrappers ..... $3–$5
Unopened pack ..... $3–$5
Unopened box ..... $100–$200
Empty display box ..... $15–$25

STAR WARS GENERAL MILLS CARDS, 1978

These cards were released in packages of General Mills cereals, and a wallet to hold the set was available through the mail. It was a fairly difficult set to acquire due to the large number of different brands of cereal that one needed to purchase.

Set of 18 cards ..... $30–$50

General Mills, Star Wars trading card and wallet

Set of 18 cards with wallet ..... $50–$75
Single cards ..... $2–$3

STAR WARS DIXIE CUPS, 1978

Cut-out photos released on the back of boxes (5″ × 6″).

Set of 8 ..... $50–$100
Single cards ..... $5–$10

STAR WARS WONDER BREAD CARDS, 1978

Wonder Bread released a sixteen-card set that was inserted one card per loaf of bread in food stores. This created a real problem at the stores as some kids were opening bread loaves and swiping the cards.

Set of 16 cards ..... $25–$35
Single cards ..... $2–$3

EMPIRE STRIKES BACK CARDS, TOPPS, 1980

Three series of cards and stickers were released by Topps for the second Star Wars movie. The stickers were different in that some of them were designed as letters of the alphabet, with pictures inside them.

Series I

Series I set, 132 cards, red/gray border, #1–132 ..... $50–$75
Series I sticker set, 33 stickers, yellow, #1–33 ..... $40–$60
Single cards ..... $0.50–$1
Single sticker ..... $1–$2
Sealed pack ..... $8–$12
Unopened box ..... $75–$125
Empty display box ..... $10–$20
Wrapper (red) ..... $3–$5

Series II

Series II set, 132 cards, blue/gray border, #132–264 ..... $40–$60
Series II sticker set, 33 stickers, blue, #32–64 ..... $40–$60
Single cards ..... $0.50–$1
Single stickers ..... $1–$2
Sealed pack ..... $8–$12
Unopened box ..... $60–$100
Empty display box ..... $10–$20
Wrapper (blue) ..... $3–$5

Series III

Series III set, 88 cards, yellow/red border, #265–354 ..... $60–$80
Series III sticker set, 22 stickers, green, #65–88 . $40–$60
Single cards ..... $0.75–$1
Single stickers ..... $2–$3
Sealed pack ..... $8–$12
Unopened box ..... $75–$125
Empty display box ..... $10–$20
Wrapper (yellow) ..... $3–$5

EMPIRE STRIKES BACK LARGE SIZE, TOPPS, 1980

These oversized (5″ × 7″) cards were issued in packs of two cards and were not as well received as Topps' other sets.

Set of 30 cards ..... $60–$75
Single cards ..... $2–$3
Sealed pack ..... $10–$12
Unopened box ..... $100–$150
Empty display box ..... $20–$30
Wrapper ..... $5–$8

STAR WARS/EMPIRE STRIKES BACK BURGER KING STRIP CARDS, 1980

A series of thirty-six cards were issued in 1980 at Burger

King and distributed in strips of three perforated cards. Twelve different strips of cards exist with scenes from the first two movies.

Set of 36 cards, 12 intact strips ....$30–$50

Burger King, Empire Strikes Back strip cards

Set of 36 cards, not in strips ....$20–$30
Single strip of 3 cards ....$3–$5
Single cards ....$0.50–$1

EMPIRE STRIKES BACK BIBB LINEN CO.

Cut-outs on side of boxes (5″ × 5″).

Set of 6 ....$30–$60
Single cards ....$5–$10

EMPIRE STRIKES BACK DIXIE CUPS, 1981

Story cards released four per box.

Set of 24 ....$50–$100
Single cards ....$3–$5

RETURN OF THE JEDI, TOPPS, 1983

Topps released two series of cards and stickers for the third Star Wars movie. The stickers for these sets were issued with several different colored borders. Values here are for the basic set without color variations.

Series I

- **Series I set,** 132 cards, red border, #1–132...........$25–$40
- **Series I sticker set,** 33 stickers, #1–33.................$15–$20
- **Single cards** ....$0.50–$0.75
- **Single sticker** ....$0.50–$0.75
- **Unopened pack** ....$4–$6
- **Unopened box** ....$50–$75
- **Wrapper,** three different...$2–$3

Series II

- **Series II set,** 88 cards, blue border, #133–222.....$50–$60
- **Series II sticker set,** 22 stickers, #34–55 ....$25–$35
- **Single cards** ....$0.50–$0.75
- **Single stickers**..$1–$2
- **Unopened pack**..$5–$8
- **Unopened box**..$75–$100
- **Wrapper,** four different...$2–$3

RETURN OF THE JEDI KELLOGG'S, 1984

Distributed inside boxes of C-3PO cereal. Peel-away sticker on top, trading card underneath.

Set of 10 stickers and 10 cards ....$50–$100
Single stickers and cards, attached...........................$5–$10
Single stickers or cards, unattached ....$2–$4

STAR WARS GALAXY, TOPPS, 1993–1995

Topps re-entered the field of Star Wars cards after an absence of ten years with their release of three series of trading cards based on all three movies, the comics and the book series. These cards were made up exclusively of artwork by some of the most popular artists in the Star Wars, comics and book fields. The inclusion of randomly inserted chase cards added to the interest in these series. The ratio of insertion of these chase cards into packs of cards is listed in parenthesis. These foil-etched spectra cards were done by Walt Simonson as a large painting that could be cut up into eighteen individual cards. This large mural continued throughout the entire three series.

Series I

- **Series I, 1993, set of 140 cards**..........................$20–$30
- **Single cards** ....$0.25–$0.50
- **S1 Darth Vader,** foil-etched chase cards (1:12), the Heroes ....$15–$20
- **S2 Han Solo,** foil-etched chase cards (1:12), the Heroes.... ....$12–$15
- **S3 Luke Skywalker,** foil-etched chase cards (1:12), the Heroes...$12–$15
- **S4 Chewbacca and C-3PO,** foil-etched chase cards (1:12), the Heroes ....$12–$15
- **S5 Yoda and Obi-Wan Kenobi,** foil-etched chase cards (1:12), the Heroes ....$12–$15
- **S6 AT-AT and Princess Leia,** foil-etched chase cards (1:12), the Heroes ....$12–$15
- **Uncut sheet of the above six cards** ....$75–$100
- **Sealed pack**..$2–$3
- **Sealed box**..$75–$100

Empty display box .... $5–$10
Wrapper .... $0.75–$1
Limited edition factory sealed set, comes in a large Millennium Falcon shaped box and contains the complete set of 140 cards, six foil cards (different foil color) and an extra card exclusive to the boxed set .... $100–$125

Series II

Series II, 1994, set of 150 cards, #141–290 .... $20–$30
Single cards .... $0.25–$0.50
S7 Granf Moff Tarkin, foil-etched chase card (1:12), the Bad Guys .... $12–$15
S8 Stormtroopers, foil-etched chase card (1:12), the Bad Guys .... $12–$15
S9 The Emperor, foil-etched chase card (1:12), the Bad Guys .... $12–$15
S10 Boba Fett, foil-etched chase card (1:12), the Bad Guys .... $15–$20
S11 Jabba the Hutt, foil-etched chase card (1:12), the Bad Guys .... $12–$15
S12 Princess Leia in Jabba's chamber, foil-etched chase card (1:12), the Bad Guys .... $12–$15
Uncut sheet of the above six cards .... $75–$100
Sealed pack .... $2–$3
Sealed box .... $60–$75
Empty display box .... $5–$8
Wrapper .... $5–$8
Limited Edition boxed set, Contains the entire 150-card set, all six foil chase cards and an exclusive card only available in the boxed set .... $60–$100

Series III

Series III, 1995, set of 90 cards and 12 "Lucasarts" foil-embossed cards, #1–90 and L1-L12 .... $20–$25
Single cards, any of the above .... $0.25–$0.50
Foil-stamp card set (First Day Production), 90 cards, (1:1) .... $60–$90
Single foil-stamped cards .... $0.75–$1
S13 Lando Calrissian, foil-etched chase cards (1:12), miscellaneous characters .... $12–$15
S14 Millennium Falcon, foil-etched chase cards (1:12), miscellaneous characters .... $12–$15
S15 Ewoks, foil-etched chase cards (1:12), miscellaneous characters .... $12–$15
S16 Jawas, foil-etched chase cards (1:12), miscellaneous characters .... $12–$15
S17 Tusken Raiders, foil-etched chase cards (1:12), miscellaneous characters .... $12–$15
S18 Jedi Spirits, foil-etched chase cards (1:12), miscellaneous characters .... $12–$15
E1 Brett Booth art, Agents of the Empire "Clearzone" cards, see-through cards with raised artwork by various artists (1:18) .... $12–$15
E2 Jeff Scott Campbell art, Agents of the Empire "Clearzone" cards, see-through cards with raised artwork by various artists (1:18) .... $12–$15
E3 Jeff Rebner art, Agents of the Empire "Clearzone" cards, see-through cards with raised artwork by various artists (1:18) .... $12–$15
E4 Joe Chiodo art, Agents of the Empire "Clearzone" cards, see-through cards with raised artwork by various artists (1:18) .... $12–$15
E5 Tom Rainey art, Agents of the Empire "Clearzone" cards, see-through cards with raised artwork by various artists (1:18) .... $12–$15
E6 Brian Denham art, Agents of the Empire "Clearzone" cards, see-through cards with raised artwork by various artists (1:18) .... $12–$15
Sealed pack .... $2–$3
Sealed box .... $50–$75
Empty display box .... $5–$8
Wrapper .... $0.75–$1

STAR WARS MASTER VISIONS, TOPPS, 1996

This oversized set (6.5″ × 10.2″) was sold as a complete set in a sealed box. The cards were created from paintings by various artists. Single cards were sometimes sold.

Complete set of 36 cards .... $50–$60
Sealed box, complete set .... $50–$60
Single cards .... $2–$3

STAR WARS FINEST, TOPPS, 1996

This set featured all-chromium cards in an attempt by Topps to produce a higher-end set of cards. This all-artwork set concentrates on the individual characters from the Star Wars saga. It consisted of ninety cards with a parallel set of ninety cards with a slightly different coloring on the reverse called refractor cards. This is somewhat similar to the foil-stamped parallel set from Star Wars Galaxy III, except that instead of being inserted one card per pack, these were inserted one card per twelve packs. The idea of a ninety-card set inserted one card per twelve packs created a need to open over 1000 packs of cards to obtain this set! Other subsets included a foil-embossed raised-printing set of six cards that combines into one larger picture and a four-card set of Topps Matrix cards.

Set of 90 cards, #1–90 .... $60–$80
Single cards .... $1–$2
Refractor card set of 90 (1:12) .... $500–$600
Single refractor cards .... $6–$10
F1 Darth Vader, embossed foil raised artwork card (1:12).... .... $12–$15
F2 Luke Skywalker, embossed foil raised artwork card (1:12) .... $12–$15
F3 Obi-Wan Kenobi, embossed foil raised artwork card (1:12) .... $12–$15
F4 Jaino Solo, embossed foil raised artwork card (1:12)........ .... $12–$15
F5 Princess Leia Organa, embossed foil raised artwork card (1:12) .... $12–$15
F6 Jacen Solo, embossed foil raised artwork card (1:12) .... $12–$15
M1 Han Solo and Chewbacca, Topps Star Wars Matrix chase card (1:18) .... $8–$10
M2 C-3PO and R2-D2, Topps Star Wars Matrix chase card (1:18) .... $8–$10

M3 Emperor Palpatine, Topps Star Wars Matrix chase card (1:18) .... $8–$10
M4 Boba Fett, Topps Star Wars Matrix chase card (1:18) .... $8–$10
Shadows of the Empire promo card, (1:18) .... $10–$12
Topps Jedi Legacy Mastervisions card, available when the redemption card (1:180) was mailed in. Large-size card showing the complete foil-embossed chase set in one picture. .... $100–$125
Redemption card for above, (expired) .... $40–$50
Sealed pack .... $3–$5
Sealed box .... $85–$100
Empty display box .... $8–$10
Wrapper .... $0.75–$1
Looseleaf album .... $20–$30

STAR WARS WIDE VISION, TOPPS, 1994–1996

In 1994 Topps reintroduced the longer- or taller-sized card that they first used with their basketball cards in the late 1960s. This time they are called "Wide Vision" cards to give the collector the effect of a cinemascope or wide-vision movie. Sets were issued for each movie, along with various insert or chase cards. The first two series of these sold out quickly.

Star Wars Wide Vision complete set of 120 cards $40–$60
Single cards .... $0.50–$1
C1 C-3PO and R2-D2, chromium chase cards (1:18) .... $20–$25
C2 Luke watches twin sunsets, chromium chase cards (1:18) .... $20–$25
C3 The Millennium Falcon, chromium chase cards (1:18) .... $20–$30
C4 Swing across the chasm, chromium chase cards (1:18) .... $20–$30
C5 Luke and Dark Lord of the Sith, chromium chase cards (1:18) .... $20–$30
C6 Millennium Falcon's escape, chromium chase cards (1:18) .... $20–$30
C7 Rebel pilots, chromium chase cards (1:18) .... $20–$30
C8 Battle in Death Star trench, chromium chase cards (1:18) .... $20–$30
C9 Rebel Starfighters, chromium chase cards (1:18) .... $20–$30
C10 Hall of the Massassi, chromium chase cards (1:18) .... $20–$30
Unopened pack .... $4–$6
Sealed box .... $75–$100
Wrapper .... $1–$1.5
Empire Strikes Back Wide Vision set of 144 cards .... $30–$40
Single cards .... $0.5–$1
C1 Probot, chromium chase cards (1:18) .... $15–$20
C2 Tauntaun, chromium chase cards (1:18) .... $15–$20
C3 AT-AT, chromium chase cards (1:18) .... $15–$20
C4 Snowspeeder, chromium chase cards (1:18) .... $15–$20
C5 Yoda, chromium chase cards (1:18) .... $15–$20
C6 Space Slug, chromium chase cards (1:18) .... $15–$20
C7 Cloud City, chromium chase cards (1:18) .... $15–$20
C8 Carbon-freezing chamber, chromium chase cards (1:18) .... $15–$20
C9 Luke dangling, chromium chase cards (1:18) .... $15–$20
C10 Rebel Cruiser, chromium chase card (1:18) .... $15–$20
MP1 Advance one-sheet, mini-poster cards (4″ × 5¾″), (1:box) .... $12–$15
MP2 Domestic one-sheet, mini-poster cards (4″ × 5¾″), (1:box) .... $12–$15
MP3 Style B domestic one-sheet, mini-poster cards (4″ × 5¾″), (1:box) .... $12–$15
MP4 Australian one-sheet, mini-poster cards (4″ × 5¾″), (1:box) .... $12–$15
MP5 German one-sheet, mini-poster cards (4″ × 5¾″), (1:box) .... $12–$15
MP6 Radio Show poster, mini-poster cards (4″ × 5¾″), (1:box) .... $12–$15
Unopened pack .... $3–$5
Sealed box .... $60–$90
Wrapper .... $0.75–$1
Return of the Jedi Wide Vision card set of 144 cards .... $25–$35
Single cards .... $0.75–$1
C1 Darth Vader arrives at Death Star, chromium chase cards (1:18) .... $12–$15
C2 Jabba's droid torture chamber, chromium chase cards (1:18) .... $12–$15
C3 Jabba's throne room, chromium chase cards (1:18) .... $12–$15
C4 Sarlac's pit, chromium chase cards (1:18) .... $12–$15
C5 Desert sail skiff, chromium chase cards (1:18) .... $12–$15
C6 Forest of Endor, chromium chase cards (1:18) .... $12–$15
C7 Space battle, chromium chase cards (1:18) .... $12–$15
C8 Father against son, chromium chase cards (1:18) .... $12–$15
C9 Luke versus the Emperor, chromium chase cards (1:18) .... $12–$15
C10 The attack of the Death Star, chromium chase cards (1:18) .... $12–$15
MP1 Advance one-sheet, mini-poster cards (4″ × 5¾″), (1:box) .... $12–$15
MP2 Style B, mini-poster cards (4″ × 5¾″), (1:box) .... $12–$15
MP3 1985 re-release, mini-poster cards (4″ × 5¾″), (1:box) .... $12–$15
MP4 Japanese poster, mini-poster cards (4″ × 5¾″), (1:box) .... $12–$15
MP5 Japanese poster, mini-poster cards (4″ × 5¾″), (1:box) .... $12–$15
MP6 Polish poster, mini-poster cards (4″ × 5¾″), (1:box) .... $12–$15
3-D Collector Redemption card (1:360), expired .... $40–$50
3-D Collector card, from redemption card .... $75–$100
Star Wars Trilogy Wide Vision set of 72 cards .... $18–$25
Single cards .... $0.25–$0.50
Sealed pack .... $2–$3
Sealed box .... $50–$70

Laser-cut chase cards (6; #L1-L6) each ....$10–$12
Star Wars 3-D Wide Vision set of 63 cards ....$80–$100
Single cards ....$1.5–$2
Sealed pack ....$4–$5
Sealed box ....$120–$150
Multi-Motion 3-D chase card (1 per box) ....$30–$40

STAR WARS 3-D LENTICULAR CARDS

Frito Lay, 1996–97. Released in packages of potato and nacho chips in two different sizes.

Round (2″) lenticular character cards, 20 different, each ....$3–$5
Set of all 20 of above ....$75–$100
Rectangular (2″ × 3″) lenticular cards, 6 different, each ....$6–$10
Set of all 6 of above ....$40–$50
More rare limited edition rectangular cards ....$20–$50

STAR WARS METALLIC TRADING CARDS

Bleachers Series of 24KT gold-plated sculptured cards. These are the same size as regular trading cards but are much thicker and are metal instead of cardboard. These all have a limited production run.

Shadows of the Empire ....$30–$35
Bounty Hunters ....$30–$35
Darth Vader ....$30–$35

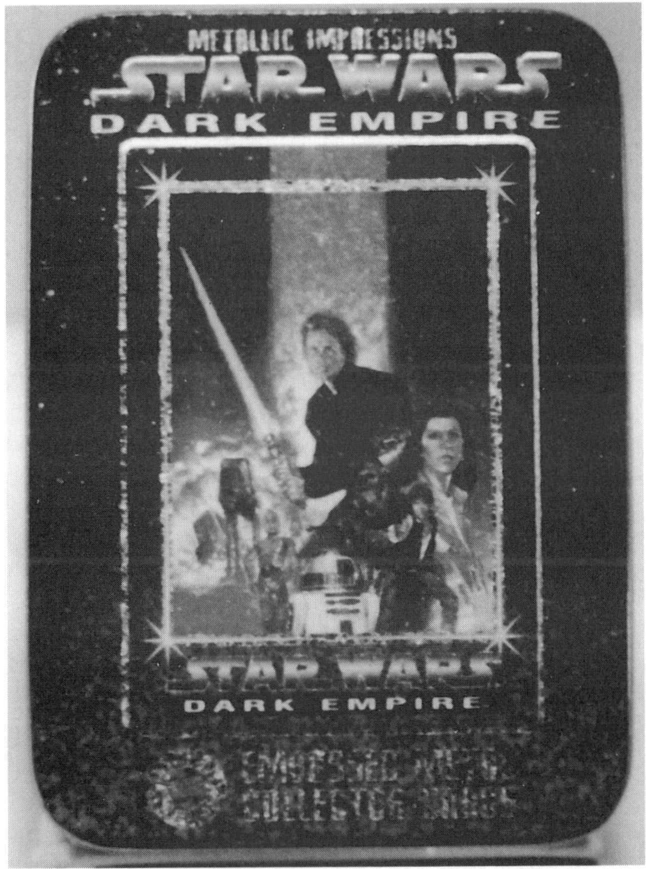

Metallic Images, Dark Empire metallic trading card

Star Wars movie poster ....$30–$35
Empire Strikes Back movie poster ....$30–$35
Return of the Jedi movie poster ....$30–$35
Darth Vader, QVC exclusive ....$30–$35
Millennium Falcon, QVC exclusive...................$30–$35

Metallic Images Series of metallic trading cards. These are sold as limited edition sets that come in a metallic box.

Star Wars Metal Card Set, 30 cards.................$60–$100
Empire Strikes Back Metal Card Set, 30 cards ....$50–$60
Return of the Jedi Metal Card Set, 30 cards .....$50–$60
Star Wars Dark Empire Metal Card Set, 6 cards ....$15–$20
Shadows of the Empire Metal Card Set, 6 cards............ ....$20–$25
Art of Ralph McQuarrie Metal Card Set, 20 cards ....$65–$75

Ceramic Trading Cards Scoreboard issued a series of three ceramic trading cards featuring the movie poster artwork.

Scoreboard Series of three ceramic trading cards featuring the movie poster artwork.

Set of three ....$50–$60

FOREIGN STAR WARS TRADING CARDS

Due to space constrictions and lack of accurate information, only the major collected foreign sets are listed here.

In the earlier years many of the foreign card sets were reissues of the American Topps sets. Sets with the same pictures were released in Canada, Mexico and England by agreement with Topps. In some cases the numbering and selection of cards differed from the American editions. In the case of the Mexican cards the distribution was so bad that few complete sets are known to exist.

In Europe several companies issued sticker sets along with albums. Due to the size of these sets (up to 400 stickers) complete sets can be hard to find. In general these sticker sets with albums are valued at between $100 and $300 per set, depending on date of release and size of set.

Australia, Streets Ice Cream Star Wars Shaped bottoms to ice cream containers.

Set of 12 ....$40–$100
Single bottoms..$5–$10

Canadian O-Pee Chee Star Wars Cards Similar to Topps series, 1978, with minor changes, text in English and French.

Set of 264 cards...$100–$200
Single cards ....$0.50–$1
Sealed pack..$5–$10
Unopened box ....$100–$200
Wrapper ....$2–$3

Canadian 3-D Lenticular Kellogg's Cereal Cards, 1997. Large, 4″ × 6″ cards on the fronts of various Kellogg's cereal boxes.

Set of three cards .... $10–$15
Set of three complete boxes with cards .... $35–$50
Dutch, Monty Cards Return of the Jedi Smaller-sized, blank-backed cards, 1983.
Set of 100 cards .... $50–$100
England, Topps Star Wars, 1978, similar to American series I and II with whiter backs.
Set of 132 .... $100–$200
Single cards .... $1–$2
Sealed pack .... $5–$10
Unopened box .... $100–$200
Wrapper .... $3–$5
Europe, Panini Star Wars Sticker Sets With albums. Issued by several countries in several languages (German, Spanish, Italian and French).
Set of 256 with album .... $100–$200
Mexico Topps Star Wars, 1978, smilar to first series of Topps U.S.
Set of 66 cards .... Rare
Single cards .... $2–$10
Sealed pack of two cards plus gum .... $8–$10
Sealed box .... $75–$150
Wrapper, three different .... $3–$5
New Zealand, Tip Top Confections Star Wars Stickers One sticker inside each wrapper of R2-D2 Ice Cream.
Set of 15 .... $50–$100
Single stickers .... $4–$8

CUSTOMIZABLE TRADING CARD GAMES

Based on the popular customizable card game Magic: The Gathering, these games have become incredibly popular. The sheer size of the sets (over 300 cards) and the scarcity of many of the cards makes these sets difficult and expensive to complete. The basic game can be played by two players each with a "starter" deck. But here is where the interest is piqued: A player can purchase additional "booster" packs that include additional cards, one of which is a "rare" and usually very powerful card. The player who accumulates the most "rare" cards will usually have a more powerful "deck" when playing the game and will have a better chance of winning.

Star Wars Customizable Card Game, Decipher 1995–1996

Decipher embarked on a series of customizable card games in much the same way they did their Star Trek: Next Generation series. The first release was a basic set consisting of 324 cards followed by several expansions of 108 cards each. Cards are divided into Light Side and Dark Side cards, by types of card and by scarcity of card.

NOTE: There are two levels of scarcity within each of the three divisions (common, uncommon and rare). This makes these sets even more difficult to complete than the Star Trek ones.

BASIC STAR WARS CUSTOMIZABLE CARD GAME, 1995

This set consists of 324 cards (108 common, 108 uncommon and 108 rare). These were issued in two editions: a black-bordered limited edition and a white-bordered unlimited edition. Due to the fact that the white-bordered versions never really sold out, most collectors only collect the black borders and demand for the white-bordered cards is not high.

Decipher, Star Wars customized card game

Complete set of black-bordered cards (324) .... $800–$1200
Complete set of white-bordered cards (324) .... $250–$500
Starter pack of black-bordered cards .... $8–$12
Single pack of black-border booster cards .... $3–$4
Sealed box of black-bordered booster cards .... $90–$110
Starter pack of white-bordered cards .... $8–$9
Single pack of white-bordered booster cards .... $60–$90
Single Cards, Divided By Type The scarcity of each card will be designated in ( ) with the abbreviations R1 (super rare), R2 (rare), UC (uncommon), and C (common). The R1 rare cards in this set are truly hard to find. There was only about one R1 card per three booster packs. The ratio of R1 rare cards: R2 rare cards: Uncommon cards: Common cards) is approximately 1:3:12:33.
Single Common (C) Cards:
Black-border limited edition .... $.25–$.50
White-border unlimited edition .... $.25–$.50
Single Uncommon (UC) Cards:
Black-border limited edition .... $.50–$1
White-border unlimited edition .... $.50–$.75
Single Rare (R1, R2) Cards:
Black-border limited edition cards are valued in the listing below. White-border unlimited editions are valued at 25–50 percent of the black border values.

Light Side Cards:
Character: Rebel

Rebel Guard (C)
Rebel Pilot (C)
Rebel Trooper (C)
General Dodonna (U)
Jek Porkins (U)
Owen Lars (U)
Pops (U)
Beru Lars (U)
Dutch (R1) .... $10–$15
Han Solo (R1) .... $30–$45
Leia Organa (R1) .... $25–$35
Luke Skywalker (R1) .... $25–$35
Obi-Wan Kenobi (R1) .... $35–$50
Red Leader (R1) .... $10–$15
Biggs Darklighter (R2) .... $5–$8

Character: Alien
Jawa (C)
Shistavanen Wolfman (C)
Talz (C)
BoShek (U)
Kabe (U)
Wioslea (U)
Figrin D'an (U)
Momaw Nadon (U)
Kal'Faini C'ndros (R1) .... $10–$15
Dice Ibegon (R2) .... $4–$6
Leesub Sirin (R2) .... $4–$6
Character: Droid
CZ-3 (C)
LIN-V8K (C)
R2-X2 (C)
R4-E1 (C)
2X-3KPR (U)
C-3PO (R1) .... $25–$35
WED-9-M1 "Bantha" Droid (R2) .... $3–$5

Starship
X-Wing (C)
Y-Wing (C)
Red 1 (U)
Corellian Corvette (U)
Millenium Falcon (R1) .... $35–$45
Gold 1 (R2) .... $4–$6
Gold 5 (R2) .... $4–$6
Red 3 (R2) .... $4–$6

Transport Vehicle
Lift Tube (C)
SoroSuub V-35 Landspeeder (C)
Luke's X-34 Landspeeder (U)
Sandcrawler (R2) .... $4–$6

Character Weapons
Blaster Rifle (C)
Blaster (C)
Jedi Lightsaber (U)
Leia's Sporting Blaster (U)
Obi-Wan's Lightsaber (R1) .... $15–$25
Han's Heavy Blaster Pistol (R2) .... $6–$8

Starship Weapons
Proton Torpedoes (C)
Quad Laser Cannon (U)

Automated Weapons
Timer Mine (C)
Tagge Seeker (R2) .... $4–$6
Tarkin Seeker (R2) .... $4–$6

Device
Electrobinoculars (C)
Fusion Generator Supply Tanks (C)
Restraining Bolt (C)
Tatooine Utility Belt (C)
Vaporator (C)
Targeting Computer (U)
Caller (U)
Hydroponics Station (U)

Location
Tatooine: Dune Sea (C)
Tatooine: Jawa Camp (C)
Tatooine: Lars; Moisture Farm (C)
Yavin 4: Jungle (C)
Death Star: Docking Bay 327 (C)
Tatooine (C)
Tatooine: Docking Bay 94 (C)
Yavin 4 (C)
Yavin 4: Docking Bay (C)
Dantooine (U)
Death Star: Trash Compactor (U)
Alderaan (U)

Death Star: Detention Block
Control Room (U)
Kessel (U)
Tatooine: Mos Eisley (U)
Yavin 4: Massassi War Room (U)
Tatooine: Obi-Wan's Hut (R1) .... $8–$12
Yavin 4: Massassi Throne Room (R1) .... $8–$12
Tatooine: Cantina (R2) .... $3–$5

Effect
Ellorrs Madak (C)
Sai'torr Kal Fas (C)
A Tremor in the Force (U)
Crash Site Memorial (U)
Eyes in the Dark (U)
Jawa Siesta (U)
Nightfall (U)
Restricted Deployment (U)
Rycar Ryjers (U)
Special Modifications (U)
Traffic Control (U)
Yavin Sentry (U)
Affect Mind (R1) .... $10–$15
Beggar (R1) .... $8–$12
Disarmed (R1) .... $8–$12
K'lor'slug (R1) .... $8–$12
Lightsaber Proficiency (R1) .... $10–$15
Obi-Wan's Cape (R1) .... $10–$15

Revolution (R1) ....$8–$12
Demotion (R2) ....$3–$5
Mantellian Savrip (R2) ....$3–$5
Rebel Planners (R2) ....$3–$5

Utinni Effect
Tusken Breath Mask (U)
Yerka Mig (U)
Plastoid Armor (U)
Death Star Plans (R1) ....$15–$20
Our Most Desperate Hour (R1) ....$15–$20
Kessel Run (R2) ....$5–$8

Lost Interrupt
Don't Underestimate Our Chances (C)
Rebel Reinforcements (C)
Surprise Assault (C)
Collision! (C)
Combined Attack (C)
Friendly Fire (C)
Old Ben (C)
Beru Stew (U)
Han's Back (U)
Leia's Back (U)
Luke's Back (U)
Return of the Jedi (U)
Cantina Brawl (R1) ....$10–$15
Don't Get Cocky (R1) ....$10–$15
Gift of the Mentor (R1) ....$10–$15
Jedi Presence (R1) ....$10–$15
Krayt Dragon Howl (R1) ....$10–$15
Skywalkers (R1) ....$15–$20
Full Throttle (R2) ....$3–$5
Noble Sacrifice (R2) ....$5–$8
On the Edge (R2) ....$3–$5
Sol Han (R2) ....$5–$8
Thank the Maker (R2) ....$3–$5
The Force is Strong in This One (R2) ....$4–$6
Warrior's Courage (R2) ....$3–$5

Used Interrupt
A Few Maneuvers (C)
Droid Shutdown (C)
Han's Dice (C)
Hear Me Baby, Hold Together (C)
Hyper Escape (C)
I've Got a Bad Feeling About This (C)
It Could Be Worse (C)
Narrow Escape (C)
Radar Scanner (C)
Rebel Barrier (C)
Scomp Link Access (C)
The Bith Shuttle (C)
We're Doomed (C)
Alter (U)
Panic (U)
Sence (U)
This Is All Your Fault (U)
Escape Pod (U)
How Did We Get Into This Mess? (U)
Nabrun Leids (U)
Out of Nowhere (U)
Spaceport Speeders (U)
Help Me Obi-Wan Kenobi (R1) ....$10–$15
Move Along (R1) ....$10–$15
Utinni! (R1) ....$10–$15
Into the Garbage Chute, Flyboy (R2) ....$3–$5

Dark Side Cards:

Character: Imperial
Death Star Trooper (C)
Imperial Pilot (C)
Imperial Trooper Guard (C)
Stormtrooper (C)
Chief Bast (U)
Coloner Wulff Yularen (U)
DS-61-2 (U)
Commander Praji (U)
Lieutenant Tanbris (U)
Darth Vader (R1) ....$50–$75
DS-61-3 (R1) ....$10–$15
Grand Moff Tarkin (R1) ....$15–$25
Admiral Motti (R2) ....$7–$10
General Tagge (R2) ....$7–$10

Character: Alien
Jawa (C)
Tusken Raider (C)
Dathcha (U)
Feltipern Trevagg (U)
Ponda Baba (U)
Profhetess (U)
M'iiyoom Onith (U)
Wuher (U)
Kitik Keed'kak (R1) ....$10–$15
Tonnika Sisters (R1) ....$10–$15
Djas Puhr (R2) ....$4–$6
Dr Evazan (R2) ....$4–$6
Garindan (R2) ....$4–$6
Labria (R2) ....$4–$6
Myo (R2) ....$4–$6

Character: Droid
LIN-V8M (C)
R1-G4 (C)
R4-M9 (C)
MSE-6 "Mouse" Droid (U)
EG-6 (U)
5D6-RA-7 (R1) ....$10–$15
WED15-1662 (R2) ....$3–$5

Starship
TIE Fighter (C)
TIE Scout (C)
Black 3 (U)
Imperial-Class Star Destroyer (U)
TIE Advanced x1 (U)
Black 2 (R1) ....$10–$15

Devastator (R1) ....$10–$15
Vader's Custom TIE (R1) ....$15–$25
Transport Vehicle
Lift Tube (C)
Ubrikkian 9000 Z001 (C)
Sandcrawler (R2)...$5–$8
Creature Vehicle
Bantha (U)
Character Weapon
Blaster Rifle (C)
Gadweffii Stick (C)
Imperial Blaster (C)
Dark Jedi Lightsaber (U)
Light Repeating Blaster Rifle (R1)........................$10–$15
Vader's Lightsaber (R1) ....$15–$25
Assault Rifle (R2)...$6–$8
Automated Weapon
Timer Mine (C)
Laser Projector (U)
Han Seeker (R2)...$4–$6
Luke Seeker (R2) ....$4–$6
Starship Weapon
Boosted TIE Cannon (U)
Ion Cannon (U)
Turbolaser Battery (R2) ....$4–$6
Device
Comlonk (C)
Droid Detector (C)
Fusion Generator Supply Tanks (C)
Restraining Bolt (C)
Stormtrooper Backpack (C)
Stormtrooper Utility Belt (C)
Blaster Scope (U)
Caller (U)
Observation Holocam (U)
Location
Death Star: Detention Block Corridor (C)
Tatooine: Jawa Camp (C)
Tatooine: Jundland Wastes (C)
Tatooine: Mos Eisley (C)
Death Star: Docking Bay 327 (C)
Tatooine (C)
Tatooine: Docking Bay 94 (C)
Yavin 4 (C)
Yavin 4: Docking Bay (C)
Dantooine (U)
Death Star: Level 4 Military Corridor (U)
Death Star: Central Core (U)
Death Star: War Room (U)
Kessel (U)
Tatooine: Lar's Moisture Farm (U)
Yavin 4: Jungle (U)
Alderaan (R1) ....$10–$15
Tatooine: Cantina (R2) ....$3–$5
Effect
Baniss Keeg (C)
Ket Maliss (C)
Macroscan (C)
A Disturbance in the Force (U)
Blaster Rack (U)
Death Star Sentry (U)
I've Lost Artoo! (U)
Jawa Pack (U)
Sunsdown (U)
Wrong Turn (U)
Your Eyes Can Deceive You (U)
Blast Door Controls (U)
Dark Hours (U)
Reactor Terminal (U)
Disarmed (R1) ....$10–$15
Expand the Empire (R1)...$10–$15
I Find Your Lack of Faith Disturbing (R1) ....$8–$12
Molator (R1) ....$8–$12
Presence of the Force (R1) ....$10–$15
Fear Will Keep Them in Line (R2) ....$3–$5
Utinni Effect
Luke? Luuuuke! (U)
Organa's Ceremonial Necklace (R1) ....$10–$15
Send a Detatchment Down (R1)...........................$10–$15
Juri Juice (R2)...$5–$8
Lateral Damage (R2) ....$5–$8
Tactical Re-Call (R2) ....$5–$8
Lost Interrupt
Counter Assault (C)
Imperial Reinforcements (C)
Kintan Strider (C)
You Overestimate Their Chances (C)
Collateral Damage (C)
Dead Jawa (C)
I've Got a Problem Here (C)
It's Worse (C)
Overload (C)
Precise Attack (C)
Set for Stun (C)
Takeel (C)
Tusken Scavengers (C)
The Empire's Back (U)
Full Scale Alert (U)
Gravel Storm (U)
Limited Resources (U)
Trooper Charge (U)
Dark Collaboration (R1)..$8–$12
Dark Jedi Presence (R1).......................................$10–$15
Local Trouble (R1) ....$8–$12
Look Sir, Trouble (R1) ....$8–$12
Physical Choke (R1)..$8–$12
The Circle Is Now Complete (R1)..........................$8–$12
Vader's Eye (R1)..$10–$15
We're All Gonna Be a Lot Thinner (R1).................$8–$12
Your Powers Are Weak, Old Man (R1)...............$10–$15
Charming to the Last (R2).......................................$3–$5
I Have You Now (R2) ....$3–$5

Lone Pilot (R2) .... $3–$5
Lone Warrior (R2) .... $3–$5
Moment of Triumph (R2) .... $3–$5
Nevar Yalnal (R2) .... $3–$5

Used Interrupt
Dark Maneuvers (C)
Imperial Barrier (C)
Imperial Code Cylinder (C)
Ommni Box (C)
Scanning Crew (C)
Tallon Roll (C)
Alter (U)
Emergency Deployment (U)
Sense (U)
Trinto Duaba (U)
Elis Helrot (U)
Evacuate? (U)
Boring Conversation Anyway (R1) .... $8–$12
Utinni! (R1) .... $15–$20

STAR WARS: A NEW HOPE EXPANSION CARDS, DECIPHER, 1996

The first expansion set contained 162 new cards, equally divided into common, uncommon and rare cards. The two levels of rare cards makes this set more difficult to complete. Cards are divided into Light Side and Dark Side just as in the original game.

Only a black-border limited edition has been released.

Complete set of 162 cards .... $400–$600
Sealed booster pack of cards .... $2–$3
Sealed box of booster packs (36) .... $75–$100
Common cards (C) .... $.25–$.50
Uncommon cards (U) .... $.50–$1
Rare cards (R2) .... $2–$3
Rare cards (R1) .... PRICED AS MARKED

Light Side Cards:

Automated Weapon
Motti Seeker (R2)

Character: Alien
Arcona (C)
Corellian (C)
Saurin (C)
Zutton (C)
Doikk Na'ts (U)
Garouf Lafoe (U)
Het Nkik (U)
Nalan Cheel (U)
Brainiac (R1) .... $15–$25
Hunchback (R1) .... $12–$20
Tzizvvt (R2)

Character: Droid
R5-D4 (Arfive-Defour) (C)
RA-7 (Aray-Seven) (C)
M-HYD "Binary" Droid (U)
R2-D2 (R2) .... $8–$10

Character: Rebel
Commander Evram Lajaie (C)
Rebel Commander (C)
Rebel Squad Leader (C)
Rebel Tech (C)
Commander Vanden Willard (U)
Tiree (U)
Wedge Antilles (R1) .... $15–$25

Character: Alien/Rebel
Chewbacca (R2) .... $8–$10

Character Weapon
Jawa Ion Gun (C)
Luke's Hunting Rifle (U)
Bowcaster (R2)

Creature Vehicle
Rogue Bantha (U)

Device
Rectenna (C)
Remote (C)
Fire Extinguisher (U)
Sensor Panel (U)
Magnetic Suction Tube (R2)

Effect
Eject! Eject! (C)
Merc Sunlet (C)
Solomahal (C)
Logistical Delay (U)
Scanner Techs (U)
Undercover (U)
Commence Recharging (R2)
Luke's Cape (R1) .... $12–$20

Epic Event
Attack Run (R2)

Immediate Effect
Grappling Hook (C)
What're You Tryin' to Push On Us? (U)

Location
Kashyyyk (C)
Yavin 4: Briefing Room (U)
Yavin 4: Massassi Ruins (U)
Clak'dor VII (R2)
Corellia (R1) .... $12–$20
Death Star: Trench (R2)
Dejarik Hologameboard (R1) .... $10–$15
Sandcrawler: Loading Bay (R1) .... $10–$15

Lost Interrupt
Blast the Door, Kid (C)
Houjix (C)
Sorry About the Mess (U)
Double Agent (R2)
Let the Wookiee Win (R1) .... $15–$25
Wookiee Roar (R1) .... $15–$25

Shuttle Vehicle
Incom T-16 Skyhopper (C)

Starship
Gold 2 (U)
Red 2 (U)

Y-Wing Assault Squadron (U)
Red 2 (R1) ....$12–$20
Red 5 (R1) ....$12–$20
Tantive IV (R1) ....$12–$20
Starship Weapon
SW-4 Ion Cannon (R2)
Used Interrupt
Corellian Slip (C)
I Have a Very Bad Feeling About This (C)
Quite a Mercenary (C)
I'm Here to Rescue You (U)
You're All Clear Kid (R1) ....$10–$15
Used or Lost Interrupt
Blue Milk (C)
Grimtaash (C)
Advance Preparation (U)
Utinni
Cell 2187 (R1) ....$12–$20
They're On Dantooine (R1) ....$10–$15

Dark Side Cards:
Automated Weapon
Leia Seeker (R2)
Character: Alien
Advoze (C)
Defel (C)
Rodian (C)
Danz Borin (U)
Lirin Car'n (U)
Mosep (U)
Reegesk (U)
Tech Mo'r (U)
URoRRuR'R'R (U)
Dannik Jerriko (R1)..$10–$15
Greedo (R1)...$12–$20
Hem Dazon (R1) ....$10–$15
Character: Droid
R2-Q2 (Artoo-Kyootoo) (C)
R5-A2 (Arfive-Aytoo) (C)
WED 15-17 "Septoid" Droid (U)
IT-O (Eyetee-Oh) (R1)..$10–$15
R3-T6 (Arthree-Teesix) (R1) ....$10–$15
U-3PO (Yoo-Threepio) (R1) ....$12–$20
Character: Imperial
Death Star Gunner (C)
Imperial Commander (C)
Imperial Squad Leader (C)
Lt. Pol Treidum (C)
Officer Evax (C)
Captain Khurgee (U)
Lt. Shann Childsen (U)
Reserve Pilot (U)
DS-61-4 (R2)
Trooper Davin Felth (R2)
Character Weapon
Jawa Blaster (C)
Creature Vehicle
Death Star Weapon
Superlaser (R2)
Device
Laser Gate (U)
Tractor Beam (U)
Death Star Tractor Beam (R2)
Hypo (R1)...$10–$15
Magnetic Suction Tube (R2)
Effect
Come With Me (C)
Imperial Justice (C)
Swilla Corey (C)
Astromech Shortage (U)
Hyperwave Scan (U)
Krayt Dragon Bones (U)
Program Trap (U)
Undercover (U)
Besieged (R2)
Dark Waters (R2)
Maneuver Check (R2)
Epic Event
Commence Primary Ignition (R2)
Immediate Effect
Tentacle (C)
There'll Be Hell to Pay (U)
Location
Kashyyyk (C)
Ralltiir (C)
Death Star: Conference Room (U)
Death Star (R2)...$8–$10
Imperial Holotable (R1) ....$10–$15
Kiffex (R1)...$10–$15
Sandcrawler: Droid Junkheep (R1) ....$15–$25
Tatooine: Bluffs (R1) ....$10–$15
Lost Interrupt
Ghhhk (C)
Stunning Leader (C)
We Have a Prisoner (C)
Sniper (U)
I'm on the Leader (R1) ....$12–$20
Retract the Bridge (R1) ....$10–$15
Shuttle Vehicle
Bespin Motors Void Spider THX 1138 (C)
Starship
TIE Vanguard (C)
Black 4 (U)
TIE Assault Squadron (U)
Victory-Class Star Destroyer (U)
Conquest (R1)..$15–$25
Starship Weapon
Enhanced TIE Laser Cannon (C)
Swamp Creature
Dianoga (R2)
Transport Vehicle
Mobquet A-1 Deluxe Floater (C)
Used Interrupt
Ng'ok (C)
Oo-ta Goo-ta, Solo? (C)
Informant (U)

This is Some Rescue! (U)
Used or Lost Interrupt
Monnok (C)
Evader (U)
Utinni Effect
Spice Mines of Kessel (R1) ....$12–$20

THE EMPIRE STRIKES BACK: HOTH SUPPLEMENT, DECIPHER, 1996

The second expansion set of cards for the Star Wars Customizable Card Game was based on the second movie and included a new set of rules inserted into every box of booster packs. Again there are 162 cards in the set and they were released as common, uncommon and rare cards as in the previous sets.

Complete set of 162 cards, black border ....$300–$500
Single booster pack ....$2.50–$3
Sealed box of booster packs (36) ....$75–$100
Common cards (C) ....$.25–$.50
Uncommon cards (U) ....$.50–$1
Rare cards (R2)...$2–$3
Rare cards (R1)...$8–$20

Light Side Cards:
Artillery Weapon
Medium Repeating Blaster Cannon (C)
Atgar Laser Cannon (U)
Golan Laser Battery (U)
Planet Defender Ion Cannon (R2)
Automated Weapon
Infantry Mine (C)
Vehicle Mine (C)
Character: Droid
EG-4 (Eegee-Four) (C)
FX-7 (Effex-Seven) (C)
R5-M2 (Arfive-Emmtoo) (C)
WED-1016 "Techie" Droid (C)
2-1B (Too-Onebee) (R1)
K-3PO (Kay-Threepio) (R1)
R-3PO (Ar-Threepio) (R2)
Character: Rebel
Echo Base Trooper (C)
Echo Base Trooper Officer (C)
Rebel Scout (C)
Rogue Gunner (C)
Tauntaun Handler (C)
Cal Alder (U)
Derek "Hobbie" Klivian (U)
Jeroen Webb (U)
Romas "Lock" Navander (U)
Shawn Valdez (U)
Tamizander Rey (U)
Tigran Jamiro (U)
Toryn Farr (U)
Wyron Sperper (U)
Commander Luke Skywalker (R1)
Dack Ralter (R2)
General Carlist Rieekan (R2)
Major Bren Derlin (R2)
Wes Janson (R2)
Zev Senesca (R2)
Character Weapon
Anakin's Lightsaber (R1)
Concussion Grenade (R1)
Combat Vehicle
Snowspeeder (U)
Rogue 1 (R1)
Rogue 2 (R2)
Rogue 3 (R1)
Creature Vehicle
Tauntaun (C)
Device
Echo Trooper Backpack (C)
Hoth Survival Gear (C)
R2 Sensor Array (C)
Artillery Remote (R2)
Effect
Frostbite (C)
Evacuation Control (U)
Tauntaun Bones (U)
Bacta Tank (R2)
Echo Base Operations (R2)
Immediate Effect
Disarming Creature (R1)
Mobile Effect
Ice Storm (U)
Location
Hoth: Defensive Perimeter (C)
Hoth: Echo Corridor (C)
Hoth: Echo Docking Bay (C)
Hoth: Echo Med Lab (C)
Hoth: North Ridge (C)
Hoth: Snow Trench (C)
Hoth (U)
Hoth: Echo Command Center (War Room) (U)
Hoth: Main Power Generators (U)
Ord Mantell (U)
Lost Interrupt
Fall Back! (C)
It Can Wait (C)
Attack Pattern Delta (U)
Walker Sighting (U)
Rug Hug (R1)
You Have Failed Me for the Last Time (R1)
You Will Go to the Dagobah System (R1)
Starship
Medium Transport (U)
Starship Weapon
Surface Defense Cannon (R2)
Used Interrupt
Nice of You Guys to Drop By (C)
Perimeter Scan (C)
One More Pass (U)
Under Attack (U)
I Thought They Smelled Bad on the Outside (R1)
Who's Scruffy Looking? (R1)

Used or Lost Interrupt
Lucky Shot (U)
Dark Dissension (R1)
Utinni Effect
The First Transport Is Away! (R1)
Vehicle Weapon
Dual Laser Cannon (U)
Power Harpoon (U)

Dark Side Cards:
Artillery Weapon
E-web Blaster (C)
Automated Weapon
Infantry Mine (C)
Vehicle Mine (C)
Character: Droid
FX-10 (Effex-ten) (C)
Probe Droid (C)
Character: Imperial
AT-AT Driver (C)
Imperial Gunner (C)
Snowtrooper (C)
Snowtrooper Officer (C)
Captain Lennox (U)
Lieutenant Cabbel (U)
Admiral Ozzel (R1)
Captain Piett (R2)
General Veers (R1)
Character Weapon
Probe Droid Laser (U)
Combat Vehicle
Blizzard Walker (U)
Blizzard 1 (R1)
Blizzard 2 (R2)
Blizzard Scout 1 (R1)
Device
Portable Fusion Generator (C)
Deflector Shield Generators (U)
Electro-Rangefinder (U)
Probe Antennae (U)
Effect
Frostbite (C)
Death Squadron (U)
Imperial Domination (U)
Silence Is Golden (U)
The Shield Doors Must Be Closed (U)
Too Cold for Speeders (U)
Image of the Dark Lord (R2)
Immediate Effect
Breached Defenses (U)
Frozen Dinner (R1)
High Anxiety (R1)
Mournful Roar (R1)
Mobile Effect
Ice Storm (U)
Epic Event
Target the Main Generator (R2)
Location
Hoth: Defensive Perimeter (C)
Hoth: Echo Docking Bay (C)
Hoth: Ice Plains (C)
Hoth: North Ridge (C)
Ord Mantell (C)
Hoth (U)
Hoth: Echo Command Center (War Room) (U)
Hoth: Echo Corridor (U)
Hoth: Wampa Cave (R2)
Lost Interrupt
A Dark Time for the Rebellion (C)
He Hasn't Come Back Yet (C)
I'd Just As Soon Kiss a Wookiee (C)
Exhaustion (U)
Exposure (U)
Wall of Fire (U)
Collapsing Corridor (R2)
Tactical Support (R2)
Used Interrupt
Cold Feet (C)
ComScan Detection (C)
Oh, Switch Off (C)
Our First Catch of the Day (C)
Probe Telemetry (C)
Stop Motion (C)
Crash Landing (U)
Lightsaber Deficiency (U)
Self-Destruct Mechanism (U)
That's It, The Rebels Are There! (U)
Walker Barrage (U)
Debris Zone (R2)
Trample (R1)
Yaggle Gakkle (R2)
Used or Lost Interrupt
Imperial Supply (C)
Turn It Off! Turn It Off! (C)
Direct Hit (U)
Furry Fury (R2)
Scruffy-Looking Nerf Herder (R2)
Snow Creature
Wampa (R2)
Starship
Stalker (R1)
Tyrant (R1)
Utinni Effect
Death Mark (R1)
Meteor Impact? (R1)
Responsibility of Command (R1)
This Is Just Wrong (R1)
Weapons Malfunction (R1)
Vehicle Weapon
AT-AT Cannon (U)

INDEX